T0214294

Lecture Notes in Computer Science 12258

More information about this series at http://www.springer.com/series/7409

Marco Manna · Andreas Pieris (Eds.)

Reasoning Web

Declarative Artificial Intelligence

16th International Summer School 2020
Oslo, Norway, June 24–26, 2020
Tutorial Lectures

 Springer

Editors
Marco Manna (iD)
Department of Mathematics
and Computer Science
University of Calabria
Rende, Italy

Andreas Pieris
School of Informatics
University of Edinburgh
Edinburgh, UK

ISSN 0302-9743   ISSN 1611-3349 (electronic)
Lecture Notes in Computer Science
ISBN 978-3-030-60066-2   ISBN 978-3-030-60067-9 (eBook)
https://doi.org/10.1007/978-3-030-60067-9

LNCS Sublibrary: SL3 – Information Systems and Applications, incl. Internet/Web, and HCI

This Springer imprint is published by the registered company Springer Nature Switzerland AG
The registered company address is: Gewerbestrasse 11, 6330 Cham, Switzerland

Preface

The Reasoning Web series of annual summer schools has become the prime educational event in the field of reasoning techniques on the Web, attracting both young and established researchers since its first initiation in 2005 by the European Network of Excellence (REWERSE). This year's summer school was part of Declarative AI 2020 (https://2020.declarativeai.net) that brought together the 4th International Joint Conference on Rules and Reasoning (RuleML+RR 2020), DecisionCAMP 2020, and the 16th Reasoning Web Summer School (RW 2020). Declarative AI 2020 was co-organized by SINTEF AS, University of Oslo, and Norwegian University of Science and Technology, under the umbrella of the SIRIUS Centre for Scalable Data Access. Declarative AI 2020 was originally planned to take place in the beautiful city of Oslo, but due to the COVID-19 pandemic, it was held as a virtual event.

The broad theme of this year's summer school was

"Declarative Artificial Intelligence"

and it covered various aspects of ontological reasoning and related issues that are of particular interest to Semantic Web and Linked Data applications. The following eight lectures have been presented during the school (further details can be found at the website of the school (https://2020.declarativeai.net/events/rw-summer-school/rw-lectures):

1. **Introduction to Probabilistic Ontologies**
   by Rafael Peñaloza (University of Milano-Bicocca, Italy).
2. **On the Complexity of Learning Description Logic Ontologies**
   by Ana Ozaki (University of Bergen, Norway).
3. **Explanation via Machine Arguing**
   by Oana Cocarascu (Imperial College London, UK), Antonio Rago (Imperial College London, UK), and Francesca Toni (Imperial College London, UK).
4. **Stream Reasoning: From Theory to Practice**
   by Emanuele Della Valle (Politecnico di Milano, Italy), Emanuele Falzone (Politecnico di Milano, Italy), and Riccardo Tommasini (University of Tartu, Estonia).
5. **Temporal Ontology-Mediated Queries and First-Order Rewritability: a Short Course**
   by Vladislav Ryzhikov (Birkbeck University of London, UK), Przemysław A. Wałęga (University of Oxford, UK), and Michael Zakharyaschev (Birkbeck University of London, UK).
6. **An Introduction to Answer Set Programming and Some of Its Extensions**
   by Wolfgang Faber (University of Klagenfurt, Austria).

7. **Declarative Data Analysis using Limit Datalog Programs**
   by Egor V. Kostylev (University of Oxford, UK).
8. **Knowledge Graphs: Research Directions**
   by Aidan Hogan (University of Chile, Chile).

This volume contains the lecture notes that complement the above lectures. All the articles are of high quality and have been written as accompanying material for the students of the summer school, in order to deepen their understanding and to serve as a reference for further detailed study. Further material, such as lecture slides and recordings, can be found at the website of the school.

We would like to thank everybody who helped make this event possible. As teaching is the main focus of a summer school, we would first like to thank all the lecturers: your hard work and commitment led to a successful event. We are also thankful to the members of the Scientific Advisory Board: your timely feedback concerning the technical program, as well as for the submitted lecture notes, helped to organize a high-quality event. Finally, we express our gratitude to the local organizers for their constant support.

August 2020   Marco Manna
                                                                   Andreas Pieris

Organization

General Chairs

Marco Manna   University of Calabria, Italy
Andreas Pieris   The University of Edinburgh, UK

Scientific Advisory Board

Leopoldo Bertossi   Universidad Adolfo Ibáñez, Chile
Thomas Eiter   TU Wien, Austria
Birte Glimm   Ulm University, Germany
Markus Krötzsch   TU Dresden, Germany
Yuliya Lierler   University of Nebraska Omaha, USA
Carsten Lutz   University of Bremen, Germany
Emanuel Sallinger   University of Oxford, UK

Contents

Introduction to Probabilistic Ontologies

Rafael Peñaloza$^{(\boxtimes)}$ (iD)

IKR3 Lab, University of Milano-Bicocca, Milan, Italy
`rafael.penaloza@unimib.it`

Abstract. There is no doubt about it; an accurate representation of a real knowledge domain must be able to capture uncertainty. As the best known formalism for handling uncertainty, probability theory is often called upon this task, giving rise to probabilistic ontologies. Unfortunately, things are not as simple as they might appear, and different choices made can deeply affect the semantics and computational properties of probabilistic ontology languages. In this tutorial, we explore the main design choices available, and the situations in which they may be meaningful or not. We then dive deeper into a specific family of probabilistic ontology languages which can express logical and probabilistic dependencies between axioms.

1 Introduction

Ontologies, in the computer-science sense of "representations of a knowledge domain" present a prominent research area of interest within the general umbrella of Artificial Intelligence, and more precisely in Knowledge Representation. Indeed, any intelligent agent should have, in one way or another, a representation of the knowledge of its active domain, so that it is able to react to observations of its environment in an adequate manner.

Within the context of the Semantic Web, ontologies have been identified as an appropriate manner to represent, combine, and in general use distributed knowledge from different sources into specific applications. Notably, beyond the general view of knowledge inter-connectivity, many industrial players, knowledge domains, and other users are building specialised ontologies for fitting their own needs. This has led not only to a large collection of ontologies dealing with all sorts of domain areas and large repositories holding them but, more importantly, with a plethora of languages which are used to build them. Abstracting from the specific peculiarities of these languages (and to avoid the need to clarify at each point which language is taken under consideration), we will see an ontology basically as a (typically finite) set of constraints that define how different elements of the knowledge domain should relate to each other. In particular, we focus on a setting where the ontology language has an underlying logical interpretation. The use of logic-based formalisms allows us to provide formal semantics, and guarantees of correctness for entailment methods. Thus, we can speak about consequences that follow from a given ontology; informally, these are pieces of knowledge that are implicitly (rather than explicitly) encoded in the ontology.

© Springer Nature Switzerland AG 2020
M. Manna and A. Pieris (Eds.): Reasoning Web 2020, LNCS 12258, pp. 1–35, 2020.
https://doi.org/10.1007/978-3-030-60067-9_1

With the success of ontology languages and the proliferation of ontologies, the usual limitations of classical logic for modelling expert knowledge come more prominently to light. One particular gap is that of representing uncertainty. Unfortunately, in many domain areas it is simply not possible to represent adequate knowledge without some level of uncertainty. A typical domain where uncertainty is commonly found is in medicine. Indeed, there are almost no certainties in medical sciences, when it comes to diagnose and cure a disease. This is because different people present different symptoms and express them in diverse manners, but also due to the limits in our capacity to observe the disease itself. Let us justify this statement with a few examples.

Suppose that a patient complains about intense abdominal pain, and very high fever. If the patient is young, and without any other known medical issues, we can expect (with a high level of certainty) that they are suffering from appendicitis; however, without additional testing and controls, this diagnosis cannot be certain. Another example appears in viral testing. Some viral infections are tested via a respiratory swab which has a limited precision, with a small possibility of error. In simple terms, a positive result in the swab provides a likelihood, but no certainty, of the infection. Finally, there exist diseases like Chronic Traumatic Encephalopathy (CTE) which cannot be diagnosed before death [21]. Indeed, although there are some signs and symptoms which may indicate the development of this ailment, the only way to know that someone suffers from CTE is to observe their brain closely.

Although medical sciences provide good and understandable examples of uncertain knowledge, uncertainty is not intrinsic to medicine only. Manufacturing processes occassionally produce defective pieces; the voting intentions of a population can be predicted by other behaviours, up to a margin of error; weather forecasts and natural disaster predictions are never fully accurate. There are countless examples which could be enumerated here.

Given the overall presence of uncertainty in these areas, it makes sense to try to include a way to represent it and use it within ontology languages. The most prominent approach for handling uncertainty is, without any doubt, probability theory. Hence, without intending to diminish any other formalisms, in this work we focus only on probabilities, with the goal of building probabilistic ontologies. From a very high level point of view, the idea is very simple: just add a probabilistic interpretation to the constraints forming the ontology, and adapt any reasoning and derivation methods to handle these probabilities. But the devil, as always, is in the details. Once we start to look closely into the formalisms, we realise that there are many choices to be made. First and foremost, how do we interpret these probabilities? Another important choice is how to combine different statements meaningfully. This is specially relevant since probabilities, in contrast to most logical formalisms, are not truth- functional; that is, one cannot compute the probability of a complex event based only on the probabilities of its components.

As there are many choices to be made about the probabilistic interpretation, several probabilistic ontology languages have been studied in the literature, many of which will be mentioned throughout this tutorial. Indeed, each classical ontology language can potentially give rise to many different probabilistic ontology languages. The field is so rich that it would be impossible to study them all in detail in a work like this. Instead, our goal is to explain the different choices, their motivation, their advantages, and their disadvantages in a manner that a user interested in representing probabilistic knowledge is able to identify the right choices. To achieve this goal, we introduce what we call the Five Golden Rules: five high-level considerations that must be kept in mind when dealing with probabilistic ontologies. These rules are by no means complete; they are not even at the same level of abstraction. They are mereley intended as a simple way to remember some of the most relevant aspects which characterise the different formalisms.

The rest of this tutorial is structured as follows. We start by providing an abstract definition of ontology languages and ontologies, which will be the base of the rest of the work. In the same section, we enumerate several examples of ontology languages, to showcase the generality of our definitions, and the scope of our work. Section 3 helps as a primer to uncertainty, and more specifically probability theory. It introduces all the notions needed for the following sections, including conditional and joint distributions, random variables, and Bayesian networks. After this general introduction, we combine both formalisms to define probabilistic ontologies in Sect. 4. We also briefly discuss some formalisms that are left out from our definition. The Five Golden Rules are presented in Sect. 5. The "rules" are given mnemonic names to help clarify their scope. The last section before the conclusions focuses on a specific probabilistic ontology language which is built by a combination of hypergraphs and databases, and different independence assumptions. It is meant as an example of a language which can be constructed from our notions, and the choices made following the golden rules.

2   Ontologies

In a very abstract sense, an ontology is merely a description of the world, or a relevant segment of it. In more practical terms, an ontology introduces all the terms of interest within a domain, and their relationships; that is, it is a representation of domain knowledge. This representation helps to understand, share, improve, and in general use the domain knowledge across applications. Depending on the domain of interest, the application at hand, and the desired properties of the description, different kinds of languages may be more or less suitable. This has motivated the introduction and study of many different knowledge representation languages.

Nowadays, the terms *ontology* or *ontology language* in the context of knowledge representation is most likely to remind us about the Web Ontology Language (OWL) from the Semantic Web [24] or, for the younger ones among us, of Knowledge Graphs (KGs). Already these two terms evoke a large variety of languages, from the different formalisms used in modern KGs [4,14], to the existing OWL 2 profiles [54], to the many description logic [2] formalisms that are less expressive than $\mathcal{SROIQ}$ [40], the logic underlying OWL 2. Despite this variety, one can easily think of features which are not covered by any one of these languages. For example, they cannot express temporal constraints, or limit the number of objects that satisfy a given property.

For most of this tutorial, we will be interested in the problem of extending ontology languages with probabilities. Since the general underlying ideas do not depend on the specific language, we will consider an abstract notion of *ontology language* which covers the examples enumerated above, but includes also other members. To make the ideas accessible, we will instantiate them in a simple language throughout several examples. Nevertheless, the reader should keep in mind that different languages satisfy different properties. These properties, their motivation, and some of the consequences of choosing them are discussed in further detail in Sect. 5.

For our purposes, an ontology language is a logical language which describes a knowledge domain by imposing constraints on how the underlying terms can be interpreted. Looking at ontology languages in this general form allows us to handle all these languages (and some more) simultaneously, without having to worry about their specific properties. In this way, we can also understand how the probabilistic component affects the notions within a language. A similar general definition of ontology has been used before, in a different context [60].

Formally, an *ontology language* is a tuple $\mathfrak{L} = (\mathfrak{A}, \mathfrak{O}, \mathfrak{C}, \models)$, where $\mathfrak{A}$ is a countable set of well-formed *axioms*, $\mathfrak{C}$ is the set of *consequences*, $\mathfrak{O} \subseteq \mathscr{P}(\mathfrak{A})$ is the set of *acceptable ontologies*—where an element $\mathcal{O} \in \mathfrak{O}$ is called an *ontology*—and $\models \subseteq \mathfrak{O} \times \mathfrak{C}$ is the *entailment relation*, which will be written using an infix notation. The only constraints imposed into these components are that the class of acceptable ontologies is closed under subsets, and that the entailment relation is monotonic. In formal terms, this means that for all $\mathcal{O}, \mathcal{O}' \subseteq \mathfrak{A}$ such that $\mathcal{O} \subseteq \mathcal{O}'$ and all $c \in \mathfrak{C}$, (i) if $\mathcal{O}' \in \mathfrak{O}$, then $\mathcal{O} \in \mathfrak{O}$, and (ii) if $\mathcal{O}' \in \mathfrak{O}$ and $\mathcal{O} \models c$, then $\mathcal{O}' \models c$. When $\mathcal{O} \models c$ we say that $\mathcal{O}$ *entails* c or that c is *entailed* by $\mathcal{O}$. Although this definition does not require it, we will often assume that an ontology is finite; that is, that it contains finitely many axioms. This makes sense in the context of knowledge representation.

Some Ontology Languages
We now present some examples of ontology languages, which will help clarify our general definition and the choices made in future sections.

Graphs. One of the simplest ontology languages one can think of is that of graphs [29]. Formally, given a countable set V of *nodes* we define the ontology language $\mathfrak{L}_\mathsf{G} := (\mathfrak{A}_\mathsf{G}, \mathfrak{O}_\mathsf{G}, \mathfrak{A}_\mathsf{G}, \models)$ where $\mathfrak{A}_\mathsf{G} := V \times V$, $\mathfrak{O}_\mathsf{G} := \mathscr{P}(\mathfrak{A}_\mathsf{G})$, and $\models$ is the reachability relation; that is, for a graph $\mathcal{G} \subseteq \mathfrak{A}_\mathsf{G}$ and nodes $u, v \in V$, we have that $\mathcal{G} \models (u, v)$ iff v is reachable from u in $\mathcal{G}$.

In this case, the axioms of the ontology are the edges in the graph, and an ontology is a set of edges. Keeping in line with the assumption mentioned before, we often restrict to finite graphs. Note that for this language—and for others which we will present later—the class of axioms and the class of consequences coincide. However, their elements are interpreted in a different manner; the pair (u, v), when seen as an axiom, represents an edge in the graph, while as a consequence it represents a question about reachability. We will see in further examples that these two classes need not coincide in general.

The attentive reader may already be wondering why we have decided to use a class of acceptable ontologies $\mathfrak{O} \subseteq \mathscr{P}(\mathfrak{A})$ rather than allowing any set of axioms to be an ontology. The reason is, of course, that for some applications, we might want to avoid an overhead or other issues caused by arbitrary sets of axioms. For example, if in our application we are only interested in *acyclic* graphs, or in *trees*, we may simply restrict the class of acceptable ontologies to reflect this fact; e.g., in the former case, we can define $\mathfrak{L}_{\mathsf{AG}} := (\mathfrak{A}_{\mathsf{G}}, \mathfrak{O}_{\mathsf{AG}}, \mathfrak{A}_{\mathsf{G}}, \models)$ where $\mathfrak{A}_{\mathsf{G}}$ and $\models$ are as before, but now $\mathfrak{O}_{\mathsf{AG}} := \{\mathcal{G} \subseteq \mathfrak{A}_{\mathsf{G}} \mid \mathcal{G} \text{ is acyclic}\}$. Note that the class $\mathfrak{O}_{\mathsf{AG}}$ is closed under subsets as required by the definition of ontology languages; that is, if $\mathcal{G}$ is an acyclic graph, then every subgraph of $\mathcal{G}$ is also acyclic. We will see other examples where considering only a restricted class of acceptable ontologies may become fundamental for the effectiveness of entailment decisions.

Prolog. Another well known formalism which can be considered an ontology language is Prolog. Here we briefly introduce only a restricted version to give the general idea. A (simplified) *Horn clause* is a logical implication of the form $\forall \mathbf{x}.(\exists \mathbf{y}.\varphi(\mathbf{x}, \mathbf{y}) \rightarrow p(\mathbf{x}))$ where $\mathbf{x}$ and $\mathbf{y}$ are vectors of variables, φ is a conjunction of predicates using the variables in $\mathbf{x}$ and $\mathbf{y}$, and p is a single predicate. A *fact* is a term $p(\mathbf{a})$, where p is a predicate and $\mathbf{a}$ is a vector of constant symbols. The language $\mathfrak{L}_{\mathsf{P}}$ is defined by the tuple $(\mathfrak{A}_{\mathsf{P}}, \mathfrak{O}_{\mathsf{P}}, \mathfrak{C}_{\mathsf{P}}, \models)$ where $\mathfrak{A}_{\mathsf{P}}$ is the class of all Horn clauses and facts, $\mathfrak{O}_{\mathsf{P}} := \mathscr{P}_{\mathsf{fin}}(\mathfrak{A}_{\mathsf{P}})$ is the set of all finite subsets of $\mathfrak{A}_{\mathsf{P}}$, $\mathfrak{C}_{\mathsf{P}}$ is the class of all facts, and $\models$ is the standard entailment relation for first-order logic, restricted to the simple implications involved. Note that in this case, the class of consequences is a strict subset of the class of axioms. In Prolog, we are not interested in finding other clauses which can be derived from an ontology, but only new facts which are implicitly encoded in it.

Databases. To include a formalism that is not typically considered an ontology language, but still fits within our definition, we consider (relational) databases. In this setting, we have a database, which is composed by a set of tables which satisfy a relational schema. The tables in the database can be abstracted to a set of ground terms $p(\mathbf{a})$ (or facts, as in the previous setting), where the arity and other properties of the predicate p are constrained by the schema, which is essentially a set of first-order formulas. Under this view, the set $\mathfrak{A}_{\mathsf{DB}}$ of axioms of the database ontology language $\mathfrak{L}_{\mathsf{DB}}$ contains all the possible facts and schema formulas; the class of acceptable ontologies $\mathfrak{O}_{\mathsf{DB}}$ includes all finite sets of axioms where the facts comply with the schema, the class of consequences $\mathfrak{C}_{\mathsf{DB}}$ is the set of all positive Boolean queries, and $\models$ is the standard entailment relation from databases to queries. In this case, the classes of axioms and consequences are different. Note also that we restrict $\mathfrak{C}_{\mathsf{DB}}$ to contain only positive queries. Indeed, if we allowed arbitrary queries, then the closed-world semantics of databases would violate the monotonicity condition over $\models$; that is, a query which uses negation may follow from a given database, and not follow anymore after a single fact has been added to it.

$\mathcal{HL}$. As a running example for this tutorial, we will consider a simple ontology language which combines the properties of (hyper)graphs and databases, with the semantics similar to what Prolog programs can do. The logic itself takes its form as a very inexpressive description logic (and hence the name), and also fits within some limited definitions of knowledge graphs (see e.g. [5]). Consider two disjoint sets N_C and N_I of *concept names* and *individual names*, respectively. An *inclusion axiom* is an expression of the form $S \to T$, where $S \subseteq N_C$ is a finite set of concept names and $T \in N_C$; a *fact* is of the form $A(a)$ with $A \in N_C$ and $a \in N_I$. We consider both, inclusion axioms and facts as axioms of our ontology language; that is, $\mathfrak{A}_{\mathsf{HL}}$ is the set of all inclusions and facts. As acceptable ontologies, we allow all finite subsets of $\mathfrak{A}_{\mathsf{HL}}$: $\mathfrak{O}_{\mathsf{HL}} := \mathscr{P}_{\mathsf{fin}}(\mathfrak{A}_{\mathsf{HL}})$. Intuitively, an $\mathcal{HL}$ ontology is composed of a finite hypergraph (defined by the inclusion axioms) and a finite set of facts; i.e., $\mathcal{HL}$ combines hypergraphs with data. For that reason, we will henceforth often refer to inclusion axioms as *hyperedges*, and a set of inclusion axioms as a *hypergraph*. The facts that form the data can be thought of as being separated from the hypergraph, which forms a kind of schema. As consequences, we consider the class $\mathfrak{C}_{\mathsf{HL}}$ of all facts. Variants of this inexpressive logic have been used to showcase the properties and understand the complexity of non-standard reasoning problems in ontology languages [58,59,61].

Strictly speaking, the inclusion axioms define a special kind of directed hypergraph [31], where hyperedges are formed by a set of *sources* and a single *target* node; i.e., given a set V of nodes, a hypergraph is a set of pairs of the form (U, v) where $U \subseteq V$ and $v \in V$. In such a hypergraph, a *path* from a set U of nodes to a node v is a sequence of hyperedges $(U_0, v_0), (U_1, v_1), \ldots, (U_n, v_n)$ such that (i) $v_n = v$ and (ii) for each $i, 0 \le i \le n$ it holds that $U_i \subseteq \{v_j \mid j < i\} \cup U$. The node v is *reachable* from the set U iff there exists a path from U to v. In this setting, we say that an ontology $\mathcal{O}$ entails the fact $A(a)$ (i.e., $\mathcal{O} \models A(a)$) iff A is reachable from some set of concepts S in the hypergraph defined by $\mathcal{O}$, such that $\{B(a) \mid B \in S\} \subseteq \mathcal{O}$. For example, Fig. 4 shows two hypergraphs representing $\mathcal{HL}$ ontologies. In both cases, if an ontology contains the facts $\mathsf{Nausea}(a)$ and $\mathsf{MemoryLoss}(a)$, we can derive the consequence $\mathsf{Observation}(a)$. The details on how to derive a consequence efficiently are explained better in Sect. 6. The choice of the language $\mathfrak{L}_{\mathsf{HL}} := (\mathfrak{A}_{\mathsf{HL}}, \mathfrak{O}_{\mathsf{HL}}, \mathfrak{C}_{\mathsf{HL}}, \models)$ as a guiding example is motivated by its simplicity, and the properties it preserves in relation to other known languages. We will make full use of all these properties in Sect. 6.

Others. As mentioned already, there exist many other logic-based formalisms which fit into our definition of ontology languages. For the sake of inclusiveness, and to motivate the generality of our discourse, we briefly mention some of them without going into much detail. The interested reader can dive deeper into any of these formalisms consulting the references provided. Before going into less obvious formalisms, we simply specify that all classical *description logics* (DLs) [2] fall into our definition of ontology language. Typically, a DL ontology is composed of a so-called TBox, which encodes the terminological knowledge of the domain, and an ABox containing all the known facts about specific individuals. Although in most cases an ontology is simply a set of axioms of these forms, it is sometimes important to restrict the class of acceptable ontologies. For example, to guarantee decidability of its reasoning services, $\mathcal{SROIQ}$ forbids combinations of some axioms involving role names (for details, see [40]). In smaller members of the family, limiting the TBox to be *acyclic* can further reduce the complexity of reasoning as well; e.g., in $\mathcal{ALC}$ the complexity drops from ExpTime for general TBoxes [66], to PSpace for acyclic ones [3]. Orthogonally, the different logics studied under the umbrella of knowledge graphs also fit this definition [25,39].

Another natural formalism to be considered is propositional logic. In this case, one can for example consider as axioms the set of all clauses, which makes a CNF formula—that is, a set of clauses—an ontology. As consequences one can consider other clauses including the empty clause used to decide satisfiability of a formula. These consequences can be derived or tested through standard methods from satisfiability testing [6]. It is perhaps less obvious to think of a temporal logic like LTL as an ontology language. In [3], LTL was used as an example of ontology language to show the power of the automata-based methods it proposed. In this context, an ontology is a set (seen as a conjunction) of temporal constraints. Independently, a language known as Declare was proposed for modelling constraints and requisites in a business process [52,62]. Declare is a graphical language, whose underlying formal semantics is based on LTL; specifically, a Declare model is a set of temporal constraints which is interpreted as the conjunction of LTL formulas (over finite time bounds) which underlie the Declare constraints. There exist, obviously, many other ontology languages that fit within our setting. Our goal is not to enumerate them all, but rather to show the generality of the definitions and of the solutions and settings that will be studied later on.

Before moving on to the main topics of this tutorial, we discuss briefly the importance of the entailment relation. In general, when studying an ontology language, one is interested in developing methods which can decide whether an ontology entails a given consequence or not. Although our definition does not require so, we are usually interested in cases where this entailment relation is decidable—in fact, all the examples mentioned in this section satisfy this property—and in developing effective methods for deciding it. When possible, these methods are also expected to be optimal w.r.t. the computational complexity of the problem. When studying ontologies languages in an abstract sense as we are doing now, all these subtleties are often lost, but that does not mean that they are not important. When possible, we will try to remind the reader of these complexity issues.

3   Uncertainty

A commonly mentioned limitation of ontology languages—specially within the context of knowledge representation—is their inability to model or handle uncertainty. Indeed, notice that we use the axioms in an ontology as absolute information, and the consequences follow (or not) from these axioms. This leaves no space for statements which are not completely certain. When dealing with natural knowledge domains, and in particular when the knowledge is built with the help of different knowledge experts and automated tools, it becomes impossible to avoid uncertainty in some axioms of every form.

Consider for example a medical application. In a very simple scenario, one could try to model the knowledge that patients showing a running nose and complaining of feeling light-headed have a common cold; for instance through an $\mathcal{HL}$ axiom like $(\{\mathsf{RunNose}, \mathsf{LightHead}\}, \mathsf{Cold})$. This rule would be correct most of the time, but ignores the fact that there exist many different maladies—some of them potentially serious—who share these same symptoms, and require additional interventions. Limiting the knowledge to this simple case could be very problematic in practice. It also ignores other potential symptoms, and additional information by patients. It would be much better to weaken the rule to express that these symptoms are *likely* associated to a common cold (with an appropriate measure of what the term "likely" means, as we will discuss later).

Importantly, uncertainty is *not* unique to medicine. As argued in the introduction, we are in fact surrounded by it. From weather reports, to potentially defective pieces of equipment, to accidents and vehicle traffic, we continuously consider and handle uncertain scenarios as any intelligent agent with automated reasoning should. Consider for instance a package delivery company which needs to schedule shipments and guarantee delivery times. All the factors just enumerated would need to be taken into account to minimize the risk of delays. Hence, it is fundamental to be able to include this uncertainty in a formal and manageable manner into our ontology languages.

Before going forward, it is worth to discuss briefly what we mean by *uncertainty*. Uncertainty is used to handle scenarios that happen or not but, due to a lack of knowledge and other factors, we do not know which is the case. That is, the outcome is precise, but our knowledge about it is not. The typical example for uncertainty is the toss of a coin: it will land in heads or not, but before performing the experiment one cannot know which one is. On the other hand, uncertainty is not about imprecise or other kinds of imperfect knowledge. For example, notions which have no precise definition such as "tall" or "close" do not express uncertainty, but rather imprecision. It is not that we do not know whether someone is tall or not, but rather that we cannot precisely define when a person is tall and when they are not.

There exist many different formalisms which can be used for measuring and handling uncertainty. Perhaps the two most prominent ones are possibility theory [30] and probability theory, where probabilities tend to be better known by average users, even though our intuitive understanding of probabilities often tends to be wrong. Since this tutorial is about probabilistic ontologies, we will consider only probability theory from now on. For completeness, before extending ontology languages with probabilities, we briefly introduce the main notions of probability theory. For a gentle introduction to the topic, we suggest [69].

3.1 Basics of Probability Theory

Probability theory measures the likelihood of occurrence of potentially interconnected events of which we do not have full certainty. The space forming these events is called the sample space. Although in the context of logic-based knowledge representation, one usually considers only *discrete* sample spaces, it makes sense to try to understand the general view on probability theory to be able to model also more complex scenarios. Nonetheless, we will try to preserves the intuition of discrete spaces as much as possible, to aid the understanding of readers who are not fully familiar with the topic.

Consider a non-empty, potentially infinite set Ω of *outcomes*, which is called the *sample space*. A *σ-algebra* over Ω is a class Σ of subsets of Ω such that $\Omega \in \Sigma$ and Σ is closed under set complementation and countable unions; that is, for all $X \subseteq \Omega$, if $X \in \Sigma$, then $\Omega \setminus X \in \Sigma$ as well; and for any countable sequence of sets $X_0, X_1, \ldots \subseteq \Omega$ the union $\bigcup_{n \in \mathbb{N}} X_n \in \Sigma$. If Σ is a σ-algebra over Ω, we call the pair (Ω, Σ) a *probability space*, and the elements of Σ are called *events*. From now on, we consider an arbitary but fixed probability space (Ω, Σ). For example, when we throw a die, the sample space is $\Omega := \{1, \ldots, 6\}$. A potential σ-algebra over this set is the powerset $\mathscr{P}(\Omega)$. Hence, for instance, the set $\{2, 4, 6\}$ is an event in this probability space which refers to the case where the roll of the die lands on an even number.

A *probability measure* is a function $P : \Sigma \to [0, 1]$ such that (i) $P(\Omega) = 1$, and (ii) if $\{X_0, X_1, \ldots\} \subseteq \Sigma$ is a countable collection of pairwise disjoint events, then $P(\bigcup_{n \in \mathbb{N}} X_i) = \sum_{n \in \mathbb{N}} P(X_i)$. In words, these conditions state that the event of all possible outcomes has probability 1—which is intuitively understood as being certain—and that the probability of the union disjoint events can be computed by adding the probabilities of each of the events. Based on these two conditions, we can derive all of the well-known properties of probabilities. For example, that for every two events $X, Y \in \Sigma$, it holds that $P(\Omega \setminus X) = 1 - P(X)$ and $P(X \cup Y) = P(X) + P(Y) - P(XY)$.[1]

Note that probabilities are defined over events, which are sets of outcomes, and not over individual outcomes in general. This is specially important when the sample space is uncountable, as it avoids the need to provide a probability value to each possible outcome. If such an assignment was required, then only a countable amount of outcomes could receive a positive probability. A simpler case is obtained when Ω is at most countable. In that case we can assume without loss of generality that the σ-algebra is simply $\mathscr{P}(\Omega)$; the class of all subsets of Ω. Moreover, it suffices to define the *probability mass function*; that is, a probability $P(\omega)$ for each outcome $\omega \in \Omega$. This implicitly yields the measure

---

[1] As is standard in probability theory, we use concatenation to denote intersection. That is, XY stands for the event $X \cap Y$.

$P(X) = \sum_{\omega \in X} P(\omega)$ for all $X \subseteq \Omega$. This is called a *discrete probability measure*. Returning to our die example, since the sample space is finite, we can define a discrete probability measure by assigning a probability to each outcome. If the die is fair, we can assign $P(i) = 1/6$ for each $i, 1 \leq i \leq 6$. In that case, we can compute the probability of observing an even number as

$$P(\{2, 4, 6\}) = P(2) + P(4) + P(6) = 3/6.$$

From the point of view of discrete probabilities, it is easy to give an intuitive reading of the notion of an event. Recall that an event is a set of outcomes, and that in a discrete probability measure, the probability of the event is just the sum of the probabilities of the outcomes it contains. This means that when we speak about the probability of an event, we are in fact measuring the likelihood of observing at least one of its outcomes.

For most notions used in ontologies and in particular in this tutorial, it suffices to consider discrete probabilities. Hence, we suggest any reader who is not familiar with probabilities or measure theory to think of this case mainly. The continuous case becomes relevant in some very specific applications and settings only.

3.2 Conditional Probabilities

A very important notion in probability theory is that of *conditioning*, which can be thought of as the adaptation of logical implication to probabilities. Intuitively, the conditional probability of X *given* Y (in symbols $P(X \mid Y)$) expresses the likelihood of observing the event X under the assumption that the event Y holds. Note that assuming the truth of Y immediately removes the possibility of many outcomes and events; in essence, any outcome that does not belong to Y is forbidden, as it contradicts the assumption that one of the outcomes in Y holds. When conditioning, we redistribute the probability of the remaining events, preserving their proportionality within the new probability space.

Formally, conditioning over an event Y defines the new probability space of outcomes in Y $(Y, \Sigma_{|Y})$ where $\Sigma_{|Y} = \{X \cap Y \mid X \in \Sigma\}$. As said before, the probability of the new events is considered to remain proportional, within the remaining set of outcomes. Hence, $P_{|Y}(X \cap Y) = P(X \cap Y)/P(Y)$. Note, however, that this definition creates a probability distribution over a new space, but we would rather prefer to be able to speak about the events of the original space. That is why the *conditional probability given Y* is defined, for every event X, as $P(X \mid Y) := P_{|Y}(XY) = P(XY)/P(Y)$. In particular this means that for any two events X, Y, $P(XY) = P(X \mid Y)P(Y)$ holds. Considering again the example with the die, if $Y = \{2, 4, 6\}$ is the event of observing an even number, and $X = \{1, 2, 3\}$ refers to observing at most a 3, then

$$P(X \mid Y) = P(XY)/P(Y) = P(\{2\})/P(Y) = \frac{1/6}{1/2} = 1/3.$$

In this case, $P(X) = P(\overline{X}) = 1/2$ but $P(X \mid Y) = 1/3$ and $P(\overline{X} \mid Y) = 2/3$.[2] That is, conditioning over another event may increase or decrease the probability of a given event.

We say that two events X, Y are *independent* iff the occurrence of one does not affect the probability of the other one. More formally, X and Y are independent iff $P(XY) = P(X)P(Y)$. Note that this means that for independent events, $P(X \mid Y) = P(X)$ and $P(Y \mid X) = P(Y)$. For example, the events $X = \{2, 4, 6\}$ and $Y = \{1, \ldots, 4\}$ are independent. Indeed, $XY = \{2, 4\}$ and we can see that $P(XY) = 1/3 = 3/6 \cdot 4/6 = P(X)P(Y)$. We extend this notion of *conditional independence* as follows. The events X and Y are *conditionally independent given Z* iff $P(XY \mid Z) = P(X \mid Z)P(Y \mid Z)$. This extension is very natural, but requires that the conditioning random variable is preserved through all the elements of the equation. Through a simple computation, it is easy to verify that for any three events X, Y, Z it holds that $P(XYZ) = P(X \mid YZ)P(Y \mid Z)P(Z)$. This idea can be easily generalised to any finite set of events. Together with conditional independence, equations of this kind will be fundamental in Sect. 3.4.

A cautious reader would have already detected an anomaly in the definition of conditional probabilities: the conditional probability given Y is only well-defined in case $P(Y) > 0$. This anomaly can be understood from our intuitive interpretation of probabilities. An event with probability 0 is one which is almost impossible to be observed, and hence assuming it to be true is akin to assuming a contradiction as the premise of a classical logical implication. In logic, this is solved by stating that everything follows from a contradiction; in probabilities, we simply disallow that special case, to guarantee that the properties of a probability distribution still hold after conditioning.

An important property of conditioning, which does not apply for classical implications is its reversibility: with enough information, we can change the conditioning and the conditioned events. Specifically, recall from the definition of conditioning that $P(X \mid Y)P(Y) = P(XY)$, but then, obviously, it is also the case that $P(Y \mid X)P(X) = P(XY)$. From these two equations we can deduce that $P(X \mid Y)P(Y) = P(Y \mid X)P(X)$. This equation, commonly known as Bayes' rule when expressed as

$$P(X \mid Y) = \frac{P(Y \mid X)P(X)}{P(Y)}$$

allows us to reverse a conditioning statement if we know the probabilities of each of the events separatedly.

3.3 Boolean Random Variables and Joint Distributions

It is often convenient to think of events X as *Boolean random variables*. Although the notion of a random variable is much more complex, it suffices for the purpose of this tutorial to equate events and random variables. More precisely, we will

---

[2] Again, as usual in probability theory, $\overline{X}$ denotes the event $\Omega \setminus X$; that is, the negation of X.

often speak about the Boolean random variable X to refer to a given event X. The reason is that, seen as a (Boolean) random variable, X can have two states: t when X holds, and f otherwise; that is, f denotes the fact that the event $\Omega \setminus X$ holds. Then X defines a probability distribution over its two states. For brevity, we will write X when the random variable is in state t, and $\overline{X}$ when it is in state f. From now on, whenever we speak about a random variable, we refer to a Boolean random variable in this sense.

Given a finite collection of random variables $X_1, \ldots, X_n$, we can build the *joint probability distribution*, which assigns a probability to each possible combination of states of the variables. Note that the specific distribution depends on the events underlying the random variables, and their probabilistic dependencies. Still, some general operations can be applied over the joint distribution. One of the most important is *marginalization*, which allows to remove a random variable from the distribution. Specifically,

$$
\begin{aligned}
P(X_2, \ldots, X_n) &= P(X_1, X_2, \ldots, X_n) + P(\overline{X}_1, X_2, \ldots, X_n) \\
&= P(X_2, \ldots, X_n \mid X_1) P(X_1) + P(X_2, \ldots, X_n \mid \overline{X}_1) P(\overline{X}_1).
\end{aligned}
$$

3.4 Bayesian Networks

Note that when building the joint probability distribution of n random variables, there is no specific pattern that the assigned probabilities should show. In the worst case, the description of the full joint probability distribution would require to provide a value for each of the 2^n different combinations of states of the random variables; that is, for all the variants of making some variables t and some f. This exponential growth becomes easily unmanageable after a few tens of variables are incorporated. For that reason, different approaches have been proposed for describing joint probability distributions more succinctly. A very prominent such approach, which exploits some conditional independence assumptions, is Bayesian networks [27,57].

In a nutshell, Bayesian networks use a graphical representation, through a directed acyclic graph (DAG) to express some conditional independence relationships between random variables (which appear as nodes in the DAG), which allow to limit the explicit probabilistic dependencies required to express the full joint probability. Formally, a *Bayesian network* is a pair $\mathcal{B} = (\mathcal{G}, \Phi)$ where $\mathcal{G}$ is a DAG whose nodes represent Boolean random variables, and Φ is a collection of conditional probability distribution tables, containing exactly one table for each node X given its parents $\pi(X)$ on G. Note that each of the tables in Φ is still exponential in the number of parents $\pi(X)$. However, assuming that the maximum in-degree in $\mathcal{G}$ is bounded, these tables are more easily handled than a full joint probability distribution table.

The graphical structure of the DAG $\mathcal{G}$ encodes an underlying conditional independence assumption between the random variables; namely, that every node is independent of all its non-successors given its parents. In other words, if the state of all the parent nodes $\pi(X)$ is known, then knowledge about any other

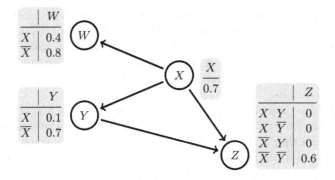

Fig. 1. A very simple Bayesian network

variable Y that is not reachable from X does not affect the likelihood of observing X itself; in formulas $P(X \mid Y\pi(X)) = P(X \mid \pi(X))$. Under this assumption, the whole joint probability distribution can be factorised as the product of all the conditional distributions appearing in Φ. That is,

$$P(\mathbf{X}) = \prod_{X \in \mathbf{X}} P(X \mid \pi(X))$$

where $\mathbf{X}$ is the set of all nodes from $\mathcal{G}$.

A very simple example of a Bayesian network is depicted in Fig. 1. In this case, the graph has four variables, and each node is depicted together with its conditional probability table. Note that describing the same joint probability distribution as a table would require 16 rows. Even at the scale of this example, we are saving almost half the space. The graphical structure expresses that the variable W is conditionally independent of both Y and Z given X. That is, if we know the state of X, any further information on Y on Z will not affect the probability of W. We can compute the probability of each possible state; for example,

$$P(W, X, \overline{Y}, \overline{Z}) = P(W \mid X)P(X)P(\overline{Y} \mid X)P(\overline{Z} \mid X\overline{Y})$$
$$= 0.4 \cdot 0.7 \cdot 0.9 \cdot 1 = 0.252.$$

Probabilistic inferences over BNs have been thoroughly studied in the literature. The simplest inference corresponds to the update of the probability distribution given some evidence; that is, computing the posterior distribution under the observation of the state of some variables of the network. In a nutshell, once we know the state of a given variable, we can use the rules of conditional probability to update our beliefs about the rest of the network, through a sort of message-passing mechanism. The same approach can also be used to compute the marginals, which in BNs is called *variable elimination*. Recall that to obtain the marginal w.r.t. a given variable X, it suffices to compute the posterior w.r.t. to each of the two possible states of X, as well as the prior probabilities of these states. Hence, it suffices to assume that we are given evidence of each of the states, and propagate this information through the network. There are many other inferences studied in the context of BNs; for instance, to find whether there are instantiations of a subset of **X** which yield a given probability of observing another variable (with or without evidence). We refer the interested reader to [27] for further details.

Importantly, although in the general case making any of these inferences is computationally hard [22,46,65], under some conditions on the structure of the underlying graph they remain tractable. For example, if the graph is a tree, or closely resembles a tree (formally, if it has a bounded *treewidth*), then there are efficient methods for propagating evidence and deriving the posterior distribution, even reducing the complexity of inferences to linear time. For example, the DAG in Fig. 1 is not a tree, but the only situation violating the tree condition is a join of two paths in a terminating node; thus, it has a low treewidth. From these, other inferences become also simpler [28].

4   Probabilistic Ontologies

We have so far introduced a general notion of ontology languages, and probabilities as a prominent theory for handling uncertainty. We now want to merge them together to be able to build and use probabilistic ontologies. At first sight, this looks as a pretty straightforward task: simply take an ontology language, and allow for probabilistic statements. However, once we try to fill in the technical details, we see that things are not as easy as they seem, and the road is paved with subtleties.

There is in fact a large space of possibilities from which to choose when extending an ontology language with probabilities. This is attested by the many different probabilistic ontology languages that can be found in the literature (see e.g. [48] for a slightly outdated survey focusing on the Semantic Web, and [19] for a more recent tutorial on probabilistic knowledge bases from a different perspective). It is very important, then, that one is aware of these choices and why they are made, lest we obtain unintended consequences from our knowledge. Before considering these choices, we introduce formally what we mean by a probabilistic ontology in the context of this work.

Definition 1 (probabilistic ontology). *Let $\mathfrak{L} = (\mathfrak{A}, \mathfrak{O}, \mathfrak{C}, \models)$ be an ontology language. A* probabilistic ontology *is a pair $(\mathcal{O}, P)$ where $\mathcal{O} \in \mathfrak{O}$ is an ontology and $P : \mathcal{O} \to [0,1]$ is a partial function assigning a probability degree to some axioms in the ontology.*

Note that probabilistic ontologies naturally generalise classical ones. Indeed, the ontology $\mathcal{O}$ can be equivalently seen as the probabilistic ontology $(\mathcal{O}, P_\emptyset)$ where $P_\emptyset$ is the empty partial function, which assigns a value to *none* of the elements of $\mathcal{O}$.

Intuitively, a probabilistic ontology is just an ontology where some of the axioms are labelled with a value in the interval $[0,1]$, which will be interpreted as their probability; that is, for a given axiom $\alpha \in \mathfrak{A}$, $P(\alpha)$ expresses the probability of α being true. Importantly, the assignment of probabilities P is a partial function, which means that not all axioms are required to get such a degree. This is fundamental to allow for cases where parts of the ontology are required to be certain. For example, in some probabilistic DLs one may expect to have only uncertain data, but certain terminological knowledge; that is, only the ABox assertions may be assigned a probability degree. Another prominent formalism that makes this restriction is ProbLog [63], a probabilistic variant of Prolog which allows facts, but not rules, to be assigned a probability. Similarly, in probabilistic databases the data tuples are uncertain, but the database schema is not [68].

One could think it is more natural to make the probabilistic assignment a total function, which assigns a probability degree to *all* the elements of $\mathcal{O}$, and using the degree 1 to express certainty. While this corresponds to the usual, intuitive understanding of probabilities—where probability 1 means certainty—it does not correspond to the mathematical properties of probabilities and, depending on the semantics chosen, may in fact produce different results. Indeed, formally speaking a probability 1 only means *almost certainty*, while probability 0 is assigned to *almost impossible* events.

Excluded Formalisms

Through our chosen notion of probabilistic ontologies, where some axioms are labelled with a real number between 0 and 1, we have in fact excluded many formalisms which have been—or could be—considered as probabilistic ontology languages as well. Prominently, it leaves out all formalisms based on log-linear interpretations of probabilities [9,55]. In those formalisms, probabilities are not assigned directly, but are rather implicitly encoded in *weights*, which can be arbitrarily large real numbers. The resulting probability is proportional to the weights used, but through a logarithmic factor, which makes it difficult to interpret the original weights. We could easily extend Definition 1 to allow these weights, but decided not to do so for clarity and conciseness of the presentation.

When trying to identify the likelihood of an axiom to hold, we often encounter the problem of finding a precise number which can be used without damaging the accuracy of the results. While the probability assigned by the function P can be interpreted as a lower or upper bound for the actual probability, in some scenarios it may become important to specify both bounds of a probability interval [16,23]. Expressing these bounds requires at least two labels per axiom, and hence does not directly fit into Definition 1. Of course, it would not be difficult to allow two functions P_L and P_U expressing the lower and upper bounds. We chose not to do so to avoid the notational overhead that it induces, but most of what will be discussed henceforth applies for this setting as well.

An important consideration is that our notion of probabilistic ontologies is intended to express uncertain knowledge, but not knowledge about uncertainty. The difference, which may seem small at first sight, is clearly observable from our definition of a probabilistic ontology: it is the knowledge (expressed through axioms) which is assigned a probability degree, but these degrees are not directly

Table 1. The five golden rules

The rules
1 Use probabilities
2 Use the right probabilities
3 To count or not to count
4 Understand the numbers
5 Be careful with independence

used within the axioms. For example, through a probabilistic ontology (based on an adequate ontology language) one can express that a person with the flu has a probability 0.8 of showing fever, but cannot express that if one has a parasitic infection with probability 0.5, then one will show fever with probability 0.8. The reason for our exclusion is that in the latter case the probabilities are an intrinsic element of the ontology language; the axioms themselves can express them already. In other words, probabilities are fundamental in the construction of the underlying ontology language. Thus, languages capable of expressing those statements (see e.g. [33,34,49]) fall into the basic definition of an ontology language from Sect. 2, rather than on the probabilistic extension of Definition 1.

Now that we have a syntactic definition of a probabilistic ontology language, we need to know how interpret these probabilistic ontologies and, more importantly, how to decide whether—and with which probability—an entailment follows from them. In addition, thinking about probabilities introduces new reasoning problems which should also be studied in these languages. As hinted already, depending on the requirements of the language and its inferences, there exist many different semantics which one could choose for interpreting the probabilities, each with a particular application scenario. Rather than enumerating them all directly, we prefer to provide five directives (the *Five Golden Rules*) which should be kept in mind when choosing the semantics, along with examples and the reasoning behind them. These examples will help the reader find probabilistic ontology languages that fall into our definition, in contrast to the excluded ones enumerated above.

5   The Five Golden Rules

Here are the five golden rules to consider when designing, choosing, or using a probabilistic ontology or probabilistic ontology language. For ease of consultation, they are also enumerated in Table 1.

5.1   Use Probabilities

This is the fundamental rule, and one who puzzles researchers and practitioners who approach the area of imperfect knowledge representation for the first time. As we have defined them, probabilistic ontologies assign a real number in $[0,1]$

to some of the axioms. As probabilities are commonly taught at schools, and we often hear probabilistic terminology in our daily lives, it is natural to associate any annotations that fall within this interval the meaning of probabilities, and this is often done in practice. However, there exist many other measures which use the same scale, but have nothing to do with probabilities or even with uncertainty.

Recall first that probabilities are a measure of *uncertainty*, meaning that they refer to events which either hold or not, and our lack of knowledge is only about which of these two possibilities holds. This goes in contrast with notions like *vagueness* or *graded truths*, where there may exist many different intermediate truth degrees, often also expressed with values in the unit interval. For example, uncertainty can express that there is a 2/3 chance that a rolled die will fall in a number smaller or equal to 4—it either does, or does not—but cannot express imprecise notions such as the concept of *nearness* or *tallness*. The latter are notions which have no precise definition, or clear-cut separations between membership and non-membership (e.g., there is no specific height at which a person starts being tall, and under which they are not). These are studied in fuzzy and many-valued logics [7,8,10,11,32,35,67]. In these logics, it is possible to express a fact like Tall(a) : 0.8 which should be interpreted as saying that a is tall with a degree 0.8. Although it may be tempting to interpret this degree as a probability, it would be a great mistake. To mention just one of the many differences between these approaches, fuzzy logics are truth-functional, while probabilities are not. That is, in fuzzy logic from the degrees of φ and ψ, one can compute the degree of $\varphi \wedge \psi$, but in probability theory this is not possible unless we know their conditional dependencies. Hence, before we can choose the appropriate semantics for our approach, we need to make sure that we are dealing with uncertainty, and not with some other kind of imperfect knowledge.

After we have confirmed that we are dealing with uncertainty, we still need to verify that probabilities are the right formalism for it. Another formalism for dealing with uncertainty, which was already mentioned before, is possibility theory [30]. While it shares many properties with probability theory, there are some important differences which make the two formalisms incompatible. Without going into too many details, in possibility theory one is more interested in a qualitative expression of the degrees of uncertainty, which is implicitly encoded by the ordering of the degrees used, rather than in the specific quantitative interpretation of these values. More specifically, in possibility theory an axiom with a degree 0.9 should only be considered *more likely* than one with degree, say 0.8, but without any specific reference to *how much more likely* it is. In addition, in possibility theory the negations are also handled differently, through an additional measure called *necessity*.

After we are convinced that probabilities are indeed the formalism that serves our purposes, we still need to make sure that we understand what these probabilities mean, and how they were obtained. Answering these questions is the focus of the remaining golden rules.

5.2 Use the Right Probabilities

When we are dealing with probabilistic knowledge, and in particular in scenarios where constraints may be shared among several individuals, it is fundamental to know how probabilities and uncertainty relate to each other and, more importantly, the scope of the uncertainty. Consider the following two statements.

1. The probability of a flight being delayed is 0.3
2. The probability of flight ZZ1900 being delayed tomorrow is 0.3

The first one can be understood as expressing that, from the whole universe of available flights, about 30% suffer delays. The second statement, however, cannot be interpreted this way; in fact, we cannot speak about the universe of "tomorrows," as there is only one such day, nor of flights ZZ1900 on that day, as again only one exists. Instead, it should be understood as expressing that from all the possible scenarios for the day (weighted according to their plausibility) about 30% involve a delay of flight ZZ1900.[3]

This difference in interpretations was already noticed by Halpern [36,37], who divided probabilistic logics into two main types. Type 1 (or *statistical*) probabilities are those that interpret statements about proportions of the world; hence, give a statistical flavour in the most basic sense of the word. Type 2 (or *subjective*) probabilities, on the other hand, interpret the statements using possible worlds; they usually express a degree of belief, which is applied to every single individual without taking into account the rest of the population.

Just as they express different kinds of views on the probability statement, they need to be interpreted differently in the semantics of a probabilistic ontology. In case of statistical probabilities, the usual semantics of the underlying classical formalism need to be overhauled. Indeed, as these statistical statements express the proportion of population elements which satisfy a given property, they implicitly assert a negation as well. In the first example above, saying that 30% of the flights are delayed means that there are also some flights (in fact, 70% of them) which are *not* delayed. This, and the semantic relationships between properties may produce new issues not foreseen in the original semantics. The usual approach to handle these issues is to partition the class of all domain individuals according to *types* (i.e., the properties they satisfy) and verify that the proportional cardinality of each partition is compatible with the associated probabilities. Some existing formalisms which use this semantics in different forms are [17,41–43,45,47,56].

The semantics of subjective probabilities are often more intuitive both in terms of understanding, and in the development of reasoning methods. In the multiple-world semantics, which are at the bottom of subjective probabilities, one builds situations in which the axiom is "believed" to be true, and others in which it is believed to be false. Each of these situations is then treated as a classical ontology containing all axioms which are assumed to hold, with its

---

[3] Alternatively, read the second statement as "the probability of rain tomorrow is 0.3".

usual semantics and entailment relation.[4] At this point, every consequence can be given a probability which is based on the probabilities of the subontologies where the entailment holds. The only problem is to identify such probabilities, which depend on the relationships between axioms, and might not be completely obvious. This issue will be discussed in more detail in Sect. 5.5. For a more general discussion on the differences between probabilistic interpretations, see e.g. [38,44].

Another important choice to make when dealing with subjective probabilities arises from the difference between an *open-world* and a *closed-world* interpretation of the probabilities and the axioms in the ontology. The simplest and most natural view is the open-world, in which an axiom which was removed from the ontology in one of the possible worlds may still hold if it is entailed by the remaining axioms. In that sense, the probability associated to the axiom serves only as a lower bound, which could be surpassed in case of knowledge redundancy or further information. This view is the one described briefly in the previous paragraph, and is shared by many formalisms including [20,63,64]. The closed-world view, on the other hand, requires that in a situation where an axiom α does not hold, this axiom must be interpreted as false. This guarantees that axioms have exactly the probability assigned to them, but may introduce many other issues. First and foremost, the ontology may become inconsistent in the presence of redundancy. Second, it may require increasing the expressivity of the underlying ontology language in ways in which existing methods may stop working. An example of a probabilistic ontology language following this view are probabilistic databases [68].

Importantly, the differences between probabilistic approaches are not always clear-cut, and may not correspond to the first intuition, or the name chosen by those who developed them. For example, ProbDeclare [51], the probabilistic extension of Declare, was developed to describe business process information extracted through a statistical analysis—each constraint is associated with the proportion of traces where it has been satisfied. However, its semantics is based on PLTL_f^0 [50], which uses a multiple-world semantics and may thus seem to represent subjective probabilities. Another example are the so-called open-world probabilistic databases [18], which apply an open-world view on the facts that *do not* appear in the database (i.e., they are not assumed impossible, but simply less likely than a given bound), but a closed-world for those that do appear—in the semantics, when a fact is chosen not to belong to the current world, then they are impossible in the given interpretation.[5]

5.3   To Count or Not to Count

The next consideration arises mainly from the difference between facts and general knowledge. While we have included them all into the name *axiom*, many

---

[4] Note that by definition of ontology languages, any subset of an ontology is also an ontology; hence this construction works without issues.

[5] The actual semantics of open-world databases is more complex than this, but we wanted to provide just a basic intuition.

```
unreliable(X) <- part-of(X,Y), unreliable(Y).
part-of(computer,chip).
part-of(chip,core).
```

Fig. 2. A Prolog program with one rule and two facts.

ontology languages make a clear distinction between them. In DLs one separates the TBox (terminological knowledge) from the ABox (the facts); databases distinguish the facts from the schema, and Prolog separates facts from rules. Even in our small language $\mathcal{HL}$, one could think of distinguishing the graph from the facts.

Facts can be either used, or not, to derive some consequences from the ontology. But more general knowledge, like rules or TBox axioms have a very different behaviour: they speak about all possible instantiations, and hence may require multiple applications within a single derivation. This behaviour is not problematic in classical ontology languages because entailments do not count; that is, they do not take into account the number of times an axiom may have to be used to derive a consequence. With probabilities, things might change. One must make a choice whether the semantics should count or not the number of applications. This issue is easier explained through examples.

Consider first a simple production scenario where the knowledge includes the statement that any component with an unreliable part is itself unreliable, together with a part-of relationship between structures. This can be expressed e.g., in Prolog through one rule and several facts as shown in Fig. 2. In this scenario it makes sense to weaken the rule into a probabilistic statement expressing that the rule holds with probability, say 0.9. That is, that components are slightly resilient to errors in their parts. Suppose that we know that the core is unreliable. What should be the probability of the computer being unreliable as well? Intuitively, a first rule application should tell us that the chip is unreliable with some probability less than 1, and hence, unreliability of computer holds with a lower probability than 0.9; assuming independence, we expect this probability to be $0.81 = 0.9 \cdot 0.9$. Thus, the fact that the rule needed to be applied more than once to deduce unreliability of computer affects the probability of this conclusion. Under the multiple-world semantics of Problog, one builds several classical Prolog programs, where the rule holds in some of them, and does not hold in others. Note that in every world that makes the rule true, the consequence unreliable(computer) holds, and in all others, it does not hold, yielding a probability 0.9 to this consequence. Hence this semantics would produce an unexpected result, simply because the multiple-world semantics does not take into account the number of times the rule is applied. For such a scenario, other semantics would be more meaningful.

Consider now a hierarchical structure expressing weather conditions, with constraints stating that cold and wet weather produces fog, and that in cold weather, urban areas have an increase in smog. Moreover, in situations of fog and smog, there is low visibility. All this can be expressed through the $\mathcal{HL}$

axioms ({Cold, Humid}, Fog), ({Cold, Urban}, Smog), and ({Fog, Smog}, LowVis). Suppose, moreover, that we know for sure that milano is an urban area with high humidity, and we predict with a 90% probability that it will be cold: Humid(milano) : 1, Urban(milano) : 1, Cold(milano) : 0.9. If we are interested in predicting the probability of low visibility, we could try to chain our axioms to the facts, and deduce first a 90% probability for each, fog and smog, and then we need to compute a probability of low visibility based on these two. If we assumed independence, we would get a probability of 0.81 of low visibility. This result has several issues, starting from the fact that fog and smog are not independent (they both depend on the cold factor),[6] but one can already see that the probability of 0.81 is a result of "counting" twice the fact that the probability of cold in Milano is 0.9. Even though this fact is used in two parts of the derivation, it is a mistake to consider the use of both applications as different. All depends on one single fact. In this case, the appropriate action is to consider a semantics that does not take into account the number of applications of an axiom. The multiple-world semantics would fit perfectly well in it.

5.4   Understand the Numbers

One of the main criticisms that probabilistic logics receive from other areas of knowledge representation is about the source of the probabilistic knowledge. More specifically, how do we compute the probabilities with which the axioms are labelled? This is a very valid criticism, and is at the heart of the applicability of these formalisms.

In many cases, we can easily justify the use of a probability as a statistical measure of what is expected to be observed. For example, a probabilistic rule under the statistical semantics may express that some proportion of the population satisfies a given property. This proportion may be computed through a full census, or approximated through different sampling techniques. Still, in some other cases the use of arbitrary numbers as probabilities—or as the expressed probabilities—is not really justified. One prominent example is the automatic population of probabilistic databases [53]. In this setting, natural language processing (NLP) techniques are applied to large corpora to extract some facts, and sometimes more advanced knowledge, which is written in the text. An advantage of using NLP is that tools often return a weight associated to each fact, which expresses the confidence on the fact. This measure can be seen as a probability, in the sense that it describes a proportion of successes in the underlying tool for sentences of the kind extracted. However, it does not refer to the likelihood of the piece of knowledge itself. In other words, the tool provides a measure of its certainty that it read the sentence correctly from the corpus, but cannot judge the correctness of this text. To put it bluntly, a well-written but falsity ridden text would provide facts with a higher confidence value than a well-researched piece with grammatical errors. This is natural, since it is not the scope of NLP to do fact checking, but only to process the written text.

---

[6] We will come back to this issue in Sect. 5.5.

Other kinds of probabilities are more problematic. For example, suppose that one is trying to model the subjective belief that a sport expert has on the likelihood of success of a specific team in a championship. As humans, we are not very good at providing adequate probabilities, and will often default back to very specific numbers which we observe continuously: 0.99, 0.9, maybe 0.8. It is very unlikely that someone would measure their confidence as, say, 0.935. Even statistical methods should be taken with a grain of salt. For example, sampling methods—which were used to justify probabilities just one paragraph above—do not really yield any specific probability which can be used directly. Rather, they can provide estimators, some of which are more likely than others, and perhaps some certainty value or confidence interval around them. If one does not understand the meaning of these notions and values, one will easily fall into a rabbit hole of misleading or erroneous interpretations of probabilistic entailments. However, this is a topic that falls outside the scope of this tutorial, and we will not go into further details.

5.5   Be Careful with Independence

The fifth golden rule refers to the notion of probabilistic independence. As we have seen throughout this section, independence is an important assumption, which is used very often for probabilistic reasoning. The reason is very simple: independence provides a flavour of truth-functionality which is not usually present in probability measures. To be more precise, for two arbitrary events X, Y, knowing $P(X)$ and $P(Y)$ does not suffice in general for knowing $P(XY)$. However, if X and Y are independent, then we know that $P(XY) = P(X)P(Y)$. Since one does not usually have enough information to compute the probability of the intersection of two events, and even if it is known, computing it may require more costly operations, one can consider independence as a simplifying assumption. Unfortunately, this assumption is often overlooked in formalism descriptions, and may not be very realistic in the first place.

We have already seen in Sect. 5.3 an example where an independence assumption yields a problematic result. An important aspect of that example is that the probabilistically dependent elements are in fact hidden from the user, and the consequence being asked. Recall that in the example we apply two different axioms that require the same fact (Cold(milano)) to be derived. The conclusions of these axioms then made no further reference to this fact, but could be further combined to derive more facts. A user querying for the probability of low visibility may have no idea that the probability of cold has any influence on it, even if they know that low visibility depends on the presence of fog and smog.

To try to convince the reader of the importance of analysing the independence assumption—despite its ubiquity in probabilistic formalisms—we present a simple example. Suppose that we are extracting information about an individual whose first name is *Andrea*. Andrea is a typical male name in Italy, but a typical female name in other parts of the world. Without further information, we cannot be certain about the gender of this individual. Suppose that one analysis concludes that there is a 50% chance that Andrea is *male*, while another one concludes that they have a 50% chance of being *female*. Note that, from our meta-knowledge perspective, these two statements are perfectly consistent with each other. They are so even if we include the constraint that Male and Female are disjoint classes. However, the independence assumption would yield the conclusion that Andrea is in the intersection of Male and Female with probability 0.25 (or yield an inconsistency together with the disjointness axiom) which is clearly wrong.

Still, one should not have the impression that it is necessarily wrong to use an independence assumption. Depending on the application, it may indeed be the right choice to make for different reasons. For example, when it is impossible to obtain a better joint probability distribution between the axioms, or in cases where representing it would be too costly. A prominent formalism where this assumption is used are tuple-independent probabilistic databases [68]. As with classical databases, in the probabilistic variant one expects to handle huge tables efficiently. Obtaining and representing a full joint probability distribution for all the tuples in the database would be prohibitive, and removing the independence assumption results in slower derivation methods. Moreover, as only the data is probabilistic and the goal is to answer queries, the multiple use of a single database tuple in different parts of the derivation is seldom an issue. Hence, while formally speaking the independence assumption is not well justified, its use allows for a practical solution. However, one should always keep in mind the limitations of the assumption, specially when extending the formalism to other uses.

6   A Specific Language

After we have seen some of the most important decisions to make when dealing with a probabilistic ontology language, we now put those notions in practice by defining a probabilistic extension of $\mathcal{HL}$ and studying some of its properties. This probabilistic ontology language can be seen as a new member of the family of Bayesian DLs which have been studied in recent years [12,20]. It can also be seen as a special case of ProbLog, with a simpler targetted syntax for expressing probabilistic rules and conditional probabilistic statements. Note that this is, in part, an artificial example for showcasing the properties and choices in the construction of ontology languages. In practice one would likely use a different language capable of expressing more complex properties.

Recall that in $\mathcal{HL}$, axioms are either hyperedges or atomic facts. In our case, we require that the probabilistic assignment of a probabilistic ontology is total; that is, every axiom in the ontology receives a probability degree. Formally, a probabilistic $\mathcal{HL}$ ontology is a finite set of $\mathcal{HL}$ axioms, where each axiom is assigned a probability degree in $[0, 1]$. For the semantics, we will choose a multiple-world approach akin to subjective probabilities, under an open-world point of view. In particular, in our approach the number of times an axiom is used to derive a consequence is irrelevant. However, we do not use the standard independence assumption, but rather assume independence only in some elements of the ontology.

Recall that we can see an $\mathcal{HL}$ ontology as being formed of two parts: a hypergraph, and a data store. Our assumption, as in many ontology languages, will be that the hypergraph will be rather small in comparison to the size of the data. Hence, we may include assumptions to manipulate the data efficiently, but can invest more computational resources dealing with the hypergraph. For this reason, we will assume tuple independence on the data (as commonly done in probabilistic databases), but provide a joint probability distribution on the hyperedges. As it will be prohibitive to express this distribution extensionally for moderately large hypergraphs,[7] we use a more compact encoding through a Bayesian network. Interestingly, this representation will allow us to express also some logical dependencies between the axioms. Formally, to achieve this, we will need to make the general notion of a probabilistic ontology slightly more precise, adding a component to the tuple.

A *probabilistic $\mathcal{HL}$ ontology* is a tuple $(\mathcal{O}, P, \mathcal{B}, B)$ where $\mathcal{O}$ is an $\mathcal{HL}$ ontology, $P : \mathcal{O} \to [0,1]$ is the *probability assignment function*, $\mathcal{B} = (\mathcal{G}, \Phi)$ is a Bayesian network with $\mathcal{G} = (V, E)$, and $B : \mathcal{O} \to \mathscr{P}(V)$ is the *context function*, which maps every hyperedge in $\mathcal{O}$ to a set of random variables in the BN $\mathcal{B}$. In essence, the context function associates each hyperedge in $\mathcal{O}$ with a class of states in the BN $\mathcal{B}$. Intuitively, this assignment expresses that the hyperedge α is true whenever all the variables in $B(\alpha)$ are made true in the BN. We require that $P, \mathcal{B}, B$ are *consistent* in the sense that $P(\alpha) = P_{\mathcal{B}}(B(\alpha))$ holds for all hyperedges α.

For example, suppose that we are interested in modelling and reasoning about the knowledge from a medical application where different co-occurring diseases are being followed. In that case, the BN from Fig. 1 represents the joint probability distribution of the diseases W, X, Y, Z. For example, variable Z could stand for CTE and W for Alzheimer's. We prefer to keep the names abstract as much as possible to avoid misunderstanding caused by existing knowledge from the user, given the artificial nature of this simplified example.[8] Consider then the probabilistic $\mathcal{HL}$ ontology $(\mathcal{O}_{\mathsf{exa}}, P_{\mathsf{exa}}, \mathcal{B}_{\mathsf{exa}}, B_{\mathsf{exa}})$ where $\mathcal{B}_{\mathsf{exa}}$ is the BN from Fig. 1 and $\mathcal{O}_{\mathsf{exa}}, P_{\mathsf{exa}}$, and B_{exa} are represented in Table 2. The hypergraph models general relationships between findings, which hold only on specific contexts. For example, in the context $\{X\}$, any patient with halucinations presents also nausea, while the converse relation (that nausea implies halucinations) only holds within the context $\{W, X\}$. Note that this means that the presence of the latter axiom necessarily implies the presence of the former. The probabilities associated to these axioms are given by the probability distribution in $\mathcal{B}_{\mathsf{exa}}$. In fact, $P_{\mathcal{B}_{\mathsf{exa}}}(\{X\}) = 0.7$. An important example is the last hyperedge $(\{\mathsf{Dementia}\}, \mathsf{Observation})$. It is associated to the empty context $\emptyset$, which expresses that it must always hold; all the RVs in $\emptyset$ are always true. Hence, it is also assigned the probability 1. In the lower part of the table we observe a few facts expressing findings present in three

---

[7] Recall that the extensional description of a joint probability distribution requires exponential space on the number of variables involved.

[8] It should go without saying, but this is only an example and should in no way be considered medical advice of any kind.

Table 2. An example probabilistic $\mathcal{HL}$ ontology. Note that the context function B_{exa} applies only to the hyperedges.

B_{exa}	P_{exa}	$\mathcal{O}_{\mathsf{exa}}$
$\{Y\}$	0.28	$(\{\mathsf{Pain}\}, \mathsf{Tachycardia})$
$\{W,Y\}$	0.196	$(\{\mathsf{Tachycardia}, \mathsf{Nausea}\}, \mathsf{Observation})$
$\{W,X\}$	0.28	$(\{\mathsf{Nausea}\}, \mathsf{Halucination})$
$\{X\}$	0.7	$(\{\mathsf{Halucination}\}, \mathsf{Nausea})$
$\{W,Z\}$	0.0432	$(\{\mathsf{Halucination}, \mathsf{MemoryLoss}\}, \mathsf{Dementia})$
$\emptyset$	1	$(\{\mathsf{Dementia}\}, \mathsf{Observation})$

P_{exa}	$\mathcal{O}_{\mathsf{exa}}$	P_{exa}	$\mathcal{O}_{\mathsf{exa}}$
0.5	$\mathsf{Dementia}(p1)$	0.8	$\mathsf{Pain}(p1)$
0.4	$\mathsf{Halucination}(p2)$	1	$\mathsf{Pain}(p2)$
0.9	$\mathsf{Nausea}(p3)$	0.7	$\mathsf{MemoryLoss}(p3)$

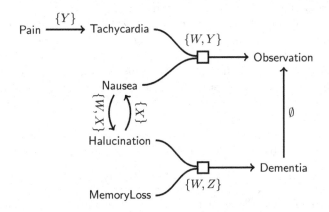

Fig. 3. The hypergraph portion of a probabilistic $\mathcal{HL}$ ontology. Each hyperedge is labelled with the set of RVs from the BN $\mathcal{B}_{\mathsf{exa}}$ given by the context function.

different patients. We assume that these finding were obtained or confirmed through imprecise indirect tests and are thus associated to a likelihood. For an easier reading, the hypergraph portion of this ontology, together with its context mapping, is depicted in Fig. 3. If we ignore for a second the probabilities, from the ontology $\mathcal{O}_{\mathsf{exa}}$ we can derive that all three patients are under observation (i.e., $\mathsf{Observation}(p_i)$ holds for $i = 1, 2, 3$). For instance, p_3 presents nausea, which implies halucinations. The latter, together with memory loss implies dementia, which itself implies observation. What we are now interested in now is taking also the probabilistic knowledge into account.

As mentioned already, we use a possible-worlds semantics to interpret the probabilities. Specifically, let $\mathsf{Fact}(\mathcal{O}) \subseteq \mathcal{O}$ be the set of all facts in $\mathcal{O}$, and let V the set of nodes in the BN $\mathcal{B}$. The set of *possible worlds* is $\mathscr{P}(\mathsf{Fact}(\mathcal{O})) \times \mathscr{P}(V)$;

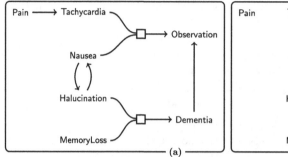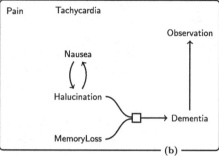

Fig. 4. The hypergraphs from the classical $\mathcal{HL}$ ontologies defined by the possible worlds (a) $w_1 = (\mathsf{Fact}(\mathcal{O}_{\mathsf{exa}}), \{W, X, Y, Z\})$ and (b) $w_2 = (\mathsf{Fact}(\mathcal{O}_{\mathsf{exa}}), \{W, X, Z\})$.

i.e., a pair containing a set of facts and a set of nodes. Each possible world $w = (\mathcal{F}, \mathbf{X})$ is assigned a probability defined as $P(w) := \prod_{\alpha \in \mathcal{F}} P(\alpha) \cdot P_{\mathcal{B}}(\mathbf{X})$. Note that for assigning the probability of a possible world, we are considering all facts as mutually independent, and independent of the hypergraph; however, the axioms in the hypergraph are not independent, but their relationship is expressed through the BN $\mathcal{B}$. In our example, these assumptions are meaningful: the probabilities in facts are obtained through tests which are assumed to be independent, but the hyperedges are probabilistically dependent according to the relationships expressed in $\mathcal{B}_{\mathsf{exa}}$.

Each possible world defines a (classical) $\mathcal{HL}$ ontology in the obvious manner. Specifically, the possible world $w = (\mathcal{F}, \mathbf{X})$ defines the $\mathcal{HL}$ ontology

$$\mathcal{O}(w) := \mathcal{F} \cup \{\alpha \in \mathcal{O} \setminus \mathsf{Fact}(\mathcal{O}) \mid B(\alpha) \subseteq \mathbf{X}\}.$$

In words, $\mathcal{O}(w)$ contains all the facts expressed by w and all the hyperedges that comply with the set $\mathbf{X}$ in their context mapping. Entailment in each ontology $\mathcal{O}(w)$ is defined exactly as in the classical case. For example, two possible worlds for our example probabilistic $\mathcal{HL}$ ontology are $w_1 = (\mathsf{Fact}(\mathcal{O}_{\mathsf{exa}}), \{W, X, Y, Z\})$ and $w_2 = (\mathsf{Fact}(\mathcal{O}_{\mathsf{exa}}), \{W, X, Z\})$. These possible worlds define the classical $\mathcal{HL}$ ontologies depicted in Fig. 4, where the facts are all those from Table 2. In the ontology defined by w_2 we can no longer derive the fact $\mathsf{Observation}(p_2)$. Perhaps surprisingly at first sight, the probability of both possible worlds is 0. In fact, a simple observation of the BN in Fig. 1 shows that any world which contains Z and either X or Y must have probability 0.

Recall that our semantics allows us to express a logical dependency between hyperedges: if α, β are two hyperedges such that $B(\alpha) \subseteq B(\beta)$, then for every possible world w it holds that if $\beta \in \mathcal{O}(w)$ then also $\alpha \in \mathcal{O}(w)$. This property is useful when trying to unify knowledge from different sources, giving a related probability to axioms provided from the same or related sources. In technical terms, it is also useful for maintaining the same syntax for $\mathcal{HL}$ axioms. Recall that hyperedges have only one target node, but it is not unrealistic to want to express that elements with some properties belong to the conjunction of two classes; e.g., that a father is a male parent. In classical $\mathcal{HL}$ this is normalised by introducing two separate axioms: fathers are male $((\{\mathsf{Father}\}, \mathsf{Male}))$, and fathers are parents $((\{\mathsf{Father}\}, \mathsf{Parent}))$, but in the probabilistic variant this normalisation would be incorrect unless we can express that both axioms must co-appear at all times.

Given a consequence $c \in \mathfrak{C}$, we define its *probability* w.r.t. $(\mathcal{O}, P, \mathcal{B}, B)$ as

$$P(c) := \sum_{w \in \mathscr{P}(\mathsf{Fact}(\mathcal{O})) \times \mathscr{P}(V), \mathcal{O}(w) \models c} P(w).$$

That is, we sum the probability of all possible worlds which entail the consequence c. Importantly, this semantics follows an open-world view of the possible world semantics: if a hyperedge or a fact is implicitly entailed by other axioms in the ontology, it might hold also in worlds where it is not explicitly required. This means that in general the probability assigned by the function P is only a lower bound, which may increase due to other dependencies. In our running example, we can see that $P(\mathsf{Observation}(p_1)) = 0.5$ because $(\{\mathsf{Dementia}\}, \mathsf{Observation})$ holds in all possible worlds, but $\mathsf{Dementia}(p_1)$ only in worlds with probability 0.5. Similarly, $P(\mathsf{Observation}(p_3)) = 0$ because for nausea and memory loss to cause dementia, both X and Z should hold which, as explained before, can only happen with probability 0. We leave as an exercise to the reader the computation of $P(\mathsf{Observation}(p_2))$.

In the construction of $\mathcal{HL}$ and its semantics, we have made several design choices. All these design choices limit the applicability of our logic to some specific scenarios, and follow the guidelines from Sect. 5. Before continuing the technical details of this language, we expand on these choices and argue about its application scenario. First of all, we repeat that we assume that the hypergraph is proportionally much smaller than the data. Hence, to allow effective reasoning, we need to be more careful about the resources involved in handling the data, than in those handling the hypergraph (reachability) task. For that reason, we have chosen to use tuple-independence within the data, which will allow us to handle the relationships between data efficiently. Although this assumption is not justified in all possible datasets, there exist situations like, e.g., when facts are being produced by sensors in a complex machinery or when individuals are being sampled, where the independence assumption is justified. On the other hand, a full independence assumption between hyperedges is particularly excessive due to the limited expressivity of the language. Indeed, inexpressive languages usually require more than one axiom to encode a single constraint. For example, suppose that we do not only want to diagnose, but also describe and explain diseases in our ontology. Then, following the example from the beginning of Sect. 3, we would like to express that a common cold usually presents a running nose and light-headedness; that is, an axiom which would look like $(\mathsf{Cold}, \{\mathsf{RunNose}, \mathsf{LightHead}\})$. However, this is not expressible in $\mathcal{HL}$. Our only choice is to divide the knowledge into two axioms $(\{\mathsf{Cold}\}, \mathsf{RunNose}), (\{\mathsf{Cold}\}, \mathsf{LightHead})$ but, clearly, these two axioms cannot be considered independent; in fact, they should always appear together because they form an atomic piece of knowledge. In our setting, both axioms will share a common context which guarantees this logical dependency. Finally, we have chosen to interpret the probabilities following the multiple-world semantics. This means that we are considering hyperedges as absolute, if they hold, but we are just not certain about the truth of the edge. This case commonly arises if the edges are being mined or extracted through automated methods from e.g., text or other web resources. In our case, we use the contextual interpretation commonly followed by Bayesian ontology languages. In this setting, we see a valuation of the variables in the BN as an uncertain context, and associate certain axioms to each context. That is, our knowledge is fully certain given the context in which it is applied, but the context itself may be uncertain. For example, we may know that in the context of osteoporosis, the bone mineral density is low, but we may not know (before a precise diagnosis) whether a patient has osteoporosis or not.

To compute the probability of a consequence c, one could simply follow the structure hinted by the definition: compute all possible worlds $w = (\mathcal{F}, \mathbf{X})$, and for each of them, compute $P(w)$ (linear in $\mathcal{F}$ but PP in the size of $\mathbf{X}$) and decide whether $\mathcal{O}(w) \models c$. This of course requires exponential time in the size of each of the components used, but by analysing each possible world independently, it is possible to limit the space usage to a polynomial bound. Although this algorithm is simple to understand and implement, it is without doubt also far from optimal in terms of the computational resources used. In order to find a better approach, we need to study deeper the properties of the language.

A slightly better approach is the following. Rather than trying to construct a classical ontology for every possible world, we produce a probabilistic ontology for each *Bayesian world*; that is, for every $\mathbf{X} \subseteq V$, but such that this ontology preserves adequate properties for probabilistic reasoning. Specifically, for each $\mathbf{X} \subseteq V$, let $\mathcal{O}(\mathbf{X}) := (\mathcal{O}', P')$ be the probabilistic ontology where

$$\mathcal{O}' := \mathsf{Fact}(\mathcal{O}) \cup \{\alpha \in \mathcal{O} \setminus \mathsf{Fact}(\mathcal{O}) \mid B(\alpha) \subseteq \mathbf{X}\}$$

and P' is the restriction of P to $\mathsf{Fact}(\mathcal{O})$. In a nutshell, $\mathcal{O}(\mathbf{X})$ includes the hypergraph that is compatible with the choice $\mathbf{X}$, but preserves the probabilistic facts as they are. Note that according to our semantics, these probabilistic facts are a probabilistic database with tuple independence. The hypergraph in $\mathcal{O}(\mathbf{X})$ still entails some implicit facts which are not explicitly encoded in the database, and need to be handled. Given a consequence c, we can compute its probability $P_{\mathbf{X}}(c)$ w.r.t. $\mathcal{O}(\mathbf{X})$ by asking a simple UCQ over the probabilistic database $(\mathsf{Fact}(\mathcal{O}), P')$, where the information of the hypergraph is encoded through a backwards propagation. For example, if $\mathbf{X} = \{W, X, Y, Z\}$ (see Fig. 4 (a)) and we are interested in the consequence $\mathsf{Observation}(p_3)$, we can construct the union of conjunctive queries by traversing the hyperedges backwards, as shown in Table 3. The first four lines (before the separation) are those from the UCQ built by $\mathbf{X} = \{W, X, Z\}$ (Fig. 4(b)). For more details see [1,15]. Note that all the components of this UCQ are simple queries with only one constant, and are thus easily manageable by modern probabilistic database systems [26]. To compute the probability of the consequence w.r.t. the original probabilistic

Table 3. Construction of a UCQ through backward traversing of a hypergraph.

Observation(p_3)
Dementia(p_3)
Halucination(p_3) $\wedge$ MemoryLoss(p_3)
Nausea(p_3) $\wedge$ MemoryLoss(p_3)
Tachycardia(p_3) $\wedge$ Nausea(p_3)
Tachycardia(p_3) $\wedge$ Halucination(p_3)
Pain(p_3) $\wedge$ Nausea(p_3)
Pain(p_3) $\wedge$ Halucination(p_3)

ontology, we need to accumulate over all Bayesian worlds, taking into account their relative likelihood by means of an arithmetic sum. Indeed, it can be shown that for every consequence $c \in \mathfrak{C}$, $P(c) = \sum_{\mathbf{X} \subseteq V} P_{\mathcal{B}}(\mathbf{X}) \cdot P_{\mathbf{X}}(c)$.

Note that this second approach would still require exponential time on the size of the probabilistic ontology; at the very least, it needs to enumerate all Bayesian worlds (i.e., all subsets of V). However, this blowup is restricted to the elements of the Bayesian network, which is assumed to be the smallest component of the whole ontology. At each Bayesian world, the probability of the consequence can be computed in polynomial time. Thus, the overall complexity of computing the probability is bounded by a polynomial on the size of the database. This is called the *data complexity*. Moreover, using a probabilistic database system allows us to make slightly more advanced derivations. One simple example is that we could substitute the constant p_3 with a variable x in the UCQ generated by our model. This would return *all* individuals that are under observation (with their respective probability), without having to query them explicitly.

7   Conclusions

In this tutorial we have introduced the basic schema of probabilistic ontologies. Our goal was not to consider a specific (probabilistic) ontology language, but rather to allow for a general view which includes as many of the existing ontology languages as possible. As a side benefit, our formalisation includes languages which may not be typically considered as ontology languages, but which can still be analysed under this view.

Just as there exists a plethora of ontology languages, which have been developed to satisfy specific needs, there are also many different possibilities for extending these languages to deal with probabilities. To get a feeling about the variety of the existing languages, one can consider the survey by Lukasiewicz and Straccia [48], which is already over a decade old. If one is interested in developing—or using—a probabilistic ontology, it is important to understand the design choices behind the underlying language and their motivations, and to ensure that these coincide with the task at hand. As a mnemonic device for the main notions to consider, we have developed *The Five Golden Rules*, which are presented in Sect. 5. The intention of these rules is to remain informed about the properties of the formalism, and the kind of consequences one should expect from them. They are, however, far from complete; a detailed analysis of each formalism, which also takes into account the properties of the underlying ontology language is always necessary. Still, if there is only one message that the reader takes home from this work, is that **there is no one-size-fits-all solution**. Each variation has its advantages and disadvantages, and they must be balanced for the applicatoin at hand. But, importantly, all the factors need to be taken into account. We often tend to focus our attention too much on the computational complexity of a problem, which in this case means ignoring important information from our knowledge domain.

As a case scenario, we have looked in some detail into a probabilistic extension of the ontology language $\mathcal{HL}$ which combines hypergraphs with a database. When building the probabilistic extension, we considered the choices to be made, and finished with the multiple-world semantics under an open-world view. We also combined an independence assumption (for all the facts in the database) with a more complex joint probability distribution on the hyperedges, which is capable of expressing probabilistic dependencies (encoded in a Bayesian network) and logical dependencies, through a mapping from the axioms to the BN. Again, we emphasise that this language is not intended to be better (or worse) than other proposals in the literature, but rather showcase the development of a probabilistic extension. Although it is possible to make blanket statements about all probabilistic extensions with some choices—e.g., that w.r.t. subjective probabilities under an open-world view, the probability of a consequence can be reduced to multiple classical entailments—being able to look at the specific formalism will usually lead to better results. In our example language, we were able to improve the overall complexity simply by knowing how the reasoning techniques work in the classical case, and adapting them for the probabilistic scenario. In general, the analysis is not so straightforward, but it is worth the effort. The example also shows that often probabilistic ontologies require more information than just a probability assignment to axioms.

In our effort to provide a general view to probabilistic ontologies without restricting to specific languages, but at the same time trying to keep the presentation simple, we had to exclude some prominent formalisms. Some of them (for example, those described at the beginning of Sect. 4) could be included without major conceptual changes, but we decided against it mainly to avoid saturating the notation, and confusing the reader with elements which only become relevant in specific cases. However, there are other languages which could not be fitted for more fundamental reasons. For example, non-monotonic logics [13], where new knowledge may defeat previously derived consequences, do not fit into our definition of ontology language. They could be problematic for the way we describe the semantics of probabilistic entailments.

Probabilities are a very natural way to represent uncertainty. There are perhaps two main causes for this naturality: first, the daily bombardment of probabilistic language to which we are submitted; and the fact that we have a solid theoretical background for obtaining and reasoning about probabilities in many different contexts. But this familiarity can also be dangerous. Typical users who are not probability experts have a faulty intuition of the meaning of probabilities, and in particular do not know the subtleties of the results of statistical methods. Case in point, the use of a sampling result as a fixed probability, ignoring the underlying sampling error, and the variability of the studied phenomenon. We thus encourage all readers to go forward, use probabilities, use them profusely, but use them carefully.

References

1. Artale, A., Calvanese, D., Kontchakov, R., Zakharyaschev, M.: The DL-Lite family and relations. J. Artif. Intell. Res. **36**, 1–69 (2009). https://doi.org/10.1613/jair.2820
2. Baader, F., Calvanese, D., McGuinness, D., Nardi, D., Patel-Schneider, P. (eds.): The Description Logic Handbook: Theory, Implementation, and Applications, 2nd edn. University Press, Cambridge (2007)
3. Baader, F., Hladik, J., Peñaloza, R.: Automata can show PSpace results for description logics. Inf. Comput. **206**(9–10), 1045–1056 (2008). https://doi.org/10.1016/j.ic.2008.03.006
4. Bellomarini, L., Benedetto, D., Gottlob, G., Sallinger, E.: Vadalog: a modern architecture for automated reasoning with large knowledge graphs. Inf. Syst., 101528 (2020). https://doi.org/10.1016/j.is.2020.101528
5. Bianchi, F., Rossiello, G., Costabello, L., Palmonari, M., Minervini, P.: Knowledge graph embeddings and explainable AI. CoRR abs/2004.14843 (2020). https://arxiv.org/abs/2004.14843
6. Biere, A., Heule, M.J.H., van Maaren, H., Walsh, T. (eds.): Handbook of Satisfiability. Frontiers in Artificial Intelligence and Applications, vol. 185. IOS Press, Amsterdam (2009)
7. Bobillo, F., Straccia, U.: Reasoning within fuzzy OWL 2 EL revisited. Fuzzy Sets Syst. **351**, 1–40 (2018). https://doi.org/10.1016/j.fss.2018.03.011
8. Borgwardt, S.: Fuzzy description logics with general concept inclusions. Ph.D. thesis, Technische Universität Dresden, Germany (2014)
9. Borgwardt, S., Ceylan, İ.İ., Lukasiewicz, T.: Ontology-mediated query answering over log-linear probabilistic data. In: Proceedings of the 33rd AAAI Conference on Artificial Intelligence, AAAI 2019, pp. 2711–2718. AAAI Press (2019). https://doi.org/10.1609/aaai.v33i01.33012711
10. Borgwardt, S., Peñaloza, R.: The complexity of lattice-based fuzzy description logics. J. Data Semant. **2**(1), 1–19 (2013). https://doi.org/10.1007/s13740-012-0013-x
11. Borgwardt, S., Peñaloza, R.: Fuzzy description logics – a survey. In: Moral, S., Pivert, O., Sánchez, D., Marín, N. (eds.) SUM 2017. LNCS (LNAI), vol. 10564, pp. 31–45. Springer, Cham (2017). https://doi.org/10.1007/978-3-319-67582-4_3
12. Botha, L., Meyer, T., Peñaloza, R.: A Bayesian extension of the description logic $\mathcal{ALC}$. In: Calimeri, F., Leone, N., Manna, M. (eds.) JELIA 2019. LNCS (LNAI), vol. 11468, pp. 339–354. Springer, Cham (2019). https://doi.org/10.1007/978-3-030-19570-0_22

13. Brewka, G.: Nonmonotonic Reasoning - Logical Foundations of Commonsense. Cambridge Tracts in Theoretical Computer Science, vol. 12. Cambridge University Press, Cambridge (1991)

14. Calì, A., Gottlob, G., Lukasiewicz, T., Pieris, A.: Datalog+/-: a family of languages for ontology querying. In: de Moor, O., Gottlob, G., Furche, T., Sellers, A. (eds.) Datalog 2.0 2010. LNCS, vol. 6702, pp. 351–368. Springer, Heidelberg (2011). https://doi.org/10.1007/978-3-642-24206-9_20

15. Calvanese, D., De Giacomo, G., Lembo, D., Lenzerini, M., Rosati, R.: Data complexity of query answering in description logics. Artif. Intell. **195**, 335–360 (2013). https://doi.org/10.1016/j.artint.2012.10.003

16. Cano, A., Cozman, F.G., Lukasiewicz, T.: Reasoning with imprecise probabilities. Int. J. Approx. Reason. **44**(3), 197–199 (2007). https://doi.org/10.1016/j.ijar.2006.09.001

17. Carvalho, R.N., Laskey, K.B., Costa, P.C.G.: PR-OWL - a language for defining probabilistic ontologies. Int. J. Approx. Reason. **91**, 56–79 (2017). https://doi.org/10.1016/j.ijar.2017.08.011

18. Ceylan, I.I., Darwiche, A., den Broeck, G.V.: Open-world probabilistic databases. In: Baral, C., Delgrande, J.P., Wolter, F. (eds.) Proceedings of the 15th International Conference on Principles of Knowledge Representation and Reasoning, KR 2016, pp. 339–348. AAAI Press (2016). http://www.aaai.org/ocs/index.php/KR/KR16/paper/view/12908

19. Ceylan, II., Lukasiewicz, T.: A tutorial on query answering and reasoning over probabilistic knowledge bases. In: d'Amato, C., Theobald, M. (eds.) Reasoning Web 2018. LNCS, vol. 11078, pp. 35–77. Springer, Cham (2018). https://doi.org/10.1007/978-3-030-00338-8_3

20. Ceylan, II., Peñaloza, R.: The Bayesian ontology language BEL. J. Autom. Reason. **58**(1), 67–95 (2017). https://doi.org/10.1007/s10817-016-9386-0

21. Concannon, L.G., Kaufman, M.S., Herring, S.A.: Counseling athletes on the risk of chronic traumatic encephalopathy. Sports Health **6**(5), 396–401 (2014). https://doi.org/10.1177/1941738114530958

22. Cooper, G.F.: The computational complexity of probabilistic inference using Bayesian belief networks. Artif. Intell. **42**(2–3), 393–405 (1990). https://doi.org/10.1016/0004-3702(90)90060-D

23. Cozman, F.G.: Graphical models for imprecise probabilities. Int. J. Approx. Reason. **39**(2–3), 167–184 (2005). https://doi.org/10.1016/j.ijar.2004.10.003

24. Cuenca Grau, B., Horrocks, I., Motik, B., Parsia, B., Patel-Schneider, P., Sattler, U.: OWL 2: The next step for OWL. J. Web Semant. **6**, 309–322 (2008)

25. Cyganiak, R., Wood, D., Lanthaler, M. (eds.): RDF 1.1 Concepts and Abstract Syntax. W3C Recommendation (25 February 2014). http://www.w3.org/TR/rdf11-concepts/

26. Dalvi, N.N., Suciu, D.: The dichotomy of probabilistic inference for unions of conjunctive queries. J. ACM **59**(6), 30:1–30:87 (2012). https://doi.org/10.1145/2395116.2395119

27. Darwiche, A.: Modeling and Reasoning with Bayesian Networks. Cambridge University Press, Cambridge (2009). http://www.cambridge.org/uk/catalogue/catalogue.asp?isbn=9780521884389

28. Dechter, R.: Bucket elimination: a unifying framework for reasoning. Artif. Intell. **113**(1–2), 41–85 (1999). https://doi.org/10.1016/S0004-3702(99)00059-4

29. Diestel, R.: Graph Theory. Graduate Texts in Mathematics, vol. 173, 5th edn. Springer, Heidelberg (2017). https://doi.org/10.1007/978-3-662-53622-3

30. Dubois, D., Prade, H.: Possibility Theory - An Approach to Computerized Processing of Uncertainty. Springer, Boston (1988). https://doi.org/10.1007/978-1-4684-5287-7

31. Gallo, G., Longo, G., Pallottino, S., Nguyen, S.: Directed hypergraphs and applications. Discret. Appl. Math. **42**(2), 177–201 (1993). https://doi.org/10.1016/0166-218X(93)90045-P

32. Gottwald, S.: Many-valued and fuzzy logics. In: Kacprzyk, J., Pedrycz, W. (eds.) Springer Handbook of Computational Intelligence, pp. 7–29. Springer, Heidelberg (2015). https://doi.org/10.1007/978-3-662-43505-2_2

33. Gutiérrez-Basulto, V., Jung, J.C., Lutz, C., Schröder, L.: A closer look at the probabilistic description logic prob-EL. In: Burgard, W., Roth, D. (eds.) Proceedings of the 25th AAAI Conference on Artificial Intelligence, AAAI 2011. AAAI Press (2011). http://www.aaai.org/ocs/index.php/AAAI/AAAI11/paper/view/3702

34. Gutiérrez-Basulto, V., Jung, J.C., Lutz, C., Schröder, L.: Probabilistic description logics for subjective uncertainty. J. Artif. Intell. Res. **58**, 1–66 (2017). https://doi.org/10.1613/jair.5222

35. Hájek, P.: Metamathematics of Fuzzy Logic. Trends in Logic, vol. 4. Springer, Dordrecht (1998). https://doi.org/10.1007/978-94-011-5300-3

36. Halpern, J.Y.: An analysis of first-order logics of probability. In: Sridharan, N.S. (ed.) Proceedings of the 11th International Joint Conference on Artificial Intelligence, IJCAI 1989, pp. 1375–1381. Morgan Kaufmann (1989). http://ijcai.org/Proceedings/89-2/Papers/084.pdf

37. Halpern, J.Y.: An analysis of first-order logics of probability. Artif. Intell. **46**(3), 311–350 (1990). https://doi.org/10.1016/0004-3702(90)90019-V

38. Halpern, J.Y.: Reasoning about Uncertainty. MIT Press, Cambridge (2005)

39. Hogan, A., et al.: Knowledge graphs. CoRR abs/2003.02320 (2020). https://arxiv.org/abs/2003.02320

40. Horrocks, I., Kutz, O., Sattler, U.: The even more irresistible $\mathcal{SROIQ}$. In: Doherty, P., Mylopoulos, J., Welty, C.A. (eds.) Proceedings of the 10th International Conference on Principles of Knowledge Representation and Reasoning, KR 2006, pp. 57–67. AAAI Press (2006)

41. Jaeger, M.: Probabilistic reasoning in terminological logics. In: Doyle, J., Sandewall, E., Torasso, P. (eds.) Proceedings of the 4th International Conference on Principles of Knowledge Representation and Reasoning, KR 1994, pp. 305–316. Morgan Kaufmann (1994)

42. Klinov, P., Parsia, B.: Pronto: a practical probabilistic description logic reasoner. In: Bobillo, F., et al. (eds.) UniDL/URSW 2008-2010. LNCS (LNAI), vol. 7123, pp. 59–79. Springer, Heidelberg (2013). https://doi.org/10.1007/978-3-642-35975-0_4

43. Koller, D., Levy, A.Y., Pfeffer, A.: P-CLASSIC: a tractable probablistic description logic. In: Kuipers, B., Webber, B.L. (eds.) Proceedings of the 14th National Conference on Artificial Intelligence, AAAI 1997, pp. 390–397. AAAI Press (1997). http://www.aaai.org/Library/AAAI/1997/aaai97-060.php

44. Kyburg Jr., H.E., Teng, C.M.: Uncertain Inference. Cambridge University Press, Cambridge (2001). https://doi.org/10.1017/CBO9780511612947

45. Laskey, K.B., da Costa, P.C.G.: Of starships and klingons: Bayesian logic for the 23rd century. In: Proceedings of the 21st Conference in Uncertainty in Artificial Intelligence, UAI 2005, pp. 346–353. AUAI Press (2005)

46. Littman, M.L., Majercik, S.M., Pitassi, T.: Stochastic Boolean satisfiability. J. Autom. Reason. **27**(3), 251–296 (2001). https://doi.org/10.1023/A:1017584715408

47. Lukasiewicz, T.: Expressive probabilistic description logics. Artif. Intell. **172**(6–7), 852–883 (2008). https://doi.org/10.1016/j.artint.2007.10.017
48. Lukasiewicz, T., Straccia, U.: Managing uncertainty and vagueness in description logics for the semantic web. J. Web Semant. **6**(4), 291–308 (2008)
49. Lutz, C., Schröder, L.: Probabilistic description logics for subjective uncertainty. In: Lin, F., Sattler, U., Truszczynski, M. (eds.) Proceedings of the 12th International Conference on Principles of Knowledge Representation and Reasoning, KR 2010. AAAI Press (2010). http://aaai.org/ocs/index.php/KR/KR2010/paper/view/1243
50. Maggi, F.M., Montali, M., Peñaloza, R.: Temporal logics over finite traces with uncertainty. In: Proceedings of the 34th AAAI Conference on Artificial Intelligence, AAAI 2020, pp. 10218–10225. AAAI Press (2020)
51. Maggi, F.M., Montali, M., Peñaloza, R., Alman, A.: Extending temporal business constraints with uncertainty. In: Proceedings of BPM-20 (2020, to appear)
52. Maggi, F.M., Montali, M., Westergaard, M., van der Aalst, W.M.P.: Monitoring business constraints with linear temporal logic: an approach based on colored automata. In: Rinderle-Ma, S., Toumani, F., Wolf, K. (eds.) BPM 2011. LNCS, vol. 6896, pp. 132–147. Springer, Heidelberg (2011). https://doi.org/10.1007/978-3-642-23059-2_13
53. Mintz, M., Bills, S., Snow, R., Jurafsky, D.: Distant supervision for relation extraction without labeled data. In: Su, K., Su, J., Wiebe, J. (eds.), Proceedings of the 47th Annual Meeting of the Association for Computational Linguistics, ACL 2009, pp. 1003–1011. The Association for Computer Linguistics (2009). https://www.aclweb.org/anthology/P09-1113/
54. Motik, B., Cuenca Grau, B., Horrocks, I., Wu, Z., Fokoue, A., Lutz, C. (eds.): OWL 2 Web Ontology Language: Profiles. W3C Recommendation (27 October 2009). http://www.w3.org/TR/owl2-profiles/
55. Niepert, M., Noessner, J., Stuckenschmidt, H.: Log-linear description logics. In: Walsh, T. (ed.) Proceedings of the 22nd International Joint Conference on Artificial Intelligence, IJCAI 2011, pp. 2153–2158. IJCAI/AAAI (2011). https://doi.org/10.5591/978-1-57735-516-8/IJCAI11-359
56. Nilsson, N.J.: Probabilistic logic. Artif. Intell. **28**(1), 71–87 (1986). https://doi.org/10.1016/0004-3702(86)90031-7
57. Pearl, J.: Probabilistic Reasoning in Intelligent Systems - Networks of Plausible Inference. Morgan Kaufmann Series in Representation and Reasoning. Morgan Kaufmann, Burlington (1989)
58. Peñaloza, R.: Inconsistency-tolerant instance checking in tractable description logics. In: Costantini, S., Franconi, E., Van Woensel, W., Kontchakov, R., Sadri, F., Roman, D. (eds.) RuleML+RR 2017. LNCS, vol. 10364, pp. 215–229. Springer, Cham (2017). https://doi.org/10.1007/978-3-319-61252-2_15
59. Peñaloza, R.: Making decisions with knowledge base repairs. In: Torra, V., Narukawa, Y., Pasi, G., Viviani, M. (eds.) MDAI 2019. LNCS (LNAI), vol. 11676, pp. 259–271. Springer, Cham (2019). https://doi.org/10.1007/978-3-030-26773-5_23
60. Peñaloza, R.: Axiom pinpointing. CoRR abs/2003.08298 (2020). https://arxiv.org/abs/2003.08298
61. Peñaloza, R., Sertkaya, B.: Understanding the complexity of axiom pinpointing in lightweight description logics. Artif. Intell. **250**, 80–104 (2017). https://doi.org/10.1016/j.artint.2017.06.002

62. Pesic, M., Schonenberg, H., van der Aalst, W.M.P.: DECLARE: full support for loosely-structured processes. In: Proceedings of the 11th IEEE International Enterprise Distributed Object Computing Conference, EDOC 2007, pp. 287–300. IEEE Computer Society (2007). https://doi.org/10.1109/EDOC.2007.14

63. Raedt, L.D., Kimmig, A., Toivonen, H.: Problog: a probabilistic prolog and its application in link discovery. In: Veloso, M.M. (ed.) Proceedings of the 20th International Joint Conference on Artificial Intelligence, IJCAI 2007, pp. 2462–2467. IJCAI (2007). http://ijcai.org/Proceedings/07/Papers/396.pdf

64. Riguzzi, F., Bellodi, E., Lamma, E., Zese, R.: Probabilistic description logics under the distribution semantics. Semant. Web **6**(5), 477–501 (2015). https://doi.org/10.3233/SW-140154

65. Roth, D.: On the hardness of approximate reasoning. Artif. Intell. **82**(1–2), 273–302 (1996). https://doi.org/10.1016/0004-3702(94)00092-1

66. Schild, K.: A correspondence theory for terminological logics: preliminary report. In: Mylopoulos, J., Reiter, R. (eds.) Proceedings of the 12th International Joint Conference on Artificial Intelligence, IJCAI 1991, pp. 466–471. Morgan Kaufmann (1991)

67. Straccia, U.: Fuzzy semantic web languages and beyond. In: Benferhat, S., Tabia, K., Ali, M. (eds.) IEA/AIE 2017. LNCS (LNAI), vol. 10350, pp. 3–8. Springer, Cham (2017). https://doi.org/10.1007/978-3-319-60042-0_1

68. Suciu, D., Olteanu, D., Ré, C., Koch, C.: Probabilistic Databases. Synthesis Lectures on Data Management. Morgan & Claypool Publishers, San Rafael (2011). https://doi.org/10.2200/S00362ED1V01Y201105DTM016

69. Tijms, H.: Understanding Probability, 3rd edn. Cambridge University Press, Cambridge (2012). https://doi.org/10.1017/CBO9781139206990

On the Complexity of Learning Description Logic Ontologies

Ana Ozaki[(✉)]

Department of Informatics, University of Bergen, Bergen, Norway
Ana.Ozaki@uib.no

Abstract. Ontologies are a popular way of representing domain knowledge, in particular, knowledge in domains related to life sciences. (Semi-) automating the process of building an ontology has attracted researchers from different communities into a field called "Ontology Learning". We provide a formal specification of the exact and the probably approximately correct learning models from computational learning theory. Then, we recall from the literature complexity results for learning lightweight description logic (DL) ontologies in these models. Finally, we highlight other approaches proposed in the literature for learning DL ontologies.

Keywords: Description logic · Exact learning · Complexity theory

1 Introduction

Ontologies have been used to build concept and role hierarchies mapping and integrating the vocabulary of data sources, to model definitional sentences in a domain of interest, to support the inference of facts in knowledge graphs, among others. However, modelling an ontology that captures in a precise and clear way the relevant knowledge of a domain can be quite time-consuming. To imagine this, consider the task of writing a text on a particular topic. The writer needs to select the right words, think about their meaning, delineate the scope, and the essential information she or he wants to convey. The knowledge of the writer needs to be clearly represented in a language, using the vocabulary and the constructs available in it. In this way, building an ontology can be seen as a similar process but often there is the additional challenge that the ontology needs to capture the knowledge of a domain in which the 'writer'—an ontology engineer—is not familiar with. The information in an ontology may need to be validated by a domain expert. Because building and maintaining ontologies are demanding tasks, several researchers have worked on developing theoretical results and practical tools for supporting this process [33, 36].

Here we consider two learning models that were applied to model the process of building an ontology. The first is the exact learning model [2]. In the exact

---

Supported by the University of Bergen.

© Springer Nature Switzerland AG 2020
M. Manna and A. Pieris (Eds.): Reasoning Web 2020, LNCS 12258, pp. 36–52, 2020.
https://doi.org/10.1007/978-3-030-60067-9_2

learning model, a learner attempts to communicate with a teacher in order to identify an abstract target concept. When instantiating the exact learning model to capture the process of building an ontology, one can consider that the teacher is a domain expert who knows the domain but cannot easily formulate it as an ontology [27]. On the other side, the role of the learner is played by an ontology engineer. The abstract target that the ontology engineer wants to identify is an ontology that reflects the knowledge of the domain expert (the teacher).

Although the teacher in the exact learning model is often described as a human (potentially a domain expert), it can also be a batch of examples [7], an artificial neural network [51,52], a Tsetlin machine [24] or any another formalism that can be used to simulate the teacher. The most studied communication protocol is based on *membership* and *equivalence* queries. A membership query gives to the learner the ability to formulate an example and ask for its classification ("does X hold in the domain?"). This mode of learning is called *active learning*. In an equivalence query, the learner asks whether a certain hypothesis is equivalent to the target. There are various results in the literature showing that the combination of these two types of queries allows the learner to correctly identify the target concept in polynomial time, with hardness results for the case in which one of the two queries is disallowed [2–4,25,40].

The second model we study is the classical probably approximately correct (PAC) learning model [46]. In the PAC model, a learner receives classified examples according to a probability distribution. Then, the learner attempts to build a hypothesis that is consistent with the examples. This mode of learning is called *passive learning* because, in contrast with the active learning mode, the learner has no control of which examples are going to be classified. One can instantiate this model to the problem of learning ontologies by considering that the ontology engineer starts attempting to collect information about the domain at random (instead of interacting with the domain expert). One can also consider the case in which, in addition to the search at random, the ontology engineer can pose membership queries to the expert. Equivalence queries are not considered in the PAC model because of a general result showing that learners that can pose equivalence queries to learn a certain target are also able to accomplish this task within the PAC model [2] (the combination is not interesting because one problem setting is 'easier' than the other, more details in Subsect. 3.3).

Having these models in mind, we first present the syntax and the semantics of the ontology language $\mathcal{ELH}$ [10,13]. This is a prototypical lightweight ontology language based on description logic (DL). Then, we formalise the exact and the PAC learning models using notions from the theory of computation. We recall from the literature complexity results for learning lightweight DL ontologies in these models and provide intuitions about these results. Finally, we point out other approaches that have been applied for learning DL ontologies.

2   Description Logic

We introduce $\mathcal{ELH}$ [10,13], a classical lightweight DL which features existential quantification ($\exists$) and conjunction ($\sqcap$). Let $\mathsf{N_C}$, $\mathsf{N_R}$, and $\mathsf{N_I}$ be countably infinite and disjoint sets of *concept* and *role* names. An $\mathcal{ELH}$ ontology (or *TBox*) is a finite set of *role inclusions* (RIs) $r \sqsubseteq s$ with $r, s \in \mathsf{N_R}$ and *concept inclusions* (CIs) $C \sqsubseteq D$ with C, D $\mathcal{EL}$ concept expressions built according to the rule

$$C, D ::= A \mid \top \mid C \sqcap D \mid \exists r.C$$

with $A \in \mathsf{N_C}$ and $r \in \mathsf{N_R}$. An $\mathcal{ELH}$ *TBox* is a finite set of RIs and CIs $C \sqsubseteq D$, with C, D being $\mathcal{EL}$ concept expressions. We denote by $\mathcal{ELH}_{lhs}$ and $\mathcal{ELH}_{rhs}$ the fragments of $\mathcal{ELH}$ that allow only a concept name on the right-hand side and on the left-hand side, respectively. That is, $\mathcal{ELH}_{lhs}$ is the language that allows *complex* $\mathcal{EL}$ expressions on the left-hand side and the same idea applies for $\mathcal{ELH}_{rhs}$. An $\mathcal{EL}$ TBox is an $\mathcal{ELH}$ TBox that does not have RIs. We may write $C \equiv D$ as a short hand for having both $C \sqsubseteq D$ and $D \sqsubseteq C$. An *assertion* is an expression of the form $r(a, b)$ or of the form $A(a)$, where $A \in \mathsf{N_C}$, $r \in \mathsf{N_R}$, and $a, b \in \mathsf{N_I}$. An *ABox* is a finite set of assertions. An $\mathcal{ELH}$ *instance query* (IQ) is of the form $C(a)$ or $r(a, b)$ with C an $\mathcal{EL}$ concept expression, $r \in \mathsf{N_R}$, and $a, b \in \mathsf{N_I}$.

We now present the usual semantics of $\mathcal{ELH}$, which is based on *interpretations*. An interpretation $\mathcal{I}$ is a pair $(\Delta^{\mathcal{I}}, \cdot^{\mathcal{I}})$ where $\Delta^{\mathcal{I}}$ is a non-empty set, called the *domain of* $\mathcal{I}$, and $\cdot^{\mathcal{I}}$ is a function mapping each $A \in \mathsf{N_C}$ to a subset $A^{\mathcal{I}}$ of $\Delta^{\mathcal{I}}$, each $r \in \mathsf{N_R}$ to a subset $r^{\mathcal{I}}$ of $\Delta^{\mathcal{I}} \times \Delta^{\mathcal{I}}$, and each $a \in \mathsf{N_I}$ to an element in $\Delta^{\mathcal{I}}$. The function $\cdot^{\mathcal{I}}$ extends to arbitrary $\mathcal{EL}$ concept expressions as follows:

$$(\top)^{\mathcal{I}} := \Delta^{\mathcal{I}}$$
$$(C \sqcap D)^{\mathcal{I}} := C^{\mathcal{I}} \cap D^{\mathcal{I}}$$
$$(\exists r.C)^{\mathcal{I}} := \{d \in \Delta^{\mathcal{I}} \mid \exists e \in C^{\mathcal{I}} \text{ such that } (d, e) \in r^{\mathcal{I}}\}$$

The interpretation $\mathcal{I}$ *satisfies* an RI $r \sqsubseteq s$ iff $R^{\mathcal{I}} \subseteq s^{\mathcal{I}}$. It satisfies a CI $C \sqsubseteq D$ iff $C^{\mathcal{I}} \subseteq D^{\mathcal{I}}$. It satisfies a TBox $\mathcal{T}$ iff $\mathcal{I}$ satisfies all RIs and CIs in $\mathcal{T}$. We write $\mathcal{I} \models \alpha$ if $\mathcal{I}$ satisfies an RI, a CI, or a TBox α. A TBox $\mathcal{T}$ *entails* a CI α (or a TBox $\mathcal{T}'$), written $\mathcal{T} \models \alpha$ (or $\mathcal{T} \models \mathcal{T}'$), iff all interpretations satisfying $\mathcal{T}$ also satisfy α (or $\mathcal{T}'$). Two TBoxes $\mathcal{T}$ and $\mathcal{T}'$ are *equivalent*, written $\mathcal{T} \equiv \mathcal{T}'$, iff $\mathcal{T} \models \mathcal{T}'$ and $\mathcal{T}' \models \mathcal{T}$. These notions can be adapted as expected for defining satisfaction and entailment of assertions, ABoxes, and IQs [10]. Given a TBox $\mathcal{T}$, the *signature* $\Sigma_{\mathcal{T}}$ of $\mathcal{T}$ is the set of concept and role names occurring in it.

Example 1. Although $\mathcal{ELH}$ is a very simple language, it is already useful to represent certain kinds of static knowledge. One can express in $\mathcal{ELH}$ that 'Penicillamine nephropathy is a renal disease' with the CI[1]:

$$\mathsf{PenicillamineNephropathy} \sqsubseteq \mathsf{RenalDisease}$$

The definitional sentence 'Penicillamine nephropathy is a renal disease of the kidney structure caused by penicillamine' can be expressed as:

$$\mathsf{PenicillamineNephropathy} \equiv \mathsf{RenalDisease} \sqcap$$

---

[1] This example follows modelling guidelines and terms found in the ontology from the medical domain SNOMED CT [45].

∃findingSite.KidneyStructure ⊓ ∃causativeAgent.Penicillamine.

An important advantage of representing domain knowledge in an ontology is that ambiguities found in natural language can be removed. For example, one can distinguish when 'is' should mean a subset relation (represented syntactically with '⊑') from when it means an equivalence (represented with the symbol '≡').

In the next section, we introduce notions from the theory of computation that are relevant to define learnability and complexity classes in the exact and PAC learning models.

3   The Complexity of Learning

Complexity classes are defined in terms of a model of computation, a type of problem, and bounds on the resources (usually time and memory) needed to solve a problem [44]. In this section, we formally define complexity classes for *learning problems* (Subsect. 3.3). Before that, we define a general model of computation that represents the communication of a learner and a teacher via queries (Subsect. 3.1). This model can be specialised for learning problems in the exact and the PAC learning models. For the exact learning model, we assume that the learner can pose membership and equivalence queries. In the PAC learning model, the learner can pose sampling queries. We describe the queries in detail in Subsect. 3.2.

3.1   Model of Computation

The main advantage of defining the model of computation is that this opens the possibility of analysing the learning phenomenon in light of the theory of computation. Our model of computation for learning problems is based on *learning systems* [50]. Learning systems are formulated using the notion of a pair (L, T) of multitape Turing machines (MTM), one for the learner, L, and one for the teacher, T. There are four kinds of tape:

- L, T share a read-only *input tape*;
- L, T share a read-write *communication tape*;
- T has a read-only tape, called *oracle tape*, not accessed by L; and
- L has a write-only *output tape*, not accessed by T.

Intuitively, the computation of the two MTMs represents the interaction of the learner and the teacher via queries, where posing a query to the teacher means writing down the input of the query in the communication tape and entering the corresponding query state. Then the teacher computes the answer, writes it in the communication tape (if the computation of the answer terminates), and enters the corresponding answer state. The learner reads the answer in the communication tape and continues its computation. This process may continue forever or halt when the learner writes its final hypothesis in the output tape and enters the final state. It is assumed that the teacher never enters the final state (only the learner can enter the final state).

In the definition of a learning system (L, T), we consider that L is a deterministic MTM (DMTM) with three tapes (input, communication, and output tapes) and that the set of states contains special elements called *query states*, one for each type of query. The teacher T is a non-deterministic MTM (NMTM) with three tapes (input, communication, and oracle tapes) and the set of states contains special elements called *answer states*, one for each type of query. We describe the types of queries for the exact and PAC learning models in Subsect. 3.2.

A DMTM with k tapes can be defined as a tuple $\mathcal{M} = (Q, \Sigma, \Theta, q_0, q_f)$ where: Q is a finite set of *states*; Σ is a finite *alphabet* containing the *blank symbol* $\sqcup$; $\Theta : (Q \setminus \{q_f\}) \times \Sigma^k \rightarrow Q \times \Sigma^k \times \{l, r\}^k$ is the *transition function*; and $\{q_0, q_f\} \subseteq Q$ are the *initial* and *final* states. The expression $\Theta(q, a_1, \ldots, a_k) = (q', b_1, \ldots, b_k, D_1, \ldots, D_k)$, with $D_i \in \{l, r\}$, means that if $\mathcal{M}$ is in state q and heads 1 through k are reading the symbols a_1 through a_k (resp.) then $\mathcal{M}$ goes to state q', the symbols $b_1, \ldots, b_k$ are written in tapes $1, \ldots, k$ (resp.) and each head i moves to the direction corresponding to D_i. An NMTM is defined in the same way as a DMTM except that $\Theta : (Q \setminus \{q_f\}) \times \Sigma^k \rightarrow \mathcal{P}(Q \times \Sigma^k \times \{l, r\}^k)$. That is, $\Theta(q, a_1, \ldots, a_k)$ is now a *set* of expressions of the form $(q', b_1, \ldots, b_k, D_1, \ldots, D_k)$.

A *configuration* of a MTM with k tapes is a k-tuple $(w_1 q w_1', \ldots, w_k q w_k')$ with $w_i, w_i' \in \Sigma^*$ and $q \in Q$, meaning that the tape i contains the word $w_i w_i'$, the machine is in state q and the head is on the position of the left-most symbol of w_i'. The notion of *successive configurations* is defined as expected in terms of the transition relations of L and T. Whenever L enters a query state, the transition relation of T is used to define a successive configuration (it may not be unique due to non-determinism of T) and whenever T enters again in an answer state then the transition relation of L defines the (unique) successive configuration (L resumes its execution). A *computation* of (L, T) on an input word w_0 is a tree whose paths are sequences of successive configurations $\alpha_0, \alpha_1, \ldots$, where $\alpha_0 = q_0 w_0$ is the *initial configuration* for the input $w_0 \in (\Sigma \setminus \{\sqcup\})^*$ and q_0 is the initial state of L. The branches of the tree correspond to the different possibilities for T to move from one state to another.

The model of computation that we presented can be generalised to the case in which there are multiple learners and multiple teachers. For our purposes, it suffices to consider only one learner and one teacher. In the following, we explain how the computational model we described can be tailored to the exact and the PAC learning models, as well as some variants of these models.

3.2 Learning Frameworks and Queries

To define the learnability in the exact and PAC models (Subsect. 3.3), we use the notion of a *learning framework* and three types of queries (membership and equivalence queries for the exact learning model and sample queries for the PAC learning model). A learning framework $\mathfrak{F}$ is a triple $(\mathcal{E}, \mathcal{L}, \mu)$ where

- $\mathcal{E}$ is a set of examples,

- $\mathcal{L}$ is a set of concept representations[2], called *hypothesis space*,
- and μ is a function that maps each element of $\mathcal{L}$ to a set of examples in $\mathcal{E}$.

We call *target* a fixed but arbitrary element of $\mathcal{L}$ that the learner wants to acquire. A *hypothesis* is an element of $\mathcal{L}$ that represents the 'idea' of the learner about the target. This element is often updated during the computation of a learning system (L, T) until L reaches its final state (if ever). Given a target $t \in \mathcal{L}$, we say that an example e is *positive* for t if $e \in \mu(t)$, and *negative* otherwise. Given a hypothesis h and a target t in $\mathcal{L}$ and an example $e \in \mathcal{E}$, we say that e is a *counterexample* for t and h if $e \in \mu(t) \oplus \mu(h)$ (where $\oplus$ denotes the symmetric difference). We may omit 'for t' and 'for t and h' if this is clear from the context.

Remark 1. Given a DL $\mathfrak{L}$, we denote by $\mathfrak{F}(\mathfrak{L})$ the learning framework $(\mathcal{E}, \mathcal{L}, \mu)$ where $\mathcal{E}$ is the set of CIs and RIs that can be formulated in $\mathfrak{L}$ (using symbols from $\mathsf{N_C}$ and $\mathsf{N_R}$), $\mathcal{L}$ is the set of all $\mathfrak{L}$ TBoxes, and

$$\mu(T) = \{\alpha \mid T \models \alpha, \text{ with } \alpha \text{ a CI or an RI in } \mathfrak{L}\}.$$

This setting is called *learning from entailments*. In the learning framework $\mathfrak{F}(\mathcal{ELH}_{rhs}) = (\mathcal{E}, \mathcal{L}, \mu)$ we have that $T = \{A \sqsubseteq \exists r.A\} \in \mathcal{L}$ and, for all $n \in \mathbb{N}$, the CI $A \sqsubseteq \exists r^n.A$ is in $\mu(T)$, where $\exists r^{n+1}.A := \exists r.\exists r^n.A$ and $\exists r^1.A := \exists r.A$.

One could define a more general notion of a learning framework, where the hypothesis space for the hypothesis of the learner differs from the hypothesis space that contains the target. Also, the mapping function μ could be adapted to represent fuzzy sets of examples. We keep the version introduced above because it is general enough for our purposes and covers classical problems in the literature [2,46]. We now describe in detail the queries that the learner can pose and how the teacher answers these queries. Consider a learning framework $\mathfrak{F} = (\mathcal{E}, \mathcal{L}, \mu)$, and a learning system (L, T) with a fixed but arbitrary target $t \in \mathcal{L}$ in the oracle tape.

- A **membership query** happens whenever L writes an example e in the communication tape and enters the membership query state. In this case, T resumes the execution and (if the computation terminates) writes 'yes' in the communication tape if $e \in \mu(t)$, otherwise, it writes 'no' (assume such answers can be formulated using symbols from the alphabets of L and T).
- An **equivalence query** happens whenever L writes a hypothesis $h \in \mathcal{L}$ in the communication tape and enters the equivalence query state. The teacher T resumes its execution and (if the computation terminates) writes some $e \in \mu(t) \oplus \mu(h)$ in the communication tape, or 'yes' if $\mu(t) = \mu(h)$.
- A **sample query** happens whenever L enters the sample query state. In this case, the teacher T resumes its execution and (if the computation terminates) writes some $(e, \ell_t(e))$ in the communication tape, where the choice of $e \in \mathcal{E}$ is according to a fixed but arbitrary probability distribution on $\mathcal{E}$ (unknown to the learner) and $\ell_t(e) = 1$, if $e \in \mu(t)$, and 0 otherwise.

---

[2] In Machine Learning, a concept representation is a way of representing a set of examples. This differs from the notion of a concept in DL.

We write $(L_{\mathfrak{F}}, T_{\mathfrak{F}}(t))$ to indicate that t is in the oracle tape and queries/answers are as just described for a learning framework $\mathfrak{F}$ (we may omit the subscript $\mathfrak{F}$ if this is clear from the context). For some learning frameworks and some types of queries, it can be assumed that the computation of answers by the teacher always terminates independently of which $t \in \mathcal{L}$ happens to be in the oracle tape. One example is when the μ function encodes the entailment relation and the entailment problem of the logic represented in $\mathcal{L}$ is decidable (e.g., entailment in $\mathcal{ELH}$ is decidable in polynomial time [9]). However, if the entailment problem is undecidable this assumption cannot be made independently of the content of the oracle tape (e.g., entailment in first-order logic).

Even if there is a teacher that always terminates depending on the content of the oracle tape, naturally, one cannot assume that all of them will terminate. So we define the following notion. Let $T(t)$ be a teacher with $t \in \mathcal{L}$ in the oracle tape. We say that $T(t)$ is *terminating for membership queries* if for every possible membership query (within a learning framework) the teacher $T(t)$ always terminates the computation of the answer. This notion can be easily adapted for other types of queries.

The multiple ways of choosing $e \in \mu(t) \oplus \mu(h)$ in an equivalence query and an example $e \in \mathcal{E}$ in a sample query is captured by the non-determinism of T (see Subsect. 3.1). For representing sample queries, one can consider the special case in which the NMTM is a multitape probabilistic Turing machine [44]. We may write $T_{\mathcal{D}}$ to indicate that, whenever a sample query is posed by L, we have that T chooses an example according to the (same) probability distribution $\mathcal{D}$, with the events of drawing examples being mutually independent (see e.g. [43] for more details on sample queries and [36] for a presentation using this notation).

3.3   Learnability and Complexity Classes

We are ready to define the notion of learnability and complexity classes for learning problems. We write $Y \in (L, T(t))(X)$ if there is a finite computation of the learning system $(L, T(t))$ with X in the input tape, t in the oracle tape, and the content written by the learner in the output tape, L, is Y. We first define learnability for the exact learning model.

Let $\mathfrak{F} = (\mathcal{E}, \mathcal{L}, \mu)$ be a learning framework. Assume that the learner can pose membership and equivalence queries and these are truthfully replied by the teacher, as described in Subsect. 3.2. We say that $\mathfrak{F}$ is *exactly learnable* if there is a learner L such that, for every $t \in \mathcal{L}$, there is a terminating $T(t)$ (for membership and equivalence queries). Moreover,

– every learning system $(L, T'(t))$ with a terminating $T'(t)$ halts and every $h \in (L, T'(t))(\Sigma_t) \cap \mathcal{L}$ satisfies $\mu(h) = \mu(t)$, where Σ_t is the signature of t.

If the number of steps made by L in each path of the computation tree is always bounded by a polynomial $p(|t|, |e|)$, where $t \in \mathcal{L}$ is the target and $e \in \mathcal{E}$ is the largest counterexample written so far in the communication tape by $T'(t)$ (in the corresponding path), then $\mathfrak{F}$ is *exactly learnable in polynomial time*.

We denote by $\textsc{El}(\mathsf{MQ},\mathsf{EQ})$ and $\textsc{Elp}(\mathsf{MQ},\mathsf{EQ})$ the classes of all learning frameworks that are, respectively, exactly learnable and exactly learnable in polynomial time with membership and equivalence queries. One can easily adapt this notation to the case in which the learner is allowed to make an exponential number of steps, denoted $\textsc{ElExp}(\mathsf{MQ},\mathsf{EQ})$, or to the case in which the learner can only pose one type of query. For representing this, we simply drop MQ or EQ from the class name (e.g., $\textsc{Elp}(\mathsf{EQ})$ is the class of all learning frameworks that are exactly learnable in polynomial time with only equivalence queries). One can also consider other types of queries, such as subset and superset queries [2], or queries that take into account the history of previous queries [38]. It follows from these definitions that $\textsc{Elp}(\mathsf{MQ},\mathsf{EQ}) \subseteq \textsc{ElExp}(\mathsf{MQ},\mathsf{EQ}) \subseteq \textsc{El}(\mathsf{MQ},\mathsf{EQ})$.

We now define learnability in the PAC model. Let $\mathfrak{F} = (\mathcal{E}, \mathcal{L}, \mu)$ be a learning framework. Assume that the learner can pose sample queries and these are replied by the teacher as in Subsect. 3.2. The goal is to build a hypothesis such that 'with high probability there is not much difference between the hypothesis and the target'. A parameter ϵ quantifies the error of the hypothesis w.r.t. the target (how different they are). Another parameter δ is used to quantify the confidence of meeting the error requirement (whether this has high probability). Both parameters are real numbers ranging between 0 and 1. Formally, we say that $\mathfrak{F}$ is *PAC learnable* if there is a function $f : (0,1)^2 \to \mathbb{N}$ and a learner L such that, for every $(\epsilon, \delta) \in (0,1)^2$, every probability distribution $\mathcal{D}$ on $\mathcal{E}$, and every target $t \in \mathcal{L}$, there is a terminating $T_{\mathcal{D}}(t)$ (for sample queries). Moreover,

- every $(L, T'(t)_{\mathcal{D}})$ with a terminating $T'(t)_{\mathcal{D}}$ halts after L poses $m \geq f(\epsilon, \delta)$ samples queries and, with probability at least $(1 - \delta)$ (over the choice of sets of m examples), $h \in (L, T'(t)_{\mathcal{D}})(\Sigma_t) \cap \mathcal{L}$ satisfies $\mathcal{D}(\mu(h) \oplus \mu(t)) \leq \epsilon$.

If the number of steps made by L in each path of the computation tree is always bounded by a polynomial function $p(|t|, |e|, 1/\epsilon, 1/\delta)$, where e is the largest example written in the communication tape by $T'(t)_{\mathcal{D}}$ (in the corresponding path), then $\mathfrak{F}$ is *PAC learnable in polynomial time*. We can easily extend these notions to the case in which the learner can also pose membership queries (with a terminating teacher for both sample and membership queries). We denote by $\textsc{Pl}$ and $\textsc{Plp}(\mathsf{SQ})$ the classes of all learning frameworks that are, respectively, PAC learnable and PAC learnable in polynomial time with sample queries. Also, we write $\textsc{Plp}(\mathsf{MQ},\mathsf{SQ})$ for the case the learner can also pose membership queries.

Remark 2. There is an important difference between the polynomial bound for the exact and the PAC learning models. In the exact model, e is the largest counterexample written *so far* by the teacher in the path of computation, while in the PAC model e is the largest example written by the teacher (at any point of the path). The more strict requirement of the exact model is to avoid a loophole in the definition [3]. Whenever the hypothesis of the learner is not equivalent, the teacher needs to provide a *counterexample*. Since this depends on both the target and the hypothesis, there could be a case in which the learner spends an exponential amount of time (in the size of the target) to discover a hypothesis that would force the teacher to provide an exponential counterexample. Then the learner would have spent a polynomial amount of time in the size of the largest counterexample but not in the size of the largest example given *so far*. This requirement is not necessary in the PAC model because the teacher does not need to provide an example that depends on the hypothesis of the learner, so there is no way the learner can 'force' the teacher to return a large example.

Theorem 1 states that positive results for the exact learning model with only equivalence queries are transferable to the PAC model and this also holds if both models allow membership queries.

Theorem 1. *The following holds* [2]*:*

- $\textsc{EL}(\textsf{EQ}) \subseteq \textsc{PL}(\textsf{SQ})$;
- $\textsc{ELP}(\textsf{EQ}) \subseteq \textsc{PLP}(\textsf{SQ})$;
- $\textsc{ELP}(\textsf{MQ}, \textsf{EQ}) \subseteq \textsc{PLP}(\textsf{MQ}, \textsf{SQ})$.

The intuition for Theorem 1 is that the learner can pose sample queries instead of equivalence queries. By posing sample queries, the learner can obtain a set of classified examples, drawn according to a fixed but arbitrary probability distribution. If the current hypothesis of the learner misclassifies one of the examples of this set then the learner has found a counterexample. So it can proceed as if it had posed an equivalence query and the teacher had returned the counterexample. Otherwise, it is shown in the proof of the theorem that if the sample is large enough then any hypothesis consistent with the sample satisfies the criteria for PAC learnability.

For presentation purposes, we have presented only *time* complexity classes for the exact and the PAC learning models. One can also consider classes that capture other ways of measuring the resources used by the learner and/or the teacher [6]. For example, one can measure the number and size of queries posed by the learner. In this way, *query* complexity classes could also be defined [5,27].

4   Learning DL Ontologies

We provide some and examples and intuitions about the notions presented so far (Subsect. 4.1). Then, in Subsect. 4.2, we recall results on learning DL ontologies in the exact and PAC learning models.

4.1   An Example

To illustrate the ideas for learning DL ontologies in the exact and the PAC learning models, we start by considering the problem of exactly learning an ontology in a toy language that allows only concept inclusions of the form $A \sqsubseteq B$ with $A, B \in \mathsf{N_C}$.

Consider the learning framework $\mathfrak{F}_{\textsf{toy}} = (\mathcal{L}, \mathcal{E}, \mu)$ with $\mathcal{L}$ and $\mathcal{E}$ being the set of all TBoxes and the set of all CIs that can be formulated in the toy language, respectively. The μ function maps TBoxes $\mathcal{T}$ in $\mathcal{L}$ to CIs in $\mathcal{E}$ entailed by $\mathcal{T}$.

$$L \qquad\qquad\qquad T(\mathcal{T})$$

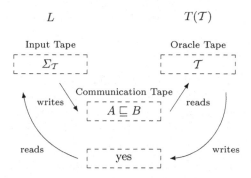

Fig. 1. Membership query in a learning system

Suppose the target $\mathcal{T} \in \mathcal{L}$ is $\{A \sqsubseteq B, B \sqsubseteq C\}$ and let $(L, T(\mathcal{T}))$ be a learning system such that on the input $\Sigma_{\mathcal{T}} = \{A, B, C\}$ (the signature of $\mathcal{T}$) returns $\mathcal{H} \equiv \mathcal{T}$. In symbols, $\mathcal{H} \in (L, T(\mathcal{T}))(\Sigma_{\mathcal{T}})$. Clearly, for all $\mathcal{T}' \in \mathcal{L}$, there is a terminating $T(\mathcal{T}')$ for membership, equivalence, and sample queries.

Figure 1 illustrates part of a computation of $(L, T(\mathcal{T}))$ on the input $\Sigma_{\mathcal{T}} = \{A, B, C\}$ where L poses the membership query $A \sqsubseteq B \in \mu(\mathcal{T})$ and receives 'yes' as an answer. A simple strategy for L is to formulate all CIs within $\Sigma_{\mathcal{T}}$ and pose membership queries with each such CI, one at a time. The CI is added to $\mathcal{H}$ if, and only if, the answer is 'yes'. With this strategy, the hypothesis $\mathcal{H}$ computed by the learner is $\{A \sqsubseteq B, A \sqsubseteq C, B \sqsubseteq C\}$. At most $|\Sigma_{\mathcal{T}}|^2$ membership queries are needed. Thus, $\mathfrak{F}_{\text{toy}} \in \text{ELP(MQ)}$.

Adding Conjunctions. Now, consider an extension of the toy language that allows conjunctions of concept names in CIs. We denote the underlying learning framework as $\mathfrak{F}_{\text{toy}}^{\sqcap}$. In this case, the strategy of posing membership queries for each possible CI formulated within the signature $\Sigma_{\mathcal{T}}$ of a target $\mathcal{T}$ still terminates (since $\Sigma_{\mathcal{T}}$ is finite). However, its does not terminate in polynomial time in $|\Sigma_{\mathcal{T}}|$ because with conjunctions one can formulate an exponential number of CIs.

In the following, we provide a simple argument showing that there is no strategy that guarantees polynomial time learnability with only membership queries. In other words, $\mathfrak{F}_{\text{toy}}^{\sqcap} \notin \text{ELP(MQ)}$.

The main idea is to define a superpolynomial set S of TBoxes in this extension of the toy language and show that any membership query can distinguish at most polynomially many elements of S. Let $\Sigma = \{A_1, \ldots, A_n, \overline{A}_1, \ldots, \overline{A}_n, M\}$. For any sequence $\sigma = \sigma^1 \ldots \sigma^n$ with $\sigma^i \in \{A_i, \overline{A}_i\}$ the expression $\sigma \sqsubseteq M$ stands for the CI $(\sigma^1 \sqcap \ldots \sqcap \sigma^n \sqsubseteq M)$. For every such sequence σ (of which there are 2^n many), consider the TBox $\mathcal{T}_\sigma$ defined as:

$$\mathcal{T}_\sigma = \{\sigma \sqsubseteq M\} \cup \mathcal{T}_0 \text{ with}$$
$$\mathcal{T}_0 = \{A_i \sqcap \overline{A}_i \sqsubseteq M \mid 1 \leq i \leq n\}$$

The CI $\sigma \sqsubseteq M$ represents a unique binary sequence for each $\mathcal{T}_\sigma$, 'marked' by the concept name M. The CIs in $\mathcal{T}_0$ are shared by all $\mathcal{T}_\sigma$ in S.

Lemma 1. *For any CI α in the extended toy language over Σ either:*

- *for every $\mathcal{T}_\sigma \in S$, we have $\mathcal{T}_\sigma \models \alpha$; or*
- *$\mathcal{T}_\sigma \models \alpha$, for at most one $\mathcal{T}_\sigma \in S$.*

Proof. Suppose there is $\mathcal{T}_\sigma \in S$ such that $\mathcal{T}_\sigma \models \alpha$ (otherwise we are done). Assume the CI α is $C \sqsubseteq D$. If D is not M then either α is a tautology or there is no $\mathcal{T}_\sigma \in S$ such that $\mathcal{T}_\sigma \models \alpha$. In both cases, we have that $\mathcal{T}_\sigma \models \alpha$ for at most one $\mathcal{T}_\sigma \in S$. Then, we can assume that D is M. Regarding C (the concept on the left side of the CI α), we make a case distinction:

- there is $1 \leq i \leq n$ such that $A_i, \overline{A}_i$ are conjuncts in C. In this case, by definition of $\mathcal{T}_0$, we have that $\mathcal{T}_\sigma \models \alpha$, for every $\mathcal{T}_\sigma \in S$.
- there is no $1 \leq i \leq n$ such that $A_i, \overline{A}_i$ are conjuncts in C. This means that $\mathcal{T}_0 \not\models \alpha$. If α is of the form $\sigma \sqsubseteq M$ then there is exactly one $\mathcal{T}_\sigma \in S$ such that $\mathcal{T}_\sigma \models \alpha$. Otherwise, there is no $\mathcal{T}_\sigma \in S$ such that $\mathcal{T}_\sigma \models \alpha$. So, $\mathcal{T}_\sigma \models \alpha$, for at most one $\mathcal{T}_\sigma \in S$.

□

Since any membership query can eliminate only polynomially many elements from S (in our case at most one), the learner cannot distinguish between the remaining elements from our initial superpolynomial set S in polynomial time. Thus, $\mathfrak{F}_{\mathsf{toy}}^{\sqcap} \notin \mathrm{ELP}(\mathsf{MQ})$.

This language can be easily translated into propositional Horn. It is known that propositional Horn expressions are exactly learnable in polynomial time if equivalence queries are also allowed [4,20]. That is, $\mathfrak{F}_{\mathsf{toy}}^{\sqcap} \in \mathrm{ELP}(\mathsf{MQ}, \mathsf{EQ})$.

Adding Existentials. We discuss here a further extension the toy language that also allows existential quantification. This language coincides with $\mathcal{EL}$, defined in Sect. 2. Our first observation is that in $\mathcal{EL}$ there is an infinite number of CIs that can be formulated with a finite signature $\Sigma_\mathcal{T}$ of a target $\mathcal{T}$. This happens because existential quantifiers can be nested in concept expressions. Moreover, due to cyclic references between concepts in an $\mathcal{EL}$ TBox, an infinite number of CIs can be entailed by a (finite) TBox (see Remark 1). This means that the strategy of posing membership queries for each possible CI formulated with the signature $\Sigma_\mathcal{T}$ of a target $\mathcal{T}$ does not terminate in this case. If equivalence queries are allowed then one can still enumerate all TBoxes of size n that can be formulated with $\Sigma_\mathcal{T}$ (up to logical equivalence) and ask equivalence queries with such TBoxes, one by one. Then one can increase n until it reaches the size of $\mathcal{T}$ (which is finite). This strategy is guaranteed to terminate, although not in polynomial time. In the next subsection, we discuss further results for $\mathcal{EL}$ extended with role inclusions (that is, $\mathcal{ELH}$) and its fragments $\mathcal{ELH}_{lhs}$ and $\mathcal{ELH}_{rhs}$, introduced in Sect. 2.

4.2   Complexity Results

We now recall from the literature polynomial time complexity results for learning DL ontologies in the exact and the PAC learning models. Figure 2 illustrates some of these results (some results and complexity classes have been omitted to simplify the presentation). Dashed lines are for the classes associated with the PAC learning model. In what follows, we give an overview of the complexity results and provide additional explanations for the complexity classes.

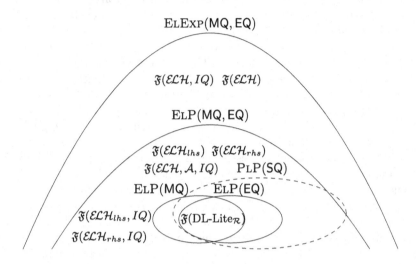

Fig. 2. Learning frameworks and complexity classes

Konev et al. [27] have shown that $\mathcal{ELH}$ (in fact already $\mathcal{EL}$) TBoxes are not exactly learnable from entailments in polynomial time while $\mathcal{ELH}_{lhs}$ and $\mathcal{ELH}_{rhs}$ are polynomially learnable [27]. In symbols, $\mathfrak{F}(\mathcal{ELH}) \notin \text{ELP}(\text{MQ}, \text{EQ})$ but $\mathfrak{F}(\mathcal{ELH}_{lhs}), \mathfrak{F}(\mathcal{ELH}_{rhs}) \in \text{ELP}(\text{MQ}, \text{EQ})$. Similar results also hold for a variant of this problem setting where the examples are pairs of the form $(\mathcal{A}, q)$ (instead of being CIs and RIs), where $\mathcal{A}$ is an ABox and q is an ($\mathcal{ELH}$) IQ [28]. In this setting, $(\mathcal{A}, q)$ is a positive example for $\mathcal{T}$ iff $(\mathcal{T}, \mathcal{A}) \models q$. We denote these learning frameworks with $\mathfrak{F}(\mathfrak{L}, IQ)$, where $\mathfrak{L}$ is the DL. In both problem settings, if the return of an equivalence query is 'yes' then this means that the hypothesis of the learner and the target are logically equivalent. Recently, it has been shown that if the ABox is fixed and one only aims at preserving IQ results w.r.t. the fixed ABox (not logical equivalence between the hypothesis and the target) then there is a polynomial time algorithm for $\mathcal{ELH}$ terminologies [37]. We denote this learning framework by $\mathfrak{F}(\mathcal{ELH}, \mathcal{A}, IQ)$ where $\mathcal{A}$ is the fixed ABox. The intuition for why the problem is 'easier' in this case is because, since the ABox is fixed, the possible counterexamples the teacher can give are constrained. The fixed ABox setting avoids the difficult scenario described in the hardness proof for the learning framework $\mathfrak{F}(\mathcal{ELH}, IQ)$ [28, Page 29 of the full version], where the teacher can give counterexamples of the form $(\mathcal{A}_\sigma, A(a))$, with $\sigma = \sigma^1, \ldots, \sigma^n$, for $\sigma^i \in \{A_i, \overline{A_i}\}$, and $\mathcal{A}_\sigma$ an ABox of the form $\{\sigma^1(a), \ldots, \sigma^n(a)\}$.

By Theorem 1, positive results in the exact learning model are transferable to the PAC model extended with membership queries. We point out that the complexity class PLP(SQ) is *not* contained in ELP(MQ, EQ). This has been discovered by Blum in 1994 [14]. He constructed an artificial counterexample to prove the result and the argument relies on cryptographic assumptions. Another (artificial) counterexample appears in the work by Ozaki et al. [37]. The argument in this case does not rely on cryptographic assumptions. Apart from these carefully constructed learning frameworks, in many cases, learning frameworks in PLP(SQ) are also in ELP(MQ, EQ).

We now explain why $\mathfrak{F}(\mathcal{ELH})$ and $\mathfrak{F}(\mathcal{ELH}, IQ)$ appear in ELEXP(MQ, EQ). In fact, they are already in ELEXP(EQ). The reason is that, as explained at the end of Subsect. 4.1, since the learning system receives the (finite) signature $\Sigma_\mathcal{T}$ of the target $\mathcal{T}$ as input, it can enumerate all TBoxes (up to logical equivalence) of a certain size and ask whether any of them is equivalent to $\mathcal{T}$, one by one, increasing this size until a TBox equivalent to $\mathcal{T}$ is found. This naive procedure clearly requires an exponential number of steps in the size of $\mathcal{T}$. The same holds for other DL languages more expressive than $\mathcal{ELH}$, as long as TBoxes can also be enumerated in this way. An exponential (but non-trivial) algorithm for $\mathcal{EL}$ terminologies and its implementation is provided by Duarte et al. [17]

It remains to explain the $\mathfrak{F}(\text{DL-Lite}_\mathcal{R})$ case. DL-Lite$_\mathcal{R}$ is a member of a well-known family of DLs [8]. What we would like to explain is that, for some ontology languages, such as DL-Lite$_\mathcal{R}$, the number of RIs and CIs that can be formulated within the (finite) signature $\Sigma_\mathcal{T}$ of a target $\mathcal{T}$ is polynomial in the size of $\Sigma_\mathcal{T}$. Since $\Sigma_\mathcal{T}$ is given as input to the learning system, this means that the learner can identify the target with only membership queries (see toy example in Subsect. 4.1), and moreover, in polynomial time in the size of $\Sigma_\mathcal{T}$. Therefore, $\mathfrak{F}(\text{DL-Lite}_\mathcal{R})$ belongs to ELP(MQ). Learning an equivalent DL-Lite$_\mathcal{R}$ TBox with only equivalence queries is also easy. This happens because there are only polynomially many counterexamples that can be given. The learner can start by posing an equivalence query with an empty hypothesis. Then, the teacher is obliged to return a positive counterexample (unless the target is equivalent to the empty hypothesis and we are done). All the learner needs to do is to add this positive counterexample to its hypothesis and then proceed by posing another equivalence query. After polynomially many equivalence queries, the learner will terminate with an equivalent hypothesis. So $\mathfrak{F}(\text{DL-Lite}_\mathcal{R}) \in$ ELP(EQ) also holds.

5   Related Work

We now highlight some other approaches from the literature for learning DL ontologies, when the focus is on finding how terms of an ontology should relate to each other using the expressivity of the ontology language at hand. These approaches are mainly based on association rule mining, formal concept analysis, inductive logic programming, and neural networks [36].

Formal concept analysis [23] has been applied to mine $\mathcal{EL}$ CIs [15] (see also [11,12,41]). In this setting, a learner receives a finite interpretation $\mathcal{I}$ as input and attempts to build a finite ontology $\mathcal{T}$ such that, for all $\mathcal{EL}$ CIs formulated in a finite signature, $\mathcal{T} \models C \sqsubseteq D$ if, and only if, $\mathcal{I} \models C \sqsubseteq D$.

This ontology, called *base*, should also satisfy certain minimality conditions. It is known that, given a finite interpretation $\mathcal{I}$, a finite base (expressed within a finite signature) always exists for the $\mathcal{EL}$ ontology language. However, this may not be the case for other ontology languages. The main difficulty in applying formal concept analysis for building ontologies is that, as originally proposed, it cannot build CIs one may expect to hold when the data is (even just slightly) incorrect. If a certain CI holds in practice but there is an element that violates it in the interpretation then the CI will not be included in the base. One could argue that this method is then useful to find such errors but the application for mining CIs has this issue.

When there is a certain threshold for tolerating errors, then association rule mining offers an interesting solution. This method is based on the measures of support and confidence [1]. The support is a metric for measuring statistical significance, while confidence measures the 'strength' of a rule, in this case, expressed as a CI in an ontology language. Many authors have already employed this method for building DL ontologies [19,48,49] (see also [42]) and for finding relational rules in knowledge graphs [22]. The usual approach is to fix the depth of the CIs in order to restrict the search space.

There is a vast literature on algorithms and techniques for learning DL *concepts* based on inductive logic programming [18,21,26,29–32] (see [34] for learning logical rules also based in inductive logic programming). One of the most well known tools for supporting the construction of DL concepts is the DL-Learner [29]. In this approach, the learner receives as input examples of assertions classified as positive and negative and the goal is to construct a DL concept expression that 'fits' the classified examples.

Deep learning has also been applied for learning DL ontologies [39]. In the mentioned work, the authors use definitional sentences labelled with their DL translation to train a recurrent neural network (see also [35] for more work on definitional sentences in a DL context). It is an interesting approach that deals extremely well with data variability. The main difficulties pointed out by the authors are how to find large amounts of classified examples to train the neural network (the authors have trained it using synthetic data) and how to capture the semantics of the ontology. The neural network could capture the syntax, for example, map the word 'and' to the logical operator '⊓'. However, as reported by the authors, the method does not really capture the semantics of the sentences and how they relate to each other. There is an extensive literature on learning assertions using neural networks [16,53] but not many works on building DL ontologies with complex concept expressions.

6 Conclusion

We have presented a formalisation of the exact and the PAC learning models and defined learning complexity classes. This opens the possibility of investigating other questions such as the problem of deciding whether a learning framework is PAC or exactly learnable. Some authors have already investigated this problem for the PAC model, with a different formalisation of PAC learnability [47].

An interesting application of exact learning algorithms is to verify neural networks, as in the already mentioned works by Weiss et al. [51,52]. These works are based on Angluin's exact learning algorithm for learning regular languages represented by deterministic finite automata with membership and equivalence queries (an abstraction of the automata is used to find counterexamples). One of the goals of this strategy is to find *adversarial inputs*: examples neither present in the training nor in the test set which were misclassified by a neural network [51, 52]. It would be interesting to investigate whether algorithms for exactly learning ontologies can also be applied to verify if a neural network captures certain rules.

References

1. Agrawal, R., Imieliński, T., Swami, A.: Mining association rules between sets of items in large databases. Spec. Interest Gr. Manag. Data SIGMOD **22**(2), 207–216 (1993)
2. Angluin, D.: Queries and concept learning. Mach. Learn. **2**(4), 319–342 (1988)
3. Angluin, D.: Negative results for equivalence queries. Mach. Learn. **5**, 121–150 (1990)
4. Angluin, D., Frazier, M., Pitt, L.: Learning conjunctions of horn clauses. Mach. Learn. **9**, 147–164 (1992)
5. Arias, M.: Exact learning of first-order expressions from queries. Ph.D. thesis, Citeseer (2004)
6. Arias, M., Khardon, R.: Complexity parameters for first order classes. Mach. Learn. **64**(1–3), 121–144 (2006)
7. Arias, M., Khardon, R., Maloberti, J.: Learning horn expressions with LOGAN-H. J. Mach. Learn. Res. **8**, 549–587 (2007)
8. Artale, A., Calvanese, D., Kontchakov, R., Zakharyaschev, M.: The DL-Lite family and relations. CoRR abs/1401.3487 (2014)
9. Baader, F., Brandt, S., Lutz, C.: Pushing the $\mathcal{EL}$ envelope. In: Kaelbling, L., Saffiotti, A. (eds.) Proceedings of the 19th International Joint Conference on Artificial Intelligence (IJCAI), pp. 364–369. Professional Book Center (2005)
10. Baader, F., Calvanese, D., McGuinness, D., Nardi, D., Patel-Schneider, P. (eds.): The Description Logic Handbook: Theory, Implementation, and Applications, Second edn. Cambridge University Press, Cambridge (2007)
11. Baader, F., Distel, F.: Exploring finite models in the description logic $\mathcal{EL}_{gfp}$. In: Ferré, S., Rudolph, S. (eds.) ICFCA 2009. LNCS (LNAI), vol. 5548, pp. 146–161. Springer, Heidelberg (2009). https://doi.org/10.1007/978-3-642-01815-2_12
12. Baader, F., Ganter, B., Sertkaya, B., Sattler, U.: Completing description logic knowledge bases using formal concept analysis. In: IJCAI, vol. 7, pp. 230–235 (2007)
13. Baader, F., Horrocks, I., Lutz, C., Sattler, U.: An Introduction to Description Logic. Cambridge University Press, Cambridge (2017)
14. Blum, A.L.: Separating distribution-free and mistake-bound learning models over the Boolean domain. SIAM J. Comput. **23**(5), 990–1000 (1994)
15. Borchmann, D., Distel, F.: Mining of $\mathcal{EL}$-GCIs. In: The 11th IEEE International Conference on Data Mining Workshops, Vancouver, Canada (2011)
16. Bordes, A., Usunier, N., García-Durán, A., Weston, J., Yakhnenko, O.: Translating embeddings for modeling multi-relational data. In: Advances in Neural Information Processing Systems. NeurIPS, pp. 2787–2795 (2013)

17. Duarte, M.R.C., Konev, B., Ozaki, A.: ExactLearner: a tool for exact learning of EL ontologies. In: KR, pp. 409–414 (2018)
18. Fanizzi, N., d'Amato, C., Esposito, F.: DL-FOIL concept learning in description logics. In: Železný, F., Lavrač, N. (eds.) ILP 2008. LNCS (LNAI), vol. 5194, pp. 107–121. Springer, Heidelberg (2008). https://doi.org/10.1007/978-3-540-85928-4_12
19. Fleischhacker, D., Völker, J., Stuckenschmidt, H.: Mining RDF data for property axioms. In: Meersman, R., et al. (eds.) OTM 2012. LNCS, vol. 7566, pp. 718–735. Springer, Heidelberg (2012). https://doi.org/10.1007/978-3-642-33615-7_18
20. Frazier, M., Pitt, L.: Learning from entailment: an application to propositional Horn sentences. In: International Conference on Machine Learning, ICML, pp. 120–127 (1993)
21. Funk, M., Jung, J.C., Lutz, C., Pulcini, H., Wolter, F.: Learning description logic concepts: when can positive and negative examples be separated? In: Proceedings of the Twenty-Eighth International Joint Conference on Artificial Intelligence, IJCAI 2019, Macao, China, 10–16 August 2019, pp. 1682–1688 (2019)
22. Galárraga, L., Teflioudi, C., Hose, K., Suchanek, F.M.: Fast rule mining in ontological knowledge bases with AMIE+. VLDB J. **24**(6), 707–730 (2015)
23. Ganter, B., Wille, R.: Formal Concept Analysis: Mathematical Foundations. Springer, Heidelberg (1997). https://doi.org/10.1007/978-3-642-59830-2
24. Granmo, O.: The Tsetlin machine - a game theoretic bandit driven approach to optimal pattern recognition with propositional logic. CoRR abs/1804.01508 (2018)
25. Hermo, M., Ozaki, A.: Exact learning: on the boundary between horn and CNF. TOCT **12**(1), 4:1–4:25 (2020)
26. Iannone, L., Palmisano, I., Fanizzi, N.: An algorithm based on counterfactuals for concept learning in the semantic web. Appl. Intell. **26**, 139–159 (2007)
27. Konev, B., Lutz, C., Ozaki, A., Wolter, F.: Exact learning of lightweight description logic ontologies. JMLR **18**(201), 1–63 (2018)
28. Konev, B., Ozaki, A., Wolter, F.: A model for learning description logic ontologies based on exact learning. In: AAAI, pp. 1008–1015 (2016)
29. Lehmann, J.: DL-learner: learning concepts in description logics. JMLR **10**, 2639–2642 (2009)
30. Lehmann, J.: Learning OWL Class Expressions, vol. 6. IOS Press, Amsterdam (2010)
31. Lehmann, J., Haase, C.: Ideal downward refinement in the EL description logic. In: ILP, pp. 73–87 (2009)
32. Lehmann, J., Hitzler, P.: Concept learning in description logics using refinement operators. Mach. Learn. **78**(1–2), 203–250 (2010)
33. Lehmann, J., Völker, J.: Perspectives on Ontology Learning, vol. 18. IOS Press, Amsterdam (2014)
34. Lisi, F.A.: AL-Quin: an onto-relational learning system for semantic web mining. Int. J. Semant. Web Inf. Syst. **7**, 1–22 (2011)
35. Ma, Y., Distel, F.: Learning formal definitions for SNOMED CT from text. In: Peek, N., Marín Morales, R., Peleg, M. (eds.) AIME 2013. LNCS (LNAI), vol. 7885, pp. 73–77. Springer, Heidelberg (2013). https://doi.org/10.1007/978-3-642-38326-7_11
36. Ozaki, A.: Learning description logic ontologies: five approaches. Where do they stand? KI - Künstl. Intell. **34**(3), 317–327 (2020). https://doi.org/10.1007/s13218-020-00656-9
37. Ozaki, A., Persia, C., Mazzullo, A.: Learning query inseparable ELH ontologies. CoRR abs/1911.07229 (2019). To appear in the proceedings of AAAI 2020

38. Ozaki, A., Troquard, N.: Learning ontologies with epistemic reasoning: the $\mathcal{EL}$ case. In: Calimeri, F., Leone, N., Manna, M. (eds.) JELIA 2019. LNCS (LNAI), vol. 11468, pp. 418–433. Springer, Cham (2019). https://doi.org/10.1007/978-3-030-19570-0_27

39. Petrucci, G., Ghidini, C., Rospocher, M.: Ontology learning in the deep. In: Blomqvist, E., Ciancarini, P., Poggi, F., Vitali, F. (eds.) EKAW 2016. LNCS (LNAI), vol. 10024, pp. 480–495. Springer, Cham (2016). https://doi.org/10.1007/978-3-319-49004-5_31

40. Pitt, L., Valiant, L.G.: Computational limitations on learning from examples. J. ACM **35**(4), 965–984 (1988)

41. Rudolph, S.: Exploring relational structures via $\mathcal{FLE}$. In: Wolff, K.E., Pfeiffer, H.D., Delugach, H.S. (eds.) ICCS-ConceptStruct 2004. LNCS (LNAI), vol. 3127, pp. 196–212. Springer, Heidelberg (2004). https://doi.org/10.1007/978-3-540-27769-9_13

42. Sazonau, V., Sattler, U.: Mining hypotheses from data in OWL: advanced evaluation and complete construction. In: d'Amato, C., et al. (eds.) ISWC 2017. LNCS, vol. 10587, pp. 577–593. Springer, Cham (2017). https://doi.org/10.1007/978-3-319-68288-4_34

43. Shalev-Shwartz, S., Ben-David, S.: Understanding Machine Learning: From Theory to Algorithms. Cambridge University Press, Cambridge (2014)

44. Sipser, M.: Introduction to the Theory of Computation Thomson Course Technology, International Edition of Second edn. Massachusetts Institute of Technology, Cambridge (2005)

45. Spackman, K.A., Campbell, K.E., Côté, R.A.: SNOMED RT: a reference terminology for health care. In: Masys, D.R. (ed.) Proceedings 1997 AMIA Annual Fall Symposium Journal of the American Medial Informatics Association, Symposium Supplement, pp. 640–644. Hanley & Belfus (1997)

46. Valiant, L.G.: A theory of the learnable. Commun. ACM **27**(11), 1134–1142 (1984)

47. Venkatraman, S., Balasubramanian, S., Sarma, R.R.: PAC-learning is undecidable. CoRR abs/1808.06324 (2018)

48. Völker, J., Fleischhacker, D., Stuckenschmidt, H.: Automatic acquisition of class disjointness. J. Web Semant. **35**, 124–139 (2015)

49. Völker, J., Niepert, M.: Statistical schema induction. In: Antoniou, G., et al. (eds.) ESWC 2011. LNCS, vol. 6643, pp. 124–138. Springer, Heidelberg (2011). https://doi.org/10.1007/978-3-642-21034-1_9

50. Watanabe, O.: A formal study of learning via queries. In: Paterson, M.S. (ed.) ICALP 1990. LNCS, vol. 443, pp. 139–152. Springer, Heidelberg (1990). https://doi.org/10.1007/BFb0032028

51. Weiss, G., Goldberg, Y., Yahav, E.: Extracting automata from recurrent neural networks using queries and counterexamples. In: ICML, pp. 5244–5253 (2018)

52. Weiss, G., Goldberg, Y., Yahav, E.: Learning deterministic weighted automata with queries and counterexamples. In: Wallach, H.M., Larochelle, H., Beygelzimer, A., d'Alché-Buc, F., Fox, E.B., Garnett, R. (eds.) NeurIPS, pp. 8558–8569 (2019)

53. Yang, B., Yih, W., He, X., Gao, J., Deng, L.: Embedding entities and relations for learning and inference in knowledge bases. In: ICLR (2015)

Explanation via Machine Arguing

Oana Cocarascu⬤, Antonio Rago⬤, and Francesca Toni⁽⊠⁾⬤

Imperial College London, London, UK
{oc511,a.rago15,ft}@imperial.ac.uk

Abstract. As AI becomes ever more ubiquitous in our everyday lives, its ability to explain to and interact with humans is evolving into a critical research area. Explainable AI (XAI) has therefore emerged as a popular topic but its research landscape is currently very fragmented. Explanations in the literature have generally been aimed at addressing individual challenges and are often ad-hoc, tailored to specific AIs and/or narrow settings. Further, the extraction of explanations is no simple task; the design of the explanations must be fit for purpose, with considerations including, but not limited to: Is the model or a result being explained? Is the explanation suited to skilled or unskilled explainees? By which means is the information best exhibited? How may users interact with the explanation? As these considerations rise in number, it quickly becomes clear that a systematic way to obtain a variety of explanations for a variety of users and interactions is much needed. In this tutorial we will overview recent approaches showing how these challenges can be addressed by utilising forms of *machine arguing* as the scaffolding underpinning explanations that are delivered to users. Machine arguing amounts to the deployment of methods from *computational argumentation* in AI with suitably mined *argumentation frameworks*, which provide abstractions of "debates". Computational argumentation has been widely used to support applications requiring information exchange between AI systems and users , facilitated by the fact that the capability of arguing is pervasive in human affairs and arguing is core to a multitude of human activities: humans argue to explain, interact and exchange information. Our lecture will focus on how machine arguing can serve as the driving force of explanations in AI in different ways, namely: by building explainable systems with argumentative foundations from linguistic data focusing on reviews), or by extracting argumentative reasoning from existing systems (focusing on a recommender system).

Keywords: Argumentation · Explanation · Explainable AI

1 Introduction

Much of AI researchers' recent efforts are being dedicated towards the extraction of explanations for results by AI tools (e.g. predictions, classifications or recommendations) and the manner in which they are provided to users (e.g. see [19, 21] for recent overviews). However, the extraction of explanations is no

© Springer Nature Switzerland AG 2020
M. Manna and A. Pieris (Eds.): Reasoning Web 2020, LNCS 12258, pp. 53–84, 2020.
https://doi.org/10.1007/978-3-030-60067-9_3

simple task; the design of the explanations must be fit for purpose, with considerations including, but not limited to: Is the model or a result being explained? Is the explanation suited to skilled or unskilled explainees? By which means is the information best exhibited? How may users interact with the explanation? As these considerations rise in number, it quickly becomes clear that a systematic way to obtain a variety of explanations for a variety of users and interactions, rather than a multitude of ad-hoc approaches lacking coherence with one another, would simplify the scope of the problem significantly, while also providing a unifying view within the research landscape. At the same time, AI systems are advancing towards providing *interactive* explanations to users. Such systems have become extremely popular in recent years; huge investments from the tech industry leaders have been devoted to developing personal assistant technology, e.g. Microsoft's *Cortana*. However, in order for these products to engage in meaningful explanatory conversations with humans they must be backed by explanatory capabilities to drive interactions.

Computational argumentation (e.g. see [2,5] for recent overviews) is a well-established field in AI focusing on the definition of so-called argumentation frameworks as abstractions of "debates" and the evaluation of the dialectical standing of positions (arguments) within these debates: for example, *abstract argumentation frameworks* [16] represent disagreements (attacks) in debates, whereas *bipolar argumentation frameworks* [9,13] represent agreements (supports) as well as disagreements . Computational argumentation has long been identified as a suitable mechanism to support explanation (e.g. as in [8,22]). Indeed, the capability of arguing is pervasive in human affairs: it is essential in certain professions, e.g. traditionally, the practice of law and politics, but also in evidence-based medicine, where evidence in favour of or against treatments is essential for decision-making. Overall, arguing is core to a multitude of human activities: humans argue to explain, interact and exchange information. As a result, various models of interactive explanation may be supported by argumentation frameworks as the underlying knowledge base. Further, given that argumentation is amenable for human consumption, it can effectively support the human desire to anthropomorphise systems.

Explainable AI can be supported by very many forms of computational argumentation, including the aforementioned abstract (with just attacks) and bipolar (with both attacks and supports) argumentation, several forms of *structured argumentation* and *quantitative bipolar argumentation* (see [7] for an overview). In some (notably abstract, bipolar and quantitative bipolar argumentation) arguments are seen as abstract entities, which can be deemed to be arguments as they are connected by dialectical relations of attack (in all cases) and possibly of support (in bipolar and quantitative bipolar argumentation). We will take this view of arguments as 'abstract' also in this lecture. Other relations are envisaged as possible in some other forms of computational argumentation, e.g. in [17]: in this lecture we will use, in addition to quantitative bipolar argumentation, also *tripolar argumentation* [23], extending bipolar argumentation with a third relation of *neutralisation*.

Computational argumentation is not just about representing arguments and relationships between them: reasoning with the represented arguments to extract semantically justified conclusion is also core to this paradigm, across all its forms. Whereas abstract argumentation, structured argumentation and bipolar argumentation predominantly use *extensions* (i.e. sets of arguments) as their semantics, quantitative bipolar argumentation uses *gradual semantics*: extensions identify sets of arguments that are collectively acceptable, from a dialectical point of view; instead, gradual semantics assign, from within a given set of values, dialectical strengths to individual arguments. In this lecture, we will make use of the second form of semantics.

Can computational argumentation support the vision of explainable AI? In order to do so, argumentation frameworks need to be extracted from the systems that need explaining. If the systems are built from scratch then argumentation for explanation can be injected within them by design, but this still requires a principled extraction from the systems' components. Moreover, the extraction of interactive explanations of various types from the extracted argumentation frameworks needs engineering. We think of the end-to-end process of extraction of argumentation framework and interactive explanations as *machine arguing*, allowing machines to engage with humans in the process of argumentation, and deployable as the scaffolding in which relevant information can be harboured so that a variety of interactive explanatory exchanges for AI systems' outputs can be extracted for various types of users. This is summarised in Fig. 1, where the AI system, in principle, may be any, based on data-centric, symbolic or hybrid methodologies. In this paper, we focus on recommender systems.

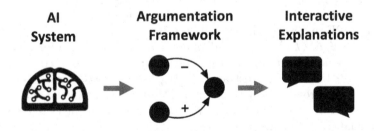

Fig. 1. Machine arguing for interactive explanations.

In this lecture we focus on two examples of this vision of machine arguing for systems' explanation: in Sect. 3 we define an explainable systems from linguistic data (i.e. reviews), so that it has argumentative foundations to support a variety of interactive explanations; and in Sect. 4 we show how interactive explanations can be extracted by argumentative reasoning from a given, non argumentative (recommender) system. In both cases, as in Fig. 1, argumentation frameworks are extracted from the underlying systems: these are quantitative bipolar argumentation frameworks in Sect. 3 and tripolar argumentation fameworks in Sect. 4.

Fig. 2. The argument graphs $\mathcal{G}_F$ for the AF $F = (\{\alpha, \beta, \gamma, \delta, \epsilon\}, \{(\beta, \alpha), (\delta, \alpha), (\gamma, \epsilon)\})$ (left) and $\mathcal{G}_F$ for the BF $F = (\{\alpha, \beta, \gamma, \delta, \epsilon\}, \{(\beta, \alpha), (\delta, \alpha), (\gamma, \epsilon)\}, \{(\gamma, \alpha), (\epsilon, \delta)\})$ (right).

Then, gradual semantics are applied to the frameworks to support the generation of interactive explanations. In Sect. 3 the gradual semantics is chosen by us (by design), and alternative gradual semantics can be applied. Instead, in Sect. 4 the semantics is dictated by the underlying recommender system, so as to match its predicted ratings, and the extraction of the argumentation framework from which explanations are drawn is regulated by the need for this semantics to be dialectically meaningful.

2   Background: Argumentation

Abstract Argumentation frameworks (AFs) are pairs consisting of a set of arguments and a binary (attack) relation between arguments [16]. Formally, an AF is any pair $\langle \mathcal{X}, \mathcal{L}^- \rangle$ where $\mathcal{L}^- \subseteq \mathcal{X} \times \mathcal{X}$. Bipolar Argumentation frameworks (BFs) extend AFs by considering two binary relations: attack and support [9]. Formally, a BF is any triple $(\mathcal{X}, \mathcal{L}^-, \mathcal{L}^+)$ where $\langle \mathcal{X}, \mathcal{L}^- \rangle$ is an AF and $\mathcal{L}^+ \subseteq \mathcal{X} \times \mathcal{X}$. If $\mathcal{L}^+ = \emptyset$, a BF $(\mathcal{X}, \mathcal{L}^-, \mathcal{L}^+)$ can be identified with an AF $\langle \mathcal{X}, \mathcal{L}^- \rangle$, so we can use the term BF to denote BFs as well as AFs.

Any $F = (\mathcal{X}, \mathcal{L}^-, \mathcal{L}^+)$ can be understood and visualised as a directed graph $\mathcal{G}_F$, also called *argument graph*, with nodes $\mathcal{X}$ and two types of edges: $\mathcal{L}^-$ and $\mathcal{L}^+$ (see e.g. [9,14]). In the illustration in Fig. 2, we show $\mathcal{G}_F$ using single ($\rightarrow$) and double ($\Rightarrow$) arrows to denote $\mathcal{L}^-$ and $\mathcal{L}^+$, respectively. In the remainder of the paper, instead, when showing $\mathcal{G}_F$, we will use arrows labelled - to denote $\mathcal{L}^-$ and arrows labelled + to denote $\mathcal{L}^+$, respectively.[1]

Semantics of AFs/BFs amount to "recipes" for determining "winning" sets of arguments or the "dialectical strength" of arguments. These semantics can be respectively defined qualitatively, in terms of *extensions* (e.g. the *grounded* extension [16], defined below), and quantitatively, in terms of a *gradual evaluation* of arguments (e.g. as in [6,7,25] – the former of which, defined below, we will use in this paper).

Given an AF $\langle \mathcal{X}, \mathcal{L}^- \rangle$, let $E \subseteq \mathcal{X}$ *defend* $a \in \mathcal{X}$ iff for all $b \in \mathcal{X}$ attacking a there exists $c \in E$ attacking b. Then, the *grounded extension* of $\langle \mathcal{X}, \mathcal{L}^- \rangle$ is $G = \bigcup_{i \geq 0} G_i$, where G_0 is the set of all *unattacked* arguments (i.e. the set of all arguments $a \in \mathcal{X}$ such that there is no argument $b \in \mathcal{X}$ with $(b, a) \in \mathcal{L}^-$)

---

[1] These alternative notations are used interchangeably in the literature, as we do here.

and $\forall i \geq 0$, G_{i+1} is the set of all arguments that G_i defends. For any $\langle \mathcal{X}, \mathcal{L}^- \rangle$, the grounded extension G always exists and is unique. As an illustration, in the simple AF in Fig. 2, left, $G = \{\beta, \delta, \gamma\}$.

On the other hand, quantitative semantics allow a *gradual evaluation* of arguments. They can be defined for BFs, as in [4], or for *Quantitative Bipolar Argumentation Frameworks* (QBFs) [6,7], of the form $(\mathcal{X}, \mathcal{L}^-, \mathcal{L}^+, \tau)$ where $(\mathcal{X}, \mathcal{L}^-, \mathcal{L}^+)$ is a BF and $\tau : \mathcal{X} \rightarrow I$ for some interval I (e.g. $I = [0, 1]$ or $I = [-1, 1]$) gives the intrinsic strength or *base score* of arguments. AFs and BFs are QBFs with special choices of τ [6], so we will sometimes use the term QBF to denote AFs and BFs. The argument graph for $\langle \mathcal{X}, \mathcal{L}^-, \mathcal{L}^+, \tau \rangle$ is the argument graph for $(\mathcal{X}, \mathcal{L}^-, \mathcal{L}^+)$.

Given a QBF $(\mathcal{X}, \mathcal{L}^-, \mathcal{L}^+, \tau)$, the strength of arguments is given by some $\sigma : \mathcal{X} \rightarrow I$. Several such notions have been defined in the literature (e.g. see [7] for an overview). We will use the notion of [25][2], where $I = [0, 1]$ and for $a \in \mathcal{X}$:
$$\sigma(a) = c(\tau(a), \mathcal{F}'(\sigma(\mathcal{L}^-(a))), \mathcal{F}'(\sigma(\mathcal{L}^+(a))))$$
such that:

(i) $\mathcal{L}^-(a)$ is the set of all arguments attacking a and if $(a_1, \ldots, a_n)$ is an arbitrary permutation of the ($n \geq 0$) elements of $\mathcal{L}^-(a)$, then $\sigma(\mathcal{L}^-(a)) = (\sigma(a_1), \ldots, \sigma(a_n))$ (similarly for supporters);

(ii) for $v_0, v_a, v_s \in [0, 1]$,
$$c(v_0, v_a, v_s) = v_0 - v_0 \cdot |v_s - v_a| \qquad \text{if } v_a \geq v_s,$$
$$c(v_0, v_a, v_s) = v_0 + (1 - v_0) \cdot |v_s - v_a| \qquad \text{if } v_a < v_s; \text{ and}$$

(iii) for $S = (v_1, \ldots, v_n) \in [0, 1]^*$ and $f'(x, y) = x + y - x \cdot y$:
if $n = 0$: $\mathcal{F}'(S) = 0$;   if $n = 1$: $\mathcal{F}'(S) = v_1$;   if $n = 2$: $\mathcal{F}'(S) = f'(v_1, v_2)$;
if $n > 2$: $\mathcal{F}'(S) = f'(\mathcal{F}'(v_1, \ldots, v_{n-1}), v_n)$.

Intuitively, the strength $\sigma(a)$ of argument a results from the combination c of three components: the base score $\tau(a)$ of a, the aggregated strength $\mathcal{F}'(\sigma(\mathcal{L}^-(a)))$ of all arguments attacking a and the aggregated strength $\mathcal{F}'(\sigma(\mathcal{L}^+(a)))$ of all arguments supporting a. The combination c decreases the base score of a if the aggregated strength of the attackers is at least as high as the aggregated strength of the supporters (with the decrement proportional to the base score and to the absolute value of the difference between the aggregated strengths). The combination c increases the base score of a otherwise, if the aggregated strength of the attackers is lower than the aggregated strength of the supporters (with the increment proportional to the distance between 1 and the base score and to the absolute value of the difference between the aggregated strengths). Finally, the aggregated strengths are defined recursively (using the probabilistic sum when there are exactly two terms to aggregate - these are either strengths of attackers or of supporters).[3]

---

[2] Note that several other notions could be used, as overviewed in [7]. we have chosen this specific notion because it satisfies some desirable properties [7] as well as performing well in practice [11].

[3] Note that this recursively defined notion treats strengths of attackers and supporters as sets, but needs to consider them in sequence (thus the mention of 'an arbitrary permutation').

As an illustration, in the BF in Fig. 2, right, if the base score of all arguments if 0.5, then $\sigma(\gamma) = \tau(\gamma) = 0.5$ and $\sigma(\epsilon) = c(0.5, 0.5, 0) = 0.5 - 0.5 \cdot 0.5 = 0.25$.

3   Building Explainable Systems with Argumentative Foundations

The use of social media has become a regular habit for many and has changed the way people interact with each other. In an age in which e-commerce and audio/video streaming are dominant markets for consumers, products' online reviews are fast becoming the preferred method of quality control for users. The aggregation of these reviews allows users to check the quality of a product while avoiding reviews which may be incoherent and irrelevant.

Within the movie domain, Rotten Tomatoes[4] (RT) is a popular review site that aggregates critics' reviews to obtain an overall percentage of critics who like the movie and critics who do not. The RT score is simplified to a binary classification for the movie of Fresh or Rotten, based on whether it is greater or equal to 60% or not, respectively. This simplification into RT score, Fresh/Rotten classification, gives users a quick way to determine whether a movie is worth watching or not. Figure 3 shows an overview of RT where each review is classified as Fresh/Rotten and the score of the movie is given by the percentage of Fresh reviews.

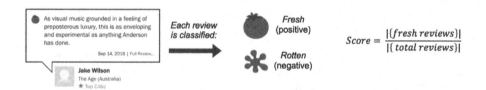

Fig. 3. Rotten Tomatoes summary.

However, the 60% threshold means that a critic's mixed review that is slightly positive overall will have the same weight as a rave review from another critic, leading to the case where a movie with a maximum RT score could be composed of only *generally* positive reviews. Also, the RT score does not take into account user preferences and so factors which decrease the RT score may not have any relevance in a user's personal selection criteria, meaning movies may be overlooked when they may actually be perfectly suited to a user's tastes. Thus, a method to *explain* the aggregation is needed so that users can decide for themselves.

To address this problem, in this section we present a method [11] that, for any given movie:

---

[4] https://www.rottentomatoes.com.

1. mines arguments from reviews;
2. extracts a QBAF and computes a dialectical strength measure as an alternative to the RT score;
3. supplements the computed strength with dialogical explanations obtained from BAFs extracted from movie reviews that empower users to interact with the system for more information about a movie's aggregated review.

The method relies upon a feature-based characterisation of reviews and mines review aggregations (RAs) from snippets drawn from reviews by critics to obtain votes (on both movies and their (sub-)features). We mine RAs from snippets and determine whether these snippets provide positive or negative votes for ((sub-)features of) movies, by looking for arguments supporting or attacking, respectively, the ((sub-)features of the) movies. The feature-characterisation along with the votes are then used to generate QBAFs, that can then provide a dialectical strength, σ of the movi.e. Our method aims to extract a QBAF for any given movie and provide a dialectical strength, σ for the movie an an alternative to the score that appears on the RT website, as can be seen in Fig. 4.

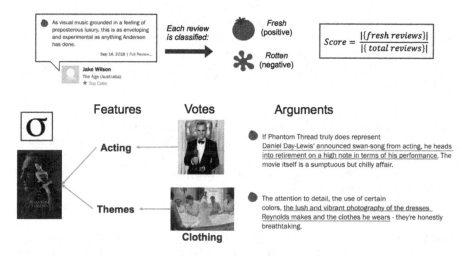

Fig. 4. The method [11] aims to match the RT score with σ computed from the QBAF extracted from the movie reviews.

3.1 Preprocessing

Definition 1. *Let $\mathcal{M}$ be a given set of movies, and $m \in \mathcal{M}$ be any movi.e. A feature-based characterisation of m is a finite set $\mathcal{F}$ of features with sub-features $\mathcal{F}' \subset \mathcal{F}$ such that each $f' \in \mathcal{F}'$ has a unique parent $p(f') \in \mathcal{F}$; for any $f \in \mathcal{F} \backslash \mathcal{F}'$, we define $p(f) = m$.*

Feature-Based Characterisation of Movies: A sub-feature is more specific than its parent feature. For example, for the movie $m = Wonder\ Wheel$, a feature may be *acting*, which may be the parent of the sub-feature *Kate Winslet*. We will refer to elements of $\mathcal{F} \backslash \mathcal{F}'$ only as features, and to elements of $\mathcal{F}'$ as sub-features. Also, we will refer to a sub-feature with parent f as a sub-feature of f.

Note that this feature-based characterisation may be obtained automatically from metadata and from the top critics' snippets that appear on the RT movie pages. By doing so, for *Wonder Wheel*, we may obtain features $\{f_A, f_D, f_W, f_T\}$, where f_A is *acting*, f_D is *directing*, f_W is *writing* and f_T is *themes*.

The sub-features in $\mathcal{F}'$ may be of different types, namely *single* (for features f_D and f_W, if we only consider movies with a single director or writer) or *multiple* (for f_A, since movies will generally have more than one actor: *Wonder Wheel* has *Kate Winslet* and *Justin Timberlake* as sub-features of f_A, and f_T, since movies will generally be associated with several themes). In the case of single sub-features, the feature can be equated with the sub-feature (for *Wonder Wheel*, *Woody Allen* is the sole director and so this sub-feature can be represented by f_D itself). Furthermore, sub-features may be *predetermined*, namely obtained from meta-data (as for the sub-features with parents f_A, f_D, f_W in the running example), or *mined* from (snippets of) reviews (for *Wonder Wheel* the sub-feature *amusement park* of f_T may be mined rather than predetermined). For example, for *Wonder Wheel*, we identify the sub-feature *amusement park* (f'_{T_1}) as several reviews mention the related terms *Coney Island* and *fairground*, as in '*like the fairground ride for which it's named, Wonder Wheel is entertaining*'.

The movie *Wonder Wheel*, its (sub-)features and how they relate are shown in Fig. 5.

Extracting Phrases Representing Potential Arguments: We analyse each critic's review independently, tokenising each review into sentences and splitting sentences into phrases when specific keywords (*but, although, though, otherwise, however, unless, whereas, despite*) occur. Each phrase may then constitute a potential argument with vote from its critic in the review aggregation.

For illustration, consider the following review for $m = $ *Wonder Wheel* from a critic:

c_1: *Despite a stunning performance by Winslet and some beautiful cinematography by Vittorio Storaro, Wonder Wheel loses its charms quickly and you'll soon be begging to get off this particular ride.*

We extract two phrases:

- p_1: *Despite a stunning performance by Winslet and some beautiful cinematography by Vittorio Storaro*
- p_2: *Wonder Wheel loses its charms quickly and you'll soon be begging to get off this particular ride*

Consider another review from a critic:

c_2: *Like the fairground ride for which it's named, it is entertaining.*

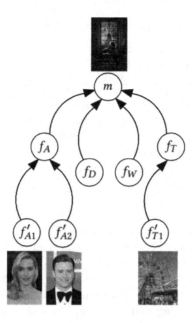

Fig. 5. Extracted (sub-)features for the movie *Wonder Wheel*.

We extract two phrases:

- p_3: *like the fairground ride for which it's named, the film is entertaining*

Finally, consider the following review from a critic:

c_3: *As we watch Allen worry and nitpick over the way women fret over aging, painting Ginny as pathetic, jealous, insecure, and clownish, it's dull, unoriginal, and offensive. Frankly, we've had enough Woody Allen takes on this subject.*
Here we extract two different phrases concerning *Woody Allen*:

- p_4: *As we watch Allen worry and nitpick over the way women fret over aging, painting Ginny as pathetic, jealous, insecure, and clownish, it's dull, unoriginal, and offensive*
- p_5: *Frankly, we've had enough Woody Allen takes on this subject.*

Using this feature-based characterisation of a movie and snippets from the movie reviews by critics, we generate votes on arguments, amounting to the movie in question and its (sub-)features. The result is a *review aggregation* for the movie, which is then transformed into a *QBAF* that we obtain as described next.

Extracting Review Aggregations: Let $m \in \mathcal{M}$ be any movie and $\mathcal{F}$ be a feature-based characterisation of m as given in Definition 1. Let $\mathcal{X}$ denote $\{m\} \cup \mathcal{F}$, referred to as the set of *arguments*. We then define the following:

Definition 2. *A review aggregation for m is a triple $\mathcal{R}(m) = \langle \mathcal{F}, \mathcal{C}, \mathcal{V} \rangle$ where*

- *$\mathcal{C}$ is a finite, non-empty set of critics;*
- *$\mathcal{V} : \mathcal{C} \times \mathcal{X} \rightarrow \{-, +\}$ is a partial function, with $\mathcal{V}(c, \alpha)$ representing the vote of critic $c \in \mathcal{C}$ on argument $\alpha \in \mathcal{X}$.*

A positive/negative vote from a critic on a (sub-)feature of the movie signifies positive/negative stance on that (sub-)feature and a positive/negative vote on m signifies positive/negative stance on the overall movi.e.

In order to determine the arguments on which the votes act, we use a *glossary* G using movie-related words for each feature as well as for movies in general. G is as follows (for any $m \in \mathcal{M}$):

$G(m) = \{movie, film, work\}$;
$G(f_D) = \{director\}$;
$G(f_A) = \{acting, cast, portrayal, performance\}$;
$G(f_W) = \{writer, writing, screenplay, screenwriter, screenwriting, script, storyline, character\}$.

We can mine votes using NLP techniques such as sentiment analysis or argument mining. For simplicity, we will use sentiment analysis, which is the process of computationally identifying and categorising opinions expressed in a piece of text to determine whether the polarity towards a particular topic, item, etc. is positive, negative, or neutral. The sentiment polarity of each phrase is translated into a (negative or positive) vote from the corresponding critic. Furthermore, we impose a threshold on the sentiment polarity to filter out phrases that can be deemed to be "neutral" and therefore cannot be considered to be votes. Votes are then assigned to arguments based on occurrences of words from G.

When determining the argument on which a vote acts, sub-features take precedence over features. A mention of "Kate Winslet" (f'_{A1}) (with or without a word from $G(f_A)$) connects with f'_{A1}, whereas a sole mention of any word from $G(f_A)$ connects with f_A. A text that contains two entities (a sub-feature or a word from the glossary) corresponding to different (sub-)features results in two arguments (and votes), one for each (sub-)feature identified.

For example, from the review from c_1, the system may extract one vote for the sub-feature "Kate Winslet" (f'_{A1}) and one for the movie in general. Thus, p_1 gives $(0.833, f'_{A1})$ therefore $\mathcal{V}(c_1, f'_{A1}) = +$, while p_2 gives $(-0.604, m)$ therefore $\mathcal{V}(c_1, m) = -$. If the neutrality threshold is 0.6 for the absolute value of the polarity, a positive vote corresponding to p_1 is assigned to f'_{A1} and a negative vote corresponding to p_2 is assigned to m. It should be noted that if a feature *cinematography* had been included in our $\mathcal{F}$ then we would have had another vote from c_1. This could be achieved by using more metadata of the movies and hence an occurrence of Storaro would correspond to a vote on cinematography. We determine the votes for the mined f_T in the same way as for the other features. For example, given p_3: *like the fairground ride for which it's named, Wonder Wheel is entertaining* leading to $(0.741, f'_{T1})$, we obtain $\mathcal{V}(c_2, f'_{T1}) = +$. If the review of a single critic results in several phrases associated with an argument with different polarities, we take the one with the highest sentiment magnitude to determine the vote on that argument. For example, given: p_5: $(-0.659, f_D)$

and p_6: $(-0.500, f_D)$, then p_5 supersedes and $\mathcal{V}(c_3, f_D) = -$. Figure 6 shows the votes extracted on the movie *Wonder Wheel* and its (sub-)features.

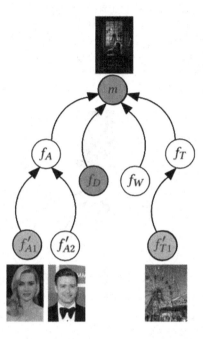

Fig. 6. Votes extracted on the movie and (sub-)features.

Augmenting Review Aggregations: A review aggregation can be *augmented* by exploiting the parent relation: a vote for/against an argument can be seen as a vote for/against the argument's parent.

In the case of f_A, which is a *multiple* feature, we also consider the augmented vote (if any) when determining whether the movie has augmented votes. This is because a movie generally has several actors, whose performances may differ. In the case of f_D and f_W, if we only consider movies with a single director or writer, the features are equated with the sub-feature. If the movie has more than one director or writer, then their augmented votes are not considered when determining the augmented votes of the movie as the contributions in directing and writing cannot be split (i.e. we cannot have director X was better than director Y for the same movie). While being a *multiple* feature, we do not consider the augmented votes of themes for the augmented votes of movies as we mine themes from texts and movies may not have themes. The importance of acting in the augmentation is also due to the fact that it appears in movie metadata, whereas themes do not.

For example, let c's vote on f_A be undefined, c's vote on sub-feature f'_{A1} of f_A be $+$ and there be no $-$ votes from c on any other sub-features of f_A. We then assume that c's overall stance on f_A is positive and therefore set c's vote on f_A to $+$. This notion of augmented review aggregation combats the brevity of the snippets causing the review aggregation being too sparsely populated.

In our example, given that f'_{A1} is positive and f'_{T1} is positive, then f_A and f_T are augmented each with a positive vote. Figure 7 shows the augmented review aggregations for the movie *Wonder Wheel*.

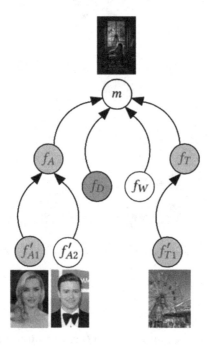

Fig. 7. Augmented review aggregations for the movie *Wonder Wheel*.

3.2 Extracting QBAFs

In order to obtain a QBAF from a review aggregation, we determine: the arguments, the arguments' base scores, and between which arguments attacks and supports are present. Having already identified the arguments, we use an aggregation of critics' votes for base scores, and we impose that a (sub-)feature attacks or supports its parent argument depending on its aggregated stance, as follows:

Definition 3. *Let $\mathcal{R}(m) = \langle \mathcal{F}, \mathcal{C}, \mathcal{V} \rangle$ be any (augmented) review aggregation for $m \in \mathcal{M}$. For any $\gamma \in \mathcal{X} = \mathcal{F} \cup \{m\}$, let $\mathcal{V}^+(\gamma) = |\{c \in \mathcal{C} | \mathcal{V}(c, \gamma) = +\}|$ and*

$\mathcal{V}^-(\gamma) = |\{c \in \mathcal{C}|\mathcal{V}(c,\gamma) = -\}|$. Then, the QBAF corresponding to $\mathcal{R}(m)$ is $\langle \mathcal{X}, \mathcal{L}^-, \mathcal{L}^+, \tau \rangle$ such that

$$\mathcal{L}^- = \{(\alpha,\beta) \in \mathcal{F}^2 | \beta = p(\alpha) \wedge \mathcal{V}^+(\beta) > \mathcal{V}^-(\beta) \wedge \mathcal{V}^+(\alpha) < \mathcal{V}^-(\alpha)\} \cup$$
$$\{(\alpha,\beta) \in \mathcal{F}^2 | \beta = p(\alpha) \wedge \mathcal{V}^+(\beta) < \mathcal{V}^-(\beta) \wedge \mathcal{V}^+(\alpha) > \mathcal{V}^-(\alpha)\} \cup$$
$$\{(\alpha,m) | \alpha \in \mathcal{F} \wedge m = p(\alpha) \wedge \mathcal{V}^+(\alpha) < \mathcal{V}^-(\alpha)\};$$
$$\mathcal{L}^+ = \{(\alpha,\beta) \in \mathcal{F}^2 | \beta = p(\alpha) \wedge \mathcal{V}^+(\beta) \geq \mathcal{V}^-(\beta) \wedge \mathcal{V}^+(\alpha) \geq \mathcal{V}^-(\alpha)\} \cup$$
$$\{(\alpha,\beta) \in \mathcal{F}^2 | \beta = p(\alpha) \wedge \mathcal{V}^+(\beta) \leq \mathcal{V}^-(\beta) \wedge \mathcal{V}^+(\alpha) \leq \mathcal{V}^-(\alpha)\} \cup$$
$$\{(\alpha,m) | \alpha \in \mathcal{F} \wedge m = p(\alpha) \wedge \mathcal{V}^+(\alpha) \geq \mathcal{V}^-(\alpha)\};$$

$$\tau(m) = 0.5 + 0.5 \cdot \frac{\mathcal{V}^+(m) - \mathcal{V}^-(m)}{|\mathcal{C}|} \text{ and } \forall f \in \mathcal{F}, \ \tau(f) = \frac{|\mathcal{V}^+(f) - \mathcal{V}^-(f)|}{|\mathcal{C}|}.$$

An attack is defined as either from a feature with dominant negative votes (with respect to positive votes) towards the movie itself or from a sub-feature with dominant negative (positive) votes towards a feature with dominant positive (negative, respectively) votes. The latter type of attack can be exemplified by a sub-feature of f_A with positive stance attacking the negative (due to other votes/arguments) feature f_A, which attacks m. Conversely, a support is defined as either from a feature with dominant positive votes towards the movie itself or from a sub-feature with dominant positive (negative) votes towards a feature with dominant positive (negative, respectively) votes. The latter type of support can be exemplified by a sub-feature of f_A with negative stance supporting the negative feature f_A, which attacks m. It should be noted that (sub-)features with equal positive and negative votes are treated as supporters, though we could have assigned no relation.

In our example, we construct the BAF as follows:

- positive argument f'_{A1} supports positive argument f_A;
- neutral argument f'_{A2} neither attacks nor supports positive argument f_A;
- positive argument f_A supports positive argument m;
- negative argument f_D attacks positive argument m;
- neutral argument f_W neither attacks nor supports positive argument m;
- positive argument f'_{T1} supports positive argument f_T;
- positive argument f_T supports positive argument m.

We adapt the base score, $\tau(m) \in [0,1]$, from [24]. Intuitively, $\tau(m) = 1$ represents all critics having a positive stance on the movie while $\tau(m) = 0$ requires universally negative stance. The base score of a (sub-)feature f is again in $[0,1]$ where, differently to movies since a feature already represents positive/negative sentiment towards the argument it supports/attacks, $\tau(f) = 0$ represents no dominant negative/positive stance from the critics on f while $\tau(f) = 1$ represents universally negative/positive stance on f.

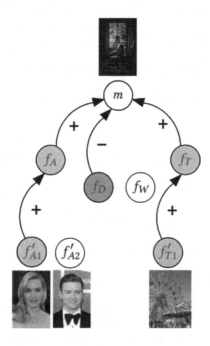

Fig. 8. The BAF obtained for the movie *Wonder Wheel*.

3.3 Explanations

The system relies on a dialogue protocol defined such that a conversation between a user and the system evolves from questions put forward by the user **U** to which the system **S** responds with explanations based on the underlying graph.

Consider the QBAF for *The Post* in Fig. 9. In Fig. 10, we can see that f_W was actually considered to be poor since it attacks m. However, the acting from Tom Hanks f'_{A1} and, particularly, Meryl Streep f'_{A2} contributed to the high strength The argumentation dialogue may then be:

U: *Why was The Post highly rated?*
S: *This movie was highly rated because the acting was great, although the writing was poor.*
U: *Why was the acting considered to be good?*
S: *The acting was considered to be good thanks to Tom Hanks and particularly Meryl Streep.*
U: *What did critics say about Meryl Streep being great?*
S: *"...Streep's hesitations, rue, and ultimate valor are soul-deep..."*

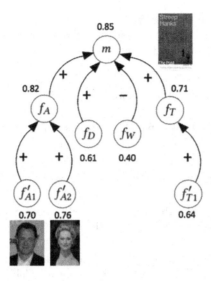

Fig. 9. QBAF for the movie *The Post.*

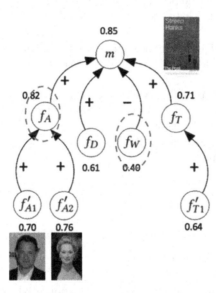

Fig. 10. The strongest supporter and strongest attacker for m.

3.4 Exercise

Given the reviews in Table 1, which represent an excerpt from the top critics reviews of the movie *Inception*:

1. identify a theme from the reviews;
2. extract votes and determine whether they have a positive or negative polarity;
3. construct the BAF from the feature-based characterisation.

Table 1. Reviews for the movie *Inception.*

R₁ A spectacular fantasy thriller based on Nolan's own original screenplay, it is the smartest CGI head-trip since The Matrix
R₂ A heist film of thrilling, almost delirious complexity
R₃ Inception is a boldly constructed wonder with plenty of – as one describes it –"paradoxical architecture"
R₄ Inception is that rare film that can be enjoyed on superficial and progressively deeper levels, a feat that uncannily mimics the mind-bending journey its protagonist takes
R₅ Mr. DiCaprio exercises impressive control in portraying a man on the verge of losing his grip, but Mr. Nolan has not, in the end, given Cobb a rich enough inner life to sustain the performance
R₆ In this smart sci-fi puzzle box, director Christopher Nolan transports the audience to a dreamscape that begins with the familiar and then takes a radical, imaginative leap
R₇ In this wildly ingenious chess game, grandmaster Nolan plants ideas in our heads that disturb and dazzle. The result is a knockout. But be warned: it dreams big
R₈ At first, Inception left me cold, feeling as if I'd just eavesdropped on somebody's bad acid trip. Now I find I can't get the film out of my mind, which is really the whole point of it, isn't it?
R₉ A devilishly complicated, fiendishly enjoyable sci-fi voyage across a dreamscape that is thoroughly compelling

3.5 Solution

The theme extracted: *dream* (Table 2).

From **R₅** the system identifies the following potential votes, with polarity:

- *Mr. DiCaprio exercises impressive control in portraying a man on the verge of losing his grip* (0.61)
- *Mr. Nolan has not, in the end, given Cobb a rich enough inner life to sustain the performance* (-0.5)

From **R₇** the system identifies the following potential votes, with polarity:

- *In this wildly ingenious chess game, grandmaster Nolan plants ideas in our heads that disturb and dazzle* (0.8)

- *The result is a knockout* (0.5)
- *be warned: it dreams big* (0.4)

From R_8 the system identifies the following potential votes, with polarity:

- *At first, Inception left me cold, feeling as if I'd just eavesdropped on somebody's bad acid trip* (−0.7)
- *now I find I can't get the film out of my mind, which is really the whole point of it, isn't it?* (0.8)

Table 2. Votes (and their polarity) extracted from the reviews in Table 1.

Feature	Vote id	Vote
movie	a_2	A heist film of thrilling, almost delirious complexity (+)
	a_3	Inception is a boldly constructed wonder with plenty of – as one describes it – "paradoxical architecture" (+)
	a_4	Inception is that rare film that can be enjoyed on superficial and progressively deeper levels, a feat that uncannily mimics the mind-bending journey its protagonist takes (+)
	a_8	Now I find I can't get the film out of my mind, which is really the whole point of it, isn't it (+)
	a_1	Augmented (+)
	a_5	Augmented (+)
	a_6	Augmented (+)
	a_7	Augmented (+)
Director Chris Nolan	a_1	A spectacular fantasy thriller based on Nolan's own original screenplay, it is the smartest cgi head-trip since the Matrix (+)
	a_6	In this smart sci-fi puzzle box, director Christopher Nolan transports the audience to a dreamscape that begins with the familiar and then takes a radical, imaginative leap (+)
	a_7	In this wildly ingenious chess game, grandmaster Nolan plants ideas in our heads that disturb and dazzle (+)
writer Chris Nolan	a_1	A spectacular fantasy thriller based on Nolan's own original screenplay, it is the smartest cgi head-trip since the Matrix (+)
acting	a_5	Augmented (+)
Leonardo DiCaprio	a_5	Mr. DiCaprio exercises impressive control in portraying a man on the verge of losing his grip (+)
themes	a_6	Augmented (+)
	a_9	Augmented (+)
dream	a_6	In this smart sci-fi puzzle box, director Christopher Nolan transports the audience to a dreamscape that begins with the familiar and then takes a radical, imaginative leap (+)
	a_9	A devilishly complicated, fiendishly enjoyable sci-fi voyage across a dreamscape that is thoroughly compelling (+)

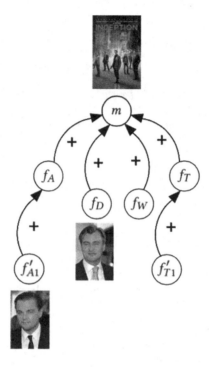

Fig. 11. BAF for movie *Inception*.

4   Extracting Argumentative Explanations from Existing AI Systems

In this section we will demonstrate how argumentative explanations may be extracted from existing AI systems. This is an extremely powerful capability as an argumentative abstraction of a system's output can provide the underlying framework for providing explanations to users in a human-like manner, given that argumentation is amenable to human consumption. This can help to alleviate some of the *black-box* issues with common AI methods since an explainable representation of the system, which is still faithful to its internal mechanisms, may be constructed.

We first introduce the *aspect-item* recommender system (RS) [23] (overviewed in Fig. 12). Here, recommendations are calculated by a hybrid method for calculating predicted ratings from ratings given by the user and by similar users. These predicted ratings (with accuracy which is competitive with the state-of-the-art) are calculated by propagating given ratings from users through an *aspect-item framework* (A-I). This underlying graphical structure comprises *item-aspects* (items and aspects) as nodes and ownership relationships from items to aspects as the edges, e.g. if an item i holds an aspect a there will be an edge (a,i) in the graph. The A-I thus houses the information used in making recommendations, thus it is from this that we define methods for extracting *tripolar argumen-*

tation frameworks (TFs) representing the reasoning for any recommendation. TFs extend classical abstract [16] and bipolar [9] argumentation frameworks by including a 'neutralising' relation (labelled 0) in addition to the standard 'attack' (labelled −) and 'support' (labelled +) relations. We will show how *argumentative explanations* (of various kinds and formats) may then be systematically generated to support interactive recommendations for users, including the opportunity for giving feedback on recommended items and their aspects. Supported formats include, amongst others, conversational and visual explanations. These explanations form the basis for interactions with users to explain recommendations and receive feedback that can be accommodated into the RS to improve its behaviour. Thus, not only are our explanations varied and diverse, but they also account (in a limited sense) for adaptable recommendations over time.

4.1 Preprocessing

Consider an RS where items (e.g. movies) are associated with aspects (e.g. comedy), which in turn have *types* (e.g. genre), and *users* may have provided *ratings* on some of the items and/or aspects. These associations may be seen to form an aspect-item framework underpinning the RS.

Definition 4. *An aspect-item framework (A-I for short) is a tuple* $\langle \mathcal{I}, \mathcal{A}, \mathcal{T}, \mathcal{L}, \mathcal{U}, \mathcal{R} \rangle$ *such that:*

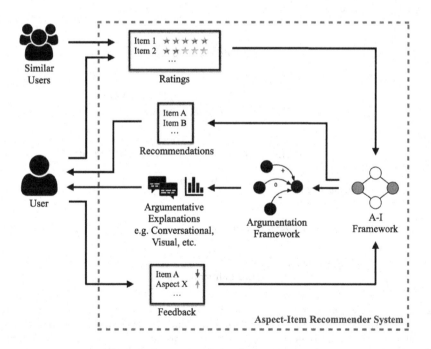

Fig. 12. Overview of the Aspect-Item RS.

- $\mathcal{I}$ is a finite, non-empty set of items;
- $\mathcal{A}$ is a finite, non-empty set of aspects and $\mathcal{T}$ is a finite, non-empty set of types such that for each aspect $a \in \mathcal{A}$ there is a (unique) type $t \in \mathcal{T}$ with t the type of a; for any $t \in \mathcal{T}$, we use $\mathcal{A}_t$ to denote $\{a \in \mathcal{A}|$ the type of a is $t\}$;
- the sets $\mathcal{I}$ and $\mathcal{A}$ are disjoint; we use $\mathcal{X}$ to denote $\mathcal{I} \cup \mathcal{A}$, and refer to it as the set of item-aspects;
- $\mathcal{L} \subseteq (\mathcal{I} \times \mathcal{A})$ is a symmetric binary relation ;
- $\mathcal{U}$ is a finite, non-empty set of users;
- $\mathcal{R} : \mathcal{U} \times \mathcal{X} \rightarrow [-1,1]$ is a partial function of ratings.

Note that each aspect has a unique type, but of course different aspects may have the same type. Thus, $\mathcal{T}$ implicitly partitions $\mathcal{A}$, by grouping together all aspects with the same type. Note also that we assume that ratings, when defined, are real numbers in the $[-1,1]$ interval. Positive (negative) ratings indicate that the user likes (dislikes, respectively) an item-aspect, with the magnitude indicating the strength of this sentiment. Other types of ratings can be translated into this format, for example a rating $x \in \{1, 2, 3, 4, 5\}$ can be translated into a rating $y \in [-1, 1]$ using $y = ((x - 1)/2) - 1$.

The $\mathcal{I}$, $\mathcal{A}$, $\mathcal{T}$ and $\mathcal{L}$ components of an A-I may be visualised as a graph (thus the term 'graphical chassis' for an A-I), as illustrated in Fig. 13. Here we use the movie domain as an example: items may be movies which are linked to the aspects of type "Genre" if they are of that genre. So the movie "Catch Me If You Can" in $\mathcal{I}$ may be linked to the aspect "Biography" in $\mathcal{A}$, which is of type "Genre" in $\mathcal{T}$, as shown in the figure.

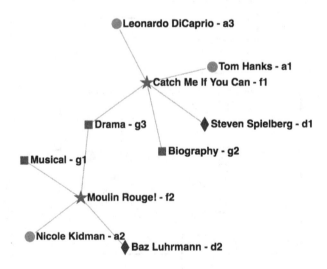

Fig. 13. Example components of an A-I visualised as a graph, with items given by red stars and types: **genres** (whose aspects are blue squares), **actors** (whose aspects are yellow circles) and **directors** (whose aspects are green diamonds). (Color figure online)

Given an A-I, predicted ratings for the items (and aspects, if required) may be calculated. In [23], we propagate the ratings through the A-I based on weightings and a *user profile* containing constants representing how much a wants a particular component to be taken into account. These aspects may be learned from data and then adjusted using feedback mechanisms, as we will show later.

The exact method used for calculating predicted ratings is not pertinent here and so we refer the reader to [23] if they wish to see an example.

4.2   Extracting TFs

We will now show how argumentation frameworks, namely TFs, may be extracted from A-Is in order to harbour the relevant information used in the calculation of a recommendation. Our aim here is to represent entities of the AI system as arguments (e.g. in the RS case, that the user likes an item-aspect) and the way in which they affect each other's evaluations (e.g. predicted ratings in the RS case) as the relations between the arguments.

For example, in the case of the RS of [23], a method for extracting a TF can be summarised as follows:

Definition 5. *Given an A-I and a user u, the corresponding TF $\langle \mathcal{X}, \mathcal{L}^-, \mathcal{L}^+, \mathcal{L}^0 \rangle$ is such that:*

- *$\mathcal{X} = \mathcal{I} \cup \mathcal{A}$ is the set of arguments that u likes each item-aspect;*

and for any $(x, y) \in \mathcal{L}$ such that $\mathcal{R}(u, y)$ is not defined (i.e. y's rating is predicted, not given) :

- *$(x, y) \in \mathcal{L}^-$ iff x had a negative effect on y's predicted rating;*
- *$(x, y) \in \mathcal{L}^+$ iff x had a positive effect on y's predicted rating;*
- *$(x, y) \in \mathcal{L}^0$ iff x had a neutralising effect on y's predicted rating.*

By defining the extraction of the TF as such, the relationships between item-aspects are categorised as argumentative relations based on the way they are used in the predicted rating calculations. In this way, the extraction function is designed to satisfy properties characterising the behaviour required by the user to support informative explanations, e.g. if an argument attacks another, its effect on the latter's predicted rating can be guaranteed to be negative.

Once again, a more explicit version of the extraction function, and the behaviour it exhibits categorised by properties, is shown in [23]. For illustration, a TF obtained from the A-I shown in Fig. 13 for user u, where $f_1 = $ *Catch Me If You Can* and $f_2 = $ *Moulin Rouge*, may be:

$$TF = \langle \{f_1, f_2, a_1, a_2, a_3, d_1, g_1, g_2, g_3\},$$

$$\{(f_2, a_2), (f_2, d_2), (f_2, g_1), (f_2, g_3), (g_3, f_1), (g_2, f_1)\},$$

$$\{(a_1, f_1), (d_1, f_1), (f_1, a_1), (f_1, g_3)\},$$

$$\{(a_3, f_1)\}\rangle,$$

as is visualised in Fig. 14. This could correspond to a situation where there are no arguments affecting f_2 since it is rated by u. Given that this rating is negative and all aspects linked to f_2 are not rated by u, f_2 attacks all such aspects. Conversely, f_1 is not rated by u but may have a positive rating from other users and thus f_1 supports all linked aspects without a rating, i.e. a_1 and g_3. The fact that f_1 is not rated by u means that all aspects linked to f_1 affect it (in an attacking, supporting or neutralising manner).

If all of the ways that item-aspects may affect one another's predicted ratings are shown by the argumentative relations, i.e. if the extraction method is *complete*, in order to explain a predicted rating for a given item-aspect, we may prune the extracted argumentation framework to be the sub-graph of the TF consisting of the item-aspects with a path to the explained item-aspect only. For example, Fig. 15 shows the sub-graph of the TF in Fig. 14, which may be seen as a qualitative explanation for the recommendation f_1 to user u, indicating all of the item-aspects which affected the recommendation.

4.3 Explanations

We will now demonstrate how argumentation frameworks extracted from this RS may be used to generate argumentative explanations to be delivered to users. TFs, like other forms of argumentation framework in different settings, form the basis for a variety of *argumentative explanations* for recommendations dictated by predicted ratings. These explanations use, as their main 'skeleton', sub-graphs

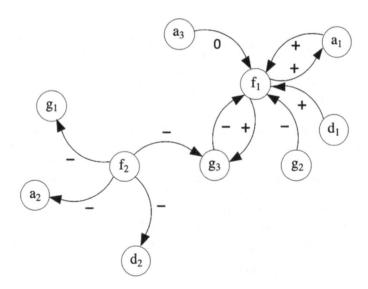

Fig. 14. A graphical representation of a possible TF extracted from the A-I in Fig. 13. Here, '+' indicates 'support' ($\mathcal{L}^+$), '-' indicates 'attack' ($\mathcal{L}^-$) and '0' indicates 'neutralises' ($\mathcal{L}^0$).

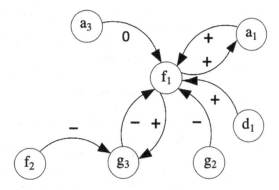

Fig. 15. Pruned version of the extracted TF in Fig. 14 for the recommendation of f_1 to u, with arguments without a path to f_1 removed.

of TFs (e.g. as in Fig. 15) providing content which can then be presented incrementally to users in different formats (e.g. as in Fig. 16) to support different styles of interaction. TFs may also point to controlled forms of feedback from users during interactions, driven by the properties they satisfy (e.g. see [23]). Thus, the use of argumentation frameworks in this manner affords great adaptability in explanations, firstly in the explanations' customisability with regards to content and format and secondly in the way it allows modifications to be made to the system via feedback mechanisms in user interactions.

4.4   Explanation Customisation

We first consider the explanation content, i.e. the information for the rationale behind a recommendation which is delivered to the user: the requirements for identifying this content obviously vary depending on user and context. We posit that the subgraph of TFs in which all nodes lead to the explained argument provides an excellent source for this information, since it represents every item-aspect which may have had an effect on the recommendation. This means that explanations that faithfully represent *how* a recommendation was determined may be drawn from this subgraph (as in Fig. 15).

The content of an explanation may be selected from this subgraph depending on the user's requirements. For example, in a basic case where the user requests information on why an item was recommended, one straightforward way to provide an explanation is for the RS to determine the positive factors which led to this result, which, in our case, would be the supporters in the sub-graph of the TF. In the case of f_1 in the example in Fig. 15, this would correspond to the content column in the first row of Table 3, which in turn could be used to obtain a linguistic explanation as in the rightmost column in Table 3, using the conjunction *because* for the argumentative relation of support and utilising the full *width* of the supporters of f_1 in the TF. If a more balanced explanation for an item being recommended is required, the style of the explanation in the

Table 3. Example variations in explanation content for f_1, with argumentative artefacts in the linguistic explanations highlighted in bold.

Requirements	Content	Linguistic explanation
All supporters of f_1	a_1, d_1	*Catch Me If You Can was recommended **because** you like Tom Tom Hanks and Steven Spielberg*
Strongest attacker and strongest supporter of f_1	a_1, g_2	*Catch Me If You Can was recommended **because** you like Tom Hanks, **despite the fact that** you dislike Biographies*
An attacker of f_1 and its own attacker	g_3, f_2	*Catch Me If You Can was not recommended **because** it inferred that you don't like Dramas, **since** you disliked Moulin Rouge*

rightmost column in the second row of Table 3 may be more appropriate, where the strongest attacker and strongest supporter in (the sub-graph of) the TF are shown, again using appropriate conjunctions for the argumentative relations. However, this still uses only width in the TF and ignores reasons for and against used arguments. In our running example, consider the case where f_1 was not recommended; the third row of Table 3 shows how depth may be used to justify the RS's inference on the user's sentiment on *Dramas*. Here, the language represents the resolutely negative effects along this chain of reasoning.

We have provided a number of examples for selecting the content of explanations from TFs, but note that other methods could be useful, e.g. including neutralisers when the RS is explaining its uncertainty about an inference. For example, [3] use templates to generate inferences of a user's sentiment on aspects in pairwise comparisons, e.g. *Catch Me If You Can was recommended* **because** *you like films by Steven Spielberg,* **especially** *those starring Tom Hanks*. Our argumentation frameworks could support such explanations by comparing the aspects of a movie with their linked items, e.g. in our running example (to use a crude method) if all the items which are linked to both d_1 and a_1 are rated more highly than those linked to d_1 but not a_1, we may construct the same argumentative explanation.

Up to now we have only considered explanations of a linguistic format but other formats are possible, and the choice of the format is an important factor in how receptive a user is towards explanations [18]. The optimal format for an explanation varies significantly based on a range of factors including the application towards which the explanation is targeted and the goals of the explainee [21]. For example, a researcher testing an RS may prefer a graphical format which is true to the TF itself, whereas a user may prefer a linguistic approach which gives the information in a natural, human-like manner. As we have shown in the previous section, argumentation frameworks themselves have been shown to be an effective way of supporting anthropomorphised *conversational* explanations. Other forms of explanations which have been shown to be beneficial in RSs include tabular explanations, e.g. as in [26], where (paraphrased in our setting) the attacking and supporting item-aspects in an explanation may be represented in a table with other attributes shown, e.g. the item-aspect's strength and distance from the recommendation. Visual explanations in the form of charts have also been shown to perform well in studies on user preferences [20].

Figure 16 shows four alternative formats (in addition to the graphical format afforded by sub-graphs of TFs) of user explanation for the example from Fig. 15. Specifically, Fig. 16i shows a visual explanation in the form of charts exploiting the width in the TF, i.e. attacking and supporting aspects coloured by type and organised by their corresponding predicted ratings, thus giving the user a clear indication of each aspect's contribution to the predicted rating of the recommended item. Figure 16ii, meanwhile, targets both depth and width in a linguistic format, which may be textual or spoken, e.g. by an AI assistant, depending on the requirements and preferences of the user. These explanations may be generated by templates or more complicated natural language generation processes, both employing the TF as the underlying knowledge base. Similar information is utilised in Fig. 16iii, which shows a tabular explanation similar to those of [26], where predicted ratings (translated to a 1–5 star scale) are shown alongside a *relevance* parameter, calculated here by inverting the distance from the recommended item. Finally, Fig. 16iv shows a conversational explanation, where the user has requested a counterfactual explanation as to why the item was not rated more highly. As the conversation progresses, the RS may step through the TF to formulate reasoning for its interactions, to which the user may respond with (possibly predetermined, as in [11]) responses. As with the linguistic explanations, conversational explanations may be textual or spoken.

i.

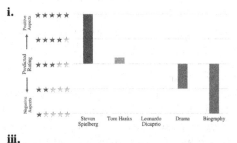

ii.

Catch Me If You Can was recommended due to:
- *your positive rating for Steven Spielberg;*
- *a positive predicted rating for Tom Hanks, due to similar users' positive ratings for Catch Me If You Can.*

This was the case despite:
- *a negative predicted rating for Dramas, due to your negative rating for Moulin Rouge.*

iii.

Aspect	Predicted Rating	Relevance
Tom Hanks	★★★☆☆	100%
Leonardo Dicaprio	★★★☆☆	100%
Biography	★☆☆☆☆	100%
Drama	★★☆☆☆	100%
Steven Spielberg	★★★★★	100%
Moulin Rouge	★☆☆☆☆	50%

iv.

user: *Why was Catch Me If You Can not given a higher predicted rating?*
RS: *...because it was predicted that you do not like Dramas.*
user: *Why was this predicted?*
RS: *...because you did not like Moulin Rouge.*

Fig. 16. Possible visual (i), linguistic (ii), tabular (iii) and conversational (iv) explanations for f_1's predicted rating in our running example.

4.5 Feedback

We now consider how argumentative explanations allow for explanation-driven feedback, regarding the way in which a user may interact with the explanation to provide the system with more information. This is an important factor for RSs particularly, as recommendations are highly unlikely to be perfect the first time and, even if they are, user preferences are dynamic and so in the ideal case an RS will adapt to their changes over time [10]. Our consideration here is whether and how the RS is able to elicit more information from the user via feedback mechanisms in these interactions.

Our explanations can leverage the argumentative reading of recommendations afforded by TFs to support feedback. For example, let us focus on explanations for a positive or negative predicted rating consisting of strong supporters or strong attackers, respectively. In both cases, if the user disagrees with the predicted rating of the recommended item being so high or so low, respectively, weakening the supporters or attackers, respectively, may be guaranteed to adjust the predicted rating as desired, depending on the definition of the extracted TF. Likewise, if a user agrees with the contribution of an attacker or supporter, strengthening it may increase the effect it has. In the visual and tabular explanations in Fig. 16, it is easy to see how this intuitive behaviour allows simple indications of potential adjustments to the predicted ratings to be integrated into the explanation format such that their effect on the recommended item's predicted rating is clearly shown to the user. For example, a modifiable bar in the chart or selectable stars in the table for *Steven Spielberg* could be shown along with an indication that any reduction in the predicted rating for *Steven Spielberg* (thus the weakening of a supporter) would in turn reduce the predicted rating of Catch Me If You Can.

Other modifications supported by argumentative explanations depending on the system being explained, e.g. for the RS in [23], adjusting the user profile or selecting a different set of similar users, could also be enacted by the argumentative explanations, e.g. if a user states that they care less/more about a particular type or that they do not consider the similar users' tastes to align with their own, respectively. In the linguistic and conversational explanations, template-based interactions could be structured to include selectable user responses initiating desired modifications. For example, if a user initiates a conversational explanation with an indicated discrepancy, e.g. *I liked Catch Me If You Can, why didn't you recommend it to me?*, then the interaction with the user may be structured to include some of the possible modifications we have mentioned, e.g. as shown in Fig. 17. In the first interaction here, the user is told that the genres, particularly *Drama*, were the main reasons (possibly obtained by determining the type with the strongest attackers) for this movie not being recommended. The user may then state they are satisfied with the explanation, reduce how much genre's are taken into account (which may be guaranteed to increase Catch Me If You Can's predicted rating due to the genres' negative effect on it) or ask for more reasons. In the illustration in the figure, the user does the latter, and in the second interaction the attacker *Moulin Rouge* is highlighted as the negative reasoning. The user may then state that they are satisfied with the explanation or give a higher rating to *Moulin Rouge* or *drama*, both of which may be guaranteed to increase *Catch Me If You Can*'s predicted rating.

Less constrained approaches may also be taken within an iterative feedback process: if some of this (unconstrained) feedback leads to temporary unintended effects on other item-aspects' predicted ratings, further interactions will provide an opportunity for recalibration to adhere to users' preferences.

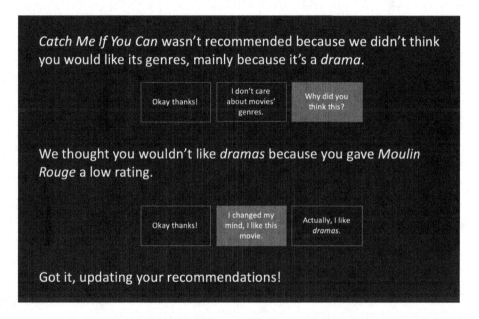

Fig. 17. An example conversational interaction driven by the argumentative explanations.

4.6   Exercise

1. The example movie RS of Fig. 12 has predicted ratings such that an item-aspect will affect another item-aspect's predicted rating negatively/positively/ neutrally if the former's predicted rating is negative/positive/zero. The ratings are as follows:

	Item-aspect	Actual Rating	Predicted Rating
Items	f_1	0.6	0.6
	f_2	–	0.2
Aspects	a_1	–	0.6
	a_2	0	0
	a_3	1	1
	d_1	–1	–1
	d_2	0.7	0.7
	g_1	–0.1	–0.1
	g_2	–	0.6
	g_3	–	0.6

(a) Sketch a graph of the RS, showing the item-aspects with edges indicating which items hold which aspects.
(b) Extract the attacks, supports and neutralisers for this RS's corresponding TF, assuming there are no ratings from similar users, and add them to the diagram.
(c) Which arguments are contained in the argumentation explanation for f_2?

Solution: This is presented, pictorially, in Fig. 18.

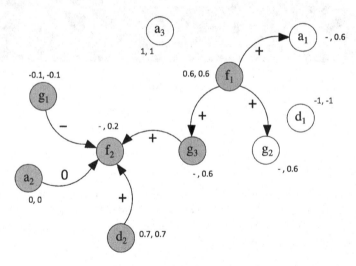

Fig. 18. Labels indicate given and predicted ratings. Arguments in the argumentation explanation for f_2 are highlighted in grey.

5   Conclusions

In this tutorial we have shown how machine arguing can be used in two distinct ways to provide explainability in AI systems. Firstly, we have shown that explainable AI systems can be built from scratch on argumentative foundations by defining a review aggregation system which allows the extraction of quantitative bipolar argumentation frameworks, which themselves support conversational interactions with users. This system is shown to produce results which are comparable with the current techniques and the capability for explainability does not induce privacy or scalability concerns. Secondly, we have shown that argumentative abstractions may be extracted from existing AI systems. To illustrate this we have focused on the domain of recommender systems, demonstrating how those which can be represented as an aspect-item framework allow the extraction of argumentative abstractions of the reasoning process in calculating a recommendation. We also show that once these argumentation frameworks have been derived, various forms of interactive explanation can be generated for users, demonstrating the flexibility of this methodology.

Various other works are based on the same "machine arguing vision" that we have demonstrated in this tutorials. In particular, within our Computational Logic and Argumentation group at Imperial College London we have contributed the following other machine-arguing-based XAI systems:

- in [15] we extract explanations from (and for) the outputs of optimsers for scheduling, and in [27] we apply them to build a system for nurse rostering, where interactive explanations are crucial; here we use abstract argumentation as the underlying form of computational argumentation;
- in [12] we extract explanations for predictions from data, building abstract argumentation frameworks from partial orders over the data; we apply the methodology to tabular data, text classification, and labelled images;
- in [1], we extract graphical explanations, which may be read as argumentative abstractions with two forms of supporting relation, from various forms of Bayesian Network Classifiers to produce counterfactual explanations.

Computational argumentation is uniquely well-placed to support XAI and various avenues for future work exist. These include, but are not limited to, a "theory" of explanations, the extraction of argumentative explanations for a broader variety of AI systems, including opaque ones (such as deep learning), and engineering aspects of machine arguing for other AI systems and applications. We conclude with some considerations relating to these avenues.

From a theoretical view point, it would be interesting to study computational aspects of the methodologies we have described, and in particular the cost of mining argumentation frameworks and explanations from them.

Different types of explanations can be defined to address the expertise of users the system targets. These range from regular users to expert users who require an understanding of the underlying model. From a theoretical point of view, the explanations need to exhibit different properties depending on the type of user the system aims to interact with, which, in turn, will also determine the level of detail included in the explanation. Different argumentation frameworks may be suited to different applications. The type of framework most relevant to the application at hand can be identified either from the properties it fulfills that match with the properties required by the application or in an empirical manner.

Other applications where machine arguing is relevant include: deception detection, fact checking and fake news detection by extracting argumentation frameworks and providing an explanation as to why a piece of text is true or deceptive/false/fake, data summarisation by means of graphical outputs extracted from argumentation frameworks, and explaining outputs of black-box models by means of argumentation frameworks which can help debug and correct the black-box models which learn from labelled data.

The works overviewed in this tutorial and the additional works mentioned here show promising uses of machine-arguing-based XAI. We hope this tutorial will enthuse others to join forces towards the several paths of future work that machine-arguing-based XAI faces, including at the forefront theoretical, empirical and experimental evaluation, as partially outlined here.

References

1. Albini, E., Rago, A., Baroni, P., Toni, F.: Relation-based counterfactual explanations for Bayesian network classifiers. In: Proceedings of the Twenty-Ninth International Joint Conference on Artificial Intelligence, IJCAI (2020, To Appear)
2. Atkinson, K., et al.: Towards artificial argumentation. AI Mag. **38**(3), 25–36 (2017)
3. Balog, K., Radlinski, F., Arakelyan, S.: Transparent, scrutable and explainable user models for personalized recommendation. In: Proceedings of the 42nd International ACM SIGIR Conference on Research and Development in Information Retrieval, SIGIR, pp. 265–274 (2019)
4. Baroni, P., Comini, G., Rago, A., Toni, F.: Abstract games of argumentation strategy and game-theoretical argument strength. In: An, B., Bazzan, A., Leite, J., Villata, S., van der Torre, L. (eds.) PRIMA 2017. LNCS (LNAI), vol. 10621, pp. 403–419. Springer, Cham (2017). https://doi.org/10.1007/978-3-319-69131-2_24
5. Baroni, P., Gabbay, D., Giacomin, M., van der Torre, L. (eds.): Handbook of Formal Argumentation. College Publications (2018)
6. Baroni, P., Rago, A., Toni, F.: How many properties do we need for gradual argumentation? In: Proceedings of the Thirty-Second AAAI Conference on Artificial Intelligence, The 30th innovative Applications of Artificial Intelligence (IAAI), and The 8th AAAI Symposium on Educational Advances in Artificial Intelligence (EAAI), pp. 1736–1743 (2018)
7. Baroni, P., Rago, A., Toni, F.: From fine-grained properties to broad principles for gradual argumentation: a principled spectrum. Int. J. Approximate Reasoning **105**, 252–286 (2019)
8. Briguez, C.E., Budán, M.C., Deagustini, C.A.D., Maguitman, A.G., Capobianco, M., Simari, G.R.: Argument-based mixed recommenders and their application to movie suggestion. Expert Syst. Appl. **41**(14), 6467–6482 (2014)
9. Cayrol, C., Lagasquie-Schiex, M.C.: On the acceptability of arguments in bipolar argumentation frameworks. In: ECSQARU, pp. 378–389 (2005)
10. Chen, X., Zhang, Y., Qin, Z.: Dynamic explainable recommendation based on neural attentive models. In: The Thirty-Third AAAI Conference on Artificial Intelligence, AAAI, The Thirty-First Innovative Applications of Artificial Intelligence Conference, IAAI, The Ninth AAAI Symposium on Educational Advances in Artificial Intelligence, EAAI, pp. 53–60 (2019)

11. Cocarascu, O., Rago, A., Toni, F.: Extracting dialogical explanations for review aggregations with argumentative dialogical agents. In: Proceedings of the 18th International Conference on Autonomous Agents and MultiAgent Systems, AAMAS, pp. 1261–1269 (2019)
12. Cocarascu, O., Stylianou, A., Cyras, K., Toni, F.: Data-empowered argumentation for dialectically explainable predictions. In: Proceedings of European Conference on Artificial Intelligence, ECAI 2020 (2020)
13. Cohen, A., Gottifredi, S., García, A.J., Simari, G.R.: A survey of different approaches to support in argumentation systems. Knowl. Eng. Rev. **29**(5), 513–550 (2014)
14. Cohen, A., Parsons, S., Sklar, E.I., McBurney, P.: A characterization of types of support between structured arguments and their relationship with support in abstract argumentation. Int. J. Approximate Reasoning **94**, 76–104 (2018)
15. Cyras, K., Letsios, D., Misener, R., Toni, F.: Argumentation for explainable scheduling. In: The Thirty-Third AAAI Conference on Artificial Intelligence, AAAI, The Thirty-First Innovative Applications of Artificial Intelligence Conference, IAAI, The Ninth AAAI Symposium on Educational Advances in Artificial Intelligence, EAAI, pp. 2752–2759. AAAI Press (2019)
16. Dung, P.M.: On the acceptability of arguments and its fundamental role in non-monotonic reasoning, logic programming and n-person games. Artif. Intell. **77**(2), 321–357 (1995)
17. Gabbay, D.M.: Logical foundations for bipolar and tripolar argumentation networks: preliminary results. J. Logic Comput. **26**(1), 247–292 (2016)
18. Gedikli, F., Jannach, D., Ge, M.: How should I explain? A comparison of different explanation types for recommender systems. Int. J. Hum. Comput. Stud. **72**(4), 367–382 (2014)
19. Guidotti, R., Monreale, A., Ruggieri, S., Turini, F., Giannotti, F., Pedreschi, D.: A survey of methods for explaining black box models. ACM Comput. Surv. **51**(5), 93:1–93:42 (2019). https://doi.org/10.1145/3236009
20. Herlocker, J.L., Konstan, J.A., Riedl, J.: Explaining collaborative filtering recommendations. In: Proceeding on the ACM Conference on Computer Supported Cooperative Work, CSCW, pp. 241–250 (2000)
21. Miller, T.: Explanation in artificial intelligence: Insights from the social sciences. Artif. Intell. **267**, 1–38 (2019). https://doi.org/10.1016/j.artint.2018.07.007
22. Naveed, S., Donkers, T., Ziegler, J.: Argumentation-based explanations in recommender systems: conceptual framework and empirical results. In: Adjunct Publication of the 26th Conference on User Modeling, Adaptation and Personalization, UMAP, pp. 293–298 (2018)
23. Rago, A., Cocarascu, O., Toni, F.: Argumentation-based recommendations: fantastic explanations and how to find them. In: Proceedings of the Twenty-Seventh International Joint Conference on Artificial Intelligence, IJCAI, pp. 1949–1955 (2018)
24. Rago, A., Toni, F.: Quantitative argumentation debates with votes for opinion polling. In: An, B., Bazzan, A., Leite, J., Villata, S., van der Torre, L. (eds.) PRIMA 2017. LNCS (LNAI), vol. 10621, pp. 369–385. Springer, Cham (2017). https://doi.org/10.1007/978-3-319-69131-2_22
25. Rago, A., Toni, F., Aurisicchio, M., Baroni, P.: Discontinuity-free decision support with quantitative argumentation debates. In: KR, pp. 63–73 (2016)

26. Vig, J., Sen, S., Riedl, J.: Tagsplanations: explaining recommendations using tags. In: Proceedings of the 14th International Conference on Intelligent User Interfaces, IUI, pp. 47–56 (2009)
27. Čyras, K., Karamlou, A., Lee, M., Letsios, D., Misener, R., Toni, F.: AI-assisted schedule explainer for nurse rostering - Demonstration. In: International Conference on Autonomous Agents and Multi-Agent Systems (2020)

Stream Reasoning: From Theory to Practice

Emanuele Falzone[1(✉)], Riccardo Tommasini[2], and Emanuele Della Valle[1]

[1] Politecnico di Milano, DEIB, Milan, Italy
{emanuele.falzone,emanuele.dellavalle}@polimi.it
[2] DataSystem Group, University of Tartu, Tartu, Estonia
riccardo.tommasini@ut.ee

Abstract. Stream Reasoning is set at the confluence of Artificial Intelligence and Stream Processing with the ambitious goal to reason on rapidly changing flows of information. The goals of the lecture are threefold: (1) Introducing students to the state-of-the-art of Stream Reasoning, (2) Deep diving into RDF Stream Processing by outlining how to design, develop and deploy a stream reasoning application, and (3) Jointly discussing the limits of the state-of-the-art and the current challenges.

1 Introduction

We live in a streaming world [8]. Data are no longer just vast and various, they are also produced faster every day. Social networks, Internet of Things deployments for healthcare or smart cities, as well as modern news infrastructures provision data continuously in the form of *data streams*, i.e., infinite sequences of timestamped data.

Since more and more streams are becoming available, the underlying Web infrastructure evolved to include new protocols for real-time data provisioning, e.g., Web Sockets[1]. Figure 1 visualizes an example of a data stream and helps us introduce the running example that we will use along this manuscript.

Example 1 (Color Stream). In our running example, we will observe a stream of colors (or colored boxes). Each element is a timestamped color observation made by a sensor.

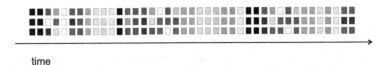

time

Fig. 1. An example of Stream Processing over a stream of colored boxes.

---

[1] https://tools.ietf.org/html/rfc6455.

© Springer Nature Switzerland AG 2020
M. Manna and A. Pieris (Eds.): Reasoning Web 2020, LNCS 12258, pp. 85–108, 2020.
https://doi.org/10.1007/978-3-030-60067-9_4

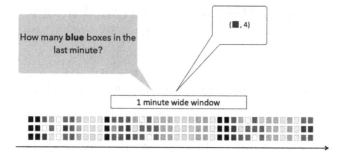

Fig. 2. An example of continuous query over the color stream. (Color figure online)

In these scenarios, data-intensive applications must deal with many new data challenges simultaneously, e.g., Data Volume and Data Velocity [17]. However, from new challenges, new opportunities arise: Stream Processing is the research field that studies how to analyze vast data streams over time. The related literature contains models, systems, and languages that lead to continuous queries and, in particular, to windowing operations [1,14].

Example 2 (Color Stream Processing (cont'd)). Continuous queries can be registered on the color stream, e.g., for counting the number of blue boxes in the last minute as shown in Fig. 2.

Additionally, data-intensive applications must deal with information coming from a variety of sources. Thus, a common problem is how to integrate data streams with background domain knowledge without violating specific time constrains. However, traditional data integration techniques are not adequate to tame variety and velocity at the same time. Indeed, such techniques are based on semantic technologies and require to put data at rest. Thus, the following research question arises.

How can we make sense, in real-time, of vast, noisy, heterogeneous data streams coming from complex domains?

The Stream Reasoning (SR) research field addresses the challenges unveiled by the research question above [8]. SR's ultimate goal is to design a new generation of systems capable of addressing Data Variety and Velocity simultaneously. To this extent, SR's research combines the lessons learned on Stream Processing with the extensive work of the Semantic Web community.

Since 2008, the results of Stream Reasoning research made an impact in both the Stream Processing and Semantic Web areas [9,18]. In particular, RDF Stream Processing (RSP) extends the Semantic Web Stack for continuous querying and reasoning upon rapidly changing information flows [12].

Example 3 (Color Stream Reasoning). Continuous queries over streams can be enriched with contextual domain knowledge. For instance, for counting the *cool*

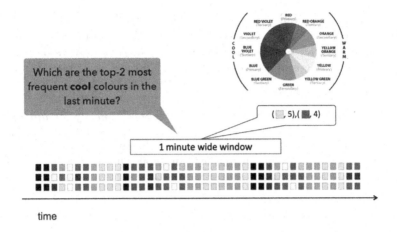

Fig. 3. An example of Stream Reasoning on a stream of colored boxes.

colors in the last minute window we must add an ontology of colors as shown in Fig. 3. Then, such ontology can be used for identifying cool colours.

In this lecture, we will walk through some prominent Stream Reasoning achievements. In particular, we focus on the area of RDF Stream Processing. We present theoretical results as well as practical guidelines and resources to build RDF Stream Processing applications.

The remainder of the paper is organized as follows: Sect. 2 presents preliminary knowledge about Continuous Processing (Sect. 2.1), RDF (Sect. 2.2) and SPARQL (Sect. 2.3). Section 3 presents the life-cycle of Streaming Linked Data. In particular, it digs into streaming data publications with five simple steps for practitioners to apply. Section 4 presents RDF Stream Processing, i.e., the last step of the Streaming Linked Data life-cycle. To this extent, the section gives an introduction to RSP-QL, i.e., the reference model for Web Stream Processing using RDF Streams. (Sect. 4.1). Moreover, the section presents canonical problems in Stream Processing on the Web. Section 5 presents the *Linear Pizza Oven*, i.e., an exercise for getting started with Streaming Linked Data and RDF Stream Processing using RSP-QL. Finally, Sect. 6 draws conclusions.

2   Preliminaries

Before providing guidelines to develop Stream Reasoning applications, we need to formalize the concepts necessary for querying and reasoning over data streams.

2.1   Continuous Queries

Continuous queries, a.k.a. persistent or standing queries, are a special class of queries that listens to updates and allow interested users to receive new results as soon as data becomes available. They are similar to traditional database queries, with the difference that they are issued once, but they run repeatedly over the input streams. This idea, known as *continuous semantics*, conveys the following intuition, i.e., the processing of an infinite input produces an infinite output [26].

Under continuous semantics, the result of a query is the set of results that would be returned if the query were executed at every instant in time.

Upon the intuition above, many query languages have been designed for writing continuous queries. Among them, the Continuous Query Language (CQL) [1] passed the test of time for what concerns relational data Stream Processing.

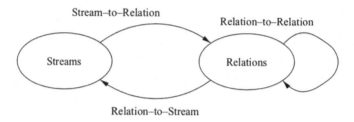

Fig. 4. The operator classes defined in CQL.

As shown in Fig. 4, CQL gives an abstract semantics to continuous queries in terms of two data types: *Streams* and *Relations.*

Definition 1. *Let T be the ordered time domain, e.g., the set of natural numbers $\mathcal{N}$. A data stream S is a possibly infinite multiset of elements $\langle o, \tau \rangle$, where o is a data item, e.g., a tuple, and $\tau \in T$ is a timestamp, e.g., a natural number.*

Definition 2. *A relation R is a mapping from each time instant $\tau \in T$ to a finite but unbounded bag of tuples belonging to a fixed schema consisting of a set of named attributes.*

Upon these two abstractions, CQL defines three classes of operators that, together, allow to write continuous queries over data streams:

- Stream-to-Relation (S2R) operators that produce a relation from a stream,
- Relation-to-Relation (R2R) operators that produce a relation from one or more other relations, and
- Relation-to-Stream (R2S) operators that produce a stream from a relation.

More specifically, S2R operators in CQL are operators that chuck a stream S into Windows. A window, denoted as W(S), is a set of elements extracted from a stream by a *window operator.* CQL describes time-based, tuple-based, and partitioned window operators. Nevertheless, in the following we will limit our scope to time-based sliding window operators.

Definition 3. *A time-based sliding window operator on a stream S takes a time interval I as a parameter and outputs at τ the relation R of $S[Range\ I]$ defined as:*

$$R(\tau) = \{s | \langle s, \tau' \rangle \wedge \tau' \leq \tau \wedge \tau' \geq max\{\tau - I, 0\}\}$$

R2R operators correspond to relational operators adapted to handle time-varying relations. Assuming the familiarity of the readers with Relational Algebra (RA), in the following we focus on the R2S operators that include:

- The *insert stream* operator that streams out all new entries w.r.t. the previous instant as per Definition 4.
- The *delete stream* operator that streams out all deleted entries w.r.t the previous instant as per Definition 5.
- The *relation stream* operator that streams out all elements at a certain instant in the source relation as per Definition 6.

Given two consecutive time instants $\tau - 1$ and τ we formally define R2S operators as follows:

Definition 4. *The insert stream operator applied to a relation R emits an element $\langle s, \tau \rangle$ if and only if the tuple s is in $R(\tau) - R(\tau - 1)$ at time τ:*

$$Istream(R) = \bigcup_{\tau \geq 0} ((R(\tau) - R(\tau - 1)) \times \{\tau\}$$

Definition 5. *The delete stream operator applied to a relation R emits an element $\langle s, \tau \rangle$ if and only if the tuple s is in $R(\tau - 1) - R(\tau)$ at time τ:*

$$Dstream(R) = \bigcup_{\tau \geq 0} ((R(\tau - 1) - R(\tau)) \times \{\tau\}$$

Definition 6. *The relation stream operator applied to a relation R emits an element $\langle s, \tau \rangle$ if and only if the tuple s is in $R(\tau)$ at time τ:*

$$Rstream(R) = \bigcup_{\tau \geq 0} (R(\tau)) \times \{\tau\}$$

2.2 Resource Description Framework

The *Resource Description Framework* (RDF) is a semistructured data model that fosters data interchange and allows publishing machine-readable representation of resources [32]. RDF requires to organize information as triples, i.e., *(subject,predicate,object)* statements.

Definition 7. *An RDF statement t is a triple*

$$(s, p, o) \in (I \cup B) \times I \times (I \cup B \cup L)$$

where I is the set of IRIs (Internationalized Resource Identifiers). B is the set of all the blank nodes, i.e., representing identifiers of anonymous resources. L is the set of literals, i.e., string values associated with their datatype. I, B, and L are disjoint from each other.

RDF triples are organized in RDF graphs (cf. Definition 8), and RDF graphs can be organized into datasets (cf. Definition 9).

Definition 8. *An RDF graph is a set of RDF triples.*

Definition 9. *An RDF Dataset DS is a set:*

$$DS = \{g_0, (u_1, g_1), (u_2, g_2), ..., (u_n, g_n)\}$$

where g_0 and g_i are RDF graphs, and each corresponding u_i is a distinct IRI. g_0 is called the default graph, while the others are called named graphs.

RDF is a data model and it can be serialized using different data formats. According to W3C, the default RDF serialization is RDF/XML[2]. However, it supports other serialization formats, e.g., Turtle[3] (TTL), JSON for Linked Data (JSON-LD)[4], NTriples[5], and TriG. In the following, we adopt mostly Turtle and JSON-LD as the default serialization because they are more readable.

```
PREFIX p: <http://example/>
<http://example/sbjct1> <http://example/pred1> <http://example/objct1> .

<http://example/subject2>
    <http://example/predicate2> <http://example/object2> ;
    <http://example/predicate3> <http://example/object3> .

p:subject4 p:predicate4 p:object4 , p:object5  .
```

Listing 1.1. Example illustrating Turtle Syntax for RDF triples.

Listing 1.1 shows at Line 2 an example of an RDF triple. Turtle syntax allows grouping triples with the same subject, separating different predicates using a semicolon (cf. Lines 5 and 6). It allows separating alternative objects for the same predicate using a comma (cf. Line 8). It allows defining prefixes for making documents more succinct. Line 1 declares a prefix IRI, which is used by the triple in the following line.

2.3   SPARQL

SPARQL is a graph query language and a protocol for RDF data. Listing 1.2 shows an example of SPARQL query which consists of three clauses, i.e., Dataset Clause, Query Form, and Where Clause. The language also includes solution modifiers such as DISTINCT, ORDER BY and GROUP BY. Finally, it is possible to associate a prefix label to an IRI.

SPARQL's Dataset Clause, indicated in Fig. 10 (a), determines the RDF dataset in the scope of the query evaluation. This clause employs the *FROM*

---

[2] https://www.w3.org/TR/rdf-syntax-grammar/.
[3] https://www.w3.org/TR/turtle/.
[4] https://www.w3.org/TR/json-ld11/.
[5] https://www.w3.org/TR/n-triples/.

```
1  PREFIX foaf:   <http://xmlns.com/foaf/0.1/>
2  SELECT ?name ?email
3  FROM <http://www.w3.org/People/Berners-Lee/card>
4  WHERE {
5      ?person foaf:name ?name ;
6              foaf:age ?age .
7      FILTER (?age > 18)
8  }
9  ORDER BY ?name
10 LIMIT 10
11 OFFSET 10
```

Listing 1.2. Example SPARQL query.

operator to load an RDF graph into the Dataset's default graph. Moreover, the *FROM NAMED* operator allows loading an RDF graph into a separated RDF graph identified by its IRI.

Definition 10. *A triple pattern t_p is a triple (sp, pp, op) s.t.*

$$(sp, pp, op) \in (I \cup B \cup V) \times (I \cup V) \times (I \cup B \cup L \cup V)$$

where I, B, and L are defined as in Definition 7, while V is the infinite set of variables.

SPARQL's Where Clause allows defining the patterns to match over an RDF dataset. During the evaluation of a query, the graph from the dataset used for matching the graph pattern is called *Active Graph*. By default, the *Active Graph* is set to the default graph of the dataset. The basic match unit in SPARQL is the Triple pattern (cf. Definition 10). Listing 1.2 presents two triple patterns (cf. Lines 5–6). A set of triple patterns is called a Basic Graph Pattern (BGP). BGPs can be named or not, and in the first case they are identified by either a variable or an IRI. BGPs can include other compound patterns defined by different algebraic operators [22]. Listing 1.2 shows an example of FILTER clause that checks whether age is higher than 18.

Last but not least, SPARQL's Query Form Clause allows specializing the query results. SPARQL includes the following forms: (i) The *SELECT* form includes a set of variables and it returns the corresponding values according to the query results. (ii) The *CONSTRUCT* form includes a graph template and it returns one or more RDF graphs filling the template variables according to the query results. (iii) The *DESCRIBE* form includes a resource identifier and it returns an RDF graph containing RDF data that describe a resource. (iv) The *ASK* form just returns a boolean value telling whether or not the query pattern has at least a solution.

Having introduced the syntax, we can now give more details about SPARQL semantics. A SPARQL query is defined as a tuple (E, DS, QS) where E is a SPARQL algebraic expression, DS an RDF dataset, and QF a query form.

The evaluation semantics of a SPARQL query algebraic expression w.r.t. an RDF dataset is defined for every operator of the algebra as $eval(DS(g), E)$ where E denotes an algebraic expression and $DS(g)$ a dataset DS with active graph g. Moreover, the evaluation semantics relies on the notion of solution mappings.

Definition 11. *A solution mapping μ is a partial function*

$$\mu : V \rightarrow I \cup B \cup L$$

from a set of Variables V to a set of RDF terms. A solution mapping μ is defined over a domain $dom(\mu) \subseteq V$, and $\mu(x)$ indicates the application of μ to x.

Following the notation of [11], we indicate with Ω a multiset of solution mappings, and with Ψ a sequence of solution mappings.

Definition 12. *Two mappings, μ_1 and μ_2, are said to be compatible, i.e., $\mu_1 \frown \mu_2$ iff:*

$$\forall x \in (dom(\mu_1) \cap dom(\mu_2)) \Rightarrow \mu_1(x) = \mu_2(x)$$

Given an RDF graph, a SPARQL query solution can be represented as a set of solution mappings, each assigning term of RDF triples in the graph to variables of the query.

The evaluation function $[\![.]\!]_D$ defines the semantics of graph pattern expressions. It takes graph pattern expressions over an RDF Dataset D as input and returns a multiset of solution mappings Ω. As in [22], the evaluation of triple patterns t, and a compound graph pattern P_i X P_j is defined as follows:

$$[\![t]\!]_D = \{\mu | dom(\mu) = var(t) \in D\}$$

$$[\![P_1\ AND\ P_2]\!] = \Omega_1 \bowtie \Omega_2 = \{\mu_1 \cup \mu_2 | \mu_1 \in \Omega_1 \wedge \mu_2 \in \Omega_2 \mu_1 \frown \mu_2\}$$

$$[\![P_1\ UNION\ P_2]\!] = \Omega_1 \cup \Omega_2 = \{\mu_1 \cup \mu_2 | \mu_1 \in \Omega_1 \vee \mu_2 \in \Omega_2 \mu_1 \frown \mu_2\}$$

$$[\![P_1\ OPTIONAL\ P_2]\!] = \Omega_1 \bowtie \Omega_2 = (\Omega_1 \bowtie \Omega_2) \cup (\Omega_1 / \Omega_2)$$

where

$$\Omega_1 / \Omega_2 = \{\mu | \mu \in \Omega_1 \wedge \nexists \mu' \in \Omega_2 \mu \frown \mu'\}$$

3   Streaming Linked Data Life-Cycle

The mechanisms to publish and consume data streams on the Web has gained attention [13] thanks to the progresses in Stream Reasoning systems and approaches. Figure 5 summarises the publication life-cycle for streaming linked data, which consists of five steps described in the following.

Name. The Step (0) aims at designing IRIs that identify the stream itself and the other resources it may contain. Linked Data best practices for good IRIs design prescribe the usage of HTTP IRIs to identify Web resources. Indeed,

Fig. 5. Streaming Linked Data Lifecycle

despite streaming extensions of the Web architecture existing (e.g., WebSocket) identification of stream as resources should still rely on HTTP IRIs [28].

To this extent, Sequeda and Corcho [25] suggested a mechanism to identify sensors and their observations. They suggested three innovative IRI schemes to identify sources, temporal, spatial, and spatio-temporal metadata [25]. Barbieri and Della Valle recommended to identify streams using IRIs that resolve a named graph containing all the relevant metadata. These named graphs also describe the current content of the window over the stream using the properties *rdfs:seeAlso* and *:receivedAt* [4]. The latter design was further developed by Mauri et al. [19] and is the approach we will adopt in the following.

To capture the essence of what a Web Stream is we provide Definition 13, which also explains how the stream itself and the element it contains are valid Web resources, i.e., they are identifiable via IRIs.

Definition 13. *A Web data stream is a Web Resource that identifies an unbounded ordered collection of pairs (o, i), where o is a Web resource, e.g., a named graph, and i is a metadata that can be used to establish an ordering relation, e.g., a timestamp.*

Example 4. (cont'd) Carrying on our running example for Step (0), the color stream that we are going to use for our running experiments is identified by the base URL http://linkeddata.stream. Moreover, we will apply the following URI schemas to identify Web Resources that are relevant for this paper:

1. http://linkeddata.stream/ontologies/{ontologyname}.
2. http://linkeddata.stream/resource/{streamname}.
3. http://linkeddata.stream/resource/{streamname}/{graphid}.

Model. Step (1) aims at describing the application domain from which data comes. To this extent, ontologies and models are designed and reused in order to capture the domain knowledge in machine-understandable way. During this step it is also critical to identify relevant resources, collect data samples, and formulate canonical information needs.

In the Stream Reasoning literature, several vocabularies have been designed, used, and adapted for representing the domain of streaming data. State-of-the-art vocabularies include but are not limited to FrAPPE [2], SAO [15], SSN [7] or SOSA [16], and SIOC [21].

Example 5. (cont'd) Carrying on our running example for Step (1), we must model the application domain for our color stream. Figure 6 exemplifies domain knowledge about colors. The role of a knowledge engineer is to design a formal model that allows a machine to understand such information.

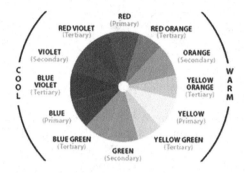

Fig. 6. Domain knowledge about colors.

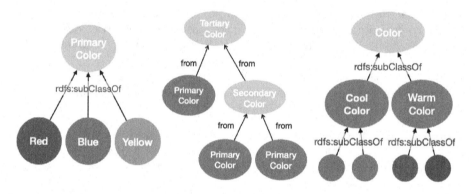

Fig. 7. Graphical representation of the color ontology.

Figures 7 exemplifies a possible way to represent the domain knowledge as a taxonomy. Notably, due to the lack of space, we represent only a sub-portion of the taxonomy. We decided to model the colors as classes in order to provide different hierarchies based on their compositions and "temperature". Consequently, individuals are instances of the colors to be identified. The OWL 2 version of such ontology is also available[6].

Describe. Step (2) aims at providing useful representations of the data streams to be consumed by humans and/or machines. It recommends to use standard vocabularies to include relevant metadata that eases the discovery of and the access to the data in the stream. For instance, during this step the data publisher shall choose an appropriate license.

Recently, Schema.org included two concepts that are relevant for stream representation, i.e., DataFeed[7] and DataFeedItem[8]. However, their adoption has not been estimated, yet.

---

[6] https://linkeddata.stream/ontologies/colors.owl.
[7] https://schema.org/DataFeed.
[8] https://schema.org/DataFeedItem.

On the other hand, Tommasini et al. [31] designed the Vocabulary & Catalog of Linked Streams (VoCaLS) with the goal of fostering interoperability between streaming services on the Web. VoCaLS consists of three modules that enable (i) Publishing streaming data following Linked Data principles, (ii) Describing streaming services, and (iii) Tracking the provenance of Stream Processing.

Example 6. (cont'd) Carrying on our running example for Step (2), we describe the color stream using an appropriate vocabulary. VoCaLS is our choice and Listing 1.3 provides an example of a stream descriptor, i.e., an RDF graph containing information about the color stream.

```
PREFIX : <http://linkeddata.stream/resource/>
PREFIX xsd: <http://www.w3.org/2001/XMLSchema#>
PREFIX rdfs: <http://www.w3.org/2000/01/rdf-schema#>
PREFIX dcat: <http://www.w3.org/ns/dcat#>
PREFIX frmt: <http://www.w3.org/ns/formats/>
PREFIX vocals: <http://w3id.org/rsp/vocals#>
PREFIX vsd: <http://w3id.org/rsp/vocals-sd#>
<> a vocals:StreamDescriptor .

:colorstream a vocals:RDFStream ;
  dcat:title "Color Stream"^^xsd:string ;
  dcat:description "Stream of primary colors"^^xsd:string ;
  dcat:license <https://creativecommons.org/licenses/by-nc/4.0/> ;
  dcat:publisher <http://linkeddata.stream> ;
  dcat:landingPage <http://linkeddata.stream/page/colorstream> ;
  vocals:hasEndpoint :ColorEndpoint  .
```

Listing 1.3. Publishing color stream with Vocals and RSP-QL

Convert. Step (3) recommends converting streaming data into a machine-readable format. As for Linked Data, RDF is the data model of choice to publish data on the Web. For streaming data, we recommend RDF Streams which are formalized by Definition 14.

Definition 14. *An RDF Stream is a data stream (cf Definition 1) where the data items o are RDF graphs, i.e., a set of RDF triples of the from (subject, predicate, object).*

Typically, streaming data is not produced directly as RDF streams. For instance, sensor push observations using a tabular format like CSV. Often, compression is also used to save bandwidth and reduce costs.

In these cases, a conversion mechanism must be set up to transform the data stream into an RDF stream. The conversion pipeline should make use of the domain ontologies designed at Step 0. Additionally, streaming data may be enriched with contextual domain knowledge, capturing the domain information collected in an ontological model.

Technologies like R2RML are adequate to set up static data conversion pipelines. Nevertheless, they present some limitations when having to deal with data streams. In particular, due to the infinite nature of streaming data, the conversion mechanism can only take into account the stream one element at a time. Alternatively, one can use a window-based Stream Processing engine to transform the input stream by means of a continuous query.

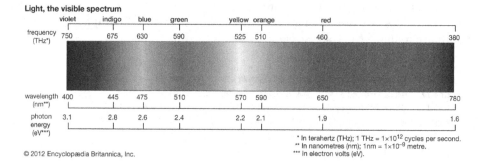

Fig. 8. Light spectrum overview.

Example 7 (cont'd). Carrying on our running example for Step (3), we exemplify an annotation process that makes use of the Color ontology to transform a sensor stream that samples the light spectrum into an RDF Stream of color instances.

According to Fig. 8, we can derive the following rules to map the sensor measurement into symbolic representations of colors:

- If the sensed frequency is between 650 and 605, the light is perceived as blue.
- If the frequency is between 605 and 545, the light is perceived as green.
- If the frequency is between 450 and 480, the light is perceived as yellow.
- If the sensed frequency is between 480 and 380, the light is perceived as red.

Table 1 shows some observation made by a sensor network about the light spectrum. Finally, Listing 1.4 displays a set of corresponding timestamped RDF graphs, denoting sample occurrences of colors.

Table 1. Sensor observation in tabular form.

ObservationID	Sensed frequency	Sensor	Timestamp
507f704d-dfb8-4fa3-97ca-64a93e56abb0	460	S1	1588684149
6e852dd4-cd3a-4516-9665-842483d5c22f	630	S2	1588684150
84b0350a-2422-4538-8689-f0e58ce1c485	590	S1	1588684152
80350a4b-4fa3-9665-8689-g46842483ds5	525	S2	1588684399

Before describing the next steps, i.e., Publish and Process, we must introduce the notion of *RSP Service*. An RSP Service is a special kind of Web service

```
 1  {
 2      "@id":"http://linkeddata.stream/streams/colorstream/1588684149",
 3      "@context":{
 4          "color":"http://linkeddata.stream/ontologies/colors#",
 5          "rdf":"http://www.w3.org/1999/02/22-rdf-syntax-ns#",
 6          "rdfs":"http://www.w3.org/2000/01/rdf-schema#"
 7      },
 8      "@graph":{
 9          "@id":"507f704d-dfb8-4fa3-97ca-64a93e56abb0",
10          "@type":"color:Red"
11      }
12  },
13  {
14      "@id":"http://linkeddata.stream/streams/colorstream/1588684150",
15      "@context":{
16          "color":"http://linkeddata.stream/ontologies/colors#",
17          "rdf":"http://www.w3.org/1999/02/22-rdf-syntax-ns#",
18          "rdfs":"http://www.w3.org/2000/01/rdf-schema#"
19      },
20      "@graph":{
21          "@id":"6e852dd4-cd3a-4516-9665-842483d5c22f",
22          "@type":"color:Blue"
23      }
24  },
25  {
26      "@id":"http://linkeddata.stream/streams/colorstream/1588684152",
27      "@context":{
28          "color":"http://linkeddata.stream/ontologies/colors#",
29          "rdf":"http://www.w3.org/1999/02/22-rdf-syntax-ns#",
30          "rdfs":"http://www.w3.org/2000/01/rdf-schema#"
31      },
32      "@graph":{
33          "@id":"84b0350a-2422-4538-8689-f0e58ce1c485",
34          "@type":"color:Green"
35      }
36  },
37  {
38      "@id":"http://linkeddata.stream/streams/colorstream/1588684399",
39      "@context":{
40          "color":"http://linkeddata.stream/ontologies/colors#",
41          "rdf":"http://www.w3.org/1999/02/22-rdf-syntax-ns#",
42          "rdfs":"http://www.w3.org/2000/01/rdf-schema#"
43      },
44      "@graph":{
45          "@id":"80350a4b-4fa3-9665-8689-g46842483ds5",
46          "@type":"color:Yellow"
47      }
48  }
```

Listing 1.4. The RDF stream of color.

that manipulates Web streams and, in particular, RDF Streams. We identify three main types of RSP services that are relevant for the streaming linked data lifecycle: (i) *Catalogs* that provide metadata about streams, their content, query endpoints and more. (ii) *Publishers* that publish RDF streams, possibly following a Linked Data compliant scheme (e.g. TripleWave in Listing 1.5). (iii) *Processors*, which model a Stream Processing service that performs any kind of transformation on streaming data, e.g. querying (by RSP engines like CSPARQL engine [3] or CQELS [23]) or reasoning (by Stream Reasoners like RDFFox [20], TrOWL [27], or MASSIF [5]), or detection (Semantic Complex Event Processors [10,29]).

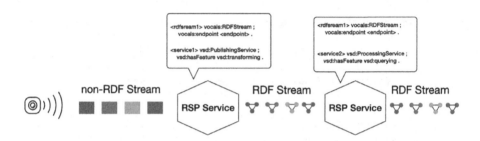

Fig. 9. Converting and publishing the sensor stream with TripleWave.

Intuitively, the first two are services relevant within streaming data publication, while the latter is relevant for processing. Due to the lack of space, in the following we focus on Publishers and Processors.

Serve. Step (4) aims at making the streaming data accessible on the Web. The goal of this step is serving the data to the audience of interest, i.e., making them available for processing.

RSP Publishers like TripleWave [19] are deployed to provision the streaming data content. TripleWave is a reusable and generic tool that enables the publication of RDF streams on the Web. It can be invoked through both pull- and push-based mechanisms, thus enabling RSP engines to automatically register and receive data from TripleWave.

```
<http://linkeddata.stream> a vsd:PublishingService ;
    vsd:hasFeature vsd:transforming .
```

Listing 1.5. The Publisher of the Color Stream.

Additionally, RSP publishing services carry on the conversion process and make the Web stream findable by publishing stream descriptors like the one presented in Listing 1.3. To this extent, VoCaLS provides additional modules for describing the provisioning service (e.g., Listing 1.5) as well as tracking the provenance of the stream transformation.

Finally, streaming data access is made possible through the publication of Stream Endpoints that refer to the appropriate protocols to the continuous or reactive consumption of Web data (e.g., WebSockets or Server-Sent Events).

```
:ColorEndpoint a vocals:StreamEndpoint ;
               dcat:format frmt:Turtle ;
               dcat:accessURL "ws://colorstream:8080" .
```

Listing 1.6. An access point to the color stream.

Example 8. (cont'd) Carrying on our running example for Step (4), Listing 1.5 and Listing 1.6 complete the stream descriptor presented in Listing 1.3 with the specification of the corresponding publishing service and access point. Additionally, Fig. 9 shows how to carry on the lifecycle consuming the sensor streams, converting it, and at the same time making the stream descriptor available. This pipeline can be realised using TripleWave [19] and the CSPARQL engine [4].

Process. Finally, the aim of Step (5) is consuming published stream for analysis. We provide details on how this is possible in the next section, making use of RSP-QL, i.e., the reference language for RDF Stream Processing [10].

4   Processing

In this section, we dig into processing Web Streams using RSP-QL. To this extent, we present an RSP-QL primer that will introduce the reader to the syntax and RSP-QL main functionalities. Furthermore, we provide a comprehensive set of analytics that builds on our running example, i.e., the color stream.

4.1   RSP-QL Primer

RSP-QL extends SPARQL 1.1 syntax and semantics to define streaming transformations over RDF Streams. The RSP-QL semantic is inspired by CQL and SECRET [14]. The formal framework includes operator classes (like CQL), and primitives to describe the operational semantics (like SECRET). In particular, it is worth mentioning that as RA corresponds to R2R operators in CQL (cf. Sect. 2), so SPARQL algebra corresponds to R2R operators in RSP-QL.

Figure 10 presents the anatomy of an RSP-QL query. As explained in Sect. 2.3, a SPARQL query consists of a Dataset Clause, a Query Form, and a Where Clause. RSP-QL extends the Dataset Clause to include Window Operators (Line 5 in Listing 1.7); it introduces the WINDOW keywords for referring to stream in the Where Clause (Line 10 in Listing 1.7), and it adds the REGISTER clause to name the R2S operators and the output streams (Line 2 in Listing 1.7). Notably, the output of an RSP-QL query with the register clause (named RSP-QL query) is not necessarily an RDF Stream. It depends on the Query Form.

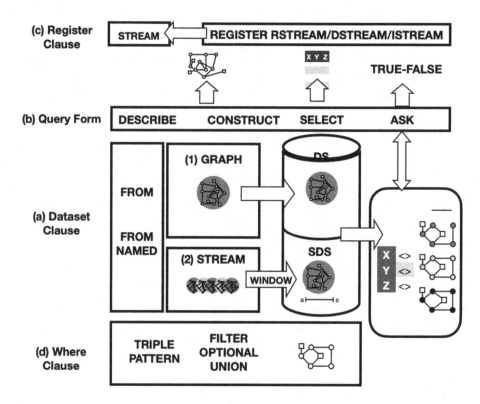

Fig. 10. The anatomy of an RSP-QL query.

```
1 PREFIX foaf:  <http://xmlns.com/foaf/0.1/>
2 REGISTER RSTREAM <sout> AS
3 SELECT ?name ?email
4 FROM <http://www.w3.org/People/Berners-Lee/card>
5 FROM NAMED WINDOW <w> ON <stream1> [RANGE PT15S STEP PT5S]
6 WHERE {
7     ?person foaf:name ?name ;
8             foaf:age ?age .
9     FILTER (?age > 18)
10    WINDOW <w> { ?person ?p ?o .}
11 }
12 ORDER BY ?name
```

Listing 1.7. Example SPARQL query.

Formally speaking, RSP-QL extends CQL for processing RDF Streams. It generalizes the concept of RDF dataset into the idea of a streaming RDF dataset called SDS (cf. Definition 17). It adds operators for continuous processing of RDF

Streams, using Time-Based Sliding Windows (cf. Definition 15), while reusing the R2S operators as defined in CQL.

Definition 15. *A Time-Based Sliding Window* $\mathbb{W}$ *is an S2R operator that takes as input an RDF stream S (cf. Definition 14) and three more parameters: (i) t_0: a time instant indicating when the operator starts processing; (ii) α: a window width; (iii) β: the window slide. These parameters characterize how the window operator divides the stream.* $\mathbb{W}(\alpha, \beta, t_0)$ *identifies a set of window intervals* $(o, c] \in \mathbb{W}$ *such that* $o, c \in T$ *and are respectively the opening and closing time instants, i.e.,* $|o_i - c_j| = \alpha$.

Once applied to an RDF Stream, an RSP-QL time-based window operator produces a *Time-Varying Graph*, i.e., a function that takes a time instant as input and produce an RDF Graph as output.

Definition 16. *A Time-Varying Graph is a function* $G_{\mathbb{W}}$ *such that*

$$G_{\mathbb{W}}(t) = \{g | (g, t) \in S \wedge (o, c] \in \mathbb{W} \wedge t \in (o, c]\}$$

The domain of the time-varying graph is the set of time instants t where time-based window operator is defined. The co-domain definition is more subtle. Indeed, the window operator chunks the RDF Stream into finite portions each containing a number of RDF Graphs. Thus, as per RSP-QL semantics, the co-domain of the time-varying graph consists of all the RDF graphs resulting from the UNION of each RDF Graph inside a window.

Definition 17. *An RSPQL dataset SDS consists of an (optional) default graph* G_{def} *and* $n(n \geq 0)$ *named Time-Varying Graphs resulting from applying Time-Based Sliding Window operators over* $m \leq n$ *RDF streams.*

Using this operator the RSP-QL users can open a time-based window over an RDF Stream and load the time-varying content into a (named) graph. To represent such concepts, RSP-QL syntax extends the SPARQL Dataset clause with a time-based Window operator. Using the following syntax (for an example see Listing 1.7 at Line 5).

FROM [NAMED] WINDOW [graph IRI] ON (stream IRI) (RANGE,STEP).

Finally, let's briefly discuss how RSP-QL extends the SPARQL evaluation semantics. To this aim, we define an RSP-QL query as follows:

Definition 18. *An RSP-QL query Q is defined as (SE, SDS, ET, QF) where:*

- *SE is an RSP-QL algebraic expression*
- *SDS is an RSP-QL dataset*
- *ET is a sequence of time instants on which the evaluation of the query occurs*
- *QF is the Query Form like in SPARQL (e.g. Select or Construct)*

Intuitively, the evaluation semantics of an RSP-QL query depends on time and is defined as

$$eval(SDS(G), SE, t) \; \forall t \in ET$$

where, SDS is a streaming dataset having G as active Time-Varying Graph, SE is an algebraic expression and t is a time instant.

The evaluation is equivalent to the SPARQL evaluation computed over the instantaneous graphs $G(t)$, i.e.,

$$eval_{SPARQL}(SDS(G(t)), SE) \; \forall t \in ET$$

The set ET of evaluation time instants is determined by the reporting policy adopted by the engine executing the query. This is known as execution semantics [14] and can in RSP-QL be described in terms of the following strategies: **CC** Content Change – the engine reports if the content of the current window changes –, **WC** Window Close – the engine reports if the current window closes –, **NC** Non-empty Content – the engine reports if the current window is not empty –, and **P** Periodic – the engine reports at regular intervals.

4.2 Putting RSP-QL into Practice

In the following, we present a comprehensive set of stream reasoning tasks and their implementation using RSP-QL as a query language for Web stream analytics. For the sake of clarity, we continue working with our running example on the color stream.

Stream Filtering. The aim of this stream reasoning task is identifying the sub-portion of the input stream that is relevant for the analysis.

Example 9 (cont'd). The previously registered color stream can be queried to retrieve the number of blue boxes in the last minute. This requires the RSP to ingest the data stream and to register a continuous query. Listing 1.8 shows the corresponding RSP-QL query.

```
1 PREFIX color: <http://linkeddata.stream/ontologies/colors#>
2 PREFIX :       <http://linkeddata.stream/resource/>
3 SELECT (COUNT(?b) as ?numBlues)
4 FROM NAMED WINDOW <bw> ON :colorstream [RANGE PT15S STEP PT5S]
5 WHERE {
6     WINDOW ?bw { ?b a color:Blue .}
7 }
```

Listing 1.8. Counting Blue Occurrences

Stream Enrichment. The aim of this stream reasoning task is joining the streaming data with contextual static knowledge to the extent of enriching the input stream and raising the level of analysis.

Example 10 (cont'd). Exploiting the sentiment ontology, we enrich the colorstream relating each color with the corresponding sentiment. Then, we count the number of color occurrences that are related to positive sentiments. The RSP-QL query is shown in Listing 1.9.

```
1  PREFIX color: <http://linkeddata.stream/ontologies/colors#>
2  PREFIX sentiment: <http://linkeddata.stream/ontologies/sentiment#>
3  PREFIX :        <http://linkeddata.stream/resource/> .
4  SELECT COUNT(?p) as ?pos
5  FROM NAMED <sentiment.rdf>
6  FROM NAMED WINDOW <rw>  ON :colorstream [RANGE PT30S STEP PT5S]
7  WHERE {
8      GRAPH <sentiment.rdf> {
9          ?c sentiment:relates [ ?s a sentiment:Positive ] .
10     }
11     WINDOW <rw> {
12         ?p a [ ?c rdfs:subClassOf color:Color .]
13         }
14 }
```

Listing 1.9. Enriching the color stream with sentiment.

Stream Crossing. The aim of this stream reasoning task is to perform analysis across two distinct RDF streams. Stream-to-Stream joining typically requires expressing window operators that provide the scope of the join execution. RSP-QL allows (i) To define different named windows over multiple stream or (ii) To define commonly named windows over different streams.

Example 11 (cont'd). Exploiting colorstream, a new stream can be built, creating new green occurrences every time yellow and blue occurs in a defined time interval. Listing 1.10 shows the corresponding RSP-QL query.

```
1  PREFIX color: <http://linkeddata.stream/ontologies/colors#>
2  PREFIX :        <http://linkeddata.stream/resource/> .
3  CONSTRUCT { ?g a color:Green ; color:from ?b, ?y . }
4  FROM NAMED WINDOW <bw> ON :bluestream [RANGE PT30S STEP PT5S]
5  FROM NAMED WINDOW <yw> ON :yellowstream [RANGE PT15S STEP PT5S]
6  WHERE {
7      WINDOW <bw> { ?b a color:Blue .}
8      WINDOW <yw> { ?y a color:Yellow .}
9      BIND( UUID() as ?g )
10 }
```

Listing 1.10. Cooking Green streams.

```
1  PREFIX color: <http://linkeddata.stream/ontologies/colors#> .
2  PREFIX :        <http://linkeddata.stream/resource/> .
3  SELECT (COUNT(?w) AS ?cntWarm) (COUNT(?c) AS ?cntCold) ((?cntWarm>?
       cntCold) as ?moreWarmThanCold)
4  FROM NAMED WINDOW <cw> ON :colorstream [RANGE PT15S STEP PT5S]
5  WHERE {
6      { WINDOW <cw> { ?w a color:Warm. } }
7      UNION
8      { WINDOW <cw> { ?c a color:Cold .} }
9  }
```

Listing 1.11. Comparing warm and cold colors.

Stream Abstraction. The aim of this stream reasoning task is leveraging background domain knowledge to raise the analysis to a higher level of abstraction. To this extent, the query answering relies on deductive reasoning.

Example 12 (cont'd). Reasoning capabilities can be exploited to continuously compare the number of cold colors versus the number of warm colors. Listing 1.11 shows the corresponding RSP-QL query.

The queries above, written in RSP-QL syntax, can be executed through YASPER [30], an RSP engine that implements RSP-QL semantics. YASPER is not just a reference implementation of RSP-QL but also a library for rapid prototyping of RSP Engines[9]. It includes different runtimes that allow for a systematic and comparative analysis of RSP-QL performance. In particular, YASPER builds on the lesson learned by realizing several working prototypes like C-SPARQL engine [3], CQELS engine [24], and Morph$_{Stream}$ [6].

5   Exercise - Linear Pizza Oven

Consider the scenario depicted in Fig. 11. The company DreamPizza bought an oven with the aim of increasing their pizza's quality. The oven is a smart one. It makes use of a conveyor belt that takes pizzas in and out of the oven. Moreover, it has several sensors that continuously produce data. Carl, a data scientist working for DreamPizza, is particularly focused on two sensors:

– **S1.** The sensor S1 is positioned at the entrance of the oven. It has a camera that, using image recognition algorithms, is capable of detecting pizza toppings. Since it is the first sensor to analyze a pizza, it also assigns to each pizza a unique id $< pid >$. The sensor S1 exploits the Pizza Ontology[10] to produce an RDF stream. An example of such a stream is shown in Listing 1.12.

---

[9] Find the most recent version at https://github.com/riccardotommasini/yasper.

[10] https://protege.stanford.edu/ontologies/pizza/pizza.owl.

Fig. 11. Linear pizza oven.

– **S2.** The sensor S2 is positioned inside the oven. It senses the temperature and, exploiting the Sensor-Observation-Sampling-Actuator ontology (SOSA[11]), outputs an RDF stream with the $< pid >$ of the pizza and the oven's temperature. Multiple measures for the same $< pid >$ are provided, denoting the temperatures of the oven during the cooking process. An example of the RDF stream produced by S2 is shown in Listing 1.13.

```
@base <http://linkeddata.stream/streams/pizza-S1/1588684149> .
@prefix : <http://www.co-ode.org/ontologies/pizza/pizza.owl#> .

<#507f704d-dfb8-4fa3-97ca-64a93e56abb0> a :Pizza ;
                                    :hasTopping :MozzarellaTopping
                                        ,
                                    :TomatoTopping .
```

Listing 1.12. The RDF stream produced by S1.

Observing the RDF streams from S1 and S2, Carl is able to observe, for each pizza, the toppings and the temperature of the oven during the cooking process. Carl wonders if it is possible to exploit such data to automatically detect the name of each pizza starting from its toppings and, analyzing the oven temperature during its cooking process, assert on the quality of such pizza. In other words, he wants to know if a pizza has been cooked correctly or not. A colleague of Carl, Frank, has a relational database containing the cooking temperature for each named pizza. A small dump of the table Cook from such database is shown in Table 2.

---

[11] https://www.w3.org/TR/vocab-ssn/.

```
@base <http://linkeddata.stream/streams/pizza-S2/1588684151> .
@prefix : <http://linkeddata.stream/streams/pizza-S1/1588684149#> .
@prefix sosa: <http://www.w3.org/ns/sosa/> .
@prefix qudt: <http://qudt.org/1.1/schema/qudt#> .
@prefix qudt-unit: <http://qudt.org/1.1/vocab/unit#> .

<#575d1e00-1b70-4a3b-9ed4-961990aaead8> a sosa:Observation ;
   sosa:hasFeatureOfInterest :507f704d-dfb8-4fa3-97ca-64a93e56abb0 ;
   sosa:hasResult [
      a qudt:QuantityValue ;
      qudt:unit qudt-unit:DegreeCelsius ;
      qudt:numericValue 280.4 ] .
```

Listing 1.13. The RDF stream produced by S2.

Table 2. Table cook from Frank's database.

NamedPizza	TempAvg	TempStd
Margherita	280	10
American	275	5

Carl needs your help to develop and deploy a Stream Reasoning application that, exploiting the data streams from the sensors and the relational database from Frank, is able to detect whether each pizza passing thought the oven is cooked correctly or not.

6   Conclusion

Social networks, sensors for Industry 4.0, smart homes, and many other devices connected to the Internet produce an ever-growing stream of data. In this context, Stream Reasoning applications are needed to integrate data streams with complex background knowledge, while addressing time-specific constraints.

In this lecture, we provide basic knowledge about data streams, continuous processing, RDF and SPARQL. We illustrate the guidelines to develop and deploy Steams Reasoning applications, analyzing the Streaming Linked Data Lifecycle and presenting concrete realizations of each step with respect to a running example based on colors. In particular, we focused on the interoperability between stream services on the Web, giving an introduction to the Vocabulary & Catalog of Linked Streams (VoCaLS), designed with the goal of solving such problems. We later depicted RSP-QL, an extension of SPARQL able to cope with data streams and that, besides introducing new operator classes, it also formalizes the operational semantics. Finally, we presented a full-stack exercise for getting started with Streaming Linked Data and RDF Stream Processing using RSP-QL.

Acknowledgments. Dr. Tommasini acknowledges support from the European Social Fund via IT Academy programme.

References

1. Arasu, A., Babu, S., Widom, J.: The CQL continuous query language: semantic foundations and query execution. VLDB J. **15**(2) (2006)
2. Balduini, M., Valle, E.D.: FraPPE: a vocabulary to represent heterogeneous spatio-temporal data to support visual analytics. In: Arenas, M., et al. (eds.) ISWC 2015. LNCS, vol. 9367, pp. 321–328. Springer, Cham (2015). https://doi.org/10.1007/978-3-319-25010-6_21
3. Barbieri, D.F., Braga, D., Ceri, S., Della Valle, E., Grossniklaus, M.: C-SPARQL: a continuous query language for RDF data streams. Int. J. Semant. Comput. **4**(1), 3–25 (2010)
4. Barbieri, D.F., Della Valle, E.: A proposal for publishing data streams as linked data - a position paper. In: LDOW. CEUR Workshop Proceedings, vol. 628. CEUR-WS.org (2010)
5. Bonte, P., Tommasini, R., Della Valle, E., Turck, F.D., Ongenae, F.: Streaming MASSIF: cascading reasoning for efficient processing of IoT data streams. Sensors **18**(11), 3832 (2018)
6. Calbimonte, J.-P., Mora, J., Corcho, O.: Query rewriting in RDF stream process-ing. In: Sack, H., Blomqvist, E., d'Aquin, M., Ghidini, C., Ponzetto, S.P., Lange, C. (eds.) ESWC 2016. LNCS, vol. 9678, pp. 486–502. Springer, Cham (2016). https://doi.org/10.1007/978-3-319-34129-3_30
7. Comton, M., et al.: The SSN ontology of the W3C semantic sensor network incu-bator group. J. Web Semant. **17**, 25–32 (2012)
8. Della Valle, E., Ceri, S., van Harmelen, F., Fensel, D.: It's a streaming world! rea-soning upon rapidly changing information. IEEE Intell. Syst. **24**(6), 83–89 (2009)
9. Della Valle, E., Dell'Aglio, D., Margara, A.: Taming velocity and variety simulta-neously in big data with stream reasoning: tutorial. In: DEBS, pp. 394–401. ACM (2016)
10. Dell'Aglio, D., Dao-Tran, M., Calbimonte, J.-P., Le Phuoc, D., Della Valle, E.: A query model to capture event pattern matching in RDF stream processing query languages. In: Blomqvist, E., Ciancarini, P., Poggi, F., Vitali, F. (eds.) EKAW 2016. LNCS (LNAI), vol. 10024, pp. 145–162. Springer, Cham (2016). https://doi.org/10.1007/978-3-319-49004-5_10
11. Dell'Aglio, D., Della Valle, E., Calbimonte, J., Corcho, Ó.: RSP-QL semantics: a unifying query model to explain heterogeneity of RDF stream processing systems. Int. J. Semant. Web Inf. Syst. **10**(4), 17–44 (2014)
12. Dell'Aglio, D., Della Valle, E., van Harmelen, F., Bernstein, A.: Stream reasoning: a survey and outlook. Data Sci. **1**(1–2), 59–83 (2017)
13. Dell'Aglio, D., Le Phuoc, D., Le-Tuan, A., Ali, M.I., Calbimonte, J.P.: On a web of data streams. In: ISWC DeSemWeb (2017)
14. Dindar, N., Tatbul, N., Miller, R.J., Haas, L.M., Botan, I.: Modeling the execution semantics of stream processing engines with SECRET. VLDB J. **22**(4), 421–446 (2013)
15. Gao, F., Ali, M.I., Mileo, A.: Semantic discovery and integration of urban data streams. In: Proceedings of the Fifth Workshop on Semantics for Smarter Cities a Workshop at the 13th International Semantic Web Conference (ISWC 2014), Riva del Garda, Italy, October 19, 2014, pp. 15–30 (2014). http://ceur-ws.org/Vol-1280/paper5.pdf

16. Janowicz, K., Haller, A., Cox, S.J.D., Phuoc, D.L., Lefrançois, M.: SOSA: a lightweight ontology for sensors, observations, samples, and actuators. J. Web Semant. **56**, 1–10 (2019)
17. Laney, D.: 3d data management: controlling data volume, velocity and variety. META Group Res. Note **6**(70), 1 (2001)
18. Margara, A., Urbani, J., van Harmelen, F., Bal, H.E.: Streaming the web: reasoning over dynamic data. J. Web Semant. **25**, 24–44 (2014)
19. Mauri, A., et al.: Triplewave: spreading RDF streams on the web. In: ISWC (2016)
20. Nenov, Y., Piro, R., Motik, B., Horrocks, I., Wu, Z., Banerjee, J.: RDFox: a highly-scalable RDF store. In: Arena, M., et al. (eds.) ISWC 2015. LNCS, vol. 9367, pp. 3–20. Springer, Cham (2015). https://doi.org/10.1007/978-3-319-25010-6_1
21. Passant, A., Bojārs, U., Breslin, J.G., Decker, S.: The SIOC project: semantically-interlinked online communities, from humans to machines. In: Padget, J., et al. (eds.) COIN -2009. LNCS (LNAI), vol. 6069, pp. 179–194. Springer, Heidelberg (2010). https://doi.org/10.1007/978-3-642-14962-7_12
22. Pérez, J., Arenas, M., Gutiérrez, C.: Semantics and complexity of SPARQL. ACM Trans. Database Syst. **34**(3), 16:1–16:45 (2009)
23. Le-Phuoc, D., Dao-Tran, M., Xavier Parreira, J., Hauswirth, M.: A native and adaptive approach for unified processing of linked streams and linked data. In: Aroyo, L., et al. (eds.) ISWC 2011. LNCS, vol. 7031, pp. 370–388. Springer, Heidelberg (2011). https://doi.org/10.1007/978-3-642-25073-6_24
24. Phuoc, D.L., Dao-Tran, M., Tuán, A.L., Duc, M.N., Hauswirth, M.: RDF stream processing with CQELS framework for real-time analysis. In: DEBS (2015)
25. Sequeda, J.F., Corcho, Ó.: Linked stream data: a position paper. In: SSN. CEUR Workshop Proceedings, vol. 522, pp. 148–157. CEUR-WS.org (2009)
26. Terry, D.B., Goldberg, D., Nichols, D.A., Oki, B.M.: Continuous queries over append-only databases. In: Stonebraker, M. (ed.) Proceedings of the 1992 ACM SIGMOD International Conference on Management of Data, San Diego, California, USA, 2–5 June 1992, pp. 321–330. ACM Press (1992). https://doi.org/10.1145/130283.130333
27. Thomas, E., Pan, J.Z., Ren, Y.: TrOWL: tractable OWL 2 reasoning infrastructure. In: Aroyo, L., et al. (eds.) ESWC 2010. LNCS, vol. 6089, pp. 431–435. Springer, Heidelberg (2010). https://doi.org/10.1007/978-3-642-13489-0_38
28. Tommasini, R.: Velocity on the web - a PhD symposium. In: WWW (Companion Volume), pp. 56–60. ACM (2019)
29. Tommasini, R., Bonte, P., Della Valle, E., Ongenae, F., De Turck, F.: A query model for ontology-based event processing over RDF streams. In: Faron Zucker, C., Ghidini, C., Napoli, A., Toussaint, Y. (eds.) EKAW 2018. LNCS (LNAI), vol. 11313, pp. 439–453. Springer, Cham (2018). https://doi.org/10.1007/978-3-030-03667-6_28
30. Tommasini, R., Della Valle, E.: Yasper 1.0: towards an RSP-QL engine. In: Proceedings of the ISWC 2017 Posters & Demonstrations and Industry Tracks Co-located with 16th International Semantic Web Conference (ISWC) (2017)
31. Tommasini, R., et al.: VoCaLS: vocabulary and catalog of linked streams. In: Vrandečić, G., et al. (eds.) ISWC 2018. LNCS, vol. 11137, pp. 256–272. Springer, Cham (2018). https://doi.org/10.1007/978-3-030-00668-6_16
32. Wood, D., Lanthaler, M., Cyganiak, R.: RDF 1.1 concepts and abstract syntax. W3C recommendation, W3C, February 2014. http://www.w3.org/TR/2014/REC-rdf11-concepts-20140225/

Temporal Ontology-Mediated Queries and First-Order Rewritability: A Short Course

V. Ryzhikov[1(✉)], P. A. Wałęga[2], and M. Zakharyaschev[1]

[1] Birkbeck, University of London, London, UK
vlad@dcs.bbk.ac.uk
[2] University of Oxford, Oxford, UK

Abstract. We discuss recent attempts to extend the ontology-based data access (aka virtual knowledge graph) paradigm to the temporal setting. Our main aim is to understand when answering temporal ontology-mediated queries can be reduced to evaluating standard first-order queries over timestamped data and what numeric predicates and operators are required in such reductions. We consider two ways of introducing a temporal dimension in ontologies and queries: using linear temporal logic *LTL* over discrete time and using metric temporal logic *MTL* over dense time.

1 Introduction

Imagine that you are an engineer and that your task is to analyse the behaviour of some complex system (such as gas turbines or drilling rigs) in order to understand what kind of undesirable events have happened in it over the past few days and why. As many others in this weird time of Covid-19 pandemic, you are working from home and can only figure out what has been going on with the system by querying the data, which is automatically collected from the system's sensors and stored in the company's databases. Your intuition and experience suggest that first you should look for *emergency stops* and unusually *high* and *low* values of *temperature, rotor speed* and other parameters read by the sensors. Then you would investigate more complex events such as '*purging is over*' that happens, according to the manual, when the main flame was on for the past 10 s and also, within the previous 10 min, there was a 30-s period when the rotor speed was above 1260 rpm and, at most 2 min before the start of that period, the rotor speed was below 1000 rpm for at least 1 min.

You might be a brilliant engineer with intimate knowledge of your equipment but alas, the odds are you have no clue where the data is stored and in which form. (Your IT expert, Joe, would have told you, if asked politely, that the equipment ID, timestamp and temperature are, respectively, in the first, tenth and fifth columns of a database table SENSOR_TEM_C, the rotor speed measurements are in a different table ROTOR_SP_RPM, and emergency stops are in a special spreadsheet—but who would you dare ask him in the time of self-isolation with three kids, a wife-mathematician and a grumpy granny in a one-bedroom flat?)

© Springer Nature Switzerland AG 2020
M. Manna and A. Pieris (Eds.): Reasoning Web 2020, LNCS 12258, pp. 109–148, 2020.
https://doi.org/10.1007/978-3-030-60067-9_5

The *ontology-based data access* (OBDA) [29,73,84]—recently rebranded as the *virtual knowledge graph* (VKG) [85]—paradigm has been introduced in the mid 2000s to facilitate access to data, make it more user-friendly, and remove the dependency on IT experts as far as formalising user queries is concerned. Informally, an OBDA system such as Mastro[1] or Ontop[2] allows the users to think that the data is always at hand in the form of a 'knowledge graph' whose vertices are individuals in the database labelled by classes they belong to and whose directed edges are labelled by relationships between those individuals. For example, the database facts that $t11$ is a gas turbine having rotor $r3$ as its moving part can be thought of as a graph edge labelled by *hasMovingPart* and going from a vertex $t11$ with label *GasTurbine* to a vertex $r3$ with label *Rotor*.

As the names of classes and relationships are familiar to the users (taken from the user manual or a textbook on the relevant domain) and the structure of the data is transparent (directed graph), formulating queries in the OBDA system should be much easier than, say, in a relational database management system (RDBMS)—especially if a visual query interface such as OptiqueVQS [77] is enabled. Moreover, the OBDA system has a secret weapon in the form of an ontology, which is supposed to capture the background knowledge about the domain. In particular, it can contain definitions and descriptions of complex classes and relationships in terms of primitive ones, which can also be utilised in user queries. Thus, the ontology provides the user with a high-level conceptual view of the data and fixes a convenient vocabulary for queries; it supports queries to multiple and possibly heterogeneous data sources, which are of no concern to the user; and it allows the system to enrich incomplete data with background knowledge, which involves reasoning.

Does it sound too good to be true? Let us make the OBDA fairy tale told above more formal and see what it amounts to computationally. Denote by $\mathcal{O}$ the ontology (designed by a domain expert). There exist dozens of ontology languages: description logics (DLs) [12,13] of different expressivity, the Web Ontology Language OWL[3] and its profiles, logic programming and deductive database languages Prolog and datalog, the perennial first-order logic (FO), etc. Let $\mathcal{O}$ be formulated in one of those languages. The knowledge graph, which the user wants to query, is a set, $\mathcal{A}$, of ground atoms of the form $A(a)$ and $P(a,b)$, where A is a unary predicate (class or concept such as *Rotor*) and P a binary predicate (relationship or property such as *hasMovingPart*) in the vocabulary of $\mathcal{O}$. The trouble is that $\mathcal{A}$ does not exist, it is virtual. It can be defined by means of a set, $\mathcal{M}$, of mappings of the form $S(\boldsymbol{x}) \leftarrow \Phi(\boldsymbol{x})$, where S is a unary or binary predicate from $\mathcal{O}$ and Φ a query over one of the datasources, $\mathcal{D}$ (say, an SQL query to a relational database). Thus, $\mathcal{A}$ can be defined as $\mathcal{M}(\mathcal{D})$. The mappings $\mathcal{M}$ are written by an expert with detailed knowledge of both $\mathcal{O}$ and $\mathcal{D}$. The users do not need to know anything about them. The users' only task is to formulate

---

[1] https://www.obdasystems.com.

[2] https://ontopic.biz.

[3] https://www.w3.org/TR/owl2-overview/.

a query $\varphi(\boldsymbol{x})$ over (imaginary) $\mathcal{A}$ in a query language such as SPARQL[4] and press the enter key. The pair $\boldsymbol{q} = (\mathcal{O}, \varphi(\boldsymbol{x}))$ is called an *ontology-mediated query*, OMQ for short. The OBDA system is then supposed to find *certain answers to $\boldsymbol{q}$* over $\mathcal{A}$—actually, over $\mathcal{D}$ as $\mathcal{A}$ does not exist—which are tuples $\boldsymbol{a}$ of individuals from $\mathcal{A}$ such that $\varphi(\boldsymbol{a})$ is a logical consequence of $\mathcal{O}$ and $\mathcal{A}$, in which case we write $\mathcal{O}, \mathcal{A} \models \varphi(\boldsymbol{a})$. Thus, the OBDA system has to somehow compute all tuples $\boldsymbol{a}$ for which $\mathcal{O}, \mathcal{M}(\mathcal{D}) \models \varphi(\boldsymbol{a})$ holds. Whether it is feasible or not depends on the ontology, mapping and query languages involved.

The crucial idea behind the OBDA paradigm is that these languages should be chosen in such a way that the *OMQ answering problem*—'is it the case that $\mathcal{O}, \mathcal{M}(\mathcal{D}) \models \varphi(\boldsymbol{a})$?'—could be reduced to the evaluation problem for standard database queries directly over $\mathcal{D}$. When $\mathcal{D}$ is a relational database, it would be great if the problem of answering $\boldsymbol{q}$ could be somehow reformulated, or *rewritten*, by the OBDA system into an SQL query $\boldsymbol{Q}(\boldsymbol{x})$ with the answer variables $\boldsymbol{x}$, which is then executed over $\mathcal{D}$ by an RDBMS at hand. In our theoretical setting we might as well assume that $\boldsymbol{Q}(\boldsymbol{x})$ is an FO-formula [1] and call an OMQ $\boldsymbol{q} = (\mathcal{O}, \varphi(\boldsymbol{x}))$ *FO-rewritable* if there is an FO-formula $\boldsymbol{Q}(\boldsymbol{x})$, a *rewriting* of $\boldsymbol{q}$, such that, for any data instance $\mathcal{D}$ and any tuple $\boldsymbol{a}$ of individuals in $\mathcal{D}$, we have $\mathcal{O}, \mathcal{M}(\mathcal{D}) \models \varphi(\boldsymbol{a})$ iff $\mathcal{D} \models \boldsymbol{Q}(\boldsymbol{a})$. If the language for mappings $\mathcal{M}$ is sufficiently simple (say, R2RML[5]), then it actually suffices to find an FO-rewriting $\boldsymbol{Q}(\boldsymbol{x})$ of $\boldsymbol{q}$ over possible virtual knowledge graphs $\mathcal{A}$, which can be later transformed to a proper SQL query over $\mathcal{D}$ by the OBDA system using the mappings (for details on this, consult [84] and references therein). Thus, we arrive to the main definition of this paper: $\boldsymbol{Q}(\boldsymbol{x})$ is an *FO-rewriting* of $\boldsymbol{q} = (\mathcal{O}, \varphi(\boldsymbol{x}))$ just in case $\mathcal{O}, \mathcal{A} \models \varphi(\boldsymbol{a})$ iff $\mathcal{A} \models \boldsymbol{Q}(\boldsymbol{a})$, for every VKG $\mathcal{A}$ (in the language of $\mathcal{O}$) and every tuple $\boldsymbol{a}$ of individuals from $\mathcal{A}$.

FO-rewritability is a very strong requirement for ontology and query languages; far from all of them satisfy it. By now, description logics and other fragments of FO that guarantee FO-rewritability are well studied and understood [84]. For example, the *OWL 2 QL* profile of the Web Ontology Language *OWL 2*[6] (underpinned by the *DL-Lite* family of description logics [6,29]) is the W3C standard ontology language for OBDA, which ensures FO-rewritability of all OMQs with an *OWL 2 QL* ontology and a SPARQL or conjunctive query. It is supported by MASTRO and Ontop. So OBDA is not a fairy tale after all.

But can you use it to spot in the sensor data those nasty events that possibly happened in your equipment? Unfortunately, not yet. Because the OBDA framework we discussed above has only been developed and implemented for querying *non-temporal* data using *atemporal* ontologies. Temporal OBDA is still largely work in progress, and the aim of this paper is to present and discuss some of the existing approaches to temporalising ontology-mediated query answering (where the authors have particular research interests). A more comprehensive recent survey of temporal OBDA can be found in [9], though the area is moving forward very fast.

---

[4] https://www.w3.org/TR/sparql11-query/.
[5] https://www.w3.org/TR/r2rml/.
[6] https://www.w3.org/TR/owl2-overview/.

2   One-Dimensional Temporal OBDA

We begin our discussion of temporal OBDA with a very simple case. Imagine that the system whose behaviour we need to analyse is equipped with a number of sensors, say $S_1, \ldots, S_n$. At certain moments of time, t, the system records in a database the current measurement of one or more sensors S_i. So we can assume that the database records take the form $S_i(t, v)$, where t is a moment of time, or a *timestamp*, and v a measurement value. When speaking of temporal events, we often classify those values into qualitative categories, which may vary from one context to another, such as *high temperature* (e.g., $v \geq 300\,°C$), *low temperature* (say, $v \leq 30\,°C$), etc. Thus, we may want to think of the record $S_3(t, 350\,°C)$ as *High(t)*: at moment t, the temperature was high. The conversion of the original quantitative 2D data $S_i(t, v)$ into qualitative 1D data of the form $A(t)$ can easily be done by mappings, for example,

$$High(t) \leftarrow \texttt{SELECT t FROM } S_3 \texttt{ WHERE v } >= \texttt{ 300}.$$

To sum up, let A_i, for $i = 1, 2, \ldots$, be a countably infinite list of unary (or monadic) predicate symbols representing such qualitative measurements. Then every data instance we want to query is simply a finite set of atoms of the form $A_i(t)$ with a timestamp t. But what is time?

In general, this is a very difficult question. Remember 'There is a time for everything. [. . .] Whatever is has already been' (Ecclesiastes) or 'Time is an illusion. Lunchtime doubly so' (Douglas Adams, The Hitchhiker's Guide to the Galaxy)? Even Computer Science uses numerous models of time: linear and branching, discrete and dense, finite and infinite, etc. [34, 36, 38, 40]. So, what can we say about our data instances?

One important property is clear: as we store data about events that have already happened, we may assume that, for any timestamps t and t', either $t < t'$ or $t = t'$, or $t > t'$. In other words, our time is *linear*. Whether the time is discrete or continuous depends on the type of the system we are dealing with. If it is *synchronous* in the sense that all records can only be made at a central clock signal, then time can be thought of as *discrete*, and so the timestamps in each data instance form a finite subset of the natural numbers $\mathbb{N}$ or the integer numbers $\mathbb{Z}$. In this paper, we prefer the integers.

Thus, in the case of discrete time, a *data instance*, $\mathcal{A}$, is a finite set of *ground atoms* of the form $A_i(\ell)$, where $\ell \in \mathbb{Z}$. We denote by $\min \mathcal{A}$ and $\max \mathcal{A}$ the minimal and maximal integer numbers occurring in $\mathcal{A}$. The *active temporal domain* of a data instance $\mathcal{A}$ is the set $\mathsf{tem}(\mathcal{A}) = \{ n \in \mathbb{Z} \mid \min \mathcal{A} \leq n \leq \max \mathcal{A} \}$. To simplify constructions and without much loss of generality, we assume that $\min \mathcal{A} = 0$ and $\max \mathcal{A} \geq 1$.

If our system is *asynchronous*, database records can be made spontaneously, for example, when the current measurement of sensor S_i differs 'substantially' from the previously recorded measurement taken by S_i. In this case, we can model time by the real numbers $\mathbb{R}$ or the rational numbers $\mathbb{Q}$. Since computer words are binary and finite, we prefer to assume that every timestamp is a *dyadic rational number* of the form $n/2^m$, where $n \in \mathbb{Z}$ and $m \in \mathbb{N}$. The set of these numbers is denoted by $\mathbb{Q}_2$. Note that although rationals such as $1/3$ are not dyadic, by Cantor's theorem, the order $(\mathbb{Q}_2, <)$ is *dense* in the sense that

$$\forall x, y \left((x < y) \rightarrow \exists z \, (x < z < y) \right)$$

and isomorphic to the order $(\mathbb{Q}, <)$. Hence, rationals can be approximated with any accuracy by dyadic rationals. In this case, a *data instance* $\mathcal{A}$ is a finite set of ground atoms of the form $A_i(\ell)$ with $\ell \in \mathbb{Q}_2$. The *active temporal domain* of $\mathcal{A}$ is the finite set $\mathsf{tem}(\mathcal{A}) = \{\ell \mid A_i(\ell) \in \mathcal{A}\}$.

Suppose we are interested in finding certain events in a given data instance. An event can be classified as *instantaneous* if it makes sense to say that it happens at a time instant (for example, an emergency stop or a power trip happened at moment t) and *extended* that can happen over a temporal interval (for example, the temperature was rising between t_1 and t_2). In this paper, we mainly consider the former type of events.

A natural language for speaking about temporal instantaneous events over $\mathbb{Z}$ is MFO($<$), *monadic first-order logic* with built-in precedence relation $<$ (cf. [30, 52]). More precisely, MFO($<$)-*formulas* are built from unary predicates $A_i(x)$ and binary predicates $x = y$, $x < y$ using the standard Boolean connectives ($\land$, $\lor$, $\rightarrow$, $\neg$) and first-order quantifiers ($\forall$ and $\exists$). They are interpreted in the usual way in structures, called (*temporal*) *interpretations*, of the form

$$\mathcal{I} = (\mathbb{Z}, <, A_1^{\mathcal{I}}, A_2^{\mathcal{I}}, \dots),$$

which have domain $(\mathbb{Z}, <)$ and interpret every predicate A_i as a subset $A_i^{\mathcal{I}} \subseteq \mathbb{Z}$. Let $\mathfrak{a}$ be an *assignment* of numbers from $\mathbb{Z}$ to individual variables in MFO($<$)-formulas. Given an MFO($<$)-formula $\varphi(\boldsymbol{x})$ with free variables $\boldsymbol{x} = (x_1, \dots, x_n)$, we write $\mathcal{I} \models \varphi(\mathfrak{a}(\boldsymbol{x}))$ to say that φ is true in $\mathcal{I}$ under the assignment $\mathfrak{a}$ (which replaces $\boldsymbol{x}$ with $\mathfrak{a}(\boldsymbol{x}) = (\mathfrak{a}(x_1), \dots, \mathfrak{a}(x_n))$).

Example 1. We illustrate what can be said in MFO($<$) by a few examples. Suppose $\varphi(t, t') = (t < t') \land \neg \exists t'' \, (t < t'' < t')$, where $t < t'' < t'$ abbreviates the formula $(t < t'') \land (t'' < t')$. Then, for any interpretation $\mathcal{I}$ and any $m, n \in \mathbb{Z}$, we have $\mathcal{I} \models \varphi(m, n)$ iff $n = m + 1$. It follows that, in MFO($<$)-formulas, we can freely use the 'functions' $t + n$ and $t - n$, for every fixed $n \in \mathbb{Z}$. This allows us to capture events such as *purging is over* from the introduction. For instance, assuming that the clock ticks every second, the following FO-formula $\varphi(t)$ says that the main flame was on for the past $10\,\mathrm{s}$ and that within the previous $10\,\mathrm{min}$, there was a 30-s period when the rotor speed was above $1260\,\mathrm{rpm}$:

$$\varphi(t) = \forall t' \left((t > t' \geq t - 10) \rightarrow \mathit{MainFlameOn}(t') \right) \land \exists t' \left[(t > t' \geq t - 600) \land \right. $$
$$\left. \forall t'' \left((t' > t'' \geq t' - 30) \rightarrow \mathit{RotorSpeedAbove1260}(t'') \right) \right].$$

We invite the reader to extend this $\varphi(t)$ to a formula $\psi(t)$ that expresses the event *purging is over* described in the introduction. Then the sentence

$$\forall t \left[\mathit{PurgingIsOver}(t) \leftrightarrow \psi(t) \right] \tag{1}$$

defines a predicate $\mathit{PurgingIsOver}(t)$ that can be used in queries.

By an MFO($<$)-*ontology* we mean any finite set, $\mathcal{O}$, of MFO($<$)-sentences. An interpretation $\mathcal{I}$ is a *model* of $\mathcal{O}$ if $\mathcal{I} \models \varphi$, for every sentence $\varphi \in \mathcal{O}$, in which case we write $\mathcal{I} \models \mathcal{O}$; $\mathcal{I}$ is a *model* of a data instance $\mathcal{A}$ if $\ell \in A^{\mathcal{I}}$ whenever $A(\ell) \in \mathcal{A}$. We write $\mathcal{O} \models \varphi$ to say that $\mathcal{I} \models \varphi$, for every model $\mathcal{I}$ of $\mathcal{O}$.

MFO($<$)-formulas $\psi(\boldsymbol{t})$ with free variables $\boldsymbol{t} = (t_1, \dots, t_m)$ can also be used as queries asking for assignments of timestamps to the *answer variables* $\boldsymbol{t}$ under which the query holds true in relevant interpretations. An *ontology-mediated query* (OMQ) in MFO($<$) is a pair $\boldsymbol{q} = (\mathcal{O}, \psi(\boldsymbol{t}))$, where $\mathcal{O}$ is an ontology and $\psi(\boldsymbol{t})$ a query, both given in MFO($<$). If $\boldsymbol{t}$ is empty ($m = 0$), then $\boldsymbol{q}$ is called a *Boolean* OMQ.

A *certain answer* to an OMQ $\boldsymbol{q} = (\mathcal{O}, \psi(\boldsymbol{t}))$ over a data instance $\mathcal{A}$ is any tuple $\boldsymbol{\ell} = (\ell_1, \dots, \ell_m)$ such that $\ell_i \in \mathsf{tem}(\mathcal{A})$, for $1 \le i \le m$, and

$$\mathcal{I} \models \psi(\boldsymbol{\ell}), \qquad \text{for every model } \mathcal{I} \text{ of } (\mathcal{O}, \mathcal{A}). \tag{2}$$

For a Boolean OMQ $\boldsymbol{q}$, a *certain answer* over $\mathcal{A}$ is 'yes' if $\mathcal{I} \models \psi$, for every model $\mathcal{I}$ of $\mathcal{O}$ and $\mathcal{A}$, and 'no' otherwise. The set of all certain answers to $\boldsymbol{q}$ over $\mathcal{A}$ is denoted by $\mathsf{ans}(\boldsymbol{q}, \mathcal{A})$. As a technical tool in our constructions, we also consider 'certain answers' that range over the whole of $\mathbb{Z}$ rather than only the active temporal domain $\mathsf{tem}(\mathcal{A})$; we denote the set of such certain answers *over $\mathcal{A}$ and $\mathbb{Z}$* by $\mathsf{ans}^{\mathbb{Z}}(\boldsymbol{q}, \mathcal{A})$.

Example 2. Suppose $\mathcal{O} = \{\, \forall t\, (A(t) \to B(t+1)),\ \forall t\, (B(t) \to A(t+1)) \,\}$ and $\mathcal{A} = \{\, A(0),\ C(1) \,\}$. Then $2n + 1 \in B^{\mathcal{I}}$, for any $n \ge 0$ and any model $\mathcal{I}$ of $(\mathcal{O}, \mathcal{A})$. It follows that, for the OMQ $\boldsymbol{q} = (\mathcal{O}, \exists t'\, ((t' = t + 2) \wedge B(t')))$, we have $\mathsf{ans}^{\mathbb{Z}}(\boldsymbol{q}, \mathcal{A}) = \{\, 2n+1 \mid n \ge -1 \,\}$, while $\mathsf{ans}(\boldsymbol{q}, \mathcal{A}) = \{1\}$ because $\mathsf{tem}(\mathcal{A}) = \{0, 1\}$.

We are now in a position to introduce the central notion of the paper that reduces answering OMQs over data instances $\mathcal{A}$ to evaluation of first-order queries over a finite first-order structure $\mathfrak{S}_{\mathcal{A}}$ with domain $\mathsf{tem}(\mathcal{A})$ ordered by $<$, in which

$$\mathfrak{S}_{\mathcal{A}} \models A(\ell) \quad \text{iff} \quad A(\ell) \in \mathcal{A},$$

for any predicate A and any $\ell \in \mathsf{tem}(\mathcal{A})$.

Definition 3 (FO-rewritability). Let $\mathcal{L}$ be a class of FO-formulas that can be interpreted over structures $\mathfrak{S}_{\mathcal{A}}$. (For example, $\mathcal{L}$ may coincide with FO($<$) or extend it with some standard numeric predicates such as $\mathrm{PLUS}(x, y, z)$, which is true iff $x + y = z$, or even with some operators such as transitive closure or relational primitive recursion.) Let $\boldsymbol{q} = (\mathcal{O}, \psi(\boldsymbol{t}))$ be an OMQ and $\boldsymbol{Q}(\boldsymbol{t})$ a constant-free $\mathcal{L}$-formula with free variables $\boldsymbol{t}$. We call $\boldsymbol{Q}(\boldsymbol{t})$ an $\mathcal{L}$-*rewriting of* $\boldsymbol{q}$ if, for any data instance $\mathcal{A}$, we have $\mathsf{ans}(\boldsymbol{q}, \mathcal{A}) = \{\boldsymbol{\ell} \subseteq \mathsf{tem}(\mathcal{A}) \mid \mathfrak{S}_{\mathcal{A}} \models \boldsymbol{Q}(\boldsymbol{\ell})\}$.[7] We say that $\boldsymbol{q}$ is $\mathcal{L}$-*rewritable* if it has an $\mathcal{L}$-rewriting.

Additionally, as a technical tool to construct $\mathcal{L}$-rewritings, we require the following notion of phantom. Given an OMQ $\boldsymbol{q} = (\mathcal{O}, \psi(\boldsymbol{t}))$ with one answer

---

[7] Here, we (ab)use set-theoretic notation for lists and write $\boldsymbol{\ell} \subseteq \mathsf{tem}(\mathcal{A})$ to say that every element of $\boldsymbol{\ell}$ is an element of $\mathsf{tem}(\mathcal{A})$.

variable t and any integer number $k \in \mathbb{Z}$, by a k-*phantom* we understand an $\mathcal{L}$-sentence Φ_q^k such that $\mathfrak{S}_\mathcal{A} \models \Phi_q^k$ iff $\max \mathcal{A} + k \in \mathsf{ans}^\mathbb{Z}(q, \mathcal{A})$, for $k > 0$, and $\mathfrak{S}_\mathcal{A} \models \Phi_q^k$ iff $k \in \mathsf{ans}^\mathbb{Z}(q, \mathcal{A})$, for $k < 0$.

We discuss the relevant classes $\mathcal{L}$ of FO-formulas in the Sects. 3 and 5.

Remark 4. In the definition above, we did not allow any constants (numbers) from $\mathbb{Z}$ in rewritings. Note, however, that the MFO($<$)-formulas $\neg \exists t' \, (t' < t)$ and $\neg \exists t' \, (t' > t)$ define the minimal and maximal numbers that occur in any given data instance. In view of this, we can use the constants min and max in FO($<$)-rewritings as syntactic sugar.

Example 5. Consider the OMQ $q = (\mathcal{O}, A(t))$, where $\mathcal{O}$ is the same as in Example 2. It is not hard to see that

$$Q(t) = \exists s \left(A(s) \wedge P(t, s) \right) \ \vee \ \exists s \left(B(s) \wedge Q(t, s) \right)$$

is a rewriting of q in MFO($<$) extended with the predicates $P(t, s)$ saying that $t - s = 2n$ for some $n \in \mathbb{N}$, and $Q(t, s)$ saying that $t - s = 2n + 1$ for some $n \in \mathbb{N}$. Note that the quantified variable s ranges between $\min \mathcal{A}$ and $\max \mathcal{A}$ in any $\mathfrak{S}_\mathcal{A}$; in particular, $t \geq s$. Finally, observe that q is *not* FO($<$)-rewritable since properties such as 't is even' are not definable by FO($<$)-formulas [64,79].

FO-rewritability of an OMQ $q = (\mathcal{O}, \psi(t))$ defined above is closely related to the data complexity of the *OMQ answering problem* for q: given a data instance $\mathcal{A}$ and a tuple ℓ of elements from $\mathsf{tem}(\mathcal{A})$, decide whether $\ell \in \mathsf{ans}(q, \mathcal{A})$. If q is regarded to be fixed and only $\mathcal{A}$ is the input, we speak of the *data complexity* of this problem; if both q and $\mathcal{A}$ are regarded as input, then we speak about the *combined complexity.* For example, evaluating standard FO-queries (without an ontology) over FO-structures—in other words, the *model checking problem*—is PSPACE-complete for combined complexity and in the class AC^0 for data complexity[8] (which is one of the smallest classes in the complexity hierarchy); see, e.g., [64, Chapter 6]. It is to be noted that, to measure the data complexity, we should assume that our data instances $\mathcal{A}$ are encoded as strings that can be given as inputs to computational devices such as Turing machines; see [56,64] for details. Now, if the OMQ q is FO($<$)-rewritable (over data instances represented as such strings), then the OMQ answering problem for q is in LOGTIME-uniform AC^0. In what follows, when discussing various types of FO-rewritablity and the corresponding complexity classes, we do not want to go into the technical details of the string representation of data instances.

---

[8] Non-uniform AC^0 is the class of languages computable by bounded-depth polynomial-size circuits with unary NOT-gates and unbounded fan-in AND- and OR-gates. Evaluation of FO($<$)-formulas extended with *arbitrary* numeric predicates is known to be in non-uniform AC^0 for data complexity. If the circuits mentioned above can be generated by a Turing machine in, say, LOGTIME, we speak about LOGTIME-uniform AC^0. For example, evaluation of FO($<$)-formulas extended with PLUS and TIMES is in LOGTIME-uniform AC^0.

For events in *asynchronous* systems, we need interpretations with a dense order (in this paper, we use $\mathbb{Q}_2$), where $FO(<)$ is not able to express the function $t + a$, for a fixed number $a \in \mathbb{Q}_2$, which is obviously needed in our purging example. To make $FO(<)$ more expressive, we extend it with built-in binary predicates $\delta_{<a}(x, y)$ and $\delta_{=a}(x, y)$, for $a \in \mathbb{Q}_2^+$ (non-negative dyadic numbers), where the former stands for $0 \le x - y < a$ and the latter for $x - y = a$. This language is denoted by $MFO(<, \delta_{\le \mathbb{Q}_2}, \delta_{=\mathbb{Q}_2})$ and interpreted in structures of the form

$$\mathcal{I} = (\mathbb{T}, <, \{\delta_{<a} \mid a \in \mathbb{Q}_2^+\}, \{\delta_{=a} \mid a \in \mathbb{Q}_2^+\}, A_1^{\mathcal{I}}, A_2^{\mathcal{I}}, \dots) \tag{3}$$

with a temporal domain $\mathbb{T} \subseteq \mathbb{Q}_2$. In fact, there are two types of semantics for $MFO(<, \delta_{\le \mathbb{Q}_2}, \delta_{=\mathbb{Q}_2})$-formulas; cf. [72]. In one of them, known as the *continuous semantics*, the temporal domain of $\mathcal{I}$ is always set to $\mathbb{T} = \mathbb{Q}_2$ in the definition (2) of the set of certain answers $\mathsf{ans}(q, \mathcal{A})$ to an OMQ q over a data instance $\mathcal{A}$. In the alternative *pointwise* (or *event*) *semantics*, for each data instance $\mathcal{A}$, we only consider those models of $(\mathcal{O}, \mathcal{A})$ in (2) that have the domain $\mathbb{T} = \mathsf{tem}(\mathcal{A})$. We illustrate the difference between these two semantics by an example.

Example 6. Consider the OMQ $q = (\mathcal{O}, A(t))$ with

$$\mathcal{O} = \big\{ \forall t \left(\forall t' \left(\delta_{<2}(t, t') \to B(t') \right) \to B'(t) \right),$$
$$\forall t \left((\exists t' (\delta_{=1}(t, t') \land B'(t'))) \to A(t) \right) \big\}.$$

Suppose first that $\mathcal{A}_1 = \{B(0), B(1/2), C(3/2)\}$ and the semantics is pointwise. In this case, possible models of $(\mathcal{O}, \mathcal{A}_1)$ have domain $\{0, 1/2, 3/2\}$, and so we obtain $\mathsf{ans}(q, \mathcal{A}_1) = \{3/2\}$ because the first axiom gives B' at 0 and then at 1/2, from which we derive A at 3/2 by the second axiom.

Note that $\mathsf{ans}(q, \mathcal{A}_2) = \emptyset$ for $\mathcal{A}_2 = \{B(0), C(3/2)\}$. Under the continuous semantics, we cannot derive B' at 0 and 1/2 because there exist time instants before 0 and between 0 and 1/2 where B' can be false. Thus, in this case, $\mathsf{ans}(q, \mathcal{A}_1) = \emptyset$.

3   Ontology-Mediated Queries with *LTL*-Ontologies

In the previous section, we argued that monadic first-order logic $MFO(<)$ provides a natural formalism for ontology-mediated queries in the synchronous case, where the time flow is discrete $(\mathbb{Z}, <)$. Temporal instantaneous events can be described then by $MFO(<)$-formulas with one free variable. We recall now that, by the celebrated Kamp Theorem [57, 74], those formulas have exactly the same expressive power as the formulas of (propositional) *linear temporal logic LTL*, which are built from propositional variables using the Booleans and the temporal operators $\bigcirc_F$ (at the next moment of time), $\Diamond_F$ (eventually),

$\Box_F$ (always in the future), $\mathcal{U}$ (until), and their past-time counterparts $\bigcirc_P$ (at the previous moment), $\Diamond_P$ (some time in the past), $\Box_P$ (always in the past) and $\mathcal{S}$ (since); see [34,40,68] and further references therein.

We give the semantics of *LTL*-formulas via their *standard* MFO($<$)-*translation* † defined inductively as follows. For an atomic proposition A, we set $A^\dagger = A(t)$. The translation † commutes with the Booleans in the sense that $(\varkappa_1 \wedge \varkappa_2)^\dagger = \varkappa_1^\dagger \wedge \varkappa_2^\dagger$, $(\neg \varkappa)^\dagger = \neg(\varkappa^\dagger)$, etc. Finally, for the temporal operators, we set:

$$
\begin{aligned}
(\bigcirc_F \varkappa)^\dagger &= \varkappa^\dagger\{t+1/t\}, \\
(\Box_F \varkappa)^\dagger &= \forall t' \left((t < t') \rightarrow \varkappa^\dagger\{t'/t\}\right), \\
(\Diamond_F \varkappa)^\dagger &= \exists t' \left((t < t') \wedge \varkappa^\dagger\{t'/t\}\right), \\
(\varkappa \mathcal{U} \lambda)^\dagger &= \exists t' \left[(t < t') \wedge \lambda^\dagger\{t'/t\} \wedge \forall t'' \left((t < t'' < t') \rightarrow \varkappa^\dagger\{t''/t\}\right)\right],
\end{aligned}
$$

and symmetrically for the 'past' operators, for instance, $(\bigcirc_P \varkappa)^\dagger = \varkappa^\dagger\{t-1/t\}$, $(\Diamond_P \varkappa)^\dagger = \exists t' \left((t > t') \wedge \varkappa^\dagger\{t'/t\}\right)$, etc. In the translation above, t' and t'' are *fresh variables* and $\{t'/t\}$ means a substitution that replaces t with t'. Given a temporal interpretation $\mathcal{I}$ and an *LTL*-formula $\varkappa$, we define the *extension* $\varkappa^\mathcal{I}$ of $\varkappa$ in $\mathcal{I}$ as the set of integers $\varkappa^\mathcal{I} = \{n \in \mathbb{Z} \mid \mathcal{I} \models \varkappa^\dagger(n)\}$.

In this section, we introduce a number of fragments of *LTL* as possible temporal ontology languages and discuss FO-rewritability of various types of OMQs with ontologies in those fragments. Having in mind the OBDA application area for these languages, we somewhat modify the standard *LTL* terminology. For instance, instead of propositional variables, we prefer to speak about atomic concepts (similarly to concept names in Description Logic).

Thus, in this paper, we think of the alphabet of *LTL* as a countably infinite set of *atomic concepts* A_i, for $i < \omega$. *Basic temporal concepts*, C, are defined by the grammar

$$
C ::= A_i \mid \Box_F C \mid \Box_P C \mid \bigcirc_F C \mid \bigcirc_P C. \tag{4}
$$

An *LTL-ontology*, $\mathcal{O}$, is a finite set of *clauses* of the form

$$
C_1 \wedge \cdots \wedge C_k \rightarrow C_{k+1} \vee \cdots \vee C_{k+m}, \tag{5}
$$

where $k, m \geq 0$ and the C_i are basic temporal concepts. As usual, we denote the empty conjunction ($k = 0$) by $\top$ and the empty disjunction ($m = 0$) by $\bot$. We often refer to the clauses in $\mathcal{O}$ as *(ontology) axioms*. Intuitively, the axioms are supposed to hold at *every moment of time*. In other words, (5) is just a shortcut for the MFO($<$)-sentence

$$
\forall t \, (C_1^\dagger \wedge \cdots \wedge C_k^\dagger \rightarrow C_{k+1}^\dagger \vee \cdots \vee C_{k+m}^\dagger). \tag{6}
$$

It is true in an interpretation $\mathcal{I}$ iff

$$
C_1^\mathcal{I} \cap \cdots \cap C_k^\mathcal{I} \subseteq C_{k+1}^\mathcal{I} \cup \cdots \cup C_{k+m}^\mathcal{I}.
$$

An ontology $\mathcal{O}$ *entails* a clause (5) if this clause is true in every model $\mathcal{I}$ of $\mathcal{O}$.

We classify ontologies by the shape of their axioms[9] and the temporal operators that occur in them. Let $c \in \{horn, krom, core, bool\}$ and $o \in \{\Box, \bigcirc, \Box\bigcirc\}$. By an LTL_c^o-*ontology* we mean any *LTL*-ontology whose clauses satisfy the following restrictions on k and m in (5) indicated by c:

horn: $m \leq 1$,
krom: $k + m \leq 2$,
core: $k + m \leq 2$ and $m \leq 1$,
bool: any $k, m \geq 0$,

and may only contain occurrences of the (future and past) temporal operators indicated in o (for example, $o = \Box$ means that only $\Box_F$ and $\Box_P$ may occur in the temporal concepts). Note that an LTL_c^o-ontology of any type may contain *disjointness axioms* of the form $C_1 \wedge C_2 \to \bot$. Although both LTL_{krom}^o- and LTL_{core}^o-ontologies may only have *binary* clauses as axioms (with at most two concepts), only the former are allowed to contain *universal covering axioms* such as $\top \to C_1 \vee C_2$; in other words, $core = krom \cap horn$.

The definition above identifies a seemingly very restricted set of *LTL*-formulas as possible ontology axioms. For example, it completely disallows the use of the standard temporal operators $\Diamond_F$ (sometime in the future), $\Diamond_P$ (sometime in the past), $\mathcal{U}$ (until) and $\mathcal{S}$ (since). Whether or not these operators can be somehow *expressed* in a given fragment LTL_c^o (in the context of OMQ answering) depends on c and o. The following example clarifies the picture.

Example 7. Observe first that the clause $\Diamond_P A \to B$ is equivalent to the $LTL_{core}^\Box$ clause $A \to \Box_F B$. Also, the former clause can be expressed in $LTL_{core}^\bigcirc$ by three clauses: $A \to \bigcirc_F X$, $X \to \bigcirc_F X$ and $X \to B$, for a fresh atomic concept X that is not supposed to occur in any data instances.

To see why, we need a few definitions. By the *signature* of an ontology we mean the set of atomic concepts that occur in it. An ontology $\mathcal{O}'$ is called a *model conservative extension* of an ontology $\mathcal{O}$ if $\mathcal{O}' \models \mathcal{O}$, the signature of $\mathcal{O}$ is contained in the signature of $\mathcal{O}'$, and every model of $\mathcal{O}$ can be expanded to a model of $\mathcal{O}'$ by providing interpretations of the fresh symbols of $\mathcal{O}'$ and leaving the domain and the interpretation of the symbols in $\mathcal{O}$ unchanged. Observe that if $q = (\mathcal{O}, \varkappa)$ is an OMQ and $\mathcal{O}'$ a model conservative extension of $\mathcal{O}$, then the certain answers to q over a data instance $\mathcal{A}$ in the signature of $\mathcal{O}$ coincide with the certain answers to $q' = (\mathcal{O}', \varkappa)$ over $\mathcal{A}$. Thus, any FO-rewriting of q' is also an FO-rewriting of q.

The ontology $\mathcal{O}'$ obtained from $\mathcal{O}$ by replacing $\Diamond_P A \to B$ with $A \to \bigcirc_F X$, $X \to \bigcirc_F X$ and $X \to B$ is a model conservative extension of $\mathcal{O}$, and so we can use it for OBDA in place of $\mathcal{O}$.

The clause $A \to \Diamond_P B$ cannot be expressed in any of the LTL_{core}^o fragments but can be expressed in $LTL_{krom}^\Box$ by $A \wedge \Box_P X \to \bot$ and $\top \to X \vee B$. The clauses of the form $A \wedge B \to C$ are in the LTL_{horn}^o fragments but not in LTL_{core}^o or

---

[9] This classification originates in the *DL-Lite* family of description logics [6].

LTL^o_{krom}. The clause $A \mathcal{U} B \to C$ can be expressed in $LTL^\bigcirc_{horn}$ by $B \to \bigcirc_P X$ and $X \wedge A \to \bigcirc_P X$ and $X \to C$, also for a fresh X. The clause $A \to B \mathcal{U} C$ can be expressed in $LTL^{\square\bigcirc}_{bool}$ using the well-known fixed-point unfolding of $B \mathcal{U} C$ as $\bigcirc_F C \vee (\bigcirc_F B \wedge \bigcirc_F (B \mathcal{U} C))$, which gives rise to 4 clauses $A \to X$, $X \to \bigcirc_F C \vee \bigcirc_F B$, $X \to \bigcirc_F C \vee \bigcirc_F X$ and $A \to \Diamond_F C$ (the $\Diamond_F$ in the last clause can be replaced with $\square_F$ as described above).

Exercise 8. Imagine that we would like to query the data about the status of a research article submitted to a certain journal. We are interested in temporal events such as *Submission, Notification, Accept, Reject, Revise, Publication*. Our background knowledge about these events can be formulated as an *LTL*-ontology $\mathcal{O}$ with the axioms below. We invite the reader to transform those axioms to the required form (5) using common sense and the previous example.

$$Notification \leftrightarrow Reject \vee Accept \vee Revise, \tag{7}$$

$$Reject \wedge Accept \to \bot, \quad Revise \wedge Accept \to \bot, \quad Reject \wedge Revise \to \bot \tag{8}$$

(at any moment of time, every notification is either a reject, accept, or revision notification, and it can only be one of them)

$$P \to \neg \Diamond_P P \wedge \neg \Diamond_F P \tag{9}$$

(for every event P we are interested in except *Notification* and *Revise*, P can happen only once for any article)

$$Publication \to \Diamond_P Accept, \quad Notification \to \Diamond_P Submission, \tag{10}$$

$$Accept \to \Diamond_F Publication, \quad Submission \to \Diamond_F Notification, \tag{11}$$

$$Revise \to \Diamond_F Notification \tag{12}$$

(obvious necessary pre-conditions for publication and notification and also the post-conditions—eventual consequences—of acceptance, submission and a revision notification; for simplicity, we assume that after a revision notification the authors always eventually receive a notification regarding a revised version)

$$Accept \vee Reject \to \neg \Diamond_F Notification \tag{13}$$

(acceptance and rejection notifications are final).

We distinguish between three types of ontology-mediated queries (OMQs) with *LTL*-ontologies:

- *Atomic* OMQs (or OMAQs, for short) take the form $q = (\mathcal{O}, A(t))$ with an atomic concept A.
- A *positive ontology-mediated instance query* (OMPIQ) $(\mathcal{O}, \varkappa(t))$ with a *positive LTL*-formula $\varkappa$, which is constructed from atoms in the standard way but using $\wedge$ and $\vee$ only (or an equivalent MFO($<$)-formula with one free variable t, which will be discussed below).

- *Quasi-positive* OMQs (or OMQPQs) $q = (\mathcal{O}, \psi(t))$ have a *quasi-positive* MFO($<$)-formula $\psi(t)$, which is recursively constructed using $\wedge$, $\vee$, $\forall$, $\exists$, as well as the *guarded* universal quantification of the form

$$\forall y\left((x < y < z) \to \varphi\right), \qquad \forall y\left((x < y) \to \varphi\right), \qquad \forall y\left((y < z) \to \varphi\right), \quad (14)$$

  where φ is a quasi-positive MFO($<$)-formula.
- Finally, general OMQs $q = (\mathcal{O}, \psi(t))$ may have arbitrary MFO($<$)-formulas $\psi(t)$.

Example 9. Consider $\mathcal{O}$ from Exercise 8. Then $(\mathcal{O}, \textit{Revise}(t))$ is an OMAQ asking when the paper was sent back for revision. As an example of OMPIQ, consider $(\mathcal{O}, (\Diamond_P \textit{Revise} \wedge \textit{Accept})(t))$ asking when (and whether) the paper was accepted after revision. As an example of OMQPQ, consider $(\mathcal{O}, \psi(t, t'))$, where

$$\psi(t, t') = \exists x\left((t < x < t') \wedge \textit{Revise}(x)\right) \wedge \textit{Submission}(t) \wedge \textit{Accept}(t'),$$

looking for time intervals $[t, t']$ over which a submitted article underwent at least one revision before acceptance. Finally, an example of a (general) OMQ is $(\mathcal{O}, \psi(t))$ with

$$\psi(t) = \textit{Submission}(t) \wedge \neg \exists t'\left((t' > t) \wedge (\textit{Accept}(t') \vee \textit{Reject}(t'))\right).$$

that checks if and when the article was submitted without accept or reject decision so far.

OMAQs are the simplest and arguably most convenient queries from the user's point of view as they presuppose that definitions of relevant events should be provided by the ontology. However, they are not suitable in situations when more than one answer variable is needed as, for example, in the query 'find all timestamps t_1 and t_3 with $t_1 < t_3$, for which there is t_2 such that $t_1 < t_2 < t_3$ and some event (say, the temperature is lower than $50\,°C$) happens everywhere in the interval $[t_1, t_2]$ and some other event (say, the temperature is higher than $90\,°C$) happens everywhere in the interval $[t_2, t_3]$'. As we shall see below, arbitrary OMQs have worse computational properties compared to OMQPQs. In fact, one can show the following version of Kamp's Theorem: every consistent quasi-positive MFO($<$)-formula $\psi(t)$ with one free variable t is equivalent over $(\mathbb{Z}, <)$ to a positive *LTL*-formula constructed using any temporal operators and the 'positive' Boolean connectives $\wedge$ and $\vee$ only [10]. Another important semantic characterisation of quasi-positive formulas is as follows. Given temporal interpretations $\mathcal{I}_1$ and $\mathcal{I}_2$, we write $\mathcal{I}_1 \preceq \mathcal{I}_2$ if $A^{\mathcal{I}_1} \subseteq A^{\mathcal{I}_2}$, for every atomic concept A. An MFO($<$)-formula $\psi(t)$ is called *monotone* if $\mathcal{I}_1 \models \psi(n)$ and $\mathcal{I}_1 \preceq \mathcal{I}_2$ imply $\mathcal{I}_2 \models \psi(n)$, for any tuple n in $\mathbb{Z}$. Now, one can show [10] that an MFO($<$)-formula is monotone iff it is equivalent over $(\mathbb{Z}, <)$ to a quasi-positive MFO($<$)-formula.

Let us now focus on rewritability of *LTL* OMQs. Is there a 'standard' query language into which any such OMQ can be rewritten? The following example shows that FO($<$), even extended with arbitrary arithmetic predicates, is not powerful enough for this purpose:

Example 10. Consider the OMAQ $q = (\mathcal{O}, B_0)$, where $\mathcal{O}$ consists of the axioms

$$\bigcirc_P B_k \wedge A_0 \rightarrow B_k \quad \text{and} \quad \bigcirc_P B_{1-k} \wedge A_1 \rightarrow B_k, \quad \text{for} \;\; k = 0, 1.$$

For every binary word $e = e_1 \ldots e_n \in \{0, 1\}^n$, we take the data instance $\mathcal{A}_e = \{B_0(0)\} \cup \{A_{e_i}(i) \mid 0 < i \le n\}$. It is not hard to check that n is a certain answer to q over $\mathcal{A}_e$ iff the number of 1s in e is even (PARITY): intuitively, the word is processed starting from the minimal timestamp and moving towards the maximal one, and the first axiom preserves B_i if the current symbol is 0, whereas the second axiom toggles B_i if the current symbol is 1. As PARITY is not in AC^0 [39], it follows that q is not FO-rewritable even if *arbitrary* numeric predicates are allowed in rewritings.

A natural and more expressive target language for rewritings is FO(RPR) that extends FO with the successor relation and *relational primitive recursion* (RPR, for short). Evaluation of FO(RPR)-formulas is known to be NC^1-complete[10] for data complexity [32], with $AC^0 \subsetneq NC^1 \subseteq L$. We remind the reader that, using RPR, we can construct formulas such as

$$\varPhi = \begin{bmatrix} Q_1(z_1, t) \equiv \Theta_1\big(z_1, t, Q_1(z_1, t-1), \ldots, Q_n(z_n, t-1)\big) \\ \ldots \\ Q_n(z_n, t) \equiv \Theta_n\big(z_n, t, Q_1(z_1, t-1), \ldots, Q_n(z_n, t-1)\big) \end{bmatrix} \varPsi,$$

where the part of $\varPhi$ within $[\ldots]$ defines recursively, via the FO(RPR)-formulas Θ_i, the interpretations of the predicates Q_i in the FO(RPR)-formula $\varPsi$ (see Example 11 below). Note that the recursion starts at $t = 0$ and assumes that $Q_i(z, -1)$ is false for all Q_i, $i = 1, \ldots, n$, and all z. Thus, the truth value of $Q_i(z, 0)$ is computed by substituting falsehood $\bot$ for all $Q_i(z, -1)$. For every $t = 1, 2, \ldots$, the recursion is then applied in the obvious way.

We illustrate relational primitive recursion by a concrete example.

Example 11. The OMQ $q = (\mathcal{O}, B_0)$ from Example 10 can be rewritten to the following FO(RPR)-formula:

$$Q(t) = \begin{bmatrix} Q_0(t) \equiv \Theta_0 \\ Q_1(t) \equiv \Theta_1 \end{bmatrix} Q_0(t),$$

where, for $k = 0, 1$,

$$\Theta_k(t, Q_0(t-1), Q_1(t-1)) = B_k(t) \vee \big(Q_k(t-1) \wedge A_0(t)\big) \vee \big(Q_{1-k}(t-1) \wedge A_1(t)\big).$$

As noted above, the recursion starts from the minimal timestamp 0 in the data instance (with $Q_i(-1)$ regarded as false) and proceeds to the maximal one.

The next theorem shows that all *LTL* OMQs can be rewritten into FO(RPR). As follows from [32, Proposition 4.3], this means that we can also rewrite our OMQs into the language MSO(<) of *monadic second-order* formulas that are built from atoms of the form $A(t)$ and $t < t'$ using the Booleans, first-order quantifiers $\forall t$ and $\exists t$, and second-order quantifiers $\forall A$ and $\exists A$ [28].

---

[10] NC^1 is the class of languages computable by a family of polynomial-size logarithmic-depth circuits with gates of at most two inputs.

Remark 12. It is worth reminding the reader (see [33, 78, 79] for details) that, by the Büchi–Elgot–Trakhtenbrot Theorem [28, 35, 81], MSO($<$)-sentences define exactly the class of regular languages. FO(RPR), extended with the predicates PLUS and TIMES or, equivalently, with one predicate BIT [56], captures exactly the languages in NC^1 (which are not necessarily regular) [32].

Theorem 13. *Every LTL OMQ is FO(RPR)- and MSO($<$)-rewritable, and so can be answered in* NC^1 *for data complexity.*

Note that the SQL:1999 ISO standard contains a WITH RECURSIVE construct that allows users to implement various FO-queries with relational primitive recursion such as the query in Example 11, which cannot be expressed in FO without recursion.

The next example shows that our OMQs can simulate arbitrary finite automata, and so FO(RPR) appears to be an optimal target language for rewritings in general (since there exist NC^1-complete regular languages).

Example 14. Let $\mathfrak{A}$ be a DFA with a tape alphabet Γ, a set of states Q, an initial state $q_0 \in Q$, an accepting state $q_1 \in Q$ and a transition function $\to$: we write $q \to_e q'$ if $\mathfrak{A}$ moves to a state $q' \in Q$ from a state $q \in Q$ while reading $e \in \Gamma$. (Without loss of generality we assume that $\mathfrak{A}$ has only one accepting state.) We take atomic concepts A_e for tape symbols $e \in \Gamma$ and atomic concepts B_q for states $q \in Q$, and consider the OMAQ $\boldsymbol{q} = (\mathcal{O}, B_{q_0})$, where

$$\mathcal{O} \;=\; \big\{\, \bigcirc_P B_{q'} \wedge A_e \to B_q \mid q \to_e q' \,\big\}.$$

For any input word $\boldsymbol{e} = (e_1 \dots e_n) \in \Gamma^*$, we set

$$\mathcal{A}_e \;=\; \big\{\, B_{q_0}(0) \,\big\} \;\cup\; \big\{\, A_{e_i}(i) \mid 0 < i \leq n \,\big\}.$$

It is easy to see that $\mathfrak{A}$ accepts $\boldsymbol{e}$ iff $\max(\mathcal{A}_e) \in \mathrm{ans}(\boldsymbol{q}, \mathcal{A}_e)$. We invite the reader to show that $\mathfrak{A}$ accepts $\boldsymbol{e}$ iff $0 \in \mathrm{ans}(\boldsymbol{q}', \mathcal{A}_e)$, where $\boldsymbol{q}' = (\mathcal{O}', \psi(t))$,

$$\mathcal{O}' \;=\; \big\{\, \overline{B}_q \wedge B_q \to \bot, \; \top \to B_q \vee \overline{B}_q \mid q \in Q \,\big\},$$

and $\psi(t)$ is the standard FO-translation of the *LTL*-formula

$$\varkappa = \; B_{q_1} \vee \bigvee_{q \to_e q'} \Diamond_P^+ (\bigcirc_P B_{q'} \wedge A_e \wedge \overline{B}_q),$$

where $\Diamond_P^+ C$ is an abbreviation for $C \vee \Diamond_P C$. (Hint: $\overline{B}_q$ represents the complement of B_q, and $\varkappa$ is equivalent to formula $\big[\, \bigwedge_{q \to_e q'} \Box_P^+ (\bigcirc_P B_{q'} \wedge A_e \to B_q) \,\big] \to B_{q_1}$, where $\Box_P^+ C$ is an abbreviation for $C \wedge \Box_P C$.)

Now we present classes of OMQs that are rewritable to FO-formulas without recursion. Namely, we have rewritings of two types. One type is the usual FO($<$)-formulas. The other one comprises FO($<, \equiv_\mathbb{N}$)-formulas that can use numeric predicates $x \equiv 0 \pmod{n}$, for any fixed $n \in \mathbb{N}$. (As shown in [16], FO($<, \equiv_\mathbb{N}$) is exactly the class of regular languages in AC^0.)

Exercise 15. Note that FO(RPR) does not contain $x < y$ or $x \equiv 0 \,(\text{mod } n)$, for $n > 1$, as atoms. We invite the reader to show that both of them can be expressed in FO(RPR) in the sense that (i) there exists an FO(RPR)-formula $\varphi_<(x,y)$ such that $\mathfrak{S} \models \varphi_<(a,b)$ iff $\mathfrak{S} \models a < b$, for any FO-structure $\mathfrak{S}$ and a, b in its domain; and (ii) for any $n > 1$, there exists an FO(RPR)-formula $\varphi_n(x)$ such that $\mathfrak{S} \models \varphi_n(a)$ iff $\mathfrak{S} \models a \equiv 0 \,(\text{mod } n)$, for any FO-structure $\mathfrak{S}$ and a in its domain. (A solution to (i) can be found in [32] and a solution to (ii) in [10].) As a consequence, we obtain that, for every FO($<, \equiv_{\mathbb{N}}$)-formula, there is an equivalent FO(RPR)-formula.

Theorem 16. *Any $LTL^{\bigcirc}_{krom}$ OMAQ is FO($<, \equiv_{\mathbb{N}}$)-rewritable, and so can be answered in AC^0 for data complexity.*

Proof (Sketch). Suppose $\boldsymbol{q} = (\mathcal{O}, A)$ is an $LTL^{\bigcirc}_{krom}$ OMAQ. By a *literal*, L, we mean an atomic concept in $\boldsymbol{q}$ or its negation. We use $\bigcirc^n L$ in place of $\bigcirc^n_F L$ if $n > 0$, L if $n = 0$, and $\bigcirc^{-n}_P L$ if $n < 0$. We write $\mathcal{O} \models L \to \bigcirc^k L'$ if $\mathcal{I} \models \forall t\,(L \to \bigcirc^k L')^\dagger$ in every model $\mathcal{I}$ of $\mathcal{O}$. For any data instance $\mathcal{A}$ consistent with $\mathcal{O}$, we have:

$$\ell \in \mathsf{ans}^{\mathbb{Z}}(\boldsymbol{q}, \mathcal{A}) \quad \text{iff} \quad \text{either } \mathcal{O} \models \top \to A$$
$$\text{or } \mathcal{O} \models B \to \bigcirc^{\ell-n} A, \text{ for some } B(n) \in \mathcal{A}.$$

Given literals L and L', let $\mathfrak{A}_{L,L'}$ be an NFA whose tape alphabet is $\{0\}$, the states are the literals, with L initial and L' accepting, and whose transitions are of the form $L_1 \to_0 L_2$, for $\mathcal{O} \models L_1 \to \bigcirc L_2$ (without loss of generality we assume that $\mathcal{O}$ does not contain nested $\bigcirc$). It is easy to see that $\mathfrak{A}_{L,L'}$ accepts 0^k $(k > 0)$ iff $\mathcal{O} \models L \to \bigcirc^k L'$. By [31,80], there are $N = O(|\mathfrak{A}_{L,L'}|^2)$ arithmetic progressions $a_i + b_i \mathbb{N} = \{a_i + b_i \cdot m \mid m \geq 0\}$, $1 \leq i \leq N$, such that $0 \leq a_i, b_i \leq |\mathfrak{A}_{L,L'}|$ and $\mathfrak{A}_{L,L'}$ accepts 0^k iff $k \in a_i + b_i \mathbb{N}$ for some i, $1 \leq i \leq N$. These progressions give rise to the FO-rewriting we need. To illustrate, suppose $\boldsymbol{q} = (\mathcal{O}, A)$ and

$$\mathcal{O} = \{A \to \bigcirc B,\ B \to \bigcirc C,\ C \to \bigcirc D,\ D \to \bigcirc A,\ D \to \bigcirc E,\ E \to \bigcirc D\}.$$

The NFA $\mathfrak{A}_{B,A}$ (more precisely, the states reachable from B) is shown below,

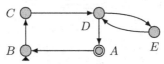

and for $L \in \{A, C, D, E\}$, $\mathfrak{A}_{L,A}$ is the same NFA but with the initial state L. It is readily seen that $\mathfrak{A}_{B,A}$ accepts 0^k iff $k \in 3 + 2\mathbb{N}$, which can be described by the formula

$$\varphi_{B,A}(t) = \exists s\,\big(B(s) \,\wedge\, (t - s \in a + b\mathbb{N})\big),$$

where $a = 3$, $b = 2$, and $(t - s \in 3 + 2\mathbb{N})$ is an abbreviation for

$$\exists n\,[(n = s + 3) \wedge (((n \equiv 0\,(\text{mod } 2)) \wedge (t \equiv 0\,(\text{mod } 2))) \vee$$
$$\exists n', t'\,((n' = n + 1) \wedge (t' = t + 1) \wedge (n' \equiv 0\,(\text{mod } 2)) \wedge (t' \equiv 0\,(\text{mod } 2))))]$$

(the reader is invited to provide the definition of $(t - s \in a + b\mathbb{N})$ for arbitrary a and b). Similarly, for $\mathfrak{A}_{E,A}$, we have $a = b = 2$. (Note that in general more than one progression is needed to characterise automata $\mathfrak{A}_{L,A}$.) To obtain an FO($<, \equiv_\mathbb{N}$)-rewriting of q, we take a disjunction of $\varphi_{L,A}(t)$, for all literals L. One can also construct any phantom $\Phi^k_{(\mathcal{O},A)}$ in FO($<, \equiv_\mathbb{N}$). $\qquad\square$

Theorem 17. *Any $LTL^\square_{bool}$ OMAQ is FO($<$)-rewritable, and so can be answered in AC^0 for data complexity.*

Proof (Sketch). Given an $LTL^\square_{bool}$-ontology $\mathcal{O}$, we construct an NFA $\mathfrak{A}$ that takes as input a data instance $\mathcal{A}$ written as the word $\mathcal{A}_0, \ldots, \mathcal{A}_k$, where $k = \max \mathcal{A}$ and $\mathcal{A}_i = \{A \mid A(i) \in \mathcal{A}\}$. Let Σ be the set of temporal concepts in $\mathcal{O}$ and their negations. Each state of $\mathfrak{A}$ is a maximal set $S \subseteq \Sigma$ that is consistent with $\mathcal{O}$; let $\boldsymbol{S}$ be the set of all such states. For $S, S' \in \boldsymbol{S}$ and a tape symbol (set of concept names) X, we set $S \to_X S'$ just in case $X \subseteq S'$, $\square_F\beta \in S$ iff $\beta, \square_F\beta \in S'$, and $\square_P\beta \in S'$ iff $\beta, \square_P\beta \in S$. A state $S \in \boldsymbol{S}$ is *accepting* if $\mathfrak{A}$ has an infinite 'ascending' chain $S \to_\emptyset S_1 \to_\emptyset \ldots$; S is *initial* if $\mathfrak{A}$ has an infinite 'descending' chain $\cdots \to_\emptyset S_1 \to_\emptyset S$. The NFA $\mathfrak{A}$ *simulates* $\mathcal{O}$ in the following sense: for any ABox $\mathcal{A}$, concept name A and $\ell \in \mathbb{Z}$, we have $\ell \in \text{ans}^\mathbb{Z}((\mathcal{O}, A), \mathcal{A})$ iff $\mathfrak{A}$ does not contain an *accepting path* $S_0 \to_{X_1} \cdots \to_{X_m} S_m$ (S_0 initial and S_m accepting) such that $A \notin S_\ell$, $X_{i+j} = \mathcal{A}_j$ if $0 \le j \le k$, and $X_j = \emptyset$ otherwise, for some i, $0 < i \le m - k$.

Define an equivalence relation, $\sim$, on $\boldsymbol{S}$ by taking $S \sim S'$ iff $S = S'$ or $\mathfrak{A}$ has a cycle with both S and S'. Let $[S]$ be the $\sim$-equivalence class of S. One can check that $S \to_X S'$ implies $S_1 \to_X S'$, for any $S_1 \in [S]$. Let $\mathfrak{A}'$ be the NFA with states $[S]$, for $S \in \boldsymbol{S}$, and transitions $[S] \to_X [S']$ iff $S_1 \to_X S'_1$, for some $S_1 \in [S]$ and $S'_1 \in [S']$. The initial (accepting) states of $\mathfrak{A}'$ are all $[S]$ with initial (accepting) S. The NFA $\mathfrak{A}'$ also simulates $\mathcal{O}$ and contains no cycles other than trivial loops, which makes it possible to express the simulation condition by an FO($<$)-formula. For example, $\mathfrak{A}'$ for $\mathcal{O} = \{A \to \square_P B, \square_P B \to C\}$ is shown below, where all states are initial and accepting, and negated concepts omitted:

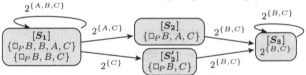

Let $q = (\mathcal{O}, C)$. Take all accepting paths π in $\mathfrak{A}'$ with pairwise distinct states at least one of which has a set without C. Thus, for $\pi = [S_1] \to_{\{A\}} [S_2] \to_\emptyset [S_3]$, a set in $[S_3]$ has no C, and the simulation condition for π, which makes sure that $\neg C$ holds at t, can be written as

$$\exists t_1, t_2 \big[\forall t' \big((t' < t_1) \to \text{loop}_{[S_1]}(t') \big) \wedge \text{sym}_{\{A\}}(t_1) \wedge$$
$$\forall t' \big((t_1 < t' < t_2) \to \text{loop}_{[S_2]}(t') \big) \wedge \text{sym}_\emptyset(t_2) \wedge$$
$$\forall t' \big((t' > t_2) \to \text{loop}_{[S_3]}(t') \big) \wedge (t \ge t_2) \wedge \neg C(t) \big],$$

where $\mathsf{sym}_{\{A\}}(t) = A(t) \wedge \neg B(t) \wedge \neg C(t)$ and $\mathsf{sym}_\emptyset(t) = \neg A(t) \wedge \neg B(t) \wedge \neg C(t)$ define transitions $\to_{\{A\}}$ and $\to_\emptyset$ in π, and $\mathsf{loop}_{[S_1]} = \top$, $\mathsf{loop}_{[S_3]} = \neg A(t)$ and $\mathsf{loop}_{[S_2]} = \bot$ say that $[S_1]$ and $[S_3]$ have loop transitions with any input and any input but A, respectively, but $[S_2]$ has no loop. To obtain an FO($<$)-rewriting of $\boldsymbol{q}$, we take a disjunction of such formulas for all accepting paths π in $\mathfrak{A}'$ and negate it. It is also possible to construct any phantom $\Phi^k_{(O,A)}$ in FO($<$). $\square$

Theorem 18. *Any* $LTL^{\square\bigcirc}_{krom}$ *OMAQ is* FO($<, \equiv_\mathbb{N}$)*-rewritable, and so can be answered in* AC^0 *for data complexity.*

Proof (Sketch). The proof utilises the monotonicity of the $\square$ operators, similarly to the proof of Theorem 17. However, the latter relies on partially-ordered NFAs accepting the models of (O, A), which do not work in the presence of $\bigcirc$. Our key observation here is that every model of (O, A) has at most $O(|O|)$ timestamps such that the same $\square$-concepts hold between any two nearest of them. The placement of these timestamps and their concept-types can be described by an FO($<$)-formula. However, to check whether these types are compatible (i.e., satisfiable in some model), we require FO($<, \equiv_\mathbb{N}$)-formulas similar to those in the proof of Theorem 16. $\square$

So far, we have considered the simplest class of OMQs with atomic queries. But what if we are interested in spotting complex events whose definitions are not provided by the available ontology? Or what if we need queries with multiple answer variables? Can we still rewrite some of the resulting OMQs into FO-queries without recursion? First, observe that we cannot use arbitrary MFO-formulas as queries if we want to achieve FO-rewritability without recursion. This is the case already for OMQs with empty ontologies as shown by Example 14. It also follows from the same example that OMQs $\boldsymbol{q} = (O, \psi(\boldsymbol{t}))$ with monotone (quasi-positive) ψ and O containing only binary disjunctions, can simulate an arbitrary DFA.

On the other hand, we show now how to obtain a strong positive rewritability result for OMQs with a Horn ontology and a monotone query. The key property of Horn ontologies required in the proof of this result is the following fact, which is well known and documented in the Prolog and datalog settings [1,4]. The *intersection* of two interpretations $\mathcal{I}_1$ and $\mathcal{I}_2$ is the interpretation $\mathcal{I}_3$ such that $A^{\mathcal{I}_3} = A^{\mathcal{I}_1} \cap A^{\mathcal{I}_2}$, for every atomic concept A.

Example 19. Consider $\mathcal{I}_1$ with $A^{\mathcal{I}_1} = \{0, 5\}$, $B^{\mathcal{I}_1} = \{n \in \mathbb{Z} \mid n > 0\}$ and $\mathcal{I}_2$ with $A^{\mathcal{I}_2} = \{-5, 0\}$, $B^{\mathcal{I}_2} = \mathbb{Z}$. Then the intersection of $\mathcal{I}_1$ and $\mathcal{I}_2$ is $\mathcal{I}_3$ with $A^{\mathcal{I}_3} = \{0\}$, $B^{\mathcal{I}_3} = \{n \in \mathbb{Z} \mid n > 0\}$.

In general, if we take a pair of models of (O, A), their intersection does not need to be a model of (O, A). The reader is invited to verify this on the simple KB $(\{A \to B \vee C\}, \{A(0)\})$. However, for O in $LTL^{\square\bigcirc}_{horn}$, the intersection of models of (O, A) will be always a model of (O, A), too. Indeed, in Example 19 both $\mathcal{I}_1$ and $\mathcal{I}_2$ are models of $(O, A) = (\{A \to \square_F B\}, \{A(0)\})$ and so is their intersection $\mathcal{I}_3$. The *canonical* (or *minimal*) *model* $\mathcal{C}_{O,A}$ of (O, A), is the intersection of all the models of (O, A). For $(\{A \to \square_F B\}, \{A(0)\})$, the canonical model is $\mathcal{I}_3$ from Example 19.

Theorem 20. Let $q = (\mathcal{O}, \psi(t))$ be an OMQPQ with an $LTL_{horn}^{\square\lozenge}$-ontology $\mathcal{O}$ and let $\mathcal{L}$ be $FO(<)$ or $FO(<, \equiv_{\mathbb{N}})$. Suppose that, for each atomic A in ψ,

- every OMAQ $(\mathcal{O}, A)$ is $\mathcal{L}$-rewritable
- there exists a phantom $\Phi_{(\mathcal{O},A)}^k$ in $\mathcal{L}$, for every $k \in \mathbb{Z}$

Then, $(\mathcal{O}, \psi(t))$ is $\mathcal{L}$-rewritable.

Proof (Sketch). To simplify presentation, we assume that $\mathcal{O}$ does not contain $\perp$. The proof relies on the fact that, for any $\mathcal{A}$, there exists a canonical model $\mathcal{C}_{\mathcal{O},\mathcal{A}}$ of $(\mathcal{O}, \mathcal{A})$. Then, using the monotonicy of ψ, one can establish the following property, for all $\ell \in \mathsf{tem}(\mathcal{A})$:

$$\ell \in \mathsf{ans}(q, \mathcal{A}) \qquad \text{iff} \qquad \mathcal{C}_{\mathcal{O},\mathcal{A}} \models \psi(\ell). \qquad (15)$$

The second important component of the proof is the fact that every OMPIQ $(\mathcal{O}, \varkappa)$ is $\mathcal{L}$-rewritable and has phantoms $\Phi_{(\mathcal{O},\varkappa)}^k$ in $\mathcal{L}$ if every OMAQ $(\mathcal{O}, A)$ with A from $\varkappa$ is such. This fact is shown by induction on the construction of $\varkappa$ using (15). As an example, we show how to construct a rewriting $\varphi_\varkappa(t)$ for $\varkappa = \lozenge_F A$ from a rewriting $\varphi_A(t)$ for A and phantoms $\Phi_{(\mathcal{O},A)}^k$. By the semantics of $\lozenge_F$, we could take

$$\varphi_\varkappa(t) = \exists t' \left((t' > t) \wedge \varphi_A(t') \right) \vee \bigvee_{k > 0} \Phi_{(\mathcal{O},A)}^k.$$

Indeed, provided that 'infinite' formulas are allowed in rewritings, it is not hard to check, using (15), that $\varphi_\varkappa(t)$ is a rewriting of $(\mathcal{O}, \varkappa)$. To avoid the 'infinite' disjunction, we need an additional *periodicity* property of the $LTL_{horn}^{\square\lozenge}$ canonical models: for every ontology $\mathcal{O}$, there are positive integers $s_\mathcal{O}$ and $p_\mathcal{O}$ such that, for any data instance $\mathcal{A}$,

$$t_\mathcal{O}(n) = t_{\mathcal{O},\mathcal{A}}(n + p_\mathcal{O}), \text{ for } n \geq \max \mathcal{A} + s_\mathcal{O}.$$

In view of this periodicity, we can finitise the 'infinite' rewriting of $(\mathcal{O}, \varkappa)$ by taking

$$\varphi_\varkappa(t) = \exists t' \left((t' > t) \wedge \varphi_A(t') \right) \vee \bigvee_{0 < k < s_\mathcal{O} + p_\mathcal{O}} \Phi_{(\mathcal{O},A)}^k.$$

The reader is invited to define phantoms $\Phi_{(\mathcal{O},\varkappa)}^k$ for $(\mathcal{O}, \varkappa)$ and $k > 0$ using the method above.

The third and last important component of this proof is that every monotone formula $\psi(t)$ is equivalent to a disjunction $\varphi(t) = \bigvee_{l=1}^k \varphi_l(t)$ of formulas of the following form, for $l = 1, \dots, k$:

$$\varphi_l(t) = \exists x_1, \dots, x_n \left[\bigwedge_{i=1}^m (t_i = x_{j_i}) \wedge (x_1 < \cdots < x_n) \wedge \bigwedge_{i=1}^n \alpha_i(x_i) \wedge \right.$$

$$\left. \bigwedge_{i=1}^{n-1} \forall y \left((x_i < y < x_{i+1}) \rightarrow \beta_i(y) \right) \right], \quad (16)$$

where the first conjunction contains $(t_i = x_1)$ and $(t_j = x_n)$ with free variables $t_i, t_j \in \boldsymbol{t}$, and the α_i and β_i are FO($<$)-formulas with one free variable equivalent to some OMPIQs $(\mathcal{O}, \varkappa_i)$ and $(\mathcal{O}, \lambda_i)$ (respectively). This equivalence result is shown using Rabinovich's proof of Kamp's Theorem [74]. Let us assume that $\psi(\boldsymbol{t})$ is a disjunction of formulas (16), and substitute in it each $\alpha_i(x_i)$ by $\varphi_{\varkappa_i}(x_i)$, where $\varphi_{\varkappa_i}(x_i)$ is a rewriting of $(\mathcal{O}, \varkappa_i)$, and similarly for $\beta_i(y)$. It is then straightforward to verify, relying on (15), that the result of this substitution is a rewriting of $(\mathcal{O}, \psi(\boldsymbol{t}))$. $\qquad\qquad\qquad\qquad\qquad\qquad\qquad\qquad\qquad\qquad\qquad\qquad\quad\square$

Corollary 21. *All monotone* $LTL^{\square\bigcirc}_{core}$ *OMQs are* FO($<, \equiv_{\mathbb{N}}$)*-rewritable, and all monotone* $LTL^{\square}_{horn}$ *OMQs are* FO($<$)*-rewritable.*

4   OBDA with Temporalised *DL-Lite*

The OMQs considered so far are one-dimensional. For example, the ontology from Exercise 8 captures background knowledge about temporal events that can happen with one article submitted to a journal. If we want to use OBDA in order to query data about other articles, authors, co-authors, editors, etc., we need a language that is capable of representing knowledge about a second dimension, a domain populated by those articles, authors, co-authors, editors, and relationships between them.

Description logics (DLs) [12,13] form a prominent family of knowledge representation formalisms designed specifically for atemporal domains of that sort. However, far from all of the existing DLs are suitable for OBDA because OMQs with DL ontologies are not necessarily rewritable to standard target query languages such as FO (which is essentially SQL) or datalog; for more details we refer the reader to the course [61]. The *DL-Lite* family of DLs was developed for OBDA with relational databases and with the aim of guaranteeing FO-rewritability of all OMQs with conjunctive queries [6,29,73,84]. *DL-Lite* logics also underpin the *OWL 2 QL* profile of the Web Ontology Language OWL 2 standardised by the W3C.

We illustrate *DL-Lite* by a simple example (borrowed from [21]); for a detailed introduction to OBDA with *OWL 2 QL*, we refer the reader to [59,61].

Example 22. Consider the following ontology $\mathcal{O}$ given in the DL syntax and, for the reader's convenience, translated into first-order logic:

$$ProjectManager \sqsubseteq \exists isAssistedBy.PA$$
$$\forall x \left(ProjectManager(x) \rightarrow \exists y \left(isAssistedBy(x, y) \wedge PA(y) \right) \right)$$
$$\exists managesProject \sqsubseteq ProjectManager$$
$$\forall x \left(\exists y \, managesProject(x, y) \rightarrow ProjectManager(x) \right)$$
$$ProjectManager \sqsubseteq Staff$$
$$\forall x \left(ProjectManager(x) \rightarrow Staff(x) \right)$$
$$PA \sqsubseteq Secretary$$
$$\forall x \left(PA(x) \rightarrow Secretary(x) \right)$$

Here, *ProjectManager*, *PA*, *Staff*, and *Secretary* are *concept names* (corresponding to the unary predicates in the FO-translations), while *isAssistedBy* as well as *managesProject* are *role names* (corresponding to the binary predicates). The conjunctive query

$$\psi(x) \;=\; \exists y \left(Staff(x) \wedge isAssistedBy(x,y) \wedge Secretary(y) \right)$$

asks for the members of staff that are assisted by secretaries. We invite the reader to verify that the following FO-query

$$\boldsymbol{Q}(x) \;=\; \exists y \left[Staff(x) \wedge isAssistedBy(x,y) \wedge (Secretary(y) \vee PA(y)) \right] \vee$$
$$ProjectManager(x) \vee \exists z \, managesProject(x,z)$$

is an *FO-rewriting* of the OMQ $\boldsymbol{Q}(x) = (\mathcal{O}, \psi(x))$ in the sense that, for any data instance $\mathcal{A}$ (which contains ground atoms such as *ProjectManager*(*bob*), *PA*(*joe*) and *isAssistedBy*(*bob, sam*)) and any individual name a from $\mathcal{A}$, we have $\mathcal{O}, \mathcal{A} \models \psi(a)$ iff $\boldsymbol{Q}(a)$ is true when evaluated directly over $\mathcal{A}$.

Being able to speak about domain concepts and roles, DL cannot say anything about their evolution in time. Following [8], we next introduce two-dimensional combinations of the *LTL* ontology languages from the previous section and various species of *DL-Lite*. The 2D language now contains *individual names* $a_0, a_1, \ldots$, *concept names* $A_0, A_1, \ldots$, and *role names* $P_0, P_1, \ldots$. *Roles S, temporalised roles R, basic concepts B*, and *temporalised concepts C* are defined by the following grammars:

$$S \;::=\; P_i \;\mid\; P_i^-, \quad R \;::=\; S \;\mid\; \Box_F R \;\mid\; \Box_P R \;\mid\; \bigcirc_F R \;\mid\; \bigcirc_P R,$$
$$B \;::=\; A_i \;\mid\; \exists S, \quad C \;::=\; B \;\mid\; \Box_F C \;\mid\; \Box_P C \;\mid\; \bigcirc_F C \;\mid\; \bigcirc_P C.$$

A *concept* or *role inclusion* takes the form

$$\vartheta_1 \sqcap \cdots \sqcap \vartheta_k \;\sqsubseteq\; \vartheta_{k+1} \sqcup \cdots \sqcup \vartheta_{k+m}, \tag{17}$$

where the ϑ_i are all temporalised concepts of the form C or, respectively, temporalised roles of the form R. When it does not matter whether we talk about concepts or roles, we refer to the ϑ_i as *terms*. A *TBox* $\mathcal{T}$ and an *RBox* $\mathcal{R}$ are finite sets of concept inclusions (CIs, for short) and, respectively, role inclusions (RIs, for short); their union $\mathcal{O} = \mathcal{T} \cup \mathcal{R}$ is called an *ontology*.

As before, we classify ontologies by the form of their inclusions and the temporal operators that occur in them. Let $\boldsymbol{c}, \boldsymbol{r} \in \{bool, horn, krom, core\}$ and $\boldsymbol{o} \in \{\Box, \bigcirc, \Box\bigcirc\}$. We denote by *DL-Lite*$_{\boldsymbol{c}/\boldsymbol{r}}^{\boldsymbol{o}}$ the *temporal description logic* whose TBoxes and RBoxes contain concept and role inclusions (17) satisfying $\boldsymbol{c}$ and $\boldsymbol{r}$, respectively, and the only temporal operators that occur in them are indicated in $\boldsymbol{o}$. Whenever $\boldsymbol{c} = \boldsymbol{r}$, we use a single subscript, that is, *DL-Lite*$_{\boldsymbol{c}}^{\boldsymbol{o}}$ = *DL-Lite*$_{\boldsymbol{c}/\boldsymbol{c}}^{\boldsymbol{o}}$.

Note that, unlike the standard atemporal *DL-Lite* logics [6,29], which can have various types of CIs but allow only *core* RIs (of the form $S_1 \sqsubseteq S_2$ and

$S_1 \sqcap S_2 \sqsubseteq \bot$), here we treat CIs and RIs in a uniform way and impose restrictions on the clausal structure of CIs and RIs separately.

An *ABox* (*data instance*, in DL parlance), $\mathcal{A}$, is a finite set of atoms of the form $A_i(a, \ell)$ and $P_i(a, b, \ell)$, where a and b are individual names and $\ell \in \mathbb{Z}$. We denote by $\mathsf{ind}(\mathcal{A})$ the set of individual names in $\mathcal{A}$; as before, we also set $\mathsf{tem}(\mathcal{A}) = \{ n \in \mathbb{Z} \mid \min \mathcal{A} \leq n \leq \max \mathcal{A} \}$. A *DL-Lite*$^o_{c/r}$ *knowledge base* (KB) is a pair $(\mathcal{O}, \mathcal{A})$, where $\mathcal{O}$ is a *DL-Lite*$^o_{c/r}$ ontology and $\mathcal{A}$ an ABox. The *size* $|\mathcal{O}|$ of an ontology $\mathcal{O}$ is the number of occurrences of symbols in $\mathcal{O}$; the size of a TBox, RBox, ABox, and knowledge base is defined analogously.

A (*temporal*) *interpretation* is a pair $\mathcal{I} = (\Delta^{\mathcal{I}}, \cdot^{\mathcal{I}(n)})$, where $\Delta^{\mathcal{I}} \neq \emptyset$ and, for each $n \in \mathbb{Z}$,

$$\mathcal{I}(n) = (\Delta^{\mathcal{I}}, a_0^{\mathcal{I}}, \dots, A_0^{\mathcal{I}(n)}, \dots, P_0^{\mathcal{I}(n)}, \dots) \tag{18}$$

is a standard (atemporal) DL interpretation with $a_i^{\mathcal{I}} \in \Delta^{\mathcal{I}}$, $A_i^{\mathcal{I}(n)} \subseteq \Delta^{\mathcal{I}}$ and $P_i^{\mathcal{I}(n)} \subseteq \Delta^{\mathcal{I}} \times \Delta^{\mathcal{I}}$. Thus, we assume that the domain $\Delta^{\mathcal{I}}$ and the interpretations $a_i^{\mathcal{I}} \in \Delta^{\mathcal{I}}$ of the individual names are the same for all $n \in \mathbb{Z}$. (However, we do not adopt the unique name assumption.) The description logic and temporal constructs are interpreted in $\mathcal{I}(n)$ as follows:

$$(P_i^-)^{\mathcal{I}(n)} = \{ (u, v) \mid (v, u) \in P_i^{\mathcal{I}(n)} \},$$
$$(\exists S)^{\mathcal{I}(n)} = \{ u \mid (u, v) \in S^{\mathcal{I}(n)}, \text{ for some } v \},$$
$$(\Box_F \vartheta)^{\mathcal{I}(n)} = \bigcap_{k > n} \vartheta^{\mathcal{I}(k)}, \qquad\qquad (\Box_P \vartheta)^{\mathcal{I}(n)} = \bigcap_{k < n} \vartheta^{\mathcal{I}(k)},$$
$$(\bigcirc_F \vartheta)^{\mathcal{I}(n)} = \vartheta^{\mathcal{I}(n+1)}, \qquad\qquad (\bigcirc_P \vartheta)^{\mathcal{I}(n)} = \vartheta^{\mathcal{I}(n-1)}.$$

As usual, $\bot$ is interpreted by $\emptyset$, and $\top$ by $\Delta^{\mathcal{I}}$ for concepts and by $\Delta^{\mathcal{I}} \times \Delta^{\mathcal{I}}$ for roles. CIs and RIs are interpreted in $\mathcal{I}$ *globally*, i.e., (17) holds in $\mathcal{I}$ if

$$\vartheta_1^{\mathcal{I}(n)} \cap \cdots \cap \vartheta_k^{\mathcal{I}(n)} \subseteq \vartheta_{k+1}^{\mathcal{I}(n)} \cup \cdots \cup \vartheta_{k+m}^{\mathcal{I}(n)}, \qquad \text{for all } n \in \mathbb{Z}.$$

Given an inclusion α, we write $\mathcal{I} \models \alpha$ if α holds in $\mathcal{I}$. We call $\mathcal{I}$ a *model* of $(\mathcal{O}, \mathcal{A})$ and write $\mathcal{I} \models (\mathcal{O}, \mathcal{A})$ if

$$\mathcal{I} \models \alpha, \text{ for all } \alpha \in \mathcal{O}, \qquad a^{\mathcal{I}} \in A^{\mathcal{I}(\ell)}, \text{ for all } A(a, \ell) \in \mathcal{A},$$
$$\text{and } (a^{\mathcal{I}}, b^{\mathcal{I}}) \in P^{\mathcal{I}(\ell)}, \text{ for all } P(a, b, \ell) \in \mathcal{A}.$$

We say that $\mathcal{O}$ is *consistent* if there is an interpretation $\mathcal{I}$, a *model of* $\mathcal{O}$, such that $\mathcal{I} \models \alpha$, for all $\alpha \in \mathcal{O}$; we also say and that $\mathcal{A}$ is *consistent with* $\mathcal{O}$ if there is a model of $(\mathcal{O}, \mathcal{A})$. For an inclusion α, we write $\mathcal{O} \models \alpha$ if $\mathcal{I} \models \alpha$ for every model $\mathcal{I}$ of $\mathcal{O}$. A concept C is *consistent with* $\mathcal{O}$ if there is a model $\mathcal{I}$ of $\mathcal{O}$ and $n \in \mathbb{Z}$ such that $C^{\mathcal{I}(n)} \neq \emptyset$; consistency of roles with $\mathcal{O}$ is defined analogously.

We now define a language for querying temporal knowledge bases, which was inspired by the SPARQL 1.1 entailment regimes [44]; see also [46,69]. The main ingredients of the language are *positive temporal concepts* $\varkappa$ and *positive temporal roles* ϱ given by the following grammars:

$$\varkappa \quad ::= \quad \top \quad | \quad A_k \quad | \quad \exists S.\varkappa \quad | \quad \varkappa_1 \sqcap \varkappa_2 \quad | \quad \varkappa_1 \sqcup \varkappa_2 \quad |$$
$$\boldsymbol{op_1}\, \varkappa \quad | \quad \varkappa_1 \, \boldsymbol{op_2} \, \varkappa_2,$$
$$\varrho \quad ::= \quad S \quad | \quad \varrho_1 \sqcap \varrho_2 \quad | \quad \varrho_1 \sqcup \varrho_2 \quad | \quad \boldsymbol{op_1}\, \varrho \quad | \quad \varrho_1 \, \boldsymbol{op_2} \, \varrho_2,$$

where $\boldsymbol{op_1} \in \{\bigcirc_F, \Diamond_F, \Box_F, \bigcirc_P, \Diamond_P, \Box_P\}$ and $\boldsymbol{op_2} \in \{\mathcal{U}, \mathcal{S}\}$. Let $\mathcal{I} = (\Delta^{\mathcal{I}}, \cdot^{\mathcal{I}(n)})$ be an interpretation. The *extensions* $\varkappa^{\mathcal{I}(n)}$ of $\varkappa$ in $\mathcal{I}$, for $n \in \mathbb{Z}$, are computed using the definition above and the following items:

$$(\exists S.\varkappa)^{\mathcal{I}(n)} = \big\{ u \in \Delta^{\mathcal{I}} \mid (u, v) \in S^{\mathcal{I}(n)}, \text{ for some } v \in \varkappa^{\mathcal{I}(n)} \big\},$$

$$(\varkappa_1 \sqcap \varkappa_2)^{\mathcal{I}(n)} = \varkappa_1^{\mathcal{I}(n)} \cap \varkappa_2^{\mathcal{I}(n)}, \qquad (\varkappa_1 \sqcup \varkappa_2)^{\mathcal{I}(n)} = \varkappa_1^{\mathcal{I}(n)} \cup \varkappa_2^{\mathcal{I}(n)},$$

$$(\Diamond_F \varkappa)^{\mathcal{I}(n)} = \bigcup_{k>n} \varkappa^{\mathcal{I}(k)}, \qquad (\Diamond_P \varkappa)^{\mathcal{I}(n)} = \bigcup_{k<n} \varkappa^{\mathcal{I}(k)},$$

$$(\varkappa_1 \mathcal{U} \varkappa_2)^{\mathcal{I}(n)} = \bigcup_{k>n} \Big(\varkappa_2^{\mathcal{I}(k)} \cap \bigcap_{n<m<k} \varkappa_1^{\mathcal{I}(m)} \Big),$$

$$(\varkappa_1 \, \mathcal{S} \, \varkappa_2)^{\mathcal{I}(n)} = \bigcup_{k<n} \Big(\varkappa_2^{\mathcal{I}(k)} \cap \bigcap_{k<m<n} \varkappa_1^{\mathcal{I}(m)} \Big).$$

The definition of $\varrho^{\mathcal{I}(n)}$ is analogous. Note that positive temporal concepts $\varkappa$ and roles ϱ include all temporalised concepts C and roles R, respectively ($\exists S$ is a shortcut for $\exists S.\top$).

A *DL-Lite$^o_{c/r}$ ontology-mediated instance query* (OMIQ) is a pair of the form $\boldsymbol{q} = (\mathcal{O}, \varkappa)$ or $\boldsymbol{q} = (\mathcal{O}, \varrho)$, where $\mathcal{O}$ is a DL-Lite$^o_{c/r}$ ontology, $\varkappa$ is a positive temporal concept and ϱ a positive temporal role (which can use all temporal operators, not necessarily only those in $\boldsymbol{o}$). If $\varkappa$ is a basic concept (i.e., A or $\exists S$) and ϱ a role, then we refer to $\boldsymbol{q}$ as an *ontology-mediated atomic query* (OMAQ, as before). A *certain answer* to an OMIQ $(\mathcal{O}, \varkappa)$ over an ABox $\mathcal{A}$ is a pair $(a, \ell) \in \mathsf{ind}(\mathcal{A}) \times \mathsf{tem}(\mathcal{A})$ such that $a^{\mathcal{I}} \in \varkappa^{\mathcal{I}(\ell)}$ for every model $\mathcal{I}$ of $(\mathcal{O}, \mathcal{A})$. A *certain answer* to $(\mathcal{O}, \varrho)$ over $\mathcal{A}$ is a triple $(a, b, \ell) \in \mathsf{ind}(\mathcal{A}) \times \mathsf{ind}(\mathcal{A}) \times \mathsf{tem}(\mathcal{A})$ such that $(a^{\mathcal{I}}, b^{\mathcal{I}}) \in \varrho^{\mathcal{I}(\ell)}$ for every model $\mathcal{I}$ of $(\mathcal{O}, \mathcal{A})$. The set of all certain answers to $\boldsymbol{q}$ over $\mathcal{A}$ is denoted, as before, by $\mathsf{ans}(\boldsymbol{q}, \mathcal{A})$.

Let $\mathcal{A}$ be any given ABox with $\mathsf{ind}(\mathcal{A}) = \{a_1, \dots, a_m\}$. We always assume, without much loss of generality, that $|\mathsf{tem}(\mathcal{A})| \geq |\mathsf{ind}(\mathcal{A})|$ (if this is not the case, we can simply add the required number of dummies with the missing time instances to $|\mathsf{tem}(\mathcal{A})|$). We represent $\mathcal{A}$ as a structure $\mathfrak{S}_{\mathcal{A}}$ with domain $\mathsf{tem}(\mathcal{A})$ ordered by $<$ such that

$$\mathfrak{S}_{\mathcal{A}} \models A(k, \ell) \quad \text{iff} \quad A(a_k, \ell) \in \mathcal{A}, \qquad \mathfrak{S}_{\mathcal{A}} \models P(k, k', \ell) \quad \text{iff} \quad P(a_k, a_{k'}, \ell) \in \mathcal{A},$$

for any concept and role names A, P and any $k, k', \ell \in \mathsf{tem}(\mathcal{A})$. To simplify notation, we often identify an individual name $a_k \in \mathsf{ind}(\mathcal{A})$ with its number representation $k \in \mathsf{tem}(\mathcal{A})$. The structure $\mathfrak{S}_{\mathcal{A}}$ represents a temporal database over which we can evaluate first-order formulas (queries) with predicates of the form $A(x, t)$, $P(x, y, t)$ and $t_1 < t_2$ as well as other standard numeric predicates and relational primitive recursion.

Definition 23 (FO-rewritability). Let $\mathcal{L}$ be one of the three languages $FO(<)$, $FO(<, \equiv_\mathbb{N})$ or $FO(RPR)$. Let $q = (\mathcal{O}, \varkappa)$ be an OMIQ and $Q(x, t)$ a constant-free $\mathcal{L}$-formula with free variables x and t. We call $Q(x, t)$ an $\mathcal{L}$-*rewriting of* q if, for any ABox $\mathcal{A}$, any $a \in \mathsf{ind}(\mathcal{A})$ and any $\ell \in \mathsf{tem}(\mathcal{A})$, we have $(a, \ell) \in \mathsf{ans}(q, \mathcal{A})$ iff $\mathfrak{S}_\mathcal{A} \models Q(a, \ell)$. Similarly, a constant-free $\mathcal{L}$-formula $Q(x, y, t)$ is an $\mathcal{L}$-*rewriting of* an OMIQ $q = (\mathcal{O}, \varrho)$ if, for any ABox $\mathcal{A}$, any $a, b \in \mathsf{ind}(\mathcal{A})$ and any $\ell \in \mathsf{tem}(\mathcal{A})$, we have $(a, b, \ell) \in \mathsf{ans}(q, \mathcal{A})$ iff $\mathfrak{S}_\mathcal{A} \models Q(a, b, \ell)$.

Having all the definitions given, it is time to recall that two-dimensional combinations of knowledge representation formalisms can be computationally very complex if any non-trivial interaction between the dimensions is available; see, e.g., [41–43, 54, 65]. Our temporalised *DL-Lite* logics are not an exception as the following theorem demonstrates:

Theorem 24. (i) *Consistency checking for DL-Lite$_{bool}^{\circ}$ KBs is undecidable.*
(ii) *There are DL-Lite$_{bool}^{\circ}$ OMAQs $q_1 = (\mathcal{O}, A)$ and $q_2 = (\mathcal{O}, S)$ such that the problems whether, for a given ABox $\mathcal{A}$, the pair $(a, 0)$ is a certain answer to q_1 over $\mathcal{A}$ and $(a, b, 0)$ is a certain answer to q_2 over $\mathcal{A}$ are undecidable.*

Proof (Sketch). (i) The proof is by reduction of the undecidable $\mathbb{N} \times \mathbb{N}$-tiling problem [19]. Given a set $\mathfrak{T} = \{1, \ldots, k\}$ of tile types, we define a *DL-Lite*$_{bool}^{\circ}$ KB $(\mathcal{O}_\mathfrak{T}, \{I(a, 0)\})$ with the following ontology $\mathcal{O}_\mathfrak{T}$, where the R_i are role names associated with the tile types $i \in \mathfrak{T}$ and $top(i)$, $bot(i)$, $right(i)$, $left(i)$ are the colours on the four edges of any tile type i:

$$I \sqsubseteq \bigsqcup_{i \in \mathfrak{T}} \exists R_i, \quad R_i \sqsubseteq \bigsqcup_{right(i) = left(j)} \bigcirc_F R_j,$$

$$\exists R_i^- \sqsubseteq \bigsqcup_{top(i) = bot(j)} \exists R_j, \quad \exists R_i \sqcap \exists R_j \sqsubseteq \bot, \quad \text{for } i \neq j.$$

It is readily checked that $\{I(a, 0)\}$ is consistent with $\mathcal{O}_\mathfrak{T}$ iff $\mathfrak{T}$ can tile the $\mathbb{N} \times \mathbb{N}$ grid.

(ii) Using the representation of the universal Turing machine by means of tiles (see, e.g., [23]), we obtain a set $\mathfrak{U}$ of tile types for which the following problem is undecidable: given a finite sequence of tile types $i_0, \ldots, i_n$, decide whether $\mathfrak{U}$ can tile the $\mathbb{N} \times \mathbb{N}$ grid so that tiles of types $i_0, \ldots, i_n$ are placed on $(0, 0), \ldots, (n, 0)$, respectively. Given such $i_0, \ldots, i_n$, we take the ABox $\mathcal{A} = \{I(a, 0), R_{i_0}(a, b, 0), \ldots, R_{i_n}(a, b, n)\}$. Then $\mathfrak{U}$ can tile $\mathbb{N} \times \mathbb{N}$ with $i_0, \ldots, i_n$ on the first row iff $\mathcal{A}$ is consistent with $\mathcal{O}_\mathfrak{U}$ iff $A(a, 0)$ is *not* a certain answer to OMAQ $(\mathcal{O}_\mathfrak{U}, A)$ over $\mathcal{A}$, where A is a fresh concept name; similar considerations apply to the case of a fresh role S. □

We can obtain better-behaved logics by restricting the expressive power of role inclusions. The proof of the following result can be found in [60].

Theorem 25. *Consistency checking for DL-Lite$_{bool/krom}^{\circ}$, DL-Lite$_{bool/horn}^{\square\circ}$ and DL-Lite$_{horn}^{\square\circ}$ is* EXPSPACE-complete *for combined complexity; for DL-Lite$_{bool/core}^{\square\circ}$ and DL-Lite$_{horn/core}^{\square\circ}$, it is* PSPACE-complete.

Let us now consider FO-rewritability of OMQs with ontologies in temporalised *DL-Lite*. To avoid many a technical detail and concentrate on the main ideas, we only discuss here OMQs with atomic queries (that is, OMAQs) and ontologies without occurrences of $\bot$ (which, therefore, are always consistent). Let $\mathcal{L}$ be one of the target languages FO($<$), FO($<, \equiv_\mathbb{N}$) or FO(RPR). We show that $\mathcal{L}$-rewritability of a $\bot$-free OMAQ with an $DL\text{-}Lite_{bool/horn}^{\Box\bigcirc}$ ontology is reducible to $\mathcal{L}$-rewritability of a role-free OMAQ. Ontologies without roles are clearly a notational variant of *LTL* ontologies; hence, in this case we can write '$LTL_{bool}^{\Box\bigcirc}$ ontologies'. We explain the reduction by instructive examples. The first two of them illustrate the interaction between the DL and temporal dimensions in $DL\text{-}Lite_{bool/horn}^{\Box\bigcirc}$ that we need to take into account when constructing the *LTL* OMAQs to which the rewritability of $\bot$-free $DL\text{-}Lite_{bool/horn}^{\Box\bigcirc}$ OMAQs is reduced.

Example 26. Suppose $\mathcal{T} = \{B \sqsubseteq \exists P, \exists Q \sqsubseteq A\}$ and $\mathcal{R} = \{P \sqsubseteq \bigcirc_F Q\}$. An obvious idea of constructing a rewriting for the OMAQ $q = (\mathcal{T} \cup \mathcal{R}, A)$ would be to find first a rewriting of the *LTL* OMAQ $(\mathcal{T}^\dagger, A^\dagger)$ obtained from $(\mathcal{T}, A)$ by replacing the basic concepts $\exists P$ and $\exists Q$ with surrogate concept names $(\exists P)^\dagger = E_P$ and $(\exists Q)^\dagger = E_Q$, respectively. This would give us the FO-query $A(x, t) \vee E_Q(x, t)$. By restoring the intended meaning of E_Q, we would then obtain $A(x, t) \vee \exists y\, Q(x, y, t)$. The second step would be to rewrite, using the RBox $\mathcal{R}$, the atom $Q(x, y, t)$ into $Q(x, y, t) \vee P(x, y, t-1)$. However, the resulting formula

$$A(x, t) \vee \exists y\, \big(Q(x, y, t) \vee P(x, y, t-1)\big)$$

is not a rewriting of q as it does not return the certain answer $(a, 1)$ over the ABox $\mathcal{A} = \{B(a, 0), C(a, 1)\}$ because so far we have not taken into account the CI $\exists P \sqsubseteq \bigcirc_F \exists Q$, which is a consequence of $\mathcal{R}$. If we now add the 'connecting axiom' $(\exists P)^\dagger \sqsubseteq \bigcirc_F (\exists Q)^\dagger$ to $\mathcal{T}^\dagger$, then in the first step we obtain $A(x, t) \vee E_Q(x, t) \vee E_P(x, t-1) \vee B(x, t-1)$, which gives us the correct FO($<$)-rewriting of q:

$$A(x, t) \vee \exists y\, \big(Q(x, y, t) \vee P(x, y, t-1)\big) \vee \exists y\, P(x, y, t-1) \vee B(x, t-1).$$

Example 27. Let $q = (\mathcal{T} \cup \mathcal{R}, A)$ with $\mathcal{T} = \{\exists Q \sqsubseteq \Box_P A\}$ and

$$\mathcal{R} = \{P \sqsubseteq \Box_F P_1,\ T \sqsubseteq \Box_F T_1,\ T_1 \sqsubseteq \Box_F T_2,\ P_1 \sqcap T_2 \sqsubseteq Q\}.$$

The two-step construction outlined in Example 26 would give us first the formula

$$\Phi(x, t) = A(x, t) \vee \exists t'\, \big((t < t') \wedge \exists y\, Q(x, y, t')\big)$$

as a rewriting of $(\mathcal{T}, A)$. It is readily checked that the following formula $\Psi(x, y, t')$ is a rewriting of $(\mathcal{R}, Q)$:

$$Q(x, y, t') \vee \big(\big[P_1(x, y, t') \vee \exists t''\, ((t'' < t') \wedge P(x, y, t''))\big] \wedge$$
$$\big[T_2(x, y, t') \vee \exists t''\, ((t'' < t') \wedge (T_1(x, y, t'') \vee$$
$$\exists t'''\, ((t''' < t'') \wedge T(x, y, t'''))))\big]\big).$$

However, the result of replacing $Q(x, y, t')$ in $\Phi(x, t)$ with $\Psi(x, y, t')$ is not an FO($<$)-rewriting of $(\mathcal{O}, A)$: when evaluated over $\mathcal{A} = \{T(a, b, 0),\ P(a, b, 1)\}$, it does not return the certain answers $(a, 0)$ and $(a, 1)$; see the picture below:

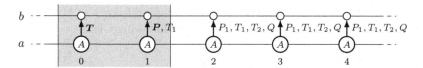

(Note that these answers would be found had we evaluated the obtained 'rewriting' over $\mathbb{Z}$ rather than $\{0,1\}$.) This time, we miss the concept inclusion $\exists (\Box_F P_1 \sqcap \Box_F T_2) \sqsubseteq \Box_F \exists Q$, which follows from $\mathcal{R}$ and $\mathcal{T}$. To fix the problem, we can take a fresh role name G_ρ, for $\rho = \{\Box_F P_1, \Box_F T_2\}$, and add the 'connecting axiom' $\exists G_\rho \sqsubseteq \Box_F \exists Q$ to $\mathcal{T}$. Then, in the first step, we rewrite the extended TBox and A to the formula

$$\Phi'(x,t) = A(x,t) \lor \exists t' \big((t < t') \land$$
$$(\exists y\, Q(x,y,t') \lor \exists t'' ((t'' < t') \land \exists y\, G_\rho(x,y,t''))) \big),$$

where we replace $Q(x,y,t')$ by $\Psi(x,y,t')$ and restore the meaning of $G_\rho(x,y,t')$ by rewriting $(\mathcal{R}, \Box_F P_1 \sqcap \Box_F T_2)$ to $P(x,y,t') \land (T_1(x,y,t') \lor \exists t'' ((t'' < t) \land T(x,y,t'')))$ and substituting it for $G_\rho(x,y,t')$ in $\Phi'(x,t)$.

We now formally define the connecting axioms for $\mathcal{O}$, assuming that $\mathcal{R}$ contains all role names in $\mathcal{T}$. Let ρ be a set of (temporalised) roles from $\mathcal{R}$ consistent with $\mathcal{R}$. Let $\boldsymbol{r}_\rho$ be the $\mathcal{R}$-canonical rod for $\{S(d,e,0) \mid S \in \rho\}$. Clearly, there are positive integers $s^\rho \le |\mathcal{R}|$ and $p^\rho \le 2^{2|\mathcal{R}|}$ with

$$\begin{aligned}
\boldsymbol{r}_\rho(n) &= \boldsymbol{r}_\rho(n - p^\rho), & \text{for } n \le -s^\rho, \\
\boldsymbol{r}_\rho(n) &= \boldsymbol{r}_\rho(n + p^\rho), & \text{for } n \ge s^\rho.
\end{aligned}$$

Then we take a fresh role name G_ρ and fresh concept names D_ρ^n, for $-s^\rho - p^\rho < n < s^\rho + p^\rho$, and construct the CIs

$$\exists G_\rho \sqsubseteq D_\rho^0, \quad D_\rho^n \sqsubseteq O_F D_\rho^{n+1}, \quad \text{for } 0 \le n < s^\rho + p^\rho - 1,$$
$$D_\rho^{s^\rho + p^\rho - 1} \sqsubseteq O_F D_\rho^{s^\rho},$$
$$D_\rho^n \sqsubseteq \exists S, \quad \text{for } S \in \boldsymbol{r}_\rho(n), \ 0 \le n < s^\rho + p^\rho,$$

and symmetrical ones for $-s^\rho - p^\rho \le n \le 0$. Let $(\mathbf{con})$ be the set of such CIs for all possible ρ. Set $\mathcal{T}_\mathcal{R} = \mathcal{T} \cup (\mathbf{con})$.

Example 28. In Example 26, for $\rho = \{P, O_F Q\}$, we have $s^\rho = 2$, $p^\rho = 1$, and so $\mathcal{T}_\mathcal{R}$ contains the CIs

$$\exists P \sqsubseteq D_\rho^0, \quad D_\rho^0 \sqsubseteq O_F D_\rho^1, \quad D_\rho^1 \sqsubseteq O_F D_\rho^2,$$
$$D_\rho^2 \sqsubseteq O_F D_\rho^2, \quad D_\rho^0 \sqsubseteq \exists P, \quad D_\rho^1 \sqsubseteq \exists Q,$$

which imply $\exists P \sqsubseteq \bigcirc_F \exists Q$. In the context of Example 27, for $\rho = \{\Box_F P_1, \Box_F T_2\}$, we have $s^\rho = 1$, $p^\rho = 1$, and so $\mathcal{T}_\mathcal{R}$ contains the following CIs:

$$\exists G_\rho \sqsubseteq D_\rho^0, \quad D_\rho^0 \sqsubseteq \bigcirc_F D_\rho^1, \quad D_\rho^1 \sqsubseteq \bigcirc_F D_\rho^1,$$

$$D_\rho^1 \sqsubseteq \exists P_1, \quad D_\rho^1 \sqsubseteq \exists T_2, \quad D_\rho^1 \sqsubseteq \exists Q.$$

We denote by $\mathcal{T}_\mathcal{R}^\dagger$ the $LTL_{bool}^{\Box\bigcirc}$ TBox obtained from $\mathcal{T}_\mathcal{R}$ by replacing every basic concept B with its surrogate $B^\dagger$.

Theorem 29. *Let* $\mathcal{L}$ *be one of* FO($<$), FO($<, \equiv_\mathbb{N}$), FO(RPR). *A DL-Lite$_{bool/horn}^{\Box\bigcirc}$ OMAQ* $(\mathcal{O}, A)$ *with a $\bot$-free* $\mathcal{O} = \mathcal{T} \cup \mathcal{R}$ *is $\mathcal{L}$-rewritable whenever*

- *the* $LTL_{bool}^{\Box\bigcirc}$ *OMAQ* $(\mathcal{T}_\mathcal{R}^\dagger, A)$ *is $\mathcal{L}$-rewritable and*

- *the* $LTL_{horn}^{\Box\bigcirc}$ *OMAQ* $(\mathcal{R}, R)$ *is $\mathcal{L}$-rewritable, for every temporalised role in $\mathcal{R}$.*

As a consequence of Theorems 13 and 29, we obtain:

Theorem 30. *Every DL-Lite$_{bool/horn}^{\Box\bigcirc}$ OMAQ is* FO(RPR)*-rewritable.*

Moreover, we also have the following:

Corollary 31. *(i) All DL-Lite$_{krom/core}^{\Box\bigcirc}$ OMAQs, and so all DL-Lite$_{core}^{\Box\bigcirc}$ OMAQs are* FO($<, \equiv_\mathbb{N}$)*-rewritable.*
(ii) All DL-Lite$_{bool/horn}^{\Box\bigcirc}$ OMAQs are FO(RPR)*-rewritable.*

These results can be extended to OMQs with more complex queries:

Theorem 32. *(i) All DL-Lite$_{horn/core}^{\Box}$ OMIQs are* FO($<$)*-rewritable.*
(ii) All DL-Lite$_{core}^{\bigcirc}$ OMIQs are FO($<, \equiv_\mathbb{N}$)*-rewritable.*
(iii) All DL-Lite$_{horn}^{\Box\bigcirc}$ OMIQs are FO(RPR)*-rewritable.*

It is to be noted that Theorem 32 holds for core and Horn *DL-Lite* logics only because even very simple disjunctive axioms lead to coNP-complete OMIQ answering problem. For example, as follows from [76], answering the atemporal *DL-Lite$_{krom}$* OMIQ

$$(\{\top \sqsubseteq A \sqcup B\}, \exists R.(\exists P_1.A \sqcap \exists P_2.A \sqcap \exists N_1.B \sqcap \exists N_2.B))$$

is coNP-complete for data complexity.

5   Ontology-Mediated Queries with *MTL* Ontologies

So far, we have discussed temporal ontologies with *LTL*-operators, which allowed us to naturally describe the behaviour of synchronous systems. Note, however, that *LTL*-representations of metric statements such as 'high temperature will be reached in at most 100 s' require long and unreadable disjunctions of the form

$$\bigcirc_F HighTemp \vee \bigcirc_F \bigcirc_F HighTemp \vee \bigcirc_F \bigcirc_F \bigcirc_F HighTemp \vee \cdots \vee \underbrace{\bigcirc_F \ldots \bigcirc_F}_{100} HighTemp.$$

Moreover, such formulas become meaningless in the case of asynchronous systems where time is dense and there is no next or previous moment.

A more suitable temporal knowledge representation formalism in this case is metric temporal logic MTL, which was introduced for modelling and reasoning about real-time systems [3,62]. Essentially, MTL-operators are obtained by indexing the LTL-operators with arbitrary intervals ϱ, which allow concise representation of metric information and which can be used over dense time. We denote the metric counterparts of the future LTL-operators $\Diamond_F$, $\Box_F$, and $\mathcal{U}$ by $\oplus_\varrho$, $\boxplus_\varrho$, and $\mathcal{U}_\varrho$, respectively; their past analogues are $\ominus_\varrho$, $\boxminus_\varrho$, and $\mathcal{S}_\varrho$. Recall from Sect. 2 that, in the case of dense time, we assume that timestamps are dyadic rational numbers (whose set is denoted by $\mathbb{Q}_2$). Each interval ϱ, indexing an MTL-operator and called its *range*, has non-negative end-points from $\mathbb{Q}_2^{\geq 0}$ or ∞.

Example 33. The formula $\oplus_{(0,100]} High\,Temp$ is regarded to be true at a time instant $t \in \mathbb{Q}_2$ if $High\,Temp$ is true at some moment in the interval $(t, t + 100]$; dually, the formula $\boxplus_{(0,100]} High\,Temp$ holds at t if $High\,Temp$ is true at every point of that interval. Note that the LTL-formula $\Diamond_F High\,Temp$ has the same meaning as the MTL-formula $\oplus_{(0,\infty)} High\,Temp$ and $\Box_F High\,Temp$ as $\boxplus_{(0,\infty)} High\,Temp$.

Similarly to the case of LTL, we treat ontology axioms with MTL-operators as (variable-free) abbreviations for monadic first-order formulas. However, since now time is dense, instead of $\mathrm{MFO}(<)$-formulas, we use $\mathrm{MFO}(<, \delta_{\leq \mathbb{Q}_2}, \delta_{= \mathbb{Q}_2})$-formulas, where $\delta_{<a}$ and $\delta_{=a}$, for $a \in \mathbb{Q}_2^+$, are additional built-in binary predicates allowing us to speak about the distance between moments of time. Recall that $\delta_{<a}(x, y)$ stands for $0 \leq x - y < a$, and $\delta_{=a}(x, y)$ for $x - y = a$. Using these predicates, for every range ϱ, we can define a predicate $\delta_\varrho(x, y)$ saying that $x - y \in \varrho$; for example, we can set

$$\delta_{[1,2)}(x, y) = \delta_{\geq 1}(x, y) \wedge \delta_{<2}(x, y).$$

We can define the *standard translation* ‡ from MTL into $\mathrm{MFO}(<, \delta_{\leq \mathbb{Q}_2}, \delta_{= \mathbb{Q}_2})$, similar to the translation † of LTL into $\mathrm{MFO}(<)$, by taking, for example

$$(\boxplus_\varrho \varkappa)^{\ddagger} = \forall t' \left(\delta_\varrho(t', t) \to \varkappa^{\ddagger}\{t/t'\} \right),$$
$$(\oplus_\varrho \varkappa)^{\ddagger} = \exists t' \left(\delta_\varrho(t', t) \wedge \varkappa^{\ddagger}\{t/t'\} \right).$$

As mentioned in Sect. 2, there are two semantics for $\mathrm{MFO}(<, \delta_{\leq \mathbb{Q}_2}, \delta_{= \mathbb{Q}_2})$ and MTL. In the *continuous semantics*, the temporal domain in the definition (2) of $\mathrm{ans}(q, \mathcal{A})$ is the whole of $\mathbb{Q}_2$; in the *pointwise semantics*, it coincides with the active domain $\mathrm{tem}(\mathcal{A})$. Under the former, $\mathrm{MFO}(<, \delta_{\leq \mathbb{Q}_2}, \delta_{= \mathbb{Q}_2})$-formulas with one free variable have the same expressive power as MTL-formulas interpreted over the reals $\mathbb{R}$ [55]. On the other hand, the satisfiability and model checking problems turn out to be undecidable in this case [50]. However, as shown in [71], both problems become decidable, albeit with non-primitive recursive complexity, if the pointwise semantics is adopted.

Let us now turn to OBDA with *MTL*-ontologies. Compared to the *LTL* OMQs, research of the *MTL* case has just begun, and very few results are known at the moment. In particular, FO-rewritability of *MTL* OMQs under the continuous semantics is practically *terra incognita*; we refer the reader to [25, 26, 82, 83] and the survey [9]. In the remainder of this section, we discuss what is known about FO-rewritability of *MTL* OMQs under the pointwise semantics following [75]. We begin with an example.

Example 34. Consider the *MTL*-ontology $\mathcal{O} = \{\boxminus_{[0,2)}B \to B', \; \diamondsuit_{[1,1]}B' \to A\}$ and the data instances $\mathcal{A}_1 = \{B(0), B(1/2), C(3/2)\}$ and $\mathcal{A}_2 = \{B(0), C(3/2)\}$. Then $\mathsf{tem}(\mathcal{A}_1) = \{0, 1/2, 3/2\}$ and $\mathsf{tem}(\mathcal{A}_2) = \{0, 3/2\}$. The minimal models $\mathcal{I}_1$ of $(\mathcal{O}, \mathcal{A}_1)$ and $\mathcal{I}_2$ of $(\mathcal{O}, \mathcal{A}_2)$ are shown in the picture below:

$\mathcal{I}_1 :$
B B'	B B'		C A
0	1/2		3/2

$\mathcal{I}_2 :$
B B'		C
0		3/2

Hence, $3/2$ is a certain answer to the OMAQ $(\mathcal{O}, A)$ over $\mathcal{A}_1$, but there is no certain answer to $(\mathcal{O}, A)$ over $\mathcal{A}_2$.

In what follows, we consider FO-rewritability of *MTL* OMAQs only. The following observation is simple and left to the reader.

Theorem 35. *Answering MTL OMAQs is in* CoNP *for data complexity.*

The next theorem establishes some lower complexity bounds for answering *MTL* OMQs, which should be compared with the data complexity of *LTL* OMQs. In this theorem, MTL^- means *MTL* with *past* operators only, with MTL^-_{horn} and MTL^-_{core} being its Horn and core fragments, respectively.

Theorem 36. *(i) Answering MTL OMAQs is* CoNP*-hard for data complexity.*
  (ii) Answering OMAQs with an MTL^-_{core} *ontology is* P*-hard for data complexity.*
  (iii) Answering OMAQs with an MTL^-_{core} *ontology containing* $\diamondsuit$ *operators only is* NL*-hard for data complexity.*

Proof (Sketch). We show (i) by reduction of the complement of the NP-complete circuit satisfiability problem [5]. Instead of presenting the details of the construction, we only consider the Boolean circuit below, which contains two input gates, one AND gate, one OR gate, and one NOT gate.

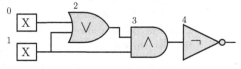

First, we enumerate the gates of the circuit with consecutive numbers starting from 0 so that if there is an edge from n to m, then $n < m$ (observe that such an enumeration always exists). Then we define a data instance $\mathcal{A}$ stating that

$\mathcal{A}$ holds in 25 timestamps. These timestamps form 5 sections, each containing 5 timestamps (as there are 5 gates in the circuit) as depicted below:

T	$T\ F$	$T\ F\ T$	$T\ F\ T\ F$	$T\ F\ T\ F\ T$
X	X	$I_1\ I_2\ D$	$I_2\ I_1\ C$	$I_0\ N$
$A\ A\ A\ A\ A$	$A\ A\ A\ A\ A$	$A\ A\ A\ A\ A$	$A\ A\ A\ A\ A$	$A\ A\ A\ A\ A$

$$\frac{0}{8}\ \frac{1}{8}\ \frac{2}{8}\ \frac{3}{8}\ \frac{4}{8} \qquad \frac{16}{8}\ \frac{17}{8}\ \frac{18}{8}\ \frac{19}{8}\ \frac{20}{8} \qquad \frac{32}{8}\ \frac{33}{8}\ \frac{34}{8}\ \frac{35}{8}\ \frac{36}{8} \qquad \frac{48}{8}\ \frac{49}{8}\ \frac{50}{8}\ \frac{51}{8}\ \frac{52}{8} \qquad \frac{64}{8}\ \frac{65}{8}\ \frac{66}{8}\ \frac{67}{8}\ \frac{68}{8}$$

The data instance $\mathcal{A}$ also contains facts about X (for the input gates), D (for the OR gate), C (for the AND gate), N (for the NOT gate), I_0 (for the input of the NOT gate), and I_1 and I_2 (for the first and the second inputs to the binary gates, i.e., OR and AND). The i-th section of $\mathcal{A}$ represents information about the i-th gate. For example, the left-most section of $\mathcal{A}$ describes the gate 0 by stating that X holds in the left-most timestamp in this section. On the other hand, the third section from the left describes the OR gate by stating that D holds in the third from the left timestamp in this section (which expresses that the gate number 2 is an OR gate), that I_1 holds in the first timestamp from the left in the section (which expresses that the gate number 0 is the first input to the OR gate), and that I_2 holds in the second timestamp from the left in the section (which expresses that the gate number 1 is the second input to the OR gate).

We can now construct an ontology that allows checking unsatisfiability of any circuit. The ontology uses two more atoms T and F, which stand for 'true' and 'false' and which allow us to simulate propagation of signals in the circuit:

$$X \to T \vee F, \qquad \diamondsuit_{[2,2]}T \to T, \qquad \diamondsuit_{[2,2]}F \to F,$$
$$N \wedge \diamondsuit_{[0,1]}(I_0 \wedge T) \to F, \qquad N \wedge \diamondsuit_{[0,1]}(I_0 \wedge F) \to T,$$
$$D \wedge \diamondsuit_{[0,1]}(I_1 \wedge T) \to T, \qquad D \wedge \diamondsuit_{[0,1]}(I_2 \wedge T) \to T,$$
$$C \wedge \diamondsuit_{[0,1]}(I_1 \wedge F) \to F, \qquad C \wedge \diamondsuit_{[0,1]}(I_2 \wedge F) \to F,$$
$$D \wedge \diamondsuit_{[0,1]}(I_1 \wedge F) \wedge \diamondsuit_{[0,1]}(I_2 \wedge F) \to F,$$
$$C \wedge \diamondsuit_{[0,1]}(I_1 \wedge T) \wedge \diamondsuit_{[0,1]}(I_2 \wedge T) \to T.$$

A possible propagation of T and F enforced by the ontology is shown in the previous picture with T and F written in grey. A given circuit is unsatisfiable iff the right-most timestamp in $\mathcal{A}$ is a certain answer to an OMAQ consisting of the above ontology and the query F.

(ii) The proof is by reduction of path system accessibility (PSA) which consists of checking whether there exists a hyperpath between two nodes in a hypergraph (the problem is well-known to be P-complete). For example, assume that a hypergraph contains vertices $0, 1, 2, 3$, and a single hyperedge $(0, 1, 2)$. Suppose we want to check whether the vertex $t = 3$ is accessible from the set of vertices $S = \{0, 1\}$, i.e., whether $t \in S$ or there are vertices u, w accessible from S and

(u, w, t) is a hyperedge. For such an instance of PSA, we construct the following data instance $\mathcal{A}$:

hyperedge (v_0, v_1, v_2)

We next define an MTL_{core}^--ontology $\mathcal{O}$ with the axioms:

$$\diamondsuit_{[2,2]} R \to R', \qquad \boxminus_{[0,1]} R' \to R'', \qquad \diamondsuit_{[2,2]} R'' \to R, \qquad \diamondsuit_{[4,4]} R \to R.$$

Then $4k + t/N$ is a certain answer to $(\mathcal{O}, R)$ over $\mathcal{A}$ iff t is accessible from S in G.

We prove (iii) by reduction of the NL-complete reachability problem in acyclic digraphs. As an example, assume that we want to check whether $t = 3$ is accessible from $s = 0$ in the following directed graph G:

To this end, we construct a data instance $\mathcal{A}_G$, whose initial segment (corresponding to the edge from 0 to 2) is depicted below:

edge $e_0 = (0, 2)$

Let $\mathcal{O}$ be a MTL_{core}^--ontology with the following rules:

$$\diamondsuit_{[2,2]} R \to R', \qquad \diamondsuit_{(0,1]} R' \to R'', \qquad \diamondsuit_{[2,2]} R'' \to R, \qquad \diamondsuit_{[4;4]} R \to R.$$

Then $4k + {}^\bullet t/N$ is a certain answer to $(\mathcal{O}, R)$ over $\mathcal{A}$ iff t is reachable from s in G.   □

In the next theorem, we show that, for each MTL_{horn}^--OMAQ, there is a rewriting to datalog queries with additional FO-formulas built from EDB predicates in their rule bodies, answering which is in P [45].

Theorem 37. *Every MTL_{horn}^--OMAQ is datalog(FO)-rewritable, and so can be answered in* P *for data complexity.*

Proof (Sketch). To illustrate how one can construct a datalog(FO)-rewriting, we consider the MTL_{horn}^--OMAQ $q = (\mathcal{O}, Alert)$, where $\mathcal{O}$ consists of the axiom:

$$\diamondsuit_{(0,600]} RotorSpeedAbove1260 \land \boxminus_{[0,10]} MainFlameOn \to Alert.$$

We construct a datalog(FO)-rewriting (Π, G) of $\boldsymbol{q}$. We will use $suc(x, y)$ stating that x is the immediate successor of the timestamp y.

The first block of Π has the following rules for every atom B occurring in $\boldsymbol{q}$:

$$B(x) \rightarrow B'(x, x), \qquad B'(x, y) \wedge B'(z, z) \wedge suc(y, z) \rightarrow B'(x, z).$$

Intuitively, instead of unary predicates $B(x)$ stating that B holds at a timestamp x, we want to obtain binary predicates $B'(x, y)$ stating that B holds in the interval $[x, y]$ (i.e., in all timestamps from the temporal domain that belong to this interval). The first rule converts $B(x)$ into $B'(x, x)$, while the second rule allows us to coalesce intervals by stating that if B holds in $[x, y]$ and in z, and moreover, there is no timestamp between y and z, then B holds in $[x, z]$.

The second block of Π consists of rules obtained by modifying axioms in $\mathcal{O}$, where every atom B not in the scope of a metric operator is replaced by $B'(x, x)$, whereas atoms in the scope of metric operators are replaced by corresponding formulas using predicates such as $\delta_{<a}$ and $\delta_{>a}$. In particular, in our example the single rule in $\mathcal{O}$ would be replaced with:

$$\big(\mathit{MainFlameOn'}(w, z) \wedge \delta_{\geq 600}(x, w) \wedge \delta_{<0}(x, z) \wedge \delta_{\geq 600}(z, w)\big) \wedge$$
$$\big(\mathit{RotorSpeedAbove1260'}(w, z) \wedge \delta_{>0}(x, w) \wedge \delta_{\leq 6000}(x, z)\big) \rightarrow \mathit{Alert'}(x, x).$$

Finally, the program Π contains the rule

$$\mathit{Alert'}(x, x) \rightarrow G(x),$$

which states that if A holds at x, then G also holds at x.

Now, for every data instance $\mathcal{A}$, t is a certain answer to $\boldsymbol{q}$ over $\mathcal{A}$ iff t is an answer to (Π, G) over $\mathcal{A}$. As a result, (Π, G) is a datalog(FO)-rewriting of $\boldsymbol{q}$.

Note that so far we have assumed that $\mathcal{A}$ is in the signature (3). However, this assumption does not differentiate between small (e.g., 0.01) and large (e.g., 1000.00000001) timestamps in $\mathcal{A}$. Instead, we can consider $\mathcal{A}$ in a different signature using $binary$ predicates $bit(i, j)$ indicating that the integer part of the timestamp i has bit j equal to 1, and analogous predicates for the fractional part. In this new representation of $\mathcal{A}$, we do not assume the predicates $\delta_{<a}(x, y)$ and $\delta_{=a}(x, y)$, however, we can express them as FO($<$)-formulas $\varphi_{<a}(x, y)$ and $\varphi_{=a}(x, y)$ with the predicates bit (see [75] for details). The predicate $suc(x, y)$ is also expressible in the new representation as $(y < x) \wedge \neg \exists z\, (y < z < x)$.   □

The next theorem establishes rewritability into FO(TC) that extends FO($<$) with the transitive closure operator. In complexity-theoretic terms, FO(TC) corresponds to NL [56].

Theorem 38. *Every MTL_{core}^{-}-OMAQ with an ontology containing $\diamondsuit_{\varrho}$ operators only is* FO(TC)-*rewritable, and so can be answered in* NL *for data complexity.*

Proof (Sketch). Let $\boldsymbol{q} = (\mathcal{O}, A)$ be an MTL_{core}^{-}-OMAQ with $\diamondsuit_{\varrho}$ operators only. First, we delete all disjointness constraints of the form $C_1 \wedge C_2 \rightarrow \bot$ from $\mathcal{O}$ and we translate the query into datalog(FO) in the same way as we did in the proof of Theorem 37. Since q is core, by the form of this translation, we obtain a linear datalog(FO) program. It is well-known that such a program can be transformed into an FO(TC)-query $\Psi_A(x)$ [45]. For every disjointness constraint $C_1 \wedge C_2 \to \bot$ in $\mathcal{O}$, we take the sentence $\exists x\, (\Psi_{C_1}(x) \wedge \Psi_{C_2}(x))$ and, finally, form a disjunction of $\Psi_A(x)$ with those sentences, which is an FO(TC)-rewriting of q.   □

The rewritability results we are going to present next impose restrictions on the range of metric operators: in particular, we consider ontologies with *unbounded* ranges of the form $\langle r, \infty)$, for $r \in \mathbb{Q}_2^{\geq 0}$ and $\langle$ being $($ or $[$, *punctual* ranges $[r, r]$, for $r \in \mathbb{Q}_2^{\geq 0}$, and *non-punctual* ranges.

Theorem 39. *Every MTL$^-$-OMAQ $q = (\mathcal{O}, A)$ with temporal operators in $\mathcal{O}$ of the form*

- $\diamondsuit_{(r,\infty)}$ *and* $\boxminus_{(r,\infty)}$ *only is* FO($<$)*-rewritable, and so can be answered in* AC^0;
- $\diamondsuit_{[r,r]}$ *and* $\boxminus_{[r,r]}$ *only is* FO(*RPR*)*-rewritable, and answering such OMAQs is* NC^1*-complete for data complexity;*
- $\diamondsuit_\varrho$ *and* $\boxminus_\varrho$, *for non-punctual* ϱ, *only is* FO(TC)*-rewritable; answering such OMAQs is in* NL *and* NC^1*-hard for data complexity.*

Moreover, MTL_{horn}^--OMAQs from the last item are also FO(DTC)-rewritable (FO with deterministic transitive closure), and so answering them is in L for data complexity. These rewritings heavily depend on the properties of the minimal models of OMAQs of a given type. For example, in the case of MTL-OMAQ with temporal operators of the forms $\diamondsuit_{(r,\infty)}$ and $\boxminus_{(r,\infty)}$ only, we can observe that the minimal model is monotonic in the sense that if $\diamondsuit_{(r,\infty)}P$ holds in a timestamp t, then the same formula holds in all timestamps greater than t. Analogously, if $\diamondsuit_{(r,\infty)}P$ does not hold in a timestamp t, then this formula holds in all timestamps smaller than t. It turns out that we can use this observation (and some additional properties of the minimal model) to construct an FO($<$)-rewriting. For more details of the constructions we refer the reader to [75].

So far in this section we discussed MTL-OMAQs. What do we know about wider classes of MTL OMQs (under the pointwise semantics)? First, we have:

Theorem 40. *Every MTL OMQ $q = (\mathcal{O}, \psi(t))$ with an* MFO($<, \delta_{\leq \mathbb{Q}_2}, \delta_{=\mathbb{Q}_2}$)*-formula $\psi(t)$ is* CONP*-complete for data complexity.*

Note that the counterpart of this result in LTL is Theorem 13. Furthermore, we say that MFO($<, \delta_{\leq \mathbb{Q}_2}, \delta_{=\mathbb{Q}_2}$)-formula is *positive*, if it is constructed using $\wedge$, $\vee$, $\forall$, $\exists$. We say that an MTL-OMQ $q = (\mathcal{O}, \psi(t))$ is *positive*, if $\psi(t)$ is a positive MFO($<, \delta_{\leq \mathbb{Q}_2}, \delta_{=\mathbb{Q}_2}$)-formula. The following result follows from [75]:

Theorem 41. *Suppose $q = (\mathcal{O}, \psi(t))$ is a positive MTL_{horn}-OMQ and $\mathcal{L}$ a language containing* FO($<$). *Suppose also that, for each atomic A in ψ, the OMAQ $(\mathcal{O}, A)$ is $\mathcal{L}$-rewritable. Then, q is also $\mathcal{L}$-rewritable.*

Therefore, by Theorems 37, 38, and 39, we obtain:

Corollary 42. (*i*) *Every positive* MTL^-_{horn}-OMQ *is datalog(FO)-rewritable.*

(*ii*) *Every positive* MTL^-_{core}-OMQ *with an ontology containing* $\diamondsuit_\varrho$ *operators only is FO(TC)-rewritable.*

(*iii*) *Every positive* MTL^--OMQ *with an ontology containing* $\diamondsuit_{(r,\infty)}$ *and* $\boxminus_{(r,\infty)}$ *operators only is FO(<)-rewritable.*

(*iv*) *Every positive* MTL^--OMQ *with an ontology containing* $\diamondsuit_{[r,r]}$ *and* $\boxminus_{[r,r]}$ *operators only is FO(RPR)-rewritable.*

(*v*) *Every positive* MTL^--OMQ *with an ontology containing* $\diamondsuit_\varrho$ *and* $\boxminus_\varrho$ *for non-punctual* ϱ *only is FO(TC)-rewritable.*

It is of interest to compare the results above to the results in the *LTL* case given by Corollary 21. The latter results also hold for positive OMQs, since every positive OMQ is also monotone. The comparison shows that, even in the case of positive Horn OMQs, the complexity landscape is more diverse for *MTL* than for *LTL*.

6   Future Research

In this paper, we have tried to overview recent developments in ontology-based access to temporal data, focusing primarily on the problem of rewriting temporal ontology-mediated queries into first-order queries over the data. For other aspects of temporal OBDA the reader is referred to the survey [9]. Compared to the classical atemporal OBDA, its temporal counterpart is still an infant, from both theoretical and especially practical points of view. In the remainder of this concluding section, we briefly discuss a few open problems and directions for future research that are related to OBDA with *LTL*, *MTL* and temporal *DL-Lite*.

LTL. The classical OBDA theory has recently investigated the fine-grained combined and parameterised complexities of OMQ answering and the succinctness problem for FO-rewritings [15,20–22]. These problems are of great importance for the temporal case, too (in particular, because the rewritings discussed above are far from optimal). Another development in the classical OBDA theory is the classification of single ontologies and even OMQs according to their data complexity and rewritability [51,66,67]. Extending this approach to temporal OMQs will most probably require totally different methods because of the linearly ordered temporal domain.

Temporal DL-Lite. The technique considered above does not seem to work for (two-sorted) conjunctive queries in place of instance queries; on the other hand, the methods of [7] indicate a somewhat different approach to deal with not necessarily tree-shaped conjunctive queries having multiple answer variables. It is of interest what happens with OMAQs when we consider Krom role inclusions. There are two open questions: the upper bound for $DL\text{-}Lite^{\square}_{bool}$ OMAQs and FO-rewritability of $DL\text{-}Lite^{\square}_{krom}$ and $DL\text{-}Lite^{\square\circ}_{krom}$ OMAQs. We conjecture that $DL\text{-}Lite_{krom}^{\square}$ OMAQs are FO($<$)-rewritable and $DL\text{-}Lite_{krom}^{\square\circ}$ OMAQs are FO($<, \equiv_{\mathbb{N}}$)-rewritable. To show this, one may need a type-based technique similar to the approach in the proof of Theorem 18 as Theorem 29 is not applicable to Krom role inclusions. Another open question is the upper bound for $DL\text{-}Lite_{bool}^{\square}$ OMAQs. On the practical side, more real-world use cases are needed to understand which temporal constructs are required to specify relevant temporal events and evaluate the performance of OMQ rewritings; for some activities in this direction we refer the reader to [17,24,25,58].

MTL. Much less is known about OMQs with *MTL*-ontologies than about ontologies with *LTL*-operators. The results presented in this paper show that some *MTL*-ontologies can be rewritten to FO (and its extensions), which indicates that reasoning with such ontologies may be feasible in practise. However, the computational properties of *MTL*-ontologies heavily depend on many aspects, such as the form of available metric operators and the type of ranges they use. The results presented in the previous section are only preliminary observations, and we are clearly far from understanding well the complexity of answering *MTL*-OMQs and classifying them accordingly. Here we mention some interesting open problems. Observe that Theorem 39 about OMAQs with non-punctual ranges contains a gap between NL and NC^1, and between L and NC^1. It would be interesting to establish tight complexity bounds for such OMAQs, as non-punctuality of ranges is a standard approach in *MTL*, which often allows one to reduce significantly the computational costs [2]. There are also many types of *MTL*-OMQs that have not been considered so far, for example, the ones with the 'since' and 'until' operators, as well as more complex queries, such as quasi-positive, or general (used in *LTL*-OMQs).

Another direction of future work concerns adopting the continuous semantics. Interestingly, such an approach has been already considered with respect to extensions of Datalog with *MTL*-operators [26,82] and applied, for example, to stream reasoning [48,49,63,83]. It is also worth mentioning that there is work on combining DLs with *MTL* [11,47]. As there is a big variety of potential applications of ontologies with *MTL*-operators, for instance, to image sequence evaluation [27], to ambient intelligence context [18,70], or to online monitoring asynchronous systems [14,37,53], among others, this direction of research looks very promising.

Acknowledgements. This work was supported by the EPSRC U.K. grants EP/S032282 'quant^{MD}: Ontology-Based Management for Many-Dimensional Quantitative Data' and EP/S032347 'OASIS: Ontology Reasoning over Frequently-Changing and Streaming Data', and by the SIRIUS Centre for Scalable Data Access (Research Council of Norway).

References

1. Abiteboul, S., Hull, R., Vianu, V.: Foundations of Databases. Addison-Wesley, Boston (1995)
2. Alur, R., Feder, T., Henzinger, T.A.: The benefits of relaxing punctuality. J. ACM (JACM) **43**(1), 116–146 (1996)
3. Alur, R., Henzinger, T.A.: Real-time logics: complexity and expressiveness. Inf. Comput. **104**(1), 35–77 (1993). http://dx.doi.org/10.1006/inco.1993.1025
4. Apt, K.R.: Logic programming. In: van Leeuwen, J. (ed.) Handbook of Theoretical Computer Science, Volume B: Formal Models and Semantics, pp. 493–574. Elsevier and MIT Press (1990). https://doi.org/10.1016/b978-0-444-88074-1.50015-9
5. Arora, S., Barak, B.: Computational Complexity: A Modern Approach, 1st edn. Cambridge University Press, New York (2009)
6. Artale, A., Calvanese, D., Kontchakov, R., Zakharyaschev, M.: The DL-Lite family and relations. J. Artif. Intell. Res. (JAIR) **36**, 1–69 (2009)
7. Artale, A., Kontchakov, R., Wolter, F., Zakharyaschev, M.: Temporal description logic for ontology-based data access. In: Proceedings of the 23rd International Joint Conference on Artificial Intelligence (IJCAI). IJCAI/AAAI (2013)
8. Artale, A., Kontchakov, R., Kovtunova, A., Ryzhikov, V., Wolter, F., Zakharyaschev, M.: First-order rewritability of temporal ontology-mediated queries. In: Proceedings of the 24th International Joint Conference on Artificial Intelligence, IJCAI 2015, pp. 2706–2712 (2015)
9. Artale, A., Kontchakov, R., Kovtunova, A., Ryzhikov, V., Wolter, F., Zakharyaschev, M.: Ontology-mediated query answering over temporal data: a survey (invited talk). In: TIME. LIPIcs, vol. 90, pp. 1:1–1:37. Schloss Dagstuhl - Leibniz-Zentrum fuer Informatik (2017)
10. Artale, A., Kontchakov, R., Kovtunova, A., Ryzhikov, V., Wolter, F., Zakharyaschev, M.: First-order rewritability of ontology-mediated queries in linear temporal logic. CoRR abs/2004.07221 (2020). https://arxiv.org/abs/2004.07221
11. Baader, F., Borgwardt, S., Koopmann, P., Ozaki, A., Thost, V.: Metric temporal description logics with interval-rigid names. In: Dixon, C., Finger, M. (eds.) FroCoS 2017. LNCS (LNAI), vol. 10483, pp. 60–76. Springer, Cham (2017). https://doi.org/10.1007/978-3-319-66167-4_4
12. Baader, F., Calvanese, D., McGuinness, D.L., Nardi, D., Patel-Schneider, P.F. (eds.): The Description Logic Handbook, 2nd edn. Cambridge University Press, Cambridge (2007)
13. Baader, F., Horrocks, I., Lutz, C., Sattler, U.: An Introduction to Description Logic. Cambridge University Press, Cambridge (2017)
14. Baldor, K., Niu, J.: Monitoring dense-time, continuous-semantics, metric temporal logic. In: Qadeer, S., Tasiran, S. (eds.) RV 2012. LNCS, vol. 7687, pp. 245–259. Springer, Heidelberg (2013). https://doi.org/10.1007/978-3-642-35632-2_24
15. Barceló, P., Feier, C., Lutz, C., Pieris, A.: When is ontology-mediated querying efficient? CoRR abs/2003.07800 (2020). https://arxiv.org/abs/2003.07800
16. Barrington, D.A.M., Compton, K.J., Straubing, H., Thérien, D.: Regular languages in nc^1. J. Comput. Syst. Sci. **44**(3), 478–499 (1992). https://doi.org/10.1016/0022-0000(92)90014-A
17. Beck, H., Dao-Tran, M., Eiter, T., Fink, M.: LARS: a logic-based framework for analyzing reasoning over streams. In: Bonet, B., Koenig, S. (eds.) Proceedings of the Twenty-Ninth AAAI Conference on Artificial Intelligence, Austin, Texas, USA, 25–30 January 2015, pp. 1431–1438. AAAI Press (2015). http://www.aaai.org/ocs/index.php/AAAI/AAAI15/paper/view/9657

18. Benfold, B., Harland, H., Bellotto, N., Bellotto, N., et al.: Cognitive visual tracking and camera control. Comput. Vis. Image Underst. **116**(3), 457–471 (2012)

19. Berger, R.: The Undecidability of the Domino Problem. American Mathematical Society (1966)

20. Bienvenu, M., Kikot, S., Kontchakov, R., Podolskii, V.V., Ryzhikov, V., Zakharyaschev, M.: The complexity of ontology-based data access with OWL 2 QL and bounded treewidth queries. In: Proceedings of the 36th ACM SIGMOD-SIGACT-SIGAI Symposium on Principles of Database Systems, PODS 2017, pp. 201–216. ACM (2017)

21. Bienvenu, M., Kikot, S., Kontchakov, R., Podolskii, V.V., Zakharyaschev, M.: Ontology-mediated queries: combined complexity and succinctness of rewritings via circuit complexity. J. ACM **65**(5), 28:1–28:51 (2018)

22. Bienvenu, M., Kikot, S., Kontchakov, R., Ryzhikov, V., Zakharyaschev, M.: On the parametrised complexity of tree-shaped ontology-mediated queries in OWL 2 QL. In: Artale, A., Glimm, B., Kontchakov, R. (eds.) Proceedings of the 30th International Workshop on Description Logics, CEUR Workshop Proceedings, Montpellier, France, 18–21 July 2017, vol. 1879 (2017). CEUR-WS.org. http://ceur-ws.org/Vol-1879/paper55.pdf

23. Börger, E., Grädel, E., Gurevich, Y.: The Classical Decision Problem. Perspectives in Mathematical Logic, Springer (1997)

24. Brandt, S., et al.: Two-dimensional rule language for querying sensor log data: a framework and use cases. In: Proceedings of the 26th International Symposium on Temporal Representation and Reasoning, TIME 2019. vol. 147, pp. 7:1–7:15. Dagstuhl Publishing (2019)

25. Brandt, S., Kalayci, E.G., Ryzhikov, V., Xiao, G., Zakharyaschev, M.: Querying log data with metric temporal logic. J. Artif. Intell. Res. **62**, 829–877 (2018)

26. Brandt, S., Kalaycı, E.G., Ryzhikov, V., Xiao, G., Zakharyaschev, M.: Querying log data with metric temporal logic. J. Artif. Intell. Res. **62**, 829–877 (2018)

27. Brzoska, C., Schäfer, K.: Temporal logic programming applied to image sequence evaluation (1995)

28. Büchi, J.: Weak second-order arithmetic and finite automata. Zeitschrift für Mathematische Logik und Grundlagen der Mathematik **6**(1–6), 66–92 (1960)

29. Calvanese, D., De Giacomo, G., Lembo, D., Lenzerini, M., Rosati, R.: Tractable reasoning and efficient query answering in description logics: the DL-Lite family. J. Autom. Reasoning **39**(3), 385–429 (2007)

30. Chomicki, J., Toman, D.: Temporal logic in information systems. In: Chomicki, J., Saake, G. (eds.) Logics for Databases and Information Systems (The Book Grow Out of the Dagstuhl Seminar 9529: Role of Logics in Information Systems, 1995), pp. 31–70. Kluwer (1998)

31. Chrobak, M.: Finite automata and unary languages. Theoret. Comput. Sci. **47**(2), 149–158 (1986)

32. Compton, K.J., Laflamme, C.: An algebra and a logic for NC^1. Inf. Comput. **87**(1/2), 240–262 (1990)

33. Compton, K.J., Straubing, H.: Characterizations of regular languages in low level complexity classes. In: Paun, G., Rozenberg, G., Salomaa, A. (eds.) Current Trends in Theoretical Computer Science, Entering the 21th Century, pp. 235–246. World Scientific (2001)

34. Demri, S., Goranko, V., Lange, M.: Temporal Logics in Computer Science. Cambridge Tracts in Theoretical Computer Science. Cambridge University Press, Cambridge (2016)

35. Elgot, C.: Decision problems of finite automata design and related arithmetics. Trans. Am. Math. Soc. **98**, 21–51 (1961)
36. Emerson, E.A.: Temporal and modal logic. In: van Leeuwen, J. (ed.) Handbook of Theoretical Computer Science, Volume B: Formal Models and Semantics, pp. 995–1072. Elsevier and MIT Press (1990). https://doi.org/10.1016/b978-0-444-88074-1.50021-4
37. Finkbeiner, B., Kuhtz, L.: Monitor circuits for LTL with bounded and unbounded future. In: Bensalem, S., Peled, D.A. (eds.) RV 2009. LNCS, vol. 5779, pp. 60–75. Springer, Heidelberg (2009). https://doi.org/10.1007/978-3-642-04694-0_5
38. Fisher, M.: Temporal representation and reasoning. In: van Harmelen, F., Lifschitz, V., Porter, B.W. (eds.) Handbook of Knowledge Representation, Foundations of Artificial Intelligence, vol. 3, pp. 513–550. Elsevier (2008). https://doi.org/10.1016/S1574-6526(07)03012-X
39. Furst, M.L., Saxe, J.B., Sipser, M.: Parity, circuits, and the polynomial-time hierarchy. Math. Syst. Theory **17**(1), 13–27 (1984)
40. Gabbay, D., Hodkinson, I., Reynolds, M.: Temporal Logic: Mathematical Foundations and Computational Aspects, vol. 1. Oxford University Press, Oxford (1994)
41. Gabbay, D., Kurucz, A., Wolter, F., Zakharyaschev, M.: Many-Dimensional Modal Logics: Theory and Applications, Studies in Logic, vol. 148. Elsevier, Amsterdam (2003)
42. Gabelaia, D., Kontchakov, R., Kurucz, A., Wolter, F., Zakharyaschev, M.: Combining spatial and temporal logics: expressiveness vs. complexity. J. Artif. Intell. Res. **23**, 167–243 (2005). https://doi.org/10.1613/jair.1537
43. Gabelaia, D., Kurucz, A., Wolter, F., Zakharyaschev, M.: Products of 'transitive' modal logics. J. Symb. Log. **70**(3), 993–1021 (2005). https://doi.org/10.2178/jsl/1122038925
44. Glimm, B., Ogbuji, C.: SPARQL 1.1 entailment regimes. W3C Recommendation (2013). http://www.w3.org/TR/sparql11-entailment
45. Grädel, E.: On transitive closure logic. In: Börger, E., Jäger, G., Kleine Büning, H., Richter, M.M. (eds.) CSL 1991. LNCS, vol. 626, pp. 149–163. Springer, Heidelberg (1992). https://doi.org/10.1007/BFb0023764
46. Gutierrez, C., Hurtado, C.A., Vaisman, A.A.: Introducing time into RDF. IEEE Trans. Knowl. Data Eng. **19**(2), 207–218 (2007)
47. Gutiérrez-Basulto, V., Jung, J.C., Ozaki, A.: On metric temporal description logics. In: Proceedings of the Twenty-second European Conference on Artificial Intelligence, pp. 837–845. IOS Press (2016)
48. Heintz, F., De Leng, D.: Spatio-temporal stream reasoning with incomplete spatial information. In: ECAI, pp. 429–434 (2014)
49. Heintz, F., Kvarnström, J., Doherty, P.: Stream reasoning in DyKnow: a knowledge processing middleware system. In: Proceedings of 1st International Workshop Stream Reasoning (2009)
50. Henzinger, T.A.: Temporal specification and verification of real-time systems. Technical report, Department of Computer Science, Stanford University, CA (1991)
51. Hernich, A., Lutz, C., Papacchini, F., Wolter, F.: Dichotomies in ontology-mediated querying with the guarded fragment. In: Proceedings of the 36th ACM SIGMOD-SIGACT-SIGAI Symposium on Principles of Database Systems, PODS 2017, pp. 185–199. ACM (2017)
52. Hirshfeld, Y., Rabinovich, A.M.: Logics for real time: decidability and complexity. Fundam. Inform. **62**(1), 1–28 (2004). http://content.iospress.com/articles/fundamenta-informaticae/fi62-1-02

53. Ho, H.-M., Ouaknine, J., Worrell, J.: Online monitoring of metric temporal logic. In: Bonakdarpour, B., Smolka, S.A. (eds.) RV 2014. LNCS, vol. 8734, pp. 178–192. Springer, Cham (2014). https://doi.org/10.1007/978-3-319-11164-3_15

54. Hodkinson, I.M., Kontchakov, R., Kurucz, A., Wolter, F., Zakharyaschev, M.: On the computational complexity of decidable fragments of first-order linear temporal logics. In: 10th International Symposium on Temporal Representation and Reasoning/4th International Conference on Temporal Logic (TIME-ICTL 2003), Cairns, Queensland, Australia, 8–10 July 2003, pp. 91–98. IEEE Computer Society (2003). https://doi.org/10.1109/TIME.2003.1214884

55. Hunter, P., Ouaknine, J., Worrell, J.: Expressive completeness for metric temporal logic. In: 28th Annual ACM/IEEE Symposium on Logic in Computer Science, LICS 2013, New Orleans, LA, USA, 25–28 June 2013, pp. 349–357. IEEE Computer Society (2013). https://doi.org/10.1109/LICS.2013.41

56. Immerman, N.: Descriptive Complexity. Springer, New York (1999). https://doi.org/10.1007/978-1-4612-0539-5

57. Kamp, H.W.: Tense logic and the theory of linear order. Ph.D. thesis, Computer Science Department, University of California at Los Angeles, USA (1968)

58. Kharlamov, E., Mehdi, G., Savkovic, O., Xiao, G., Kalayci, E.G., Roshchin, M.: Semantically-enhanced rule-based diagnostics for industrial Internet of Things: the SDRL language and case study for Siemens trains and turbines. J. Web Semant. **56**, 11–29 (2019)

59. Kontchakov, R., Rodriguez-Muro, M., Zakharyaschev, M.: Ontology-based data access with databases: A short course. In: Reasoning Web. Semantic Technologies for Intelligent Data Access - 9th International Summer School 2013, Proceedings, Mannheim, Germany, 30 July–2 August 2013, pp. 194–229 (2013). https://doi.org/10.1007/978-3-642-39784-4_5

60. Kontchakov, R., Ryzhikov, V., Wolter, F., Zakharyaschev, M.: Boolean role inclusions in DL-Lite with and without time (2020). Manuscript

61. Kontchakov, R., Zakharyaschev, M.: An introduction to description logics and query rewriting. In: Reasoning Web. Reasoning on the Web in the Big Data Era - 10th International Summer School 2014, Proceedings, Athens, Greece, 8–13 September 2014, pp. 195–244 (2014). https://doi.org/10.1007/978-3-319-10587-1_5

62. Koymans, R.: Specifying real-time properties with metric temporal logic. Real-Time Syst. **2**(4), 255–299 (1990). http://dx.doi.org/10.1007/BF01995674

63. de Leng, D., Heintz, F.: Approximate stream reasoning with metric temporal logic under uncertainty. In: Proceedings of the AAAI Conference on Artificial Intelligence, vol. 33, pp. 2760–2767 (2019)

64. Libkin, L.: Elements of Finite Model Theory. Springer, Heidelberg (2004). https://doi.org/10.1007/978-3-662-07003-1

65. Lutz, C., Wolter, F., Zakharyaschev, M.: Temporal description logics: a survey. In: Proceedings of the 15th International Symposium on Temporal Representation and Reasoning (TIME 2008), pp. 3–14 (2008)

66. Lutz, C., Sabellek, L.: Ontology-mediated querying with the description logic EL: trichotomy and linear datalog rewritability. In: Sierra, C. (ed.) Proceedings of the Twenty-Sixth International Joint Conference on Artificial Intelligence, IJCAI 2017, Melbourne, Australia, 19–25 August 2017, pp. 1181–1187 (2017). https://doi.org/10.24963/ijcai.2017/164. ijcai.org

67. Lutz, C., Wolter, F.: The data complexity of description logic ontologies. Logical Methods Comput. Sci. **13**(4) (2017). https://doi.org/10.23638/LMCS-13(4:7)2017

68. Manna, Z., Pnueli, A.: The Temporal Logic of Reactive and Concurrent Systems-Specification. Springer, New York (1992). https://doi.org/10.1007/978-1-4612-0931-7
69. Motik, B.: Representing and querying validity time in RDF and OWL: a logic-based approach. J. Web Semant. **12**, 3–21 (2012)
70. Münch, D., IJsselmuiden, J., Arens, M., Stiefelhagen, R.: High-level situation recognition using fuzzy metric temporal logic, case studies in surveillance and smart environments. In: 2011 IEEE International Conference on Computer Vision Workshops (ICCV Workshops), pp. 882–889. IEEE (2011)
71. Ouaknine, J., Worrell, J.: On the decidability of metric temporal logic. In: 20th Annual IEEE Symposium on Logic in Computer Science (LICS 2005), pp. 188–197. IEEE (2005)
72. Ouaknine, J., Worrell, J.: Some recent results in metric temporal logic. In: Cassez, F., Jard, C. (eds.) FORMATS 2008. LNCS, vol. 5215, pp. 1–13. Springer, Heidelberg (2008). https://doi.org/10.1007/978-3-540-85778-5_1
73. Poggi, A., Lembo, D., Calvanese, D., De Giacomo, G., Lenzerini, M., Rosati, R.: Linking data to ontologies. In: Spaccapietra, S. (ed.) Journal on Data Semantics X. LNCS, vol. 4900, pp. 133–173. Springer, Heidelberg (2008). https://doi.org/10.1007/978-3-540-77688-8_5
74. Rabinovich, A.: A proof of Kamp's theorem. Logical Methods Comput. Sci. **10**(1), 1–16 (2014)
75. Ryzhikov, V., Wałęga, P.A., Zakharyaschev, M.: Data complexity and rewritability of ontology-mediated queries in metric temporal logic under the event-based semantics. In: Kraus, S. (ed.) Proceedings of the Twenty-Eighth International Joint Conference on Artificial Intelligence, IJCAI 2019, Macao, China, 10–16 August 2019, pp. 1851–1857 (2019). https://doi.org/10.24963/ijcai.2019/256. ijcai.org
76. Schaerf, A.: On the complexity of the instance checking problem in concept languages with existential quantification. J. Intell. Inf. Syst. **2**(3), 265–278 (1993)
77. Soylu, A., Giese, M., Jimenez-Ruiz, E., Vega-Gorgojo, G., Horrocks, I.: Experiencing OptiqueVQS: a multi-paradigm and ontology-based visual query system for end users. Univ. Access Inf. Soc. **15**(1), 129–152 (2016)
78. Straubing, H., Weil, P.: An introduction to finite automata and their connection to logic. CoRR abs/1011.6491 (2010)
79. Straubing, H.: Finite Automata, Formal Logic, and Circuit Complexity. Birkhauser Verlag, Basel (1994)
80. To, A.W.: Unary finite automata vs. arithmetic progressions. Inf. Process. Lett. **109**(17), 1010–1014 (2009)
81. Trakhtenbrot, B.: Finite automata and the logic of one-place predicates. Siberian Math. J. **3**, 103–131 (1962). English translation in: AMS Transl. 59 (1966) 23–55
82. Wałęga, P.A., Cuenca Grau, B., Kaminski, M., Kostylev, E.: DatalogMTL: computational complexity and expressive power. In: International Joint Conferences on Artificial Intelligence (IJCAI) (2019)
83. Wałęga, P.A., Kaminski, M., Grau, B.C.: Reasoning over streaming data in metric temporal datalog. In: Proceedings of the AAAI Conference on Artificial Intelligence, vol. 33, pp. 3092–3099 (2019)

84. Xiao, G., et al.: Ontology-based data access: a survey. In: Lang, J. (ed.) Proceedings of the Twenty-Seventh International Joint Conference on Artificial Intelligence, IJCAI 2018, Stockholm, Sweden, 13–19 July 2018, pp. 5511–5519 (2018). https://doi.org/10.24963/ijcai.2018/777. ijcai.org

85. Xiao, G., Ding, L., Cogrel, B., Calvanese, D.: Virtual knowledge graphs: an overview of systems and use cases. Data Intell. 1(3), 201–223 (2019). https://doi.org/10.1162/dint_a_0001110.1162/dint_a_00011

An Introduction to Answer Set Programming and Some of Its Extensions

Wolfgang Faber[✉]

University of Klagenfurt, 9020, Klagenfurt am Wörthersee, Austria
wolfgang.faber@aau.at

Abstract. Answer Set Programming (ASP) is a rule-based language rooted in traditional Logic Programming, Databases, Knowledge Representation, and Non-monotonic Reasoning. It offers a flexible language for declarative problem solving, with support of efficient general-purpose solvers and reasoners. The larger part of this article provides an introduction to ASP, with a historical perspective, a definition of the core language, a guideline to knowledge representation, and an overview of existing ASP solvers. One part focuses on one commonly used feature: aggregates and generalized atoms. The inclusion of aggregates in ASP (and Logic Programming at large) has long been motivated, however there are some issues with semantics to be addressed, in particular when aggregates occur in recursive definitions. Very similar considerations are needed when coupling ASP with other formalisms, which we collectively refer to as "generalized atoms". An overview of these semantic challenges and proposals for addressing them is provided, along with an overview of complexity results and system support.

1 Introduction

Traditional software engineering is focussed on an imperative, algorithmic approach, in which a computer is basically being told what steps should be followed in order to solve a given problem. Finding good algorithms for hard problems is often not obvious and requires substantial skill and knowledge. Despite these efforts, solutions provided in this way typically lack flexibility: when the specification of the given problem changes only slightly, for example because additional information on the nature of the problem becomes available, major re-engineering is often necessary, in the worst case from scratch. The main problem with this approach is that the knowledge about the problem and its solutions is not represented explicitly, but only implicitly, hidden inside the algorithm. Especially in Artificial Intelligence, it does not seem like the best idea to solve problems in this way, as that would yield inflexible, and hence arguably unintelligent agents. John McCarthy has coined the term *elaboration tolerance* [129] in the 1980s for the ease of modifying problem representations to take into account new phenomena. He argues that natural languages fare well regarding elaboration tolerance in "human" use; clearly, algorithmic representations are not particularly elaboration tolerant.

Declarative programming is an alternative, which suits elaboration tolerance much better. In this approach, the problem and its solutions are specified explicitly. That is, the

---

Parts of this work are based on [70].

M. Manna and A. Pieris (Eds.): Reasoning Web 2020, LNCS 12258, pp. 149–185, 2020.
https://doi.org/10.1007/978-3-030-60067-9_6

features of the problem and its solution are represented, rather than a method for how solutions are to be obtained. Methods like this actually come natural in science, but also in everyday life. Before we try to work out how to solve a problem, we usually first try to understand it and determine out how a solution would look like, before trying to find a method to obtain a solution. One of the first to put this approach into perspective in computer science was the same John McCarthy mentioned earlier in the 1950s [128]. He also postulated that the most natural language for specifying problems and solutions would be logic, and in particular predicate logic.

In fact, logic is an excellent candidate for declarative programming: it provides a simple and abstract formalism, and in addition, it has the potential for automation. Similar to an abstract or electronic machine which can execute an algorithm, computational logic has produced tools that allow for automatically obtaining solutions, given a declarative specification in logic. Indeed, many people nowadays use this way of solving problems: Queries to relational databases together with the database schemata are examples of declarative specifications that allow for obtaining answers to the queries. The probably most widely used database query language, SQL, essentially is predicate logic written in a specific way [1].

However, in many cases one wants to go beyond databases as they are used today. It has been shown that relational databases and query languages like SQL can only represent fairly simple problems. For instance, problems like finding the cheapest tour of a number of cities, or filling a container with items of different size, such that the value transported in the container is maximized, are typical problems that can probably not be solved using SQL. It might seem strange to use the word "probably" here, but underlying this conjecture is one of the most famous open problems in Computer Science—the question whether P equals NP. These are complexity classes; basically every problem has some intrinsic complexity, indicating how many resources are required to solve it on a standard machine model, in terms of the size of the problem input. P is the class of problems that require at most polynomial amount of time in the input size (which is variable). NP is just a slight alteration, in which one also gets a polynomial-size certificate that can be verified in time polynomial in the input. The crucial question is how to obtain this certificate for a given input, and indeed so far nobody has succeeded to prove convincingly either that this can always be done in polynomial time or that it cannot be done in polynomial time. In other words, it is unknown whether P and NP are different or equal, see for example [14, 93].

Logic Programming is an attempt to use declarative programming with logic that goes beyond SQL, and often beyond P. The main construct in logic programming is a rule, an expression that looks like $Head \leftarrow Body$, where $Body$ is a logic conjunction possibly involving negation, and $Head$ is either an atomic formula or a logic disjunction. This can be seen as a logic formula ($\leftarrow$ denoting implication, and universal quantification being implicit), with the special meaning that $Head$ is defined by that rule. At the time of the establishment of the field (as described in the following section), logic programming actually attempted to become a full-scale programming language. Its most famous language, Prolog [48], aimed at this, but had to renounce to full declarativity in order to achieve that goal. For instance, in Prolog rules the order of elements inside $Body$ matters, as does the order among rules (most notably for termination). Moreover, Prolog also has a number of non-logical constructs.

Answer Set Programming (ASP) is a branch of logic programming, which does not aspire to create a full-scale language. In this respect, it is influenced by database languages, as also these are not general-purpose languages, but suffice for a particular class of problems. ASP does however attempt to enlarge the class of problems which can be expressed by the language. While, as mentioned earlier, SQL probably cannot express hard problems in NP, ASP definitely can. Actually, ASP can uniformly express all problems in the complexity class Σ_2^P and its complement Π_2^P, which are similar to NP and co-NP, respectively, with an NP-hard oracle, that is, at each step of the computation a problem in NP might have to be solved. If it turns out that P = NP, then all of these classes coincide. For details on these complexity classes, see [14,93], for a survey of expressivity and complexity in ASP, see [53].

In ASP, the rule construct $Head \leftarrow Body$ (where $Head$ can be a disjunction) is read like a formula in nonmonotonic logics, rather than classical logic. Nonmonotonic logics are an effort to formulate a logic of common sense, that is, adapting the semantics of logic such that it corresponds better to our everyday reasoning, which is characterized by the presence of incomplete knowledge, hypothetical reasoning and default assumptions. It can be argued that nonmonotonic logics are much better suited in such a setting than classical logic. One salient feature in ASP is that the truth of elements needs justifications, that is, for an atom to be true there must be a rule in the program that supports its truth. In this respect, the formula is related to intuitionistic or constructive logic, and indeed ASP has been characterized by means of an intermediate logic that is situated between classical and intuitionistic logic [136].

A common and natural language feature in declarative languages are aggregate statements. In fact, the aggregate statement COUNT and SUM are widely used in SQL, and are covered in any serious introduction to databases. Since ASP has (via Datalog) roots in databases, aggregate constructs appeared fairly soon after the consolidation of the core language. Including these constructs is, however, only straightforward when they are used as in database queries. Other uses, especially in recursive definitions, proved to be difficult in terms of defining the "correct" meaning. Indeed, to date there is still controversy on this matter. As a sidenote, also newer versions of SQL allow for recursive definitions, but using aggregates in these is prohibited in the standardization document. Also the current ASP standard "ASP-Core-2" [42] does not allow aggregates in recursive definitions, but some ASP systems do support that.

Summarizing, ASP is a formalism that has emerged syntactically from logic programming, with strong influences from database theory, nonmonotonic logics, knowledge representation, symbolic artificial intelligence, and more. Its main representation feature is the rule, which is interpreted according to common sense principles. It allows for declarative specifications of a rich class of programs, generalizing the declarative approach of databases. In ASP, one writes a program (a collection of rules), which represents a problem to be solved. This program, together with some input, which is also expressed by a collection of factual rules, possesses a collection of solutions (possibly also no solution), which correspond to the solutions of the modelled problem. Since these solutions are usually sets, the term Answer Set has been coined.

Concerning terminology, ASP is sometimes used in a somewhat broader sense, referring to any declarative formalism representing a solution as a set. However, the more frequent understanding is the narrower reading adopted in this article, which has been coined in [91]. Moreover, since ASP is the most prominent branch of logic programming in which rule heads may be disjunctive, sometimes the term Disjunctive Logic Programming can be found referring explicitly to ASP. Yet other terms for ASP are A-Prolog, AnsProlog, and Stable Logic Programming. For complementary introductory material on ASP, we refer to [18] and [89].

2   History of ASP from a Logic Programming Perspective

The roots of Answer Set Programming lie predominantly in Logic Programming, Nonmonotonic Reasoning and Databases. In this section we give an overview on the history of Logic Programming from the perspective of Answer Set Programming. It therefore does not cover several important subfields of Logic Programming, such as Constraint Logic Programming [127] or Abductive Logic Programming [105]. We should also note that this is an informed, but personal perspective.

As mentioned in the introduction, one of the first to suggest logic, and in particular predicate logic, as a programming language was John McCarthy in the 1950s [128]. McCarthy's motivating example was set in Artificial Intelligence, and involved planning as its main task, an agenda that was continuously elaborated, see for instance [130].

Developments in Computational Logic, most notably the specification of the Resolution principle and unification as a computational method by J. Alan Robinson in 1965 [149], acted as a catalyst for the rise of Logic Programming. This field can besaid to have started with Prolog, a working system developed by a group around Alain Colmerauer in Marseilles [48]. A few other, somewhat more restricted systems had been available before, but Prolog was to make the breakthrough for Logic Programming.

One of the prime advocates of what would become known as the Logic Programming paradigm has been Robert Kowalski, who provided the philosophical basis and concretizations of the paradigm, for instance in [107] and [108]. Kowalski also collaborated with Colmerauer on Prolog, and within his group in Edinburgh, alternative implementations of Prolog were created. There has also been a standardization effort for the language, which would become known as Edinburgh Prolog and served as the de facto specification of Prolog for many years until the definition of ISO Prolog in 1995 [103].

However, Logic Programming, and Prolog in particular, was inspired by, but not the same as classical first-order logic. Initially the differences were not entirely clear. The first effort to provide a formal definition for the semantics of Logic Programming is also due to Kowalski, who together with Maarten van Emden gave a semantics based on fixpoints of operators for a restricted class of logic programs (Horn programs, also called positive programs) in [160]. This fixpoint semantics essentially coincided with minimal Herbrand models and with resolution-based query answering on Horn programs. The major feature missing in Horn programs is negation—however Prolog did have a negation operator.

Indeed, the quest for finding a suitable semantics in the spirit of minimal models for programs containing negation turned out to be far from straightforward. The first attempt was made by Keith Clark in [47] by defining a transformation of the programs to formulas in classical logic, which are then interpreted using the classical model semantics. However, the approach gave arguably unintuitive results for programs with positive recursion. In particular, the obtained semantics does not coincide with the minimal model semantics on positive programs.

At about the same time, Raymond Reiter formulated the Closed World Assumption in [146], which can be seen as the philosophical basis of the treatment of negation.

A further milestone in the research on the intended semantics for programs with negation has been the definition of what later became known uniformly as perfect model semantics for programs that can be stratified on negation, in [13] and [161]. The basic idea of stratification is that programs can be partitioned into subprograms (strata) such that the rules of each stratum contain negative predicates only if they are are defined in lower strata. In this way, it is possible to evaluate the program by separately evaluating its partitions in such a way that a given "stratum" is processed whenever the ones from which it (negatively) depends have already been processed.

While stratification was an important step forward, it is obvious that not all logic programs are stratified. In particular, programs which are recursive through negation are never stratified, and the problem of assigning a semantics to non-stratified programs still remained open. There were essentially two approaches for finding suitable definitions.

The first approach was giving up the classical setting of models that assign two truth values, and introduce a third value, intuitively representing "unknown". This approach required a somewhat different definition, because in the two-valued approach one would give a definition only for positive values, implicitly stating that all other constructs are considered to be negative. For instance, for minimal models, one minimizes the true elements, implicitly stating that all elements not contained in the minimal model will be false. With three truth values this strategy is no longer applicable, as elements which are not true can be either false or undefined. In order to resolve this issue, Allen Van Gelder, Kenneth Ross, and John Schlipf introduced the notion of unfounded sets in [162], in order to define which elements of the program should be considered false given some partial valuation. Combining existing techniques for defining the minimal model with unfounded sets, they defined the notion of a well-founded model. In this way, any program would still be guaranteed to have a single model, just like there is a unique minimal model for positive programs and a unique perfect model for stratified programs.

The second approach consisted of viewing logic programs as formulas in nonmonotonic logics (see for instance [125] for an overview) rather than formulas of classical logic (with an additional minimality criterion), and as a corollary, abandoning the unique model property. Among the first to concretize this was Michael Gelfond in [87], who proposed to view logic programs as formulas of autoepistemic logic, and Nicole Bidoit and Christine Froidevaux in [23], who proposed to view logic programs as formulas of default logic. Both of these developments have been picked up by Michael Gelfond and Vladimir Lifschitz, who in [90] defined the notion of stable models, which is inspired by nonmonotonic logics, however does not refer explicitly to these, but rather relies on a reduct which effectively emulates nonmonotonic inference. It was this surprisingly simple formulation, which did not require previous knowledge on non-classical logics that has become well-known, and forms the basis of ASP. While any program admits exactly one well-founded model, programs may admit no, one or many stable models. However, well-founded and stable models are closely related, for instance the well-founded model of a program is contained in each stable model, cf. [163]. Moreover, both approaches coincide with perfect models on stratified programs.

Yet another line of research, somewhat orthogonal to finding the right semantics for programs with negation, concerned the use of disjunction in rule heads. This construct is appealing, because it allows for direct nondeterministic definitions. Prolog and many other logic programming languages traditionally do not provide such a feature, being restricted to so-called definite rules. Jack Minker has been a pioneer and advocate of having disjunctions in programs. In [131] he formulated the Generalized Closed World Assumption (GCWA), which gave a simple and intuitive semantics for disjunctive logic programs. This concept has been elaborated on over the years, most notably by the Extended GCWA defined in [167]. Eventually, also the stable model semantics has been extended to disjunctive programs in [144] by just minimally altering the definition of [90]. On the other hand, defining an extension of well-founded models for disjunctive programs remains a controversial matter to this date with various rivalling definitions, cf. [164].

The final step towards Answer Set Programming in the traditional sense has been the addition of a second kind of negation, which has a more classical reading than negation as failure. This second negation is often known as true, strong, or classical negation. Combining this feature with disjunctive stable models of [144] led to the definition of answer sets in [91].

Since then, several other features in ASP were introduced, leading to the definition of the ASP standard "ASP-Core-2" [42]. This standard was essentially already created in 2013 out of a standardization effort for the 2013 edition of the ASP Competition [3], and is an evolution of "ASP-Core" as used in the preceding ASP Competition [45], which was in turn based on a sketch done by the LPNMR steering committee in 2004[1].

3   ASP Language

In what follows, we provide a formal definition of the syntax and semantics of the core Answer Set Programming language in the sense of [91], that is, disjunctive logic programming involving two kinds of negation (referred to as strong negation and negation as failure), under the answer sets semantics.

3.1   Core ASP

Syntax. Following a convention dating back to Prolog, strings starting with uppercase letters denote logical variables, while strings starting with lower case letters denote constants. A *term* is either a variable or a constant. Note that here function symbols are not considered.

An *atom* is an expression $p(t_1, \ldots, t_n)$, where p is a *predicate* of arity n and $t_1, \ldots, t_n$ are terms. A *classical literal* l is either an atom p (in this case, it is *positive*), or a negated

---

[1] https://www.mat.unical.it/aspcomp2011/files/Corelang2004.pdf.

atom $\neg p$ (in this case, it is *negative*). A *negation as failure (NAF) literal* ℓ is of the form l or not l, where l is a classical literal; in the former case ℓ is *positive*, and in the latter case *negative*. Unless stated otherwise, by *literal* we mean a classical literal.

Given a classical literal l, its *complementary* literal $\neg l$ is defined as $\neg p$ if $l = p$ and p if $l = \neg p$. A set L of literals is said to be *consistent* if, for every literal $l \in L$, its complementary literal is not contained in L.

A *disjunctive rule* (*rule*, for short) r is a construct

$$a_1 \lor \cdots \lor a_n \leftarrow b_1, \cdots, b_k, \text{ not } b_{k+1}, \cdots, \text{ not } b_m. \tag{1}$$

where $a_1, \cdots, a_n, b_1, \cdots, b_m$ are classical literals and $n \geq 0$, $m \geq k \geq 0$. The disjunction $a_1 \lor \cdots \lor a_n$ is called the *head* of r, while the conjunction $b_1, \ldots, b_k$, not b_{k+1}, ..., not b_m is referred to as the *body* of r. A rule without head literals (i.e., $n = 0$) is usually referred to as an *integrity constraint*. A rule having precisely one head literal (i.e., $n = 1$) is called a *normal rule*. If the body is empty (i.e., $k = m = 0$), it is called a *fact*, and in this case the "$\leftarrow$" sign is usually omitted.

Integrity constraints (or sometimes just constraints for short) can be viewed as rules with $\bot$ (falsity) in the head; after all, $\bot$ is the neutral element for disjunction. The intended meaning therefore is that the body of the integrity constraint should not become true.

The following notation will be useful for further discussion. If r is a rule of form (1), then $H(r) = \{a_1, \ldots, a_n\}$ is the set of literals in the head and $B(r) = B^+(r) \cup B^-(r)$ is the set of the body literals, where $B^+(r)$ (the *positive body*) is $\{b_1, \ldots, b_k\}$ and $B^-(r)$ (*the negative body*) is $\{b_{k+1}, \ldots, b_m\}$.

An *ASP program* $\mathcal{P}$ is a finite set of rules. A not-free program $\mathcal{P}$ (i.e., such that $\forall r \in \mathcal{P} : B^-(r) = \emptyset$) is called *positive* or *Horn*,[2] and a $\lor$-free program $\mathcal{P}$ (i.e., such that $\forall r \in \mathcal{P} : |H(r)| \leq 1$) is called *normal logic program*.

In ASP, rules in programs are usually required to be safe. The motivation of safety comes from the field of databases, where safety has been introduced as a means to guarantee that queries (programs in the case of ASP) do not depend on the universe (the set of constants) considered. As an example, a fact $p(X)$. gives rise to the truth of $p(a)$ when the universe $\{a\}$ is considered, while it gives rise to the truth of $p(a)$ and $p(b)$ when the universe $\{a, b\}$ is considered. Safe programs do not suffer from this problem when at least the constants occurring in the program are considered. For a detailed discussion, we refer to [1].

A rule is *safe* if each variable in that rule also appears in at least one positive literal in the body of that rule. An ASP program is safe, if each of its rules is safe, and in the following we will only consider safe programs.

A term (an atom, a rule, a program, etc.) is called *ground*, if no variable appears in it. Sometimes a ground program is also called *propositional* program.

---

[2] In positive programs negation as failure (not) does not occur, while strong negation ($\neg$) may be present.

Example 1. Consider the following program:

r_1: $a(X) \lor b(X) \leftarrow c(X,Y), d(Y),$ not $e(X)$.
r_2: $\leftarrow c(X,Y), k(Y), e(X),$ not $b(X)$
r_3: $m \leftarrow n, o, a(1)$.
r_4: $c(1,2)$.

r_1 *is a disjunctive rule with* $H(r_1) = \{a(X), b(X)\}$, $B^+(r_1) = \{c(X,Y), d(Y)\}$, *and* $B^-(r_1) = \{e(X)\}$. r_2 *is an integrity constraint with* $B^+(r_2) = \{c(X,Y), k(Y), e(X)\}$, *and* $B^-(r_2) = \{b(X)\}$. r_3 *is a ground, positive, and non-disjunctive rule with* $H(r_3) = \{m\}$, $B^+(r_3) = \{n, o, a(1)\}$, *and* $B^-(r_3) = \emptyset$. r_4, *finally, is a fact (note that* $\leftarrow$ *is omitted). Moreover, all of the rules are safe.*   □

Semantics. We next describe the semantics of ASP programs, which is based on the answer set semantics originally defined in [91]. However, different to [91] only consistent answer sets are considered, as it is now standard practice.

We note that in ASP the availability of some pre-interpreted predicates is assumed, such as $=, <, >$. However, it would also be possible to define them explicitly as facts, so they are not treated in a special way here.

Herbrand Universe and Literal Base. For any program $\mathcal{P}$, the *Herbrand universe*, denoted by $U_\mathcal{P}$, is the set of all constants occurring in $\mathcal{P}$. If no constant occurs in $\mathcal{P}$, $U_\mathcal{P}$ consists of one arbitrary constant[3]. The *Herbrand literal base* $B_\mathcal{P}$ is the set of all ground (classical) literals constructable from predicate symbols appearing in $\mathcal{P}$ and constants in $U_\mathcal{P}$ (note that, for each atom p, $B_\mathcal{P}$ contains also the strongly negated literal $\neg p$).

Example 2. Consider the following program:
$\mathcal{P}_0 = \{$
r_1: $a(X) \lor b(X) \leftarrow c(X,Y)$.
r_2: $e(X) \leftarrow c(X,Y),$ not $b(X)$.
r_4: $c(1,2)$.
$\}$
then, the universe is $U_{\mathcal{P}_0} = \{1, 2\}$, *and the base is* $B_{\mathcal{P}_0} = \{a(1), a(2), b(1), b(2), e(1), e(2), c(1,1), c(1,2), c(2,1), c(2,2), \neg a(1), \neg a(2), \neg b(1), \neg b(2), \neg e(1), \neg e(2), \neg c(1,1), \neg c(1,2), \neg c(2,1), \neg c(2,2)\}$.   □

Ground Instantiation. For any rule r, $Ground(r)$ denotes the set of rules obtained by replacing each variable in r by constants in $U_\mathcal{P}$ in all possible ways. For any program $\mathcal{P}$, its ground instantiation is the set $Ground(\mathcal{P}) = \bigcup_{r \in \mathcal{P}} Ground(r)$. Note that for propositional programs, $\mathcal{P} = Ground(\mathcal{P})$ holds.

---

[3] Actually, since the language does not contain function symbols and since rules are required to be safe, this extra constant is not needed. However, we have kept the classic definition in order to avoid confusion.

Example 3. Consider again program $\mathcal{P}_0$ of Example 2. Its ground instantiation is:

$Ground(\mathcal{P}_0) = \{$

$\qquad g_1: a(1) \vee b(1) \leftarrow c(1,1).\qquad g_2: a(1) \vee b(1) \leftarrow c(1,2).$

$\qquad g_3: a(2) \vee b(2) \leftarrow c(2,1).\qquad g_4: a(2) \vee b(2) \leftarrow c(2,2).$

$\qquad g_5: e(1) \leftarrow c(1,1), \text{not } b(1).\ \ g_6: e(1) \leftarrow c(1,2), \text{not } b(1).$

$\qquad g_7: e(2) \leftarrow c(2,1), \text{not } b(2).\ \ g_8: e(2) \leftarrow c(2,2), \text{not } b(2).$

$\qquad g_9: c(1,2).$

$\qquad \}$

Note that, the the atom $c(1,2)$ was already ground in $\mathcal{P}_0$, while the rules $g_1, \ldots, g_4$ (resp. $g_5, \ldots, g_8$) are obtained by replacing the variables in r_1 (resp. r_2) with constants in $U_{\mathcal{P}_0}$. □

Answer Sets. For every program $\mathcal{P}$, its answer sets are defined using its ground instantiation $Ground(\mathcal{P})$ in two steps: First the answer sets of positive disjunctive programs are defined, then the answer sets of general programs are defined by a reduction to positive disjunctive programs and a stability condition.

An interpretation I is a consistent set of ground classical literals $I \subseteq B_{\mathcal{P}}$ w.r.t. a program $\mathcal{P}$. A consistent interpretation $X \subseteq B_{\mathcal{P}}$ is called *closed under* $\mathcal{P}$(where $\mathcal{P}$ is a positive disjunctive Datalog program), if, for every $r \in Ground(\mathcal{P})$, $H(r) \cap X \neq \emptyset$ whenever $B(r) \subseteq X$. An interpretation which is closed under $\mathcal{P}$ is also called *model* of $\mathcal{P}$. An interpretation $X \subseteq B_{\mathcal{P}}$ is an *answer set* for a positive disjunctive program $\mathcal{P}$, if it is minimal (under set inclusion) among all (consistent) interpretations that are closed under $\mathcal{P}$.

Example 4. The positive program $\mathcal{P}_1 = \{a \vee \neg b \vee c.\}$ has the answer sets $\{a\}$, $\{\neg b\}$, and $\{c\}$; note that they are minimal and correspond to the multiple ways of satisfying the disjunction. Its extension $\mathcal{P}_2 = \mathcal{P}_1 \cup \{\leftarrow a.\}$ has the answer sets $\{\neg b\}$ and $\{c\}$, since the additional constraint is not satisfied by interpretation $\{a\}$. Moreover, the positive program $\mathcal{P}_3 = \mathcal{P}_2 \cup \{\neg b \leftarrow c.\ ;\ c \leftarrow \neg b.\}$ has the single answer set $\{\neg b, c\}$ (indeed, the remaining consistent closed interpretation $\{a, \neg b, c\}$ is not minimal). while, it is easy to see that, $\mathcal{P}_4 = \mathcal{P}_3 \cup \{\leftarrow c\}$ has no answer set. □

The *reduct* or *Gelfond-Lifschitz transform* of a ground program $\mathcal{P}$ w.r.t. a set $X \subseteq B_{\mathcal{P}}$ is the positive ground program $\mathcal{P}^X$, obtained from $\mathcal{P}$ by

- deleting all rules $r \in \mathcal{P}$ for which $B^-(r) \cap X \neq \emptyset$ holds;
- deleting the negative body from the remaining rules.

An *answer set* of a program $\mathcal{P}$ is a set $X \subseteq B_{\mathcal{P}}$ such that X is an answer set of $Ground(\mathcal{P})^X$.

Example 5. For the negative ground program $\mathcal{P}_5 = \{a \leftarrow \text{not } b.\}$, $A = \{a\}$ is the only answer set, as $\mathcal{P}_5^A = \{a.\}$. For example for $B = \{b\}$, $\mathcal{P}_5^B = \emptyset$, and so B is not an answer set. □

Example 6. Consider again program $\mathcal{P}_0$ of Example 2, whose ground instantiation $Ground(\mathcal{P}_0)$ has been reported in Example 3. A naïve way to compute the answer sets of $\mathcal{P}_0$ is to consider all possible interpretations, checking whether they are answer sets of $Ground(\mathcal{P}_0)$.

For instance, consider the interpretation $I_0 = \{c(1,2), a(1), e(1)\}$. The corresponding reduct $Ground(\mathcal{P}_0)^{I_0}$ contains the rules g_1, g_2, g_3, g_4, g_9, plus $e(1) \leftarrow c(1,1)$, $e(1) \leftarrow c(1,2)$, $e(2) \leftarrow c(2,1)$ and $e(2) \leftarrow c(2,2)$, obtained by canceling the negative literals from g_5, g_6, g_7 and g_8, respectively. We can thus verify that I_0 is an answer set for $Ground(\mathcal{P}_0)^{I_0}$ and therefore also an answer set for $Ground(\mathcal{P}_0)$ and $\mathcal{P}_0$.

Let us now consider the interpretation $I_1 = \{c(1,2), b(1), e(1)\}$, which is a model of $Ground(\mathcal{P}_0)$. The reduct $Ground(\mathcal{P}_0)^{I_1}$ contains the rules g_1, g_2, g_3, g_4, g_9 plus both $e(2) \leftarrow c(2,1)$ and $e(2) \leftarrow c(2,2)$ (note that both g_5 and g_6 are deleted because $b(1) \in I_1$). I_1 is not an answer set of $Ground(\mathcal{P}_0)^{I_1}$ because $\{c(1,2), b(1)\} \subset I_1$ is. As a consequence I_1 is not an answer set of $\mathcal{P}_0$.

It can be verified that $\mathcal{P}_0$ has two answer sets, I_0 and $\{c(1,2), b(1)\}$. □

Example 7. Given the ASP program $\mathcal{P}_5 = \{a \vee \neg b \leftarrow c. \; ; \; \neg b \leftarrow \text{not } a, \text{not } c. \; ; \; a \vee c \leftarrow \text{not } \neg b.\}$ and $I = \{\neg b\}$, the reduct $\mathcal{P}_5^I$ is $\{a \vee \neg b \leftarrow c. \; ; \; \neg b.\}$. It is easy to see that I is an answer set of $\mathcal{P}_5^I$, and for this reason it is also an answer set of $\mathcal{P}_5$.

Now consider $J = \{a\}$. The reduct $\mathcal{P}_5^J$ is $\{a \vee \neg b \leftarrow c. \; ; \; a \vee c.\}$ and it can be easily verified that J is an answer set of $\mathcal{P}_5^J$, so it is also an answer set of $\mathcal{P}_5$.

If, on the other hand, we take $K = \{c\}$, the reduct $\mathcal{P}_5^K$ is equal to $\mathcal{P}_5^J$, but K is not an answer set of $\mathcal{P}_5^K$: for the rule $r : a \vee \neg b \leftarrow c$, $B(r) \subseteq K$ holds, but $H(r) \cap K \neq \emptyset$ does not. Indeed, it can be verified that I and J are the only answer sets of $\mathcal{P}_5$.

In some cases, it is possible to emulate disjunction by unstratified normal rules by "shifting" the disjunction to the body [21,61,116], as shown in the following example. Consider $\mathcal{P}_5 = \{a \vee b.\}$ and its "shifted version" $\mathcal{P}_5' = \{a \leftarrow \text{not } b. \; ; \; b \leftarrow \text{not } a.\}$. Both programs have the same answer sets, namely $\{a\}$ and $\{b\}$.

However, this is not possible in general. For example, consider $\mathcal{P}_6 = \{a \vee b. \; ; \; a \leftarrow b. \; ; \; b \leftarrow a.\}$. It has $\{a, b\}$ as its single answer set, while its "shifted version" $\mathcal{P}_6' = \{a \leftarrow \text{not } b. \; ; \; b \leftarrow \text{not } a. \; ; \; a \leftarrow b. \; ; \; b \leftarrow a.\}$ has no answer set at all.

As a side note, there has been a lot of work in the ASP community on (equivalent) replaceability of program parts, the most common notion being strong equivalence [122]. Two programs are said to be strongly equivalent if they can be replaced in any context such without altering answer sets. The considerations above prove that $\mathcal{P}_5$ and $\mathcal{P}_5'$ are not strongly equivalent. However, there is no deep relationship between "shifted" programs and strong equivalence: They can be strongly equivalent (e.g. $\mathcal{P}_5 \cup \{\leftarrow a, b.\}$ and $\mathcal{P}_5' \cup \{\leftarrow a, b.\}$), equivalent (e.g. $\mathcal{P}_5$ and $\mathcal{P}_5'$), or not equivalent at all (e.g. $\mathcal{P}_6$ and $\mathcal{P}_6'$).

ASP inherits its main two reasoning tasks from nonmonotonic reasoning: *brave reasoning* (also called credulous reasoning) and *cautious reasoning* (also called skeptical reasoning). Given a program $\mathcal{P}$ and a formula ϕ without variables, $\mathcal{P} \models_b \phi$ if ϕ is true in some answer set of $\mathcal{P}$, $\mathcal{P} \models_c \phi$ if ϕ is true in all answer sets of $\mathcal{P}$. While these definitions work for any formula, in ASP ϕ is often restricted to an atom, a literal, or a conjunction of literals. When ϕ contains variables, one is asking for those substitutions[4] σ for which $\mathcal{P} \models_b \phi\sigma$ (or $\mathcal{P} \models_c \phi\sigma$).

3.2 Semantic Characterizations

While the semantic definition given in the previous section is the one originally given in [91], several other definitions have been shown to be equivalent to it.

For instance, Pearce showed in [136] how to link stable models and answer sets to the intermediate logic HT ("Here and There") proposed by Heyting [100] (corresponding also to the three-valued Gödel Logic $G3$) by essentially adding an equilibrium criterion.

Another characterization has been provided by means of a simplified reduct that became known as the *FLP reduct* [75,76]. The FLP reduct of a ground program $\mathcal{P}$ w.r.t. a set $X \subseteq B_{\mathcal{P}}$ is the ground program $\mathcal{P}^X$, obtained from $\mathcal{P}$ by

- deleting all rules $r \in \mathcal{P}$ for which the body is false (i.e., $B^+(r) \not\subseteq X$ or $B^-(r) \cap X \neq \emptyset$ holds).

The definition of an answer set then remains the same except for the replacement of Gelfond-Lifschitz reduct by FLP reduct. The motivation for this reduct was a language extension by aggregates (cf. the next section), but it also significantly simplifies the handling of standard programs, as rules that are not deleted by the reduct remain intact.

Further characterizations have been provided by Lifschitz in [120] and [121].

3.3 Language Extensions

The work on ASP started with rules as introduced here so far, but fairly soon implementations extending the basic language started to emerge. The most important extensions to the ASP language can be grouped in three main classes:

- *Optimization Constructs*
- *Aggregates and External Atoms*
- *Function Symbols and Existential Quantifiers*
- *Arbitrary Formulas as Programs*
- *Preference Handling*

Optimization Constructs. The basic ASP language can be used to solve complex search problems, but does not natively provide constructs for specifying optimization problems (i.e., problems where some goal function must be minimized or maximized). Two extension of ASP have been conceived for solving optimization problems: *Weak Constraints* [32,115] and *Optimize Statements* [154].

In the basic language, constraints are rules with empty head, and represent a condition that *must* be satisfied, and for this reason they are also called *strong* constraints.

---

[4] A substitution here is a set of instructions for replacing variables by terms (here constants). An application of these replacements is denoted by postfixing the substitution to the structure, in which the replacements should be applied.

Contrary to strong constraints, *weak constraints* allow us to express desiderata, that is, conditions that *should* be satisfied. Thus, they may be violated, and their semantics involves minimizing the number of violated instances of weak constraints. In other words, the presence of strong constraints modifies the semantics of a program by discarding all models which do not satisfy some of them; while weak constraints identify an approximate solution, that is, one in which (weak) constraints are satisfied as much as possible.

From a syntactic point of view, a weak constraint is like a strong one where the implication symbol $\leftarrow$ is replaced by $\leftsquigarrow$. The informal meaning of a weak constraint $\leftsquigarrow B$ is "try to falsify B," or "B should preferably be false." Additionally, a weight and a priority level for the weak constraint may be specified after the constraint enclosed in brackets (by means of positive integers or variables). When not specified, the weak constraint is assumed to have weight 1 and priority level 1, respectively.

In this case, we are interested in the answer sets which minimize the sum of weights of the violated (unsatisfied) weak constraints in the highest priority level and, among them, those which minimize the sum of weights of the violated weak constraints in the next lower level, and so on. In other words, the answer sets are considered along a lexicographic ordering along the priority levels over the sum of weights of violated weak constraints. Therefore, higher values for weights and priority levels allow for marking weak constraints of higher importance (e.g., the most important constraints are those having the highest weight among those with the highest priority level).

As an example consider the Traveling Salesman Problem (TSP). TSP is a variant of the Hamiltonian Cycle problem, which amounts to finding the shortest (minimal cost) Hamiltonian cycle (that is, a cycle including all vertices of the graph) in a directed *numerically labeled* graph. This problem can be solved by adapting the encoding of the Hamiltonian Path problem given in Sect. 5 (and discussed in detail there) in order to deal with labels, by adding only one weak constraint.

Suppose that the graph G is specified by predicates *node* (unary) and *arc* (ternary), and that one starting node is specified by the predicate *start* (unary).

The ASP program with weak constraints solving the TSP problem is thus as follows:

$r_1: inPath(X, Y, C) \lor outPath(X, Y, C) \leftarrow arc(X, Y, C).$
$r_2: reached(X) \leftarrow start(X).$
$r_3: reached(X) \leftarrow reached(Y), inPath(Y, X).$
$r_4: \leftarrow inPath(X, Y, \_), inPath(X, Y_1, \_), Y <> Y_1.$
$r_5: \leftarrow inPath(X, Y, \_), inPath(X_1, Y, \_), X <> X_1.$
$r_6: \leftarrow node(X), \text{not } reached(X).$
$r_7: startreached \leftarrow start(X), inPath(Y, X, C).$
$r_8: \leftarrow \text{not } startreached.$
$r_9: \leftsquigarrow inPath(X, Y, C)[C, 1].$

Different to the Hamiltonian Path program of Sect. 5, *arc*, *inPath*, and *outPath* now have a third argument, indicating the cost associated with the arc.

Otherwise the only differences with respect to the Hamiltonian Path program of Sect. 5 are rule r_7 and constraint r_8, which ensure cyclicity of the path, and the weak constraint r_9, which states the preference to avoid taking arcs with high cost in the path, and has the effect of selecting those answer sets for which the total cost of arcs selected by $inPath$ (which coincides with the length of the path) is the minimum (i.e., the path is the shortest) .

The TSP encoding provided above is an example of the "guess, check and optimize" programming pattern [115], which extends the original "guess and check" (see Sect. 5) by adding an additional "optimization part" which mainly contains weak constraints. In the example above, the optimization part contains only the weak constraint r_8.

Optimize Statements are syntactically somewhat simpler. They assign numeric values to a set of ground literals, and thereby select those answer sets for which the sum of the values assigned to literals which are true in the respective answer sets are maximal or minimal. It is not hard to see that Weak Constraints can emulate Optimize Statements, but not vice versa. For details on how they can be emulated, we refer to the ASP-Core-2 standard in [42].

Aggregates and Generalized Atoms.   There are some simple properties, often arising in real-world applications, which cannot be encoded in a simple and natural manner using ASP. Especially properties that require the use of arithmetic operators on a set of elements satisfying some conditions (like sum, count, or maximum) need rather cumbersome encodings (often also necessitating an "external" ordering relation over terms), if one is confined to classic ASP. In order to deal with such properties, one might like to have an "external" definition for such properties. On an abstract level, this can be viewed like having an "external atom," which use some external evaluator to determine truth or falsity. The best-known type of programs with such external atoms are HEX programs, which evolved from dl-programs that use description logics as external evaluators [66].

A related concept is known as Constraint Answer Set Programming (CASP, see for example [118]). There are quite significant differences, though: while there are "external atoms" in CASP, their truth values usually do not depend on truth values of other atoms.

In order to capture this more general view, the term *generalized atom* has also been used in order to refer to external atoms, aggregate atoms, and related constructs. The crucial feature is that the truth value of such a generalized atom is determined by the truth values of several atoms, rather than the truth value of just one atom. In the following, we will stick with the more traditional numeric aggregates for simplicity.

Similar observations have also been made in related domains, notably database systems, which led to the definition of aggregate functions. Especially in database systems this concept is now both theoretically and practically fully integrated. When ASP systems became used in real applications, it was apparent that aggregates are often needed also here. First, cardinality and weight constraints [154], which are special cases of aggregates, have been introduced. However, in general one might want to use also other aggregates (like minimum, maximum, or average), and it is not clear how to generalize the framework of cardinality and weight constraints to allow for arbitrary aggregates. To overcome this deficiency, ASP has been extended with special atoms handling aggregate functions [43,57,59,73,75,98,141]. Intuitively, an aggregate function can be thought of as a (possibly partial) function mapping multisets of constants to a constant.

An *aggregate function* is of the form $f(S)$, where S is a set term of the form $\{$ *Vars*: *Conj*$\}$, where *Vars* is a list of variables and *Conj* is a conjunction of standard atoms, and f is an *aggregate function symbol*.

The most common aggregate functions compute the number of terms, the sum of non-negative integers, and minimum/maximum term in a set.

Aggregates are especially useful when real-world problems have to be dealt with. Consider the following example application:[5] A project team has to be built from a set of employees according to the following specifications:

1. At least a given number of different skills must be present in the team.
2. The sum of the salaries of the employees working in the team must not exceed the given budget.

Suppose that our employees are provided by a number of facts of the form *emp*(*EmpId, Skill, Salary*); the minimum number of different skills and the budget are specified by the facts $nSkill(N)$ and $budget(B)$. We then encode each property stated above by an aggregate atom, and enforce it by an integrity constraint:

$$r_1: in(I) \ \lor \ out(I) \leftarrow emp(I, Sk, Sa).$$
$$r_3: \leftarrow nSkill(M), \text{not } \#count\{Sk : emp(I, Sk, Sa), in(I)\} >= M.$$
$$r_4: \leftarrow budget(B), \text{not } \#sum\{Sa, I : emp(I, Sk, Sa), in(I)\} <= B.$$

Intuitively, the disjunctive rule "guesses" whether an employee is included in the team or not, while the two constraints correspond one-to-one to the requirements. Indeed, the function $\#count$ counts the number of employees in the team, while $\#sum$ sums the salaries of the employees which are part of the team.

In Sect. 4, we will discuss the semantics for aggregates and generalized atoms in more detail.

Function Symbols and Existential Quantifiers. Since ASP evolved from Datalog, traditional ASP languages do not allow for function symbols or existential quantification. However, often it is convenient to use function symbols for simple reasons like grouping arguments together; they are also needed for creating and managing more complex data structures like lists, as available in standard logic programming languages like Prolog. Also in applications concerning ontologies or the Semantic Web, often existential quantifications in rule heads would be required in order to model unknown entities. Of course, the two approaches are related, as usually it is possible to eliminate existential quantifiers by introducing Skolem functions.

A major difficulty is that extensions either by function symbols or existential quantifiers immediately lead to undecidability of the respective computational problems. A major quest is therefore the identification of significant decidable subclasses of the language.

Concerning extensions with (uninterpreted) function symbols, there are essentially two groups of proposals:

---

[5] In the example, we adopted the syntax of the DLV system, the same aggregate functions can be specified also by exploiting other ASP dialects.

Syntactically restricted fragments, such as ω-*restricted programs* [158], λ-*restricted programs* [86], *finite-domain programs* [39], *argument-restricted programs* [119], FDNC *programs* [152], *bidirectional programs* [67], and the proposal of [123]; these approaches introduce syntactic constraints (which can be easily checked at small computational cost) or explicit domain restrictions, thus allowing computability of answer sets and/or decidability of querying.

Semantically restricted fragments, such as *finitely ground programs* [39], *finitary programs* [24,25], *disjunctive finitely-recursive programs* [20] and *queries* [11,40]; with respect to syntactically restricted fragments, these approaches aim at identifying broader classes of programs for which computational tasks such as querying are decidable. However, deciding the membership of a given program in these fragments is undecidable in general.

There have been a few other proposals that treat function symbols not in the traditional logic programming sense, but as in classical logic, where most prominently the unique names assumption does not hold. We refer to [33] for an overview.

Concerning existential quantifiers in rule heads, most proposals are confined to positive, non-disjunctive programs, often referred to as Datalog$^\pm$. The decidable subclasses in this case rely on four main syntactic paradigms, called *guardedness* [35], *weak-acyclicity* [77], *stickiness* [37,38], and *shyness* [114]. Extensions of these decidable classes to positive, but disjunctive programs have been proposed in [12,94], and [143]. A condition which combines weak acyclicity and guardedness has been proposed in [109]. Guardedness has been extended to stratified negation in [36].

Arbitrary Formulas as Programs. There have been several attempts at generalizing the input language to arbitrary formulas, rather than rules, with the intention of identifying the "ASP logic." Pearce had provided equilibrium logic in the 1990s [136], but it was confined to propositional logic and had only one kind of negation (negation as failure). This logic has more recently been extended to quantified equilibrium logic in [139]. Moreover, there were attempts at defining semantics of arbitrary formulas by means of a second-order sentence reminiscent of circumscription. This had first been done for propositional formulas [79], and was later extended to first-order formulas [81]. In contrast to the languages discussed in the previous sections, the goal here is to define an ASP semantics for languages that are as general as possible. Reasoning tasks for first-order theories clearly suffer from undecidability issues.

Preference Handling. ASP programs usually follow a "guess and check" programming pattern (see Sect. 5), where a set of rules (the guessing part) is used to guess a solution (or equivalently, to generate answer set candidates); while another set of rules, called checking part, is added to discard solutions which are not admissible. This methodology allows the programmer to distinguish between solutions and non-solutions. However, in many realistic applications the possibility to make more fine grained distinctions is required; and, in particular, distinctions between more and less preferred solutions are needed (see [28] for a discussion). For this reason, there has been a substantial amount of work on extending ASP programs with preferences, and in particular, the major focus has been on qualitative approaches. This stems from the fact that for a variety of applications numerical information is hard to obtain (preference elicitation is rather difficult) and often turns out to be unnecessary (see [28]). Still, language extensions based on quantitative information, such as weak constraints mentioned above, emulate qualitative preferences under certain conditions, and vice versa.

There are two basic possibilities for representing qualitative preferences. In one approach, the preference is specified among rules, mirroring the fact that some rules may be more reliable than others, and striving to use a set of rules that is as preferred as possible for giving reason to an answer. In the second approach, the preferences are specified among literals, reflecting information on either the likelihood or the desirability of the affirmations represented by the literals.

In the first kind of formalisms, preferences are specified by means of an ordering among rules. Formally, an *ordered logic program* is a pair $(\Pi, <)$ where Π is a logic program and $< \subseteq (\Pi \times \Pi)$ is a strict partial order. Given, $r_1, r_2 \in \Pi$, the relation $r_1 < r_2$ expresses that r_2 has higher priority than r_1. For example, consider the following program:

$$r_1 : \neg a. \qquad r_2 : b \leftarrow \neg a, \text{not } c. \qquad r_3 : c \leftarrow \text{not } b.$$

This program has two answer sets, one given by $\{\neg a, b\}$ and the other given by $\{\neg a, c\}$. For the first answer set, rules r_1 and r_2 are applied; for the second, r_1 and r_3. However, assume that we have reason to prefer r_2 to r_3, expressed by $r_3 < r_2$. In this case we would want to obtain just the first answer set. In this case we say that the first is a *preferred answer set*.

In general, defining which answer sets should be the preferred ones in this setting is not always as obvious as in the example above, and indeed several approaches have been proposed. A comprehensive comparison of three major semantics, defined by Delgrande, Schaub, Tompits [56], by Brewka and Eiter [29], and by Wang, Zhou, Lin [165], has been presented in [151].

In the second representational approach, preferences are represented among atoms, literals or formulas.

One way of specifying this has been proposed in [27] is the use of *ordered disjunction* in rule heads. In particular, the operator $\times$ in rule heads acts as a disjunction specifying also preferences. The meaning of a rule $a_1 \times \ldots \times a_n \leftarrow body.$ is that if the body is satisfied then some a_i must be in the answer set, most preferably a_1, if this is impossible then a_2, and so on. The formal semantics is defined by means of answer sets of split programs and of rule satisfaction degrees. There are some degrees of freedom when aggregating the satisfaction degrees of several rules, leading to different semantics, the main ones being cardinality-based, set-inclusion-based, and Pareto-based.

In the ordered disjunction approach the construction of answer sets is amalgamated with the expression of preferences. *Optimization programs* [30], on the other hand, strictly separate these two aspects. An optimization program is a pair (P_{gen}, P_{pref}). Here, P_{gen} is an arbitrary logic program used to generate answer sets. All we require is that it produces sets of literals as its answer sets. P_{pref} is a preference program. Preference programs consist of preference rules of the form $c_1 > \ldots > c_n \leftarrow body$, where the c_i are Boolean combinations of literals built from $\vee, \wedge, \neg$ and not. As in the case of ordered disjunction, the semantics of these programs is based on the degree of satisfaction of preference rules, and as in the case of ordered disjunctions, there are several options for aggregating these satisfaction degrees for defining semantics.

Another ASP extension suitable for preference handling has been presented in [17]. There, standard ASP has been enriched by introducing consistency-restoring rules (cr-rules) and preferences, leading to the CR-Prolog language. Basically, in this language, besides standard ASP rules one may specify CR-rules, that are expressions of the form: $r{:}a_1 \vee \ldots \vee a_n \leftarrow^+ body$ ($n \geq 1$). The intuitive meaning of CR-rule$r$ is: if $body$ is true then one of $a_1, \ldots, a_n$ is "possibly" believed to be true. Importantly, the name of CR-prolog rules can be directly exploited to specify preferences among them. In particular, if the fact $prefer(r_1, r_2)$ is added to a CR-program, then rule r_1 is preferred over rule r_2. This allows one to encode partial orderings among preferred answer sets by explicitly writing preferences among CR-rules.

Other Extensions. ASP has been extended in other directions in order to meet requirements of different application domains, hence there is a number of interesting languages having the roots on ASP. For instance, ASP has been exploited for defining and implementing *action languages* (i.e., languages conceived for dealing with actions and change) $\mathcal{K}$ [64], and $\mathcal{E}$ [60]; while, in [142] a framework for *abduction with penalization* has been proposed and implemented as a front-end for the ASP system DLV. A logic language called *ID-Logic* [126] has been introduced to deal with classical logic with inductive definitions (which correspond semantically to logic rules). Other ASP extensions have been conceived to deal with *Ontologies* (i.e., abstract models of a complex domain). In particular, in [148] an ASP-based language for ontology specification and reasoning has been proposed, which extends ASP in order to deal with complex real-world entities, like classes, objects, compound objects, axioms, and taxonomies. In [99] an open world semantics for ASP programs has been proposed. Moreover, in [65] an extension of ASP, called *HEX-Programs*, which supports higher-order atoms as well as external atoms has been proposed. External atoms allows for embedding external sources of computation in a logic program. Thus, HEX-programs are useful for various tasks, including meta-reasoning, data type manipulations, and reasoning on top of Description Logic (DL) [15] ontologies. *Template predicates* have been introduced in [44]. Template predicates are special intensional predicates defined by means of generic reusable subprograms, which have been conceived for easing coding and improving readability and compactness of programs. Finally, nested programs, allowing for nested logical expressions to occur in rules have also been studied [137, 138].

4 Semantics of Aggregates and Generalized Atoms

The main issue with the semantics for aggregates and generalized atoms is when they occur in recursive definitions, and the fact that an aggregate atom can behave like a positive literal, a negative literal, or neither of them.

Example 8. Consider the following simple programs, all of which contain recursion "through" aggregates:

$P_1 = \{p(a) \leftarrow \#\texttt{count}\{X : p(X)\} > 0.\}$

$P_2 = \{p(a) \leftarrow \#\texttt{count}\{X : p(X)\} < 1.\}$

$P_3 = \{p(a) \leftarrow \#\texttt{count}\{X : p(X)\} \neq 1., p(b) \leftarrow \#\texttt{count}\{X : p(X)\} \neq 1.\}$

It is quite straightforward that P_1 should behave like $P_1' = \{p(a) \leftarrow p(a).\}$ and yield an empty answer set, and that P_2 should behave like $P_2' = \{p(a) \leftarrow \text{not } p(a).\}$ and yield no answer set. But P_3 is less clear. Indeed, while $\#\text{count}\{X : p(X)\} > 0$ has the same satisfaction pattern as $p(a)$, and $\#\text{count}\{X : p(X)\} < 1$ has the same satisfaction pattern as $\text{not} p(a)$, there is no standard ASP literal that has the same satisfaction pattern as $\#\text{count}\{X : p(X)\} \neq 1$ (namely true for $\emptyset$ and $\{p(a), p(b)\}$, false for $\{p(a)\}$ and $\{p(b)\}$).

Still, early approaches like [58, 88, 106] also assigned unintuitive answer sets to P_1, which is assigned $\emptyset$ and $\{p(a)\}$ as answer sets in those approaches, as they essentially treated aggregates like negative literals.

Indeed, later work identified the classes of *monotone* and *antimonotone* generalized atoms, that behave, respectively, like positive and negative literals. A monotone generalized atom a has the property that if I satisfies a, then also any $I' \supseteq I$ (assigning more standard atoms to true) satisfies a as well. Antimonotone generalized atoms exhibit opposite behavior, namely if I satisfies a, then also any $I' \subseteq I$ (assigning more standard atoms to false) satisfies a as well. Positive literals are monotone, while negative literals are antimonotone. There is also the notion of convex generalized atoms, which can be seen as a combination of monotone and antimonotone properties, namely if there is an interval $[I, J]$ of interpretations such that a is true for all K such that $I \subseteq K \subseteq J$ and false for all other interpretations. For monotone generalized atoms, the upper interval bound is the Herbrand base, while for antimonotone generalized atoms, the lower bound is the empty set.

When attempting to resolve these issues, there emerged essentially two strands of semantics. One semantics, defined independently, and by different means, by Pelov, Denecker, and Bruynooghe [140, 141] and by Son and Pontelli [156], avoids "jumping over gaps" like $\{p(a)\}$ and $\{p(b)\}$ in P_3. We refer to this kind of semantics as *PSP* semantics. The other type of semantics, defined by the author, Leone, and Pfeifer [75, 76], and independently, and for a larger class of programs, by Ferraris [79, 80], is based on a reduct and minimality condition. We refer to that kind of semantics as *FLP* semantics.

In [6] it was shown that the PSP and FLP semantics coincide up to convex generalized atoms. It was already established earlier that each PSP answer set is also an FLP answer set, but not vice versa. For programs containing non-convex generalized atoms, some FLP answer sets are not PSP answer sets. In particular, there are programs that have FLP answer sets but no PSP answer sets.

However, in [7] it was argued that even the FLP semantics is still too restrictive, and an attempt to improve the situation was made, defining the supportedly stable or SFLP (supportedly FLP) semantics. However, while SFLP solves some issues, it also introduces new ones. A further attempt was published in [8]. The motivation in both cases was that P_3 of Example 8 should have one answer set, namely $\{p(a), p(b)\}$. This answer set could be derived by a simple inflationary operator, starting with $\emptyset$, then deriving $\{p(a), p(b)\}$, as the rules defining these atoms evaluate to true in $\emptyset$. $\{p(a), p(b)\}$ is then a fixpoint, as the rule bodies still evaluate to true with respect to $\{p(a), p(b)\}$. PSP semantics do not admit this answer set, as the operators there cannot "move over the gaps" $\{p(a)\}$ and $\{p(b)\}$ in the satisfaction pattern of the generalized atoms, while for FLP the reduct for $\{p(a), p(b)\}$ has minimal models $\{p(a)\}$ and $\{p(b)\}$ and not $\{p(a), p(b)\}$, barring $\{p(a), p(b)\}$ from being an FLP answer set.

The semantics defined in [7,8] do allow for the answer set $\{p(a), p(b)\}$ of P_3, but all of them show other anomalies.

An orthogonal development has been published in [92]. However, the observations in [7,8] apply also to that semantics, in the sense that they do not assign any answer set to P_3 of Example 8.

As a bottom line, there seems to be general agreement on the semantics of convex generalized atoms. Concerning non-convex generalized atoms, both PSP and FLP semantics are popular, yet it can be argued that they do not treat some programs (such as P_3) as one would intuitively expect. We believe that more research is still needed in order to settle this issue convincingly.

While the ASP-Core-2 standard explicitly forbids aggregates in recursions, some systems do support them: clingo [84] supports the FLP semantics (the Ferraris version) and uses the transformation defined in [9], which rewrites programs with arbitrary aggregates to equivalent ones with monotone aggregates only. IDP [46] uses a different syntax to ASP-Core-2, but allows for definitions involving recursive generalized atoms unde the PSP semantics.

5   Knowledge Representation and Reasoning in ASP

ASP has been used in several domains, ranging from artificial intelligence over traditional databases to semantic web applications. ASP can be used to encode problems in a declarative fashion; indeed, the power of disjunctive rules allows for expressing problems which are more complex than NP, and the (optional) separation of a fixed, non-ground program from an input database allows one to obtain uniform solutions over varying instances.

More in detail, many problems of comparatively high computational complexity can be solved in a natural manner by following a "Guess&Check" programming methodology, originally introduced in [63] and refined in [115]. The idea behind this method can be summarized as follows: a database of facts is used to specify an instance of the problem, while a set of (usually disjunctive[6]) rules, called "guessing part", is used to define the search space; solutions are then identified in the search space by another (optional) set of rules, called "checking part", which impose some admissibility constraint. Basically, the answer sets of the program, which combines the input database with the guessing part, represent "solution candidates"; those candidates are then filtered, by adding the checking part, which guarantee that the answer sets of the resulting program represent precisely the admissible solutions for the input instance. To grasp the intuition behind the role of both the guessing and checking parts, consider the following example.

---

[6] Some ASP variants use *choice rules* as guessing part (see [133, 154, 159]), Moreover, in some cases, it is possible to emulate disjunction by unstratified normal rules by "shifting" the disjunction to the body [21,61,116], but this is not possible in general.

Example 9. Suppose that we want to partition a set of persons in two groups, while avoiding that father and children belong to the same group. Following the guess&check methodology, we use a disjunctive rule to "guess" all the possible assignments of persons to groups as follows:

$$group(P, 1) \vee group(P, 2) \leftarrow person(P).$$

To understand what this rule does, consider a simple instance of the problem, in which there are two persons: joe *and his father* john. *This instance is represented by four facts*

$$person(john).person(joe).father(john, joe).$$

We can verify that the answer sets of the resulting program (facts plus disjunctive rule) correspond to all possible assignments of the three persons to two groups:

$\{person(john), person(joe), father(john, joe), group(john, 1), group(joe, 1)\}$
$\{person(john), person(joe), father(john, joe), group(john, 1), group(joe, 2)\}$
$\{person(john), person(joe), father(john, joe), group(john, 2), group(joe, 1)\}$
$\{person(john), person(joe), father(john, joe), group(john, 2), group(joe, 2)\}$

However, we want to discard assignments in which father and children belong to the same group. To this end, we add the checking part by writing the following constraint:

$$\leftarrow group(P1, G), group(P2, G), father(P1, P2).$$

The answer sets of the augmented program are then the intending ones, where the checking part has acted as a sort of filter:

$\{person(john), person(joe), father(john, joe), group(john, 1), group(joe, 2)\}$
$\{person(john), person(joe), father(john, joe), group(john, 2), group(joe, 1)\}$

□

In the following, we illustrate the usage of ASP as a tool for knowledge representation and reasoning by example. In particular, we first deal with a problem motivated by classical deductive database applications; then we exploit the "Guess&Check" programming style to show how a number of well-known harder problems can be encoded in ASP.

Reachability. Given a finite directed graph $G = (V, A)$, we want to compute all pairs of nodes $(a, b) \in V \times V$ such that b is reachable from a through a nonempty sequence of arcs in A. In different terms, the problem amounts to computing the transitive closure of the relation A.

The input graph is encoded by assuming that A is represented by the binary relation $arc(X, Y)$, where a fact $arc(a, b)$ means that G contains an arc from a to b, i.e., $(a, b) \in A$; while, the set of nodes V is not explicitly represented, since the nodes appearing in the transitive closure are implicitly given by these facts.

The following program then defines a relation $reachable(X, Y)$ containing all facts $reachable(a, b)$ such that b is reachable from a through the arcs of the input graph G:

$$r_1 : reachable(X, Y) \leftarrow arc(X, Y).$$
$$r_2 : reachable(X, Y) \leftarrow arc(X, U), reachable(U, Y).$$

The first rule states that that node Y is reachable from node X if there is an arc in the graph from X to Y, while the second rule represents the transitive closure by stating that node Y is reachable from node X if there exists a node U such that U is directly reachable from X (there is an arc from X to U) and Y is reachable from U.

As an example, consider a graph represented by the following facts:

$$arc(1, 2). \quad arc(2, 3). \quad arc(3, 4).$$

The single answer set of the program reported above together with these three facts program is

$$\{reachable(1, 2), reachable(2, 3), reachable(3, 4), reachable(1, 3),$$
$$reachable(2, 4), reachable(1, 4), arc(1, 2), arc(2, 3), arc(3, 4).\}$$

The first three reported literals are justified by the rule r_1, while the other literals containing the predicate $reachable$ are justified by rule r_2.

In the following, we describe the usage of the "Guess&Check" methodology.

Hamiltonian Path. Given a finite directed graph $G = (V, A)$ and a node $a \in V$ of this graph, does there exist a path in G starting at a and passing through each node in V exactly once?

This is a classical NP-complete problem in graph theory. Suppose that the graph G is specified by using facts over predicates $node$ (unary) and arc (binary), and the starting node a is specified by the predicate $start$ (unary). Then, the following program $\mathcal{P}_{hp}$ solves the *Hamiltonian Path* problem:

$$r_1 : inPath(X, Y) \lor outPath(X, Y) \leftarrow arc(X, Y).$$
$$r_2 : reached(X) \leftarrow start(X).$$
$$r_3 : reached(X) \leftarrow reached(Y), inPath(Y, X).$$
$$r_4 :\leftarrow inPath(X, Y), inPath(X, Y_1), Y <> Y_1.$$
$$r_5 :\leftarrow inPath(X, Y), inPath(X_1, Y), X <> X_1.$$
$$r_6 :\leftarrow node(X), not\ reached(X), not\ start(X).$$

The disjunctive rule (r_1) guesses a subset S of the arcs to be in the path, while the rest of the program checks whether S constitutes a Hamiltonian Path. Here, an auxiliary predicate $reached$ is defined, which specifies the set of nodes which are reached from the starting node. Doing this is very similar to reachability, but the transitivity is defined over the guessed predicate $inPath$ using rule r_3. Note that $reached$ is completely determined by the guess for $inPath$, no further guessing is needed.

In the checking part, the first two constraints (namely, r_4 and r_5) ensure that the set of arcs S selected by $inPath$ meets the following requirements, which any Hamiltonian Path must satisfy: (i) there must not be two arcs starting at the same node, and (ii) there must not be two arcs ending in the same node. The third constraint enforces that all nodes in the graph are reached from the starting node in the subgraph induced by S.

Let us next consider an alternative program $\mathcal{P}'_{hp}$, which also solves the *Hamiltonian Path* problem, but intertwines the reachability with the guess:

$$r_1 : inPath(X,Y) \ \vee \ outPath(X,Y) \leftarrow reached(X), \ arc(X,Y).$$
$$r_2 : inPath(X,Y) \ \vee \ outPath(X,Y) \leftarrow start(X), \ arc(X,Y).$$
$$r_3 : reached(X) \leftarrow inPath(Y,X).$$
$$r_4 :\leftarrow inPath(X,Y), \ inPath(X,Y_1), Y <> Y_1.$$
$$r_5 :\leftarrow inPath(X,Y), \ inPath(X_1,Y), X <> X_1.$$
$$r_6 :\leftarrow node(X), \ not \ reached(X), \ not \ start(X).$$

Here, the two disjunctive rules (r_1 and r_2), together with the auxiliary rule r_3, guess a subset S of the arcs to be in the path, while the rest of the program checks whether S constitutes a Hamiltonian Path. Here, $reached$ is defined in a different way. In fact, $inPath$ is already defined in a way that only arcs reachable from the starting node will be guessed. The remainder of the checking part is the same as in $\mathcal{P}_{hp}$.

Ramsey Numbers. In the previous example, we have seen how a search problem can be encoded in an ASP program whose answer sets correspond to the problem solutions. We now build a program whose answer sets witness that a property does not hold, i.e., the property at hand holds if and only if the program has no answer set. We next apply the above programming scheme to a well-known problem of number and graph theory.

The Ramsey number $R(k, m)$ is the smallest integer n such that, no matter how we color the arcs of the complete undirected graph (clique) with n nodes using two colors, say red and blue, there is a red clique with k nodes (a red k-clique) or a blue clique with m nodes (a blue m-clique).

Ramsey numbers exist for all pairs of positive integers k and m [145]. We next show a program $\mathcal{P}_{ra}$ that allows us to decide whether a given integer n is *not* the Ramsey Number $R(3, 4)$. By varying the input number n, we can determine $R(3, 4)$, as described below. Let $\mathcal{F}_{ra}$ be the collection of facts for input predicates *node* and *arc* encoding a complete graph with n nodes. $\mathcal{P}_{ra}$ is the following program:

$$r_1 : blue(X,Y) \ \vee \ red(X,Y) \leftarrow arc(X,Y).$$
$$r_2 :\leftarrow red(X,Y), \ red(X,Z), \ red(Y,Z).$$
$$r_3 :\leftarrow blue(X,Y), \ blue(X,Z), \ blue(Y,Z), \ blue(X,W), \ blue(Y,W), \ blue(Z,W).$$

Intuitively, the disjunctive rule r_1 guesses a color for each edge. The first constraint (r_2) eliminates the colorings containing a red clique (i.e., a complete graph) with 3 nodes, and the second constraint (r_3) eliminates the colorings containing a blue clique with 4 nodes. The program $\mathcal{P}_{ra} \cup \mathcal{F}_{ra}$ has an answer set if and only if there is a coloring of the edges of the complete graph on n nodes containing no red clique of size 3 and no blue clique of size 4. Thus, if there is an answer set for a particular n, then n is *not* $R(3, 4)$, that is, $n < R(3, 4)$. On the other hand, if $\mathcal{P}_{ra} \cup \mathcal{F}_{ra}$ has no answer set, then $n \geq R(3, 4)$. Thus, the smallest n such that no answer set is found is the Ramsey number $R(3, 4)$.

Strategic Companies. In the examples considered so far, the complexity of the problems is located at most on the first level of the Polynomial Hierarchy [135] (in NP or co-NP). We next demonstrate that also more complex problems, located at the second level of the Polynomial Hierarchy, can be encoded in ASP. To this end, we now consider a knowledge representation problem, inspired by a common business situation, which is known under the name *Strategic Companies* [34].

Suppose there is a collection $C = \{c_1, \ldots, c_m\}$ of companies c_i owned by a holding, a set $G = \{g_1, \ldots, g_n\}$ of goods, and for each c_i we have a set $G_i \subseteq G$ of goods produced by c_i and a set $O_i \subseteq C$ of companies controlling (owning) c_i. O_i is referred to as the *controlling set* of c_i. This control can be thought of as a majority in shares; companies not in C, which we do not model here, might have shares in companies as well. Note that, in general, a company might have more than one controlling set. Let the holding produce all goods in G, i.e., $G = \bigcup_{c_i \in C} G_i$.

A subset of the companies $C' \subseteq C$ is a *production-preserving* set if the following conditions hold: (1) The companies in C' produce all goods in G, i.e., $\bigcup_{c_i \in C'} G_i = G$. (2) The companies in C' are closed under the controlling relation, i.e., if $O_i \subseteq C'$ for some $i = 1, \ldots, m$ then $c_i \in C'$ must hold.

A subset-minimal set C', which is *production-preserving*, is called a *strategic set*. A company $c_i \in C$ is called *strategic*, if it belongs to some strategic set of C.

This notion is relevant when companies should be sold. Indeed, intuitively, selling any non-strategic company does not reduce the economic power of the holding. Computing strategic companies is on the second level of the Polynomial Hierarchy [34].

In the following, we consider a simplified setting as considered in [34], where each product is produced by at most two companies (for each $g \in G \, | \{c_i \mid g \in G_i\}| \leq 2$) and each company is jointly controlled by at most three other companies, i.e., $|O_i| \leq 3$ for $i = 1, \ldots, m$. Assume that for a given instance of Strategic Companies, $\mathcal{F}_{st}$ contains the following facts:

- $company(c)$ for each $c \in C$,
- $prod\_by(g, c_j, c_k)$, if $\{c_i \mid g \in G_i\} = \{c_j, c_k\}$, where c_j and c_k may possibly coincide,
- $contr\_by(c_i, c_k, c_m, c_n)$, if $c_i \in C$ and $O_i = \{c_k, c_m, c_n\}$, where c_k, c_m, and c_n are not necessarily distinct.

We next present a program $\mathcal{P}_{st}$, which characterizes this hard problem using only two rules:

$$r_1 : strat(Y) \ \vee \ strat(Z) \leftarrow prod\_by(X, Y, Z).$$
$$r_2 : strat(W) \leftarrow contr\_by(W, X, Y, Z), \, strat(X), \, strat(Y), \, strat(Z).$$

Here $strat(X)$ means that company X is a strategic company. The guessing part of the program consists of the disjunctive rule r_1, and the checking part consists of the normal rule r_2. The program $\mathcal{P}_{st}$ is surprisingly succinct, given that Strategic Companies is a hard problem.

The program $\mathcal{P}_{st}$ exploits the minimization which is inherent to the semantics of answer sets for the check whether a candidate set C' of companies that produces all goods and obeys company control is also minimal with respect to this property.

The guessing rule r_1 intuitively selects one of the companies c_1 and c_2 that produce some item g, which is described by $prod\_by(g, c_1, c_2)$. If there was no company control information, minimality of answer sets would naturally ensure that the answer sets of $\mathcal{F}_{st} \cup \{r_1\}$ correspond to the strategic sets; no further checking would be needed. However, in case control information is available, the rule r_2 checks that no company is sold that would be controlled by other companies in the strategic set, by simply requesting that this company must be strategic as well. The minimality of the strategic sets is automatically ensured by the minimality of answer sets.

The answer sets of $\mathcal{F}_{st} \cup \mathcal{P}_{st}$ correspond one-to-one to the strategic sets of the holding described in $\mathcal{F}_{st}$; a company c is thus strategic iff $strat(c)$ is in some answer set of $\mathcal{F}_{st} \cup \mathcal{P}_{st}$.

An important note here is that the checking "constraint" r_2 interferes with the guessing rule r_1: applying r_2 may "spoil" the minimal answer set generated by r_1. For example, suppose the guessing part gives rise to a ground rule

$$r_3 : strat(c1) \ \lor \ strat(c2) \leftarrow prod\_by(g, c1, c2)$$

and the fact $prod\_by(g, c1, c2)$ is given in $\mathcal{F}_{st}$. Now suppose the rule is satisfied in the guessing part by making $strat(c1)$ true. If, however, in the checking part an instance of rule r_2 is applied which derives $strat(c2)$, then the application of the rule r_3 to derive $strat(c1)$ is invalidated, as the minimality of answer sets implies that rule r_3 cannot justify the truth of $strat(c1)$, if another atom in its head is true.

6   Implementations and Applications

In this section we consider some additional topics that allow the reader to have a broader picture of ASP. In particular, we introduce the general architecture of ASP systems, and we briefly describe several applications of ASP.

6.1   System algorithms

Initially somewhat impeded by complexity considerations, reasonable algorithms and systems supporting ASP became available in the second half of the 1990s. The first widely used ones were Smodels [153, 154], supporting non-disjunctive ASP, and DLV [115], supporting ASP (with disjunction) as defined in [91]. These two systems have been improved over the years and are still in widespread use. Later-on, more systems for non-disjunctive ASP, like ASSAT [124, 168], Cmodels [16], and Clasp [85] became available, and also more disjunctive ASP systems became available with the advent of GnT [104], cmodels-3 [117], and ClaspD [62]. As of writing, the most widely used systems are clingo [83, 84] and DLV-2.0 [4, 41].

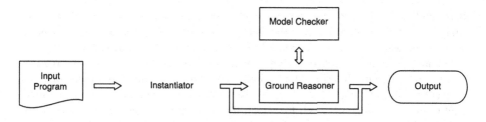

Fig. 1. General architecture of an ASP system.

While, as discussed below, the systems do not use the same techniques, they basically agree on the general architecture depicted in Fig. 1.

The evaluation flow of the computation is outlined in detail. Upon startup, the input specified by the user is parsed and transformed into the internal data structures of the system.[7]

In general, an input program $\mathcal{P}$ contains variables, and the first step of a computation of an ASP system is to eliminate these variables, generating a ground instantiation $ground(\mathcal{P})$ of $\mathcal{P}$. This variable-elimination process is called *instantiation* of the program (or *grounding*), and is performed by the *Instantiator* module (see Fig. 1).

A naïve Instantiator would produce the full ground instantiation $Ground(\mathcal{P})$ of the input, which is, however, undesirable from a computational point of view, as in general many useless ground rules would be generated. All of the systems therefore employ different procedures, which are geared towards keeping the instantiated program as small as possible. A necessary condition is, of course, that the instantiated program must have the same answer sets as the original program. However, it should be noted that the Instantiator solves a problem, which is in general EXPTIME-hard, the produced ground program being potentially of exponential size with respect to the input program. Optimizations in the Instantiator therefore often have a big impact, as its output is the input for the following modules, which implement computationally hard algorithms. Moreover, if the input program is normal and stratified, the Instantiator module is, in some cases, able to directly compute its stable model (if it exists).

The subsequent computations, which constitute the non-deterministic part of an ASP system, are then performed on $ground(\mathcal{P})$ by both the *Ground Reasoner* and the *Model Checker*. Roughly, the former produces some "candidate" answer set, whose stability is subsequently verified by the latter.

The existing ASP systems mainly differ in the technique employed for implementing the *Ground Reasoner* . There are basically two approaches, that we will refer to as *search-based* and *rewriting-based*. In the search-based approach, the *Ground Reasoner* implements a backtracking search algorithm, which works directly on the ground instantiation of the input program. Search-based systems, like e.g. DLV and Smodels, are often referred to as "native" ASP systems, because the employed algorithms directly manipulate logic programs and are optimized for those. In the rewriting-based

---

[7] The input is usually read from text files, but some systems also interface to relational databases for retrieving facts stored in relational tables.

approach, the *Ground Reasoner* transforms the ground program into a propositional formula and then invokes a Boolean satisfiability solver for finding answer set candidates.

As previously pointed out, the *Model Checker* verifies whether an answer set candidate at hand is an answer set for the input program. This task is as hard as the problem solved by the Ground Reasoner for disjunctive programs, while it is trivial for non-disjunctive programs. However, there is also a class of disjunctive programs, called Head-Cycle-Free programs [21], for which the task solved by the Model Checker is provably simpler, which is exploited in the system algorithms.

Finally, once an answer set has been found, ASP systems typically print it in text format, and possibly the *Ground Reasoner* resumes in order to look for further answer sets.

In order to implement query answering, an important technique is a generalization of the Magic Set algorithm, originally proposed for Datalog programs. It has been extended to ASP without negation and integrity constraints in [97] and [50], and extended to certain classes of programs containing negation but no disjunction in [71,72]. In [10] the technique is described for programs with both disjunction and negation (but in a limited form, also integrity constraints are not permitted), and in [5] a large fragment of programs has been identified, for which this technique is correct. It has been implemented in the ASP system DLV, and also inside the system KAON2 [101, 102].

There are also some solvers, notably ALPHA [166] and some earlier efforts like GASP [134], ASPeRiX [110], and OMiGA [54], which avoid the Instantiator step, which can be particularly costly, especially in terms of memory use.

6.2 Applications

Answer Set Programming has been successfully applied to many areas including:

– *Information integration.* ASP has been exploited for supporting consistent query answering, in information integration systems under the so-called Global-as-View approach [111–113], also in presence of data inconsistencies and data incompleteness.
– *Configuration and Verification management.* In product configuration [155], ASP has been used as a declarative semantics providing formal definitions for main concepts in product configuration, including configuration models, requirements, and valid configurations. And, in particular, in the field of software configuration, a prototype configurator for the complete Debian Linux system distribution has been implemented by using ASP [157].
– *Knowledge Management.* ASP has a strong potential for exploitation in the area of knowledge management and semantic technologies.
  An ASP-based system for ontology representation and reasoning, called OntoDLV [148], is employed in many real-world applications, ranging from e-learning to enterprise ontologies and agent-based applications. In [150] an ASP-based approach to the problem of recognizing and extracting information from unstructured documents has been presented. While, in [51,52] a system for content classification, called OLEX, is presented, which exploits ASP to extract concepts and semantic metadata from documents.

– *Security engineering.* In [2] it is shown how security protocols can be specified and verified efficiently and effectively by embedding reasoning about actions into logic programming. In particular, two significant case studies in protocol verification have been modeled: the classical Needham-Schroeder public-key protocol, and the Aziz-Diffie key agreement protocol for mobile communication.

Moreover, applications from various areas can be found in the literature, including auctions [19], scheduling [74], policy description [22], workflow management [96], outlier detection [95], linguistics [69], multi agent systems [31,49,82], and E-learning [82].

A more recent survey of industrial applications can be found in [78].

At this point, we would like to note that there is also a field that is dedicated to software engineering for ASP, see for instance [55], and prototype tools are available (see [26,44,55,68,147,148]).

Acknowledgements. The author thanks all his co-authors over the years, for the discussions and the work that laid the foundation to this overview; in particular Nicola Leone and Francesco Ricca, with whom I co-authored a description, on which the present work has been partially based. The author would also like to thank the ASP community at large, it is great to be part of such a stimulating and critical, yet amiable crowd.

References

1. Abiteboul, S., Hull, R., Vianu, V.: Foundations of Databases. Addison-Wesley, Boston (1995)
2. Aiello, L.C., Massacci, F.: Verifying security protocols as planning in logic programming. ACM Trans. Comput. Logic **2**(4), 542–580 (2001)
3. Alviano, M., et al.: The fourth answer set programming competition: preliminary report. In: Cabalar, P., Son, T.C. (eds.) Logic Programming and Nonmonotonic Reasoning, 12th International Conference, LPNMR 2013, Corunna, Spain, 15–19 September 2013. Proceedings. Lecture Notes in Computer Science, vol. 8148, pp. 42–53. Springer (2013). https://doi.org/10.1007/978-3-642-40564-8_5
4. Alviano, M., et al.: The ASP system DLV2. In: Balduccini, M., Janhunen, T. (eds.) Logic Programming and Nonmonotonic Reasoning - 14th International Conference, LPNMR 2017, Espoo, Finland, July 3–6, 2017, Proceedings. Lecture Notes in Computer Science, vol. 10377, pp. 215–221. Springer (2017). https://doi.org/10.1007/978-3-319-61660-5_19
5. Alviano, M., Faber, W.: Dynamic magic sets and super-coherent answer set programs. AI Commun. Eur. J. Artif. Intell. **24**(2), 125–145 (2011). https://doi.org/10.3233/AIC-2011-0492
6. Alviano, M., Faber, W.: The complexity boundary of answer set programming with generalized atoms under the FLP semantics. In: Cabalar, P., Tran, S.C. (eds.) Logic Programming and Nonmonotonic Reasoning – 12th International Conference (LPNMR 2013), Lecture Notes in AI (LNAI), vol. 8148, pp. 67–72. Springer, Heidelberg (2013). https://doi.org/10.1007/978-3-642-40564-8_7
7. Alviano, M., Faber, W.: Supportedly stable answer sets for logic programs with generalized atoms. In: Ten Cate, B., Mileo, A. (eds.) 9th International Conference on Web Reasoning and Rule Systems (RR 2015). Lecture Notes in Computer Science, vol. 9209, pp. 30–44. Springer, Heidelberg (2015). https://doi.org/10.1007/978-3-319-22002-4_4

8. Alviano, M., Faber, W.: Chain answer sets for logic programs with generalized atoms. In: Calimeri, F., Leone, N., Manna, M. (eds.) Proceedings of the 16th European Conference on Logics in Artificial Intelligence (JELIA 2019). Lecture Notes in AI (LNAI), vol. 11468, pp. 462–478. Springer, Heidelberg (2019). https://doi.org/10.1007/978-3-030-19570-0_30

9. Alviano, M., Faber, W., Gebser, M.: Rewriting recursive aggregates in answer set programming: back to monotonicity. In: Theory and Practice of Logic Programming, 31st International Conference on Logic Programming (ICLP 2015) Special Issue, vol. 15, no. 4–5, 5, pp. 59–573 (2015). https://doi.org/10.1017/S1471068415000228

10. Alviano, M., Faber, W., Greco, G., Leone, N.: Magic sets for disjunctive datalog programs. Artif. Intell. **187–187**, 156–192 (2012). https://doi.org/10.1016/j.artint.2012.04.008, http://arxiv.org/abs/1204.6346

11. Alviano, M., Faber, W., Leone, N.: Disjunctive ASP with functions: decidable queries and effective computation. In: Theory and Practice of Logic Programming, 26th International Conference on Logic Programming (ICLP 2010) Special Issue, vol. 10, no. 4–6, pp. 497–512 (2010). https://doi.org/10.1017/S1471068410000244

12. Alviano, M., Faber, W., Leone, N., Manna, M.: Disjunctive datalog with existential quantifiers: Semantics, decidability, and complexity issues. Theory and Practice of Logic Programming, 28th International Conference on Logic Programming (ICLP 2012) Special Issue, vol. 12, no. 4–5, pp. 701–718 (2012). https://doi.org/10.1017/S1471068412000257

13. Apt, K.R., Blair, H.A., Walker, A.: Towards a Theory of Declarative Knowledge. In: Minker [132], pp. 89–148 (1988)

14. Arora, S., Barak, B.: Computational Complexity: A Modern Approach. Cambridge University Press, Cambridge (2009)

15. Baader, F., Calvanese, D., McGuinness, D.L., Nardi, D., Patel-Schneider, P.F. (eds.): The Description Logic Handbook: Theory, Implementation, and Applications. Cambridge University Press, Cambridge (2003)

16. Lierler, Y., Maratea, M.: Cmodels-2: SAT-based answer set solver enhanced to non-tight programs. In: Lifschitz, V., Niemela, I. (eds.) Logic Programming and Nonmonotonic Reasoning. LPNMR 2004. Lecture Notes in Computer Science, vol. 2923 (2003). Springer, Heidelberg. https://doi.org/10.1007/978-3-540-24609-1_32, http://www.cs.utexas.edu/users/tag/cmodels.html

17. Balduccini, M., Gelfond, M.: Logic programs with consistency-restoring rules. In: Doherty, J.P., McCarthy, M.W. (ed.) International Symposium on Logical Formalization of Commonsense Reasoning, AAAI 2003 Spring Symposium Series (2003). citeseer.ist.psu.edu/balduccini03logic.html

18. Baral, C.: Knowledge Representation, Reasoning and Declarative Problem Solving. Cambridge University Press, Cambridge (2003)

19. Baral, C., Uyan, C.: Declarative specification and solution of combinatorial auctions using logic programming. In: Eiter, T., Faber, W., Truszczyński, M. (eds.) Proceedings of the 6th International Conference on Logic Programming and Nonmonotonic Reasoning (LPNMR-01). Lecture Notes in AI (LNAI), vol. 2173, pp. 186–199. Springer, Heidelberg (2001). https://doi.org/10.1007/3-540-45402-0_14

20. Baselice, S., Bonatti, P.A., Criscuolo, G.: On finitely recursive programs. Theory Pract. Logic Program. **9**(2), 213–238 (2009)

21. Ben-Eliyahu, R., Dechter, R.: Propositional semantics for disjunctive logic programs. Ann. Math. Artif. Intell. **12**, 53–87 (1994). https://doi.org/10.1007/BF01530761

22. Bertino, E., Mileo, A., Provetti, A.: User preferences vs minimality in PPDL. In: Buccafurri, F. (ed.) Proceedings of the Joint Conference on Declarative Programming APPIA-GULP-PRODE 2003, pp. 110–122, September 2003

23. Bidoit, N., Froidevaux, C.: Minimalism subsumes default logic and circumscription in stratified logic programming. In: Proceedings of the Symposium on Logic in Computer Science (LICS 1987), pp. 89–97. IEEE (1987)

24. Bonatti, P.A.: Reasoning with infinite stable models II: disjunctive programs. In: Proceedings of the 18th International Conference on Logic Programming (ICLP 2002). LNCS, vol. 2401, pp. 333–346. Springer, Heidelberg (2002). https://doi.org/10.1007/3-540-45619-8_23

25. Bonatti, P.A.: Reasoning with infinite stable models. Artif. Intell. **156**(1), 75–111 (2004)

26. Brain, M., De Vos, M.: Debugging logic programs under the answer set semantics. In: de Vos, M., Provetti, A. (eds.) Proceedings ASP05 - Answer Set Programming: Advances in Theory and Implementation, Bath, UK, July 2005

27. Brewka, G.: Logic programming with ordered disjunction. In: Proceedings of the 9th International Workshop on Non-Monotonic Reasoning (NMR 2002), pp. 67–76, April 2002

28. Brewka, G.: Answer sets: from constraint programming towards qualitative optimization. In: Lifschitz, V., Niemelä, I. (eds.) Proceedings of the 7th International Conference on Logic Programming and Non-Monotonic Reasoning (LPNMR-7). LNAI, vol. 2923, pp. 34–46. Springer, Heidelberg (2004). https://doi.org/10.1007/978-3-540-24609-1_6

29. Brewka, G., Eiter, T.: Preferred answer sets for extended logic programs. Artif. Intell. **109**(1–2), 297–356 (1999)

30. Brewka, G., Niemelä, I., Truszczyński, M.: Answer set optimization. In: Gottlob, G., Walsh, T. (eds.) IJCAI-03, Proceedings of the Eighteenth International Joint Conference on Artificial Intelligence, Acapulco, Mexico, pp. 867–872. Morgan Kaufmann (2003)

31. Buccafurri, F., Caminiti, G.: A Social Semantics for Multi-agent Systems. In: Baral, C., Greco, G., Leone, N., Terracina, G. (eds.) Logic Programming and Nonmonotonic Reasoning – 8th International Conference, LPNMR'05, Diamante, Italy. Lecture Notes in Computer Science, vol. 3662, pp. 317–329. Springer, Heidelberg (2005). https://doi.org/10.1007/11546207_25

32. Buccafurri, F., Leone, N., Rullo, P.: Enhancing disjunctive datalog by constraints. IEEE Trans. Knowl. Data Eng. **12**(5), 845–860 (2000)

33. Cabalar, P.: Partial functions and equality in answer set programming. In: Proceedings of the 24th International Conference on Logic Programming (ICLP 2008). Lecture Notes in Computer Science, vol. 5366, pp. 392–406. Springer, Heidelberg (2008). https://doi.org/10.1007/978-3-540-89982-2_36

34. Cadoli, M., Eiter, T., Gottlob, G.: Default logic as a query language. IEEE Trans. Knowl. Data Eng. **9**(3), 448–463 (1997)

35. Calì, A., Gottlob, G., Kifer, M.: Taming the infinite chase: query answering under expressive relational constraints. In: Brewka, G., Lang, J. (eds.) Proceedings of the Eleventh International Conference on Principles of Knowledge Representation and Reasoning (KR 2008), pp. 70–80. AAAI Press (2008)

36. Calì, A., Gottlob, G., Lukasiewicz, T.: A general datalog-based framework for tractable query answering over ontologies. J. Web Semant. **14**, 57–83 (2012)

37. Calì, A., Gottlob, G., Pieris, A.: Advanced processing for ontological queries. Proc. VLDB Endow. **3**(1), 554–565 (2010)

38. Calì, A., Gottlob, G., Pieris, A.: Towards more expressive ontology languages: the query answering problem. Artif. Intell. **193**, 87–128 (2012)

39. Calimeri, F., Cozza, S., Ianni, G., Leone, N.: Computable functions in ASP: theory and implementation. In: Proceedings of the 24th International Conference on Logic Programming (ICLP 2008). Lecture Notes in Computer Science, vol. 5366, pp. 407–424. Springer, Heidelberg (2008). https://doi.org/10.1007/978-3-540-89982-2_37

40. Calimeri, F., Cozza, S., Ianni, G., Leone, N.: Magic sets for the bottom-up evaluation of finitely recursive programs. In: Erdem, E., Lin, F., Schaub, T. (eds.) Logic Programming and Nonmonotonic Reasoning – 10th International Conference (LPNMR 2009). Lecture Notes in Computer Science, vol. 5753, pp. 71–86. Springer, Heidelberg (2009). https://doi.org/10.1007/978-3-642-04238-6_9

41. Calimeri, F., Dodaro, C., Fuscà, D., Perri, S., Zangari, J.: Efficiently coupling the I-DLV grounder with ASP solvers. Theory Pract. Log. Program. **20**(2), 205–224 (2020). https://doi.org/10.1017/S1471068418000546

42. Calimeri, F., et al.: Asp-core-2 input language format. Theory Pract. Logic Program. **20**(2), 294–309 (2020). https://doi.org/10.1017/S1471068419000450

43. Calimeri, F., Faber, W., Leone, N., Perri, S.: Declarative and computational properties of logic programs with aggregates. In: Nineteenth International Joint Conference on Artificial Intelligence (IJCAI 2005), pp. 406–411, August 2005

44. Calimeri F., Ianni G., Ielpa G., Pietramala A., Santoro M.C.: A system with template answer set programs. In: Alferes, J.J., Leite, J. (eds.) Logics in Artificial Intelligence. JELIA 2004. Lecture Notes in Computer Science, vol. 3229. Springer, Heidelberg (2004). https://doi.org/10.1007/978-3-540-30227-8_59

45. Calimeri, F., Ianni, G., Ricca, F.: The third open answer set programming competition. Theory Pract. Logic Program. **14**(1), 117–135 (2014). https://doi.org/10.1017/S1471068412000105

46. Cat, B.D., Bogaerts, B., Bruynooghe, M., Janssens, G., Denecker, M.: Predicate logic as a modeling language: the IDP system. In: Kifer, M., Liu, Y.A. (eds.) Declarative Logic Programming: Theory, Systems, and Applications, pp. 279–323. ACM/Morgan & Claypool (2018). https://doi.org/10.1145/3191315.3191321

47. Clark, K.L.: Negation as failure. In: Gallaire, H., Minker, J. (eds.) Logic and Data Bases, pp. 293–322. Plenum Press, New York (1978)

48. Colmerauer, A., Roussel, P.: The Birth of Prolog. ACM, New York (1996)

49. Costantini, S., Tocchio, A.: The DALI logic programming agent-oriented language. In: Alferes, J.J., Leite, J. (eds.) Proceedings of the 9th European Conference on Artificial Intelligence (JELIA 2004). Lecture Notes in AI (LNAI), vol. 3229, pp. 685–688. Springer, Heidelberg (2004). https://doi.org/10.1007/978-3-540-30227-8_57

50. Cumbo, C., Faber, W., Greco, G., Leone, N.: Enhancing the magic-set method for disjunctive datalog programs. In: Proceedings of the the 20th International Conference on Logic Programming - ICLP 2004. Lecture Notes in Computer Science, vol. 3132, pp. 371–385. Springer, Heidelberg (2004). https://doi.org/10.1007/978-3-540-27775-0_26

51. Cumbo, C., Iiritano, S., Rullo, P.: Reasoning-based knowledge extraction for text classification. In: Suzuki, E., Arikawa, S. (eds.) DS 2004. LNCS (LNAI), vol. 3245, pp. 380–387. Springer, Heidelberg (2004). https://doi.org/10.1007/978-3-540-30214-8_34

52. Curia, R., Ettorre, M., Gallucci, L., Iiritano, S., Rullo, P.: Textual document pre-processing and feature extraction in OLEX. In: Proceedings of Data Mining 2005, Skiathos, Greece (2005)

53. Dantsin, E., Eiter, T., Gottlob, G., Voronkov, A.: Complexity and expressive power of logic programming. ACM Comput. Surv. **33**(3), 374–425 (2001)

54. Dao-Tran, M., Eiter, T., Fink, M., Weidinger, G., Weinzierl, A.: OMiGA: an open minded grounding on-the-fly answer set solver. In: del Cerro, L.F., Herzig, A., Mengin, J. (eds.) JELIA 2012. LNCS (LNAI), vol. 7519, pp. 480–483. Springer, Heidelberg (2012). https://doi.org/10.1007/978-3-642-33353-8_38

55. De Vos, M., Schaub, T. (eds.): SEA 2007: software engineering for answer set programming, vol. 281. CEUR (2007). http://CEUR-WS.org/Vol-281/

56. Delgrande, J.P., Schaub, T., Tompits, H.: A Framework for Compiling Preferences in Logic Programs. Theory Pract. Logic Program. **3**(2), 129–187 (2003)

57. Dell'Armi, T., Faber, W., Ielpa, G., Leone, N., Pfeifer, G.: Aggregate functions in disjunctive logic programming: semantics, complexity, and implementation in DLV. In: Proceedings of the 18th International Joint Conference on Artificial Intelligence (IJCAI) 2003, pp. 847–852. Morgan Kaufmann Publishers, Acapulco (2003)

58. Dell'Armi, T., Faber, W., Ielpa, G., Leone, N., Pfeifer, G.: Aggregate functions in DLV. In: de Vos, M., Provetti, A. (eds.) Proceedings ASP03 - Answer Set Programming: Advances in Theory and Implementation, Messina, Italy, pp. 274–288 (2003). http://CEUR-WS.org/Vol-78/

59. Denecker, M., Pelov, N., Bruynooghe, M.: Ultimate well-founded and stable semantics for logic programs with aggregates. In: Codognet, P. (eds) Logic Programming. ICLP 2001. Lecture Notes in Computer Science, vol. 2237, pp. 212–226. Springer, Heidelberg (2001). https://doi.org/10.1007/3-540-45635-X_22

60. Dimopoulos, Y., Kakas, A.C., Michael, L.: Reasoning about actions and change in answer set programming. In: Lifschitz, V., Niemelä, I. (eds.) LPNMR 2004. LNCS (LNAI), vol. 2923, pp. 61–73. Springer, Heidelberg (2003). https://doi.org/10.1007/978-3-540-24609-1_8

61. Dix, J., Gottlob, G., Marek, V.W.: Reducing disjunctive to non-disjunctive semantics by shift-operations. Fundam. Inform. **28**, 87–100 (1996)

62. Drescher, C., Gebser, M., Grote, T., Kaufmann, B., König, A., Ostrowski, M., Schaub, T.: Conflict-driven disjunctive answer set solving. In: Brewka, G., Lang, J. (eds.) Proceedings of the Eleventh International Conference on Principles of Knowledge Representation and Reasoning (KR 2008), pp. 422–432. AAAI Press, Sydney (2008)

63. Eiter, T., Faber, W., Leone, N., Pfeifer, G.: Declarative problem-solving using the DLV system. In: Minker, J. (ed.) Logic-Based Artificial Intelligence, pp. 79–103. Kluwer Academic Publishers (2000)

64. Eiter, T., Faber, W., Leone, N., Pfeifer, G., Polleres, A.: A logic programming approach to knowledge-state planning: semantics and complexity. ACM Trans. Comput. Logic **5**(2), 206–263 (2004)

65. Eiter, T., Ianni, G., Schindlauer, R., Tompits, H.: A uniform integration of higher-order reasoning and external evaluations in answer set programming. In: International Joint Conference on Artificial Intelligence (IJCAI) 2005, Edinburgh, UK, pp. 90–96, August 2005

66. Eiter, T., Lukasiewicz, T., Schindlauer, R., Tompits, H.: Combining answer set programming with description logics for the semantic web. In: Principles of Knowledge Representation and Reasoning: Proceedings of the Ninth International Conference (KR2004), Whistler, Canada, pp. 141–151: Extended report RR-1843-03-13, p. 2003. Institut für Informationssysteme, TU Wien (2004)

67. Eiter, T., Simkus, M.: Bidirectional answer set programs with function symbols. In: Boutilier, C. (ed.) Proceedings of the 21st International Joint Conference on Artificial Intelligence (IJCAI-09), Pasadena, CA, USA, pp. 765–771, July 2009

68. El-Khatib, O., Pontelli, E., Son, T.C.: Justification and debugging of answer set programs in ASP. In: Jeffery, C., Choi, J.D., Lencevicius, R. (eds.) Proceedings of the Sixth International Workshop on Automated Debugging, California, USA. ACM (2005)

69. Erdem, E., Lifschitz, V., Nakhleh, L., Ringe, D.: Reconstructing the evolutionary history of Indo-European languages using answer set programming. In: Dahl, V., Wadler, P. (eds.) Practical Aspects of Declarative Languages, 5th International Symposium (PADL 2003). Lecture Notes in Computer Science, vol. 2562, pp. 160–176. Springer, Heidelberg (2003). https://doi.org/10.1007/3-540-36388-2_12

70. Faber, W.: Answer set programming. In: Rudolph, S., Gottlob, G., Horrocks, I., van Harmelen, F. (eds.) Reasoning Web. Semantic Technologies for Intelligent Data Access - 9th International Summer School 2013, Mannheim, Germany, 30 July–2 August 2013, Proceedings, vol. 8067, pp. 162–193. Lecture Notes in Computer Science. Springer, Heidelberg (2013). https://doi.org/10.1007/978-3-642-39784-4_4

71. Faber, W., Greco, G., Leone, N.: Magic sets and their application to data integration. In: Eiter, T., Libkin, L. (eds.) ICDT 2005. LNCS, vol. 3363, pp. 306–320. Springer, Heidelberg (2004). https://doi.org/10.1007/978-3-540-30570-5_21

72. Faber, W., Greco, G., Leone, N.: Magic sets and their application to data integration. J. Comput. Syst. Sci. **73**(4), 584–609 (2007). https://doi.org/10.1016/j.jcss.2006.10.012

73. Faber, W., Leone, N.: On the complexity of answer set programming with aggregates. In: Baral, C., Brewka, G., Schlipf, J.S. (eds.) Logic Programming and Nonmonotonic Reasoning – 9th International Conference, LPNMR 2007. Lecture Notes in AI (LNAI), vol. 4483, pp. 97–109. Springer, Heidelberg (2007)

74. Faber, W., Leone, N., Pfeifer, G.: Representing school timetabling in a disjunctive logic programming language. In: Egly, U., Tompits, H. (eds.) Proceedings of the 13th Workshop on Logic Programming (WLP'98), Vienna, Austria, pp. 43–52, October 1998

75. Faber, W., Leone, N., Pfeifer, G.: Recursive aggregates in disjunctive logic programs: semantics and complexity. In: Alferes, J.J., Leite, J. (eds.) JELIA 2004. LNCS (LNAI), vol. 3229, pp. 200–212. Springer, Heidelberg (2004). https://doi.org/10.1007/978-3-540-30227-8_19

76. Faber, W., Leone, N., Pfeifer, G.: Semantics and complexity of recursive aggregates in answer set programming. Artif. Intell. **175**(1), 278–298 (2011). https://doi.org/10.1016/j.artint.2010.04.002. Special Issue: John McCarthy's Legacy

77. Fagin, R., Kolaitis, P.G., Miller, R.J., Popa, L.: Data exchange: semantics and query answering. Theoret. Comput. Sci. **336**(1), 89–124 (2005)

78. Falkner, A.A., Friedrich, G., Schekotihin, K., Taupe, R., Teppan, E.C.: Industrial applications of answer set programming. KI **32**(2–3), 165–176 (2018). https://doi.org/10.1007/s13218-018-0548-6

79. Ferraris, P.: Answer sets for propositional theories. In: Baral, C., Greco, G., Leone, N., Terracina, G. (eds.) Logic Programming and Nonmonotonic Reasoning – 8th International Conference, LPNMR 2005, Diamante, Italy, September 2005, Proceedings. Lecture Notes in Computer Science, vol. 3662, pp. 119–131. Springer, Heidelberg (2005). https://doi.org/10.1007/11546207_10

80. Ferraris, P.: Logic programs with propositional connectives and aggregates. ACM Trans. Comput. Logic **12**(4), 25 (2011). https://doi.org/10.1145/1970398.1970401

81. Ferraris, P., Lee, J., Lifschitz, V.: A new perspective on stable models. In: Twentieth International Joint Conference on Artificial Intelligence (IJCAI 2007), pp. 372–379, January 2007

82. Garro, A., Palopoli, L., Ricca, F.: Exploiting agents in e-learning and skills management context. AI Commun. Eur. J. Artif. Intell. **19**(2), 137–154 (2006)

83. Gebser, M., Kaminski, R., Kaufmann, B., Schaub, T.: Clingo = ASP + control: Preliminary report. CoRR abs/1405.3694 (2014)

84. Gebser, M., Kaminski, R., Kaufmann, B., Schaub, T.: Multi-shot ASP solving with clingo. Theory Pract. Log. Program. **19**(1), 27–82 (2019). https://doi.org/10.1017/S1471068418000054

85. Gebser, M., Kaufmann, B., Neumann, A., Schaub, T.: Conflict-driven answer set solving. In: Twentieth International Joint Conference on Artificial Intelligence (IJCAI-07), pp. 386–392. Morgan Kaufmann Publishers (2007)

86. Gebser, M., Schaub, T., Thiele, S.: GrinGo: a new grounder for answer set programming. In: Baral, C., Brewka, G., Schlipf, J. (eds.) LPNMR 2007. LNCS (LNAI), vol. 4483, pp. 266–271. Springer, Heidelberg (2007). https://doi.org/10.1007/978-3-540-72200-7_24

87. Gelfond, M.: On stratified autoepistemic theories. In: Proceedings of the Sixth National Conference on Artificial Intelligence (AAAI 1987), pp. 207–211 (1987)

88. Gelfond, M.: Representing knowledge in A-Prolog. In: Kakas, A.C., Sadri, F. (eds.) Computational Logic: Logic Programming and Beyond. LNCS (LNAI), vol. 2408, pp. 413–451. Springer, Heidelberg (2002). https://doi.org/10.1007/3-540-45632-5_16

89. Gelfond, M., Leone, N.: Logic Programming and knowledge representation - the A-Prolog perspective. Artif. Intell. **138**(1–2), 3–38 (2002)

90. Gelfond, M., Lifschitz, V.: The stable model semantics for logic programming. In: Logic Programming: Proceedings Fifth International Conference and Symposium, pp. 1070–1080. MIT Press, Cambridge (1988)

91. Gelfond, M., Lifschitz, V.: Classical negation in logic programs and disjunctive databases. New Gener. Comput. **9**, 365–385 (1991). https://doi.org/10.1007/BF03037169

92. Gelfond, M., Zhang, Y.: Vicious circle principle, aggregates, and formation of sets in ASP based languages. Artif. Intell. **275**, 28–77 (2019). https://doi.org/10.1016/j.artint.2019.04.004

93. Goldreich, O.: Computational Complexity: A Conceptual Perspective. Cambridge University Press, Cambridge (2008)

94. Gottlob, G., Manna, M., Morak, M., Pieris, A.: On the complexity of ontological reasoning under disjunctive existential rules. In: Rovan, B., Sassone, V., Widmayer, P. (eds.) Proceedings of the 37th International Symposium Mathematical Foundations of Computer Science (MFCS 2012). Lecture Notes in Computer Science, vol. 7464, pp. 1–18. Springer, Heidelberg (2012). https://doi.org/10.1007/978-3-642-32589-2_1

95. Greco, G., Greco, S., Zumpano, E.: A logical framework for querying and repairing inconsistent databases. IEEE Trans. Knowl. Data Eng. **15**(6), 1389–1408 (2003)

96. Greco, G., Guzzo, A., Saccà, D.: A logic programming approach for planning workflows evolutions. In: Buccafurri, F. (ed.) Proceedings of the Joint Conference on Declarative Programming APPIA-GULP-PRODE 2003, pp. 75–85, September 2003

97. Greco, S.: Binding propagation techniques for the optimization of bound disjunctive queries. IEEE Trans. Knowl. Data Eng. **15**(2), 368–385 (2003)

98. Hella, L., Libkin, L., Nurmonen, J., Wong, L.: Logics with aggregate operators. J. ACM **48**(4), 880–907 (2001)

99. Heymans, S., Van Nieuwenborgh, D., Vermeir, D.: Semantic Web reasoning with conceptual logic programs. In: Antoniou, G., Boley, H. (eds.) RuleML 2004. LNCS, vol. 3323, pp. 113–127. Springer, Heidelberg (2004). https://doi.org/10.1007/978-3-540-30504-0_9

100. Heyting, A.: Die formalen Regeln der intuitionistischen Logik. Sitzungsberichte der Preussischen Akademie der Wissenschaften, Physikalisch-Mathematische Klasse, pp. 42–56 (1930)

101. Hustadt, U., Motik, B., Sattler, U.: Reducing SHIQ-description logic to disjunctive datalog programs. In: Principles of Knowledge Representation and Reasoning: Proceedings of the Ninth International Conference (KR2004), Whistler, Canada, pp. 152–162 (2004)

102. Hustadt, U., Motik, B., Sattler, U.: Reasoning in description logics by a reduction to disjunctive datalog. J. Autom. Reason. **39**(3), 351–384 (2007). https://doi.org/10.1007/s10817-007-9080-3

103. International Organization for Standardization: ISO/IEC 13211–1:1995: Information technology – Programming languages – Prolog – Part 1: General core. International Organization for Standardization, Geneva, Switzerland (1995)

104. Janhunen, T., Niemelä, I., Seipel, D., Simons, P., You, J.H.: Unfolding partiality and disjunctions in stable model semantics. Technical report, cs.AI/0303009. arXiv.org (2003)

105. Kakas, A.C., Kowalski, R.A., Toni, F.: Abductive logic programming. J. Logic Comput. **2**(6), 719–770 (1992)
106. Kemp, D.B., Stuckey, P.J.: Semantics of logic programs with aggregates. In: Saraswat, V.A., Ueda, K. (eds.) Proceedings of the International Symposium on Logic Programming (ISLP 1991), pp. 387–401. MIT Press (1991)
107. Kowalski, R.A.: Predicate logic as programming language. In: IFIP Congress, pp. 569–574 (1974)
108. Kowalski, R.A.: Algorithm = Logic + Control. Commun. ACM **22**(7), 424–436 (1979)
109. Krötzsch, M., Rudolph, S.: Extending decidable existential rules by joining acyclicity and guardedness. In: Walsh, T. (ed.) Proceedings of the 22nd International Joint Conference on Artificial Intelligence (IJCAI-11), pp. 963–968 (2011)
110. Lefèvre, C., Béatrix, C., Stéphan, I., Garcia, L.: ASPeRiX, a first-order forward chaining approach for answer set computing. Theory Pract. Log. Program. **17**(3), 266–310 (2017). https://doi.org/10.1017/S1471068416000569
111. Lembo, D., Lenzerini, M., Rosati, R.: Integrating inconsistent and incomplete data sources. In: Proceedings of SEBD 2002, Portoferraio, Isola d'Elba, pp. 299–308 (2002)
112. Lembo, D., Lenzerini, M., Rosati, R.: Source inconsistency and incompleteness in data integration. In: Proceedings of the Knowledge Representation meets Databases International Workshop (KRDB-02). CEUR Electronic Workshop Proceedings, Toulouse, France (2002). http://sunsite.informatik.rwth-aachen.de/Publications/CEUR-WS/Vol-54/
113. Leone, N., et al.: The INFOMIX system for advanced integration of incomplete and inconsistent data. In: Proceedings of the 24th ACM SIGMOD International Conference on Management of Data (SIGMOD 2005), Baltimore, Maryland, USA, pp. 915–917. ACM Press (2005)
114. Leone, N., Manna, M., Terracina, G., Veltri, P.: Efficiently computable datalog$^\exists$ programs. In: Brewka, G., Eiter, T., McIlraith, S. (eds.) Proceedings of the 13th International Conference on Principles of Knowledge Representation and Reasoning (KR 2012). AAAI Press (2012)
115. Leone, N., et al.: The DLV system for knowledge representation and reasoning. ACM Trans. Comput. Logic **7**(3), 499–562 (2006)
116. Leone, N., Rullo, P., Scarcello, F.: Disjunctive stable models: unfounded sets, fixpoint semantics and computation. Inf. Comput. **135**(2), 69–112 (1997)
117. Lierler, Y.: Disjunctive answer set programming via satisfiability. In: Baral, C., Greco, G., Leone, N., Terracina, G. (eds.) Logic Programming and Nonmonotonic Reasoning – 8th International Conference, LPNMR'05, Diamante, Italy, September 2005, Proceedings. Lecture Notes in Computer Science, vol. 3662, pp. 447–451. Springer, Heidelberg (2005). https://doi.org/10.1007/11546207_44
118. Lierler, Y.: Relating constraint answer set programming languages and algorithms. Artif. Intell. **207**, 1–22 (2014). https://doi.org/10.1016/j.artint.2013.10.004
119. Lierler, Y., Lifschitz, V.: One more decidable class of finitely ground programs. In: Hill, P.M., Warren, D.S. (eds.) ICLP 2009. LNCS, vol. 5649, pp. 489–493. Springer, Heidelberg (2009). https://doi.org/10.1007/978-3-642-02846-5_40
120. Lifschitz, V.: Twelve definitions of a stable model. In: Garcia de la Banda, M., Pontelli, E. (eds.) ICLP 2008. LNCS, vol. 5366, pp. 37–51. Springer, Heidelberg (2008). https://doi.org/10.1007/978-3-540-89982-2_8
121. Lifschitz, V.: Thirteen definitions of a stable model. In: Blass, A., Dershowitz, N., Reisig, W. (eds.) Fields of Logic and Computation, Essays Dedicated to Yuri Gurevich on the Occasion of His 70th Birthday, Lecture Notes in Computer Science, vol. 6300, pp. 488–503. Springer, Heidelberg (2010). https://doi.org/10.1007/978-3-642-15025-8_24
122. Lifschitz, V., Pearce, D., Valverde, A.: Strongly equivalent logic programs. ACM Trans. Comput. Logic **2**(4), 526–541 (2001)

123. Lin, F., Wang, Y.: Answer set programming with functions. In: Proceedings of Eleventh International Conference on Principles of Knowledge Representation and Reasoning (KR2008), Sydney, Australia, pp. 454–465. AAAI Press (2008)
124. Lin, F., Zhao, Y.: ASSAT: computing answer sets of a logic program by SAT solvers. In: Proceedings of the Eighteenth National Conference on Artificial Intelligence (AAAI-2002), Edmonton, Alberta, Canada. AAAI Press/MIT Press (2002)
125. Marek, V.W., Truszczyński, M.: Nonmonotonic Logics - Context-Dependent Reasoning. Springer, Heidelberg (1993)
126. Mariën, M., Gilis, D., Denecker, M.: On the relation between ID-logic and answer set programming. In: Alferes, J.J., Leite, J. (eds.) JELIA 2004. LNCS (LNAI), vol. 3229, pp. 108–120. Springer, Heidelberg (2004). https://doi.org/10.1007/978-3-540-30227-8_12
127. Marriott, K., Stuckey, P.J.: Programming with Constraints: An Introduction. MIT Press, Cambridge (1998)
128. McCarthy, J.: Programs with common sense. In: Proceedings of the Teddington Conference on the Mechanization of Thought Processes, pp. 75–91. Her Majesty's Stationery Office (1959)
129. McCarthy, J.: Elaboration Tolerance (1999). http://www-formal.stanford.edu/jmc/elaboration.html
130. McCarthy, J., Hayes, P.J.: Some philosophical problems from the standpoint of artificial intelligence. In: Meltzer, B., Michie, D. (eds.) Machine Intelligence, vol. 4, pp. 463–502. Edinburgh University Press (1969)
131. Minker, J.: On indefinite data bases and the closed world assumption. In: Loveland, D.W. (ed.) Proceedings 6th Conference on Automated Deduction (CADE '82). Lecture Notes in Computer Science, vol. 138, pp. 292–308. Springer, New York (1982). https://doi.org/10.1007/BFb0000066
132. Minker, J. (ed.): Foundations of Deductive Databases and Logic Programming. Morgan Kaufmann Publishers Inc., Washington DC (1988)
133. Niemelä, I., Simons, P.: Smodels—an implementation of the stable model and well-founded semantics for normal logic programs. In: Dix, J., Furbach, U., Nerode, A. (eds.) LPNMR 1997. LNCS, vol. 1265, pp. 420–429. Springer, Heidelberg (1997). https://doi.org/10.1007/3-540-63255-7_32
134. Palù, A.D., Dovier, A., Pontelli, E., Rossi, G.: GASP: answer set programming with lazy grounding. Fundam. Inform. 96(3), 297–322 (2009). https://doi.org/10.3233/FI-2009-180
135. Papadimitriou, C.H.: Computational Complexity. Addison-Wesley, Boston (1994)
136. Pearce, D.: Equilibrium logic. Ann. Math. Artif. Intell. 47(1–2), 3–41 (2006). https://doi.org/10.1007/s10472-006-9028-z
137. Pearce, D., Sarsakov, V., Schaub, T., Tompits, H., Woltran, S.: A polynomial translation of logic programs with nested expressions into disjunctive logic programs: preliminary report. In: Proceedings of the 9th International Workshop on Non-Monotonic Reasoning (NMR 2002) (2002)
138. Pearce, D., Tompits, H., Woltran, S.: Encodings for equilibrium logic and logic programs with nested expressions. In: Brazdil, P., Jorge, A. (eds.) EPIA 2001. LNCS (LNAI), vol. 2258, pp. 306–320. Springer, Heidelberg (2001). https://doi.org/10.1007/3-540-45329-6_31
139. Pearce, D., Valverde, A.: Quantified equilibrium logic and foundations for answer set programs. In: Garcia de la Banda, M., Pontelli, E. (eds.) ICLP 2008. LNCS, vol. 5366, pp. 546–560. Springer, Heidelberg (2008). https://doi.org/10.1007/978-3-540-89982-2_46
140. Pelov, N.: Semantics of logic programs with aggregates. Ph.D. thesis, Katholieke Universiteit Leuven, April 2004
141. Pelov, N., Denecker, M., Bruynooghe, M.: Well-founded and stable semantics of logic programs with aggregates. Theory Pract. Logic Program. 7(3), 301–353 (2007)

142. Perri, S., Scarcello, F., Leone, N.: Abductive logic programs with penalization: semantics, complexity and implementation. Theory Pract. Logic Program. **5**(1–2), 123–159 (2005)
143. Pierre Bourhis, M.M., Pieris, A.: The impact of disjunction on ontological query answering under guarded-based existential rules. In: Proceedings of the 23rd International Joint Conference on Artificial Intelligence (IJCAI-13) (2013)
144. Przymusinski, T.C.: Stable semantics for disjunctive programs. New Gener. Comput. **9**, 401–424 (1991). https://doi.org/10.1007/BF03037171
145. Radziszowski, S.P.: Small ramsey numbers. Electron. J. Comb. **1** (1994). Revision 9: 15 July 2002
146. Reiter, R.: On closed world data bases. In: Gallaire, H., Minker, J. (eds.) Logic and Data Bases, pp. 55–76. Plenum Press, New York (1978)
147. Ricca, F.: The DLV Java wrapper. In: de Vos, M., Provetti, A. (eds.) Proceedings ASP03 - Answer Set Programming: Advances in Theory and Implementation, pp. 305–316. Messina, Italy, September 2003. http://CEUR-WS.org/Vol-78/
148. Ricca, F., Leone, N.: Disjunctive logic programming with types and objects: the DLV$^+$ system. J. Appl. Logics **5**(3), 545–573 (2007)
149. Robinson, J.A.: A machine-oriented logic based on the resolution principle. J. ACM **12**(1), 23–41 (1965)
150. Ruffolo, M., Leone, N., Manna, M., Saccà, D., Zavatto, A.: Exploiting ASP for semantic information extraction. In: de Vos, M., Provetti, A. (eds.) Proceedings ASP05 - Answer Set Programming: Advances in Theory and Implementation, Bath, UK, pp. 248–262, July 2005
151. Schaub, T., Wang, K.: A comparative study of logic programs with preference. In: Proceedings of the Seventeenth International Joint Conference on Artificial Intelligence (IJCAI) 2001, pp. 597–602. Morgan Kaufmann Publishers, Seattle (2001)
152. Šimkus, M., Eiter, T.: FDNC: decidable non-monotonic disjunctive logic programs with function symbols. In: Dershowitz, N., Voronkov, A. (eds.) LPAR 2007. LNCS (LNAI), vol. 4790, pp. 514–530. Springer, Heidelberg (2007). https://doi.org/10.1007/978-3-540-75560-9_37
153. Simons, P.: Smodels, since 1996. http://www.tcs.hut.fi/Software/smodels/
154. Simons, P., Niemelä, I., Soininen, T.: Extending and implementing the stable model semantics. Artif. Intell. **138**, 181–234 (2002)
155. Soininen, T., Niemelä, I.: Developing a declarative rule language for applications in product configuration. In: Gupta, G. (ed.) PADL 1999. LNCS, vol. 1551, pp. 305–319. Springer, Heidelberg (1998). https://doi.org/10.1007/3-540-49201-1_21
156. Son, T.C., Pontelli, E.: A constructive semantic characterization of aggregates in ASP. Theory Pract. Logic Program. **7**, 355–375 (2007)
157. Syrjänen, T.: A rule-based formal model for software configuration. Technical report A55, Digital Systems Laboratory, Department of Computer Science, Helsinki University of Technology, Espoo, Finland (1999)
158. Syrjänen, T.: Omega-restricted logic programs. In: Eiter, T., Faber, W., Truszczyński, M. (eds.) LPNMR 2001. LNCS (LNAI), vol. 2173, pp. 267–280. Springer, Heidelberg (2001). https://doi.org/10.1007/3-540-45402-0_20
159. Syrjänen, T.: Lparse 1.0 User's Manual (2002). http://www.tcs.hut.fi/Software/smodels/lparse.ps.gz
160. van Emden, M.H., Kowalski, R.A.: The semantics of predicate logic as a programming language. J. ACM **23**(4), 733–742 (1976)
161. Van Gelder, A.: Negation as failure using tight derivations for general logic programs. In: Minker [132], pp. 1149–1176 (1989)
162. Van Gelder, A., Ross, K.A., Schlipf, J.S.: Unfounded sets and well-founded semantics for general logic programs. In: Proceedings of the Seventh Symposium on Principles of Database Systems (PODS 1988), pp. 221–230 (1988)

163. Van Gelder, A., Ross, K.A., Schlipf, J.S.: The well-founded semantics for general logic programs. J. ACM **38**(3), 620–650 (1991)
164. Wang, K., Zhou, L.: Comparisons and computation of well-founded semantics for disjunctive logic programs. ACM Trans. Comput. Logic **6**(2), 295–327 (2005)
165. Wang, K., Zhou, L., Lin, F.: Alternating fixpoint theory for logic programs with priority. In: Lloyd, J., et al. (eds.) CL 2000. LNCS (LNAI), vol. 1861, pp. 164–178. Springer, Heidelberg (2000). https://doi.org/10.1007/3-540-44957-4_11
166. Weinzierl, A.: Blending lazy-grounding and CDNL search for answer-set solving. In: Balduccini, M., Janhunen, T. (eds.) Logic Programming and Nonmonotonic Reasoning - 14th International Conference, LPNMR 2017, Espoo, Finland, 3–6 July 2017, Proceedings. Lecture Notes in Computer Science, vol. 10377, pp. 191–204. Springer, Heidelberg (2017). https://doi.org/10.1007/978-3-319-61660-5_17
167. Yahya, A.H., Henschen, L.J.: Deduction in non-horn databases. J. Autom. Reason. **1**(2), 141–160 (1985). https://doi.org/10.1007/BF00244994
168. Zhao, Y.: ASSAT, since 2002. http://assat.cs.ust.hk/

Declarative Data Analysis Using Limit Datalog Programs

Egor V. Kostylev[✉][iD]

University of Oxford, Oxford, UK
egor.kostylev@cs.ox.ac.uk

Abstract. Currently, data analysis tasks are often solved using code written in standard imperative programming languages such as Java and Scala. However, in recent years there has been a significant shift towards declarative solutions, where the definition of the task is clearly separated from its implementation, and users describe what the desired output is, rather than how to compute it. For example, instead of computing shortest paths in a graph by a concrete algorithm, one first describes what a path length is and then selects only paths of minimum length. Such specification is independent of evaluation details, allowing analysts to focus on the task at hand rather than implementation details. In these notes we will give an overview of Limit Datalog, a recent declarative query language for data analysis. This language extends usual Datalog with integer arithmetic (and hence many forms of aggregation) to naturally capture data analytics tasks, but at the same time carefully restricts the interaction of recursion and arithmetic to preserve decidability of reasoning. We concentrate on the positive language, but also discuss several generalisations and fragments of positive Limit Datalog, with various complexity and expressivity.

Keywords: Constraint and logic programming · Database query languages · Logic and databases

1 Introduction

One of the main trends in information systems is the analysis of complex datasets. In this context, 'data analysis' covers a broad range of tasks including complex query answering and data aggregations. In practice, such tasks are often solved using imperative programming languages such as Java and Scala. However, recently we have witnessed a significant interest in declarative solutions, where the definition of the task is clearly separated from its implementation [1,24,33,34,37]. Here, the main idea is that users describe *what* the desired output is, rather than *how* it is computed; for instance, instead of computing shortest paths in a graph using a concrete algorithm, one first describes what a

The author thanks Mark Kaminski, Bernardo Cuenca Grau, Boris Motik, and Ian Horrocks for their participation in the preparation of these notes.

ⓒ Springer Nature Switzerland AG 2020
M. Manna and A. Pieris (Eds.): Reasoning Web 2020, LNCS 12258, pp. 186–222, 2020.
https://doi.org/10.1007/978-3-030-60067-9_7

path length is and then selects the paths of minimum length. Such a specification does not depend on evaluation details, and thus allows analysts to focus on the task itself. An evaluation strategy can be selected independently, typically using efficient general algorithms 'for free'.

An vital component for declarative data analysis is a logic-based language to represent the analysis tasks. Datalog [10], a well-established logic-based formalism, is a prime candidate due to its support for recursion, which is required to express problems such as shortest path. However, standard Datalog supports neither arithmetic nor aggregation, which is required by many basic data analysis tasks aiming to capture quantitative aspects of data (e.g., the length of a shortest path). Research on extending recursive rule languages with numeric computations started several decades ago [3, 7, 13, 22, 27, 29, 36], and is currently experiencing a revival [12, 25, 39]. This body of work, however, focuses primarily on integrating recursion with arithmetic and aggregation in a coherent semantic framework on a conceptual level. However, little is known about the computational properties of such languages, other than the fact that a straightforward combination of recursion and arithmetic is undecidable [10]. This applies to the languages of existing Datalog-based tools such as BOOM [1], DeALS [38], LogicBlox [2], Myria [37], SociaLite [33], Overlog [23], Dyna [11], and Yedalog [5].

The primary goal of these notes is to give an in-depth presentation of limit $Datalog_{\mathbb{Z}}$ [9, 18–20], a recent extension of Datalog that is powerful and flexible enough to naturally capture many important analysis tasks, and that yet exhibit favourable computational properties of reasoning. This language, together with its several fragments, provides a formal basis for reasoning engines supporting complex analytical tasks and at the same time gives correctness, robustness, scalability, and extensibility guarantees. They can also serve as a unified logical framework providing a basis for understanding the expressive power of the key data analysis constructs. In fact, we mostly concentrate on *positive* limit $Datalog_{\mathbb{Z}}$, presented in [19], which is enough for a demonstration of the main ideas, leaving the extensions with various types of negation for further more advanced studies [18, 20]. The secondary goal is to master several advanced techniques for establishing formal properties of knowledge representation languages, such as reduction to Presburger arithmetic and Turing machine simulation.

We will depart from (positive) $Datalog_{\mathbb{Z}}$—a direct extension of (positive) Datalog with integer arithmetic and comparisons, which is also the starting point for several languages combining recursion and aggregation, such as the formalism of Ross and Sagiv [29]. After basic definitions in Sect. 2, in Sect. 3.1 we will present our language, positive *limit* $Datalog_{\mathbb{Z}}$, which can be seen as either a semantic or a syntactic restriction of $Datalog_{\mathbb{Z}}$. In limit $Datalog_{\mathbb{Z}}$, all intensional predicates with numeric arguments are *limit* predicates keeping the maximal or the minimal bound on the numeric values for each tuple of the other arguments. For example, if a directed edge-weighted graph is encoded by means of a ternary predicate E, then the following rules over a min limit predicate *dst* compute the length of a shortest path from a source node a_s to each node in the graph:

$$\rightarrow dst(a_s, 0), \tag{1}$$

$$dst(x, m) \wedge E(x, y, n) \rightarrow dst(y, m + n). \tag{2}$$

Intuitively, Rule (2) says that, if x is reachable from a_s by a path of length at most m and (x, y) is an edge of length n, then y is reachable from a_s with length at most $m + n$. If these rules and a dataset entail $dst(a, \ell)$, then the length of a shortest path from a_s to a is at most ℓ; thus, $dst(a, k)$ holds for each $k \geq \ell$ since the length of a shortest path is also at most k. This is the key difference with ordinary $Datalog_{\mathbb{Z}}$, where $dst(a, \ell)$ and $dst(a, k)$ are not semantically connected. In Sect. 3.2, we show that fact entailment remains undecidable for limit $Datalog_{\mathbb{Z}}$ programs. Thus, to ensure decidability, we introduce *limit-linear* $Datalog_{\mathbb{Z}}$, which essentially disallows multiplication of numeric variables. In Sect. 3.3, we will present several examples that show how positive limit-linear $Datalog_{\mathbb{Z}}$ can capture data analysis tasks relevant in practice.

In Sect. 4, we will study fact entailment—that is, the main reasoning problem for Datalog-related languages—and establish its decidability and coNP-completeness for positive limit-linear $Datalog_{\mathbb{Z}}$. This complexity is *data complexity*, in the sense that only the dataset part of the program is considered as part of the input while the rest is fixed; however, our proofs can be easily adapted to coNEXP-completeness in *combined complexity*. Our upper coNP bound is obtained by a reduction to the evaluation problem for sentences of a specific shape in Presburger arithmetic (i.e., the first-order theory of the integer numbers with addition). Finally, in Sect. 4.3 we show that the coNP bound is tight.

The results of Sect. 4 establish intractability of reasoning for positive limit-linear programs, which is not always practical. Thus, in Sect. 5, we will identify fragments of our language for which reasoning is tractable in data complexity, and which are therefore well-suited for data-intensive applications. In particular, using the idea of *cyclic dependency* detection, in Sect. 5.1 we will introduce *stable* programs that allow reasoning to become P-complete in data complexity as well as EXP-complete in combined complexity—that is, no harder than for usual Datalog without arithmetic. Stability, however, is a semantic condition that is hard to check; thus, in Sect. 5.2, we will present a syntactic *type-consistency* condition, which implies stability and can be easily checked rule by rule. We then argue that all analysis tasks discussed in our examples can be captured using type-consistent $Datalog_{\mathbb{Z}}$ programs.

Finally, in Sect. 6, we compare limit $Datalog_{\mathbb{Z}}$ with the formalisms underpinning several existing rule-based systems for data analysis, such as the formalism of Ross and Sagiv [29].

2   Syntax and Semantics of Positive Datalog$_{\mathbb{Z}}$

We assume familiarity with the basic concepts of logic and rule-based query languages for databases and knowledge representation. We assume standard definitions of the basic time computational complexity classes such as P, NP, coNP, EXP, NEXP, and coNEXP.

In the rest of this section, we recapitulate the syntax and semantics of positive Datalog and arithmetic over the integers, which we call positive $Datalog_{\mathbb{Z}}$. Our formalism is standard, and closely related to constraint logic programming (CLP) over the structure $(\mathbb{Z}, \leq, <, +, -, \cdot, \times, 0, \pm 1, \pm 2, \dots)$, for $\mathbb{Z}$ the set of integers [8,10]. When looking at the formalisation, it worths to remember that positive $Datalog_{\mathbb{Z}}$ without numbers, numeric variables, numeric predicates, and arithmetic functions is just the usual positive Datalog.

2.1   Syntax

We assume countably infinite and mutually disjoint sets of *objects*, *object variables*, *numeric variables*, and *predicates*. Each predicate has an *arity* from the set $\mathbb{N}$ of natural numbers with zero, and each position of each predicate is of either *object* or *numeric sort*. The set of predicates includes the usual binary *comparison* predicates $\leq$ and $<$ with both positions numeric. We refer to all other predicates as *standard* to distinguish them from the comparison predicates.

An *object term* is an object or an object variable. A *numeric term* is an integer, a numeric variable, or an expression of the form $s_1 + s_2$, $s_1 - s_2$ or $s_1 \times s_2$, where s_1 and s_2 are numeric terms, while $+$, $-$ and $\times$ are the usual *arithmetic functions*. A *constant* is an object or an integer.

A *standard atom* is an expression of the form $A(t_1, \dots, t_v)$, where A is a standard predicate of arity v and each t_i is a term matching the sort of position i of A. A *comparison atom* is of the form $(s_1 \lhd s_2)$, where s_1 and s_2 are numeric terms and $\lhd$ is a comparison predicate. We use standard abbreviations concerning comparison atoms, such as $(s_1 \geq s_2)$ for $(s_2 \leq s_1)$, $(s_1 \doteq s_2)$ for $(s_1 \leq s_2) \wedge (s_2 \leq s_1)$, and $(s_1 \leq s_2 < s_3)$ for $(s_1 \leq s_2) \wedge (s_2 < s_3)$.

A (positive) *rule* ρ is a first-order sentence of the form

$$\forall \mathbf{x}. \; \varphi \to \alpha, \tag{3}$$

where the *body* φ of ρ is a conjunction of (standard and comparison) atoms, the *head* α of ρ is a standard atom, and $\mathbf{x}$ is the tuple of all variables in φ and α; the quantifier $\forall \mathbf{x}$ is often omitted for brevity.

A rule ρ is *safe* if each variable in ρ occurs in the body of ρ. As usual in Datalog, safety ensures (object) *domain independence*—that is, that the semantics of a set of rules does not depend on objects in the vocabulary not explicitly mentioned in the rules. Note, however, that the rules such as $(n \leq n) \to C(n)$ for a numeric variable n and a predicate C with a numeric position is also considered safe in our context; this may seem counterintuitive for the first look, but does not impose any difficulties as unsafe rules in usual Datalog, because, intuitively, we assume that all integers $\mathbb{Z}$ are always in the domain.

A *fact* is a (safe) rule with empty body and where all the terms in the head are constants (i.e., objects and integers, but not variables or terms with arithmetic functions). A *dataset* is a finite set of facts. We do not usually distinguish between facts and their head atoms, and often omit $\to$ when writing facts.

A standard predicate A is *intensional* (*IDB*) in a set $\mathcal{P}$ of rules if it occurs in $\mathcal{P}$ in the head of a rule that is not a fact; otherwise, A is *extensional* (*EDB*) in $\mathcal{P}$. A positive (*Datalog$_\mathbb{Z}$*) *program* is a finite set of safe rules.

Example 1. As a simple example of a positive *Datalog$_\mathbb{Z}$* program we may consider the one in the introduction: it consists of Fact (1) and Rule (2), which use a ternary (i.e., of arity 3) EDB predicate E and binary (of arity 2) IDB predicate *dst*, as well as a dataset of an appropriate number of facts of the form $E(a_1, a_2, k)$ encoding a directed edge-weighted graph. Note that the last positions of both predicates are numeric, while others are object. In Rule (2), x is an object variable, while m and n are numeric variables. This program does not have any comparison atoms, but uses arithmetic function $+$.   ◁

2.2   Semantics

We adopt the standard notion of *substitutions*—that is, sort-compatible partial mappings of variables to constants. For E an expression (such as a term, atom, or rule) and σ a substitution, $E\sigma$ is the expression obtained by replacing with $\sigma(x)$ each occurrence of every variable x in E on which σ is defined. An expression E' is an *instance* of E if $E' = E\sigma$ for some substitution σ. An expression is *ground* if it mentions no variables (note that each fact is ground by definition, but not every ground atom is a fact, because it may mention arithmetic functions). A substitution σ is a *grounding* of an expression E if $E\sigma$ is ground.

A *(Herbrand) interpretation* is a (possibly infinite) set of facts (e.g., a dataset is an interpretation). An interpretation $\mathcal{I}$ *satisfies* a ground atom λ, written $\mathcal{I} \models \lambda$, if one of the following holds:

- λ is a standard atom and $\mathcal{I}$ contains each fact obtained from λ by evaluating all the numeric terms under the usual semantics of integer arithmetic;
- λ is a comparison atom that evaluates to *true* under the usual semantics of arithmetic functions and comparisons.

Note that satisfaction of a comparison atom does not actually depend on $\mathcal{I}$, and this case is included only for uniformity. The notion of satisfaction extends to conjunctions of ground atoms, rules, and programs in a standard way (i.e., as in first-order logic). An interpretation $\mathcal{I}$ is a *model* of a program $\mathcal{P}$ if $\mathcal{I} \models \mathcal{P}$.

We next define the notion of entailment for positive *Datalog$_\mathbb{Z}$* programs. Analogously to the case of usual Datalog, it is formulated in terms of the least fixpoint of an *immediate consequence operator* $\mathcal{S}$, which is defined as follows: for $\mathcal{I}$ an interpretation and $\mathcal{P}$ a positive program, $\mathcal{S}_\mathcal{P}(\mathcal{I})$ is the interpretation defined as the set of all facts γ for which there exists a ground instance $\varphi \to \alpha$ of a rule in $\mathcal{P}$ such that $\mathcal{I} \models \varphi$ and γ can be obtained from α by evaluating all numeric terms. By definition, an interpretation $\mathcal{I}$ is a model of a positive program $\mathcal{P}$ if and only if $\mathcal{S}_\mathcal{P}(\mathcal{I}) \subseteq \mathcal{I}$. Also, for each positive program $\mathcal{P}$, operator $\mathcal{S}_\mathcal{P}$ is monotonic with respect to set inclusion—that is, $\mathcal{S}_\mathcal{P}(\mathcal{I}_1) \subseteq \mathcal{S}_\mathcal{P}(\mathcal{I}_2)$ for every two interpretations $\mathcal{I}_1$ and $\mathcal{I}_2$ such that $\mathcal{I}_1 \subseteq \mathcal{I}_2$. Hence we can define the semantics of as the fixpoint of the immediate consequence operator: the *partial* *materialisation* $\mathcal{M}^\kappa$ of a positive program $\mathcal{P}$, for $\kappa \in \mathbb{N}$, is an interpretation that is defined by induction on κ as follows:

$$\mathcal{M}^0 = \emptyset, \qquad\qquad \mathcal{M}^\kappa = \mathcal{S}_\mathcal{P}(\mathcal{M}^{\kappa-1}), \qquad \text{if } \kappa \geq 1.$$

The *materialisation* $\mathcal{M}(\mathcal{P})$ of $\mathcal{P}$ is then the union of all partial materialisations:

$$\mathcal{M}(\mathcal{P}) = \bigcup_{\kappa \in \mathbb{N}} \mathcal{M}^\kappa.$$

It is immediate to check that $\mathcal{M}(\mathcal{P}) \models \mathcal{P}$—that is, the materialisation of a program $\mathcal{P}$ is a model of $\mathcal{P}$.

A positive program $\mathcal{P}$ *entails* a fact γ, written $\mathcal{P} \models \gamma$, if $\gamma \in \mathcal{M}(\mathcal{P})$. Given such $\mathcal{P}$ and γ, checking whether $\mathcal{P} \models \gamma$ holds is a key problem in Datalog applications, and it is the main subject of this paper. Note that fact entailment subsumes conjunctive query answering, since we can encode a query as a rule.

Observe that our definition of entailment coincides with the usual first-order notion—that is, for a positive program $\mathcal{P}$ and a fact γ, we have that $\mathcal{P} \models \gamma$ if and only if $\gamma \in \mathcal{I}$ for every $\mathcal{I}$ such that $\mathcal{I} \models \mathcal{P}$, or, in other words, that $\mathcal{M}(\mathcal{P}) = \bigcap_{\mathcal{I} \models \mathcal{P}} \mathcal{I}$. Furthermore, if program $\mathcal{P}$ does not use arithmetic functions, then the number of steps in the naive construction of the partial materialisation can be bounded by a finite number, and this yields a procedure is often used for checking fact entailment in many practical Datalog engines. The boundedness property, however, no longer holds when $\mathcal{P}$ uses arithmetic.

Example 2. Let $\mathcal{P}$ be a *Datalog*$_\mathbb{Z}$ program containing a fact $B(1)$ and rule $B(m) \to B(m+1)$, where predicate B has a single numeric position. Applying $\mathcal{P}$ iteratively derives $B(1), B(2), \dots$ without stopping: the partial materialisation $\mathcal{M}^\kappa$ consists of $B(1), \dots, B(\kappa)$ for each $\kappa \in \mathbb{N}$. As a result, the materialisation $\mathcal{M}(\mathcal{P})$ contains $B(k)$ for each $k \geq 1$ and is thus infinite. $\triangleleft$

Despite Example 2, the construction of $\mathcal{M}(\mathcal{P})$ is still well defined if we consider the possibly infinite 'limit' of rule application (the existence of the least fixpoint of such applications is guaranteed by the Knaster-Tarski theorem). However, such a 'computation' of $\mathcal{M}(\mathcal{P})$ does not give us an algorithm for checking fact entailment in *Datalog*$_\mathbb{Z}$ with full arithmetic. Moreover, one can exploit the fact that $\mathcal{M}(\mathcal{P})$ can be infinite to show that checking fact entailment is undecidable even for positive programs without multiplication and subtraction that use standard predicates with at most one numeric position [10,19]. Our goal is thus to identify restrictions that, on the one hand, provide us with languages rich enough to capture interesting data analysis problems and, on the other hand, support decidable or even tractable fact entailment.

For the decidable languages, we then consider *combined complexity*, which assumes that both a program $\mathcal{P}$ and a fact γ form the input of the problem, and *data complexity*, which assumes that $\mathcal{P} = \mathcal{P}' \cup \mathcal{D}$ for $\mathcal{P}'$ a program and $\mathcal{D}$ a dataset, and that only $\mathcal{D}$ and γ form the input while $\mathcal{P}'$ is fixed (in this case, we may say that $\mathcal{D}$ is the *dataset part* of $\mathcal{P}$). In fact, we mostly concentrate on data complexity, which is relevant in practice, and discuss combined complexity only briefly. In these studies, we usually assume that all integers in the input to fact entailment are coded in binary, and denote by $\|E\|$ the size of the representation of an expression (e.g., term, atom, program) E assuming this coding of numbers. All our theorems on complexity bounds, however, hold also under unary encoding of integers, so the choice of encoding is immaterial for all results in these notes.

3   Positive Limit-Linear Datalog$_\mathbb{Z}$

In this section, we first introduce *limit positive Datalog$_\mathbb{Z}$*, which can be seen as either a semantic or a syntactic restriction of positive *Datalog$_\mathbb{Z}$*. To overcome the undecidability of entailment, we then restrict the use of multiplication and thus arrive to *limit-linear* programs. Finally, we present several application examples.

3.1   Syntax and Semantics of Limit Programs

As illustrated in Example 2, one of the main problems in *Datalog$_\mathbb{Z}$* is that the materialisation of a program can be infinite. Towards a decidable fragment of *Datalog$_\mathbb{Z}$*, we first introduce *limit* positive programs. As we shall see, the materialisations of such programs can be represented using finite structures. The key feature of limit programs is that their IDB predicates are partitioned into *object* and *limit* predicates, as specified in the following definition.

Definition 1. *A predicate is* object *if it has only object positions, and it is* numeric *if its last position is numeric and its other positions are object; moreover, each numeric predicate is either* exact *or* limit, *and each limit predicate is either* min *or* max. *A limit (Datalog$_\mathbb{Z}$) positive program is a positive program that uses only object and numeric predicates, and where all exact predicates are EDB.*

The notions in Definition 1 transfer to atoms in the obvious way; for example, a standard atom is max if its predicate is max. For C a limit predicate, we write $\preceq_C$ for $\leq$ if C is max, and for $\geq$ if C is min, with $\prec_C$, $\succeq_C$, and $\succ_C$ defined accordingly; similarly, for S a set of integers, we write $\max_C S$ for $\max S$ if C is max, and for $\min S$ if C is min.

Object and exact numeric predicates are essentially the same as predicates in ordinary *Datalog$_\mathbb{Z}$*. The intuition behind limit predicates is that they keep only the upper, in case of max, or only the lower, in case of min, bounds on the numeric values for each tuple of object arguments. For example, assume that a positive program $\mathcal{P}$ consists only of facts $C(a,5)$ and $C(a,7)$, where C is a numeric predicate and a is an object. If $\mathcal{P}$ is an ordinary *Datalog$_\mathbb{Z}$* program, then the materialisation $\mathcal{M}(\mathcal{P})$ coincides with $\mathcal{P}$. If, however, $\mathcal{P}$ is limit and C is max, then the semantics of limit *Datalog$_\mathbb{Z}$* ensures that every model of $\mathcal{P}$ contains the fact $C(a,k)$ for each $k \leq 7$, and moreover $\mathcal{M}(\mathcal{P})$ consists precisely of these facts. Thus, 7 is the limit value of C on a in $\mathcal{M}(\mathcal{P})$, and we can finitely represent $\mathcal{M}(\mathcal{P})$ as just $C(a,7)$.

We next define the direct model-theoretic semantics of limit $Datalog_\mathbb{Z}$. In this semantics, the intended meaning of limit predicates is captured by requiring all the models $\mathcal{I}$ of a program to be closed for limit predicates—that is, whenever $\mathcal{I}$ contains a limit fact γ, it also contains all facts implied by γ according to the predicate type.

Definition 2. *An interpretation $\mathcal{I}$ is* limit-closed *if $C(\mathbf{a}, k') \in \mathcal{I}$ for each limit fact $C(\mathbf{a}, k) \in \mathcal{I}$ and each integer k' such that $k' \preceq_C k$.*

The semantics of fact entailment is then defined in terms of an immediate consequence operator acting on limit-closed interpretations, as specified next.

Definition 3. *Given a limit positive program $\mathcal{P}$ and a limit-closed interpretation $\mathcal{I}$ let $\mathcal{S}_\mathcal{P}(\mathcal{I})$ be the least limit-closed superset of $\mathcal{S}_{\mathcal{P}'}(\mathcal{I})$, where $\mathcal{S}_{\mathcal{P}'}$ is the ordinary immediate consequence operator applied to program $\mathcal{P}'$ that is $\mathcal{P}$ seen as an ordinary positive $Datalog_\mathbb{Z}$ program (see Sect. 2.2). The* partial materialisations *and the* materialisation $\mathcal{M}(\mathcal{P})$ *of a limit positive program $\mathcal{P}$ are defined as the partial materialisations and materialisation of an ordinary program but using the immediate consequence operator for limit programs instead of the operator for ordinary programs. A limit program $\mathcal{P}$* entails *a fact γ, written $\mathcal{P} \models \gamma$, if and only if $\gamma \in \mathcal{M}(\mathcal{P})$.*

The definition of materialisation for limit programs is correct by the Knaster-Tarski theorem (in the sense that the least fixpoint exists), since the monotonicity property holds as in the ordinary case (i.e., $\mathcal{S}_\mathcal{P}(\mathcal{I}_1) \subseteq \mathcal{S}_\mathcal{P}(\mathcal{I}_2)$ for each positive limit program $\mathcal{P}$ and limit-closed interpretations $\mathcal{I}_1$ and $\mathcal{I}_2$ that satisfy $\mathcal{I}_1 \subseteq \mathcal{I}_2$ and coincide on the EDB predicates).

Having direct semantics of limit programs at hand, we next argue that they can be easily rewritten to ordinary $Datalog_\mathbb{Z}$ programs. Indeed, the semantics of limit predicates can be axiomatised in $Datalog_\mathbb{Z}$ by extending the program with the following rule for each max predicate C and analogously for min predicates:

$$C(\mathbf{x}, m) \wedge (n \leq m) \to C(\mathbf{x}, n).$$

The following example illustrates the intuitions of the definitions we presented thus far.

Example 3. Let, as in Example 1, $\mathcal{P}$ be the positive program containing Rules (1) and (2) from the introduction, and the facts that describe a directed graph with edge lengths using predicate E. When computing the lengths of the shortest paths from a_s, we need not remember the length of each path from a_s: it suffices to keep just the lengths of the shortest paths found so far. Thus, we can make dst a min predicate, which is tantamount to extending $\mathcal{P}$ with the following rule:

$$dst(x, m) \wedge (m \leq n) \to dst(x, n).$$

As a consequence of this change, a fact $dst(a, \ell)$ follows from $\mathcal{P}$ if and only if the distance from the source node a_s to a is *at most* ℓ; hence, each $dst(a, k)$ with $k \geq \ell$ then follows as well. Note that only dst is a limit predicate: E is EDB and so it can be exact, which is necessary to correctly encode the graph structure. $\triangleleft$

Finally, we observe that each limit program can be easily rewritten into an equivalent *homogeneous* program that uses only max (or only min) predicates. This can be done by replacing all min predicates with fresh max predicates of the same arities and negating the corresponding numeric arguments in atoms with the replaced predicates.

3.2   Undecidability and Limit-Linear Programs

We now start our investigation of the computational properties of limit positive *Datalog*$_\mathbb{Z}$. However, our first result is negative: the ability to finitely represent materialisations does not ensure decidability.

Theorem 1. *The fact entailment problem for positive limit programs is undecidable.*

Proof. The proof is by reduction of Hilbert's tenth problem, which is to determine, given a polynomial $p(m_1, \ldots, m_v)$ over variables $m_1, \ldots, m_v$ with integer coefficients, whether the equation $p(m_1, \ldots, m_v) = 0$ has an integer solution. For every such polynomial p, let $\mathcal{P}_p$ be the positive limit program consisting of the following single rule with A a nullary object predicate:

$$(p(m_1, \ldots, m_v) \doteq 0) \to A.$$

Thus, $\mathcal{P}_p \models A$ if and only if $p(m_1, \ldots, m_v) = 0$ has an integer solution. □

The main reason for undecidability in Theorem 1 is that, due to multiplication, checking whether the body of a rule matches an interpretation (i.e., checking rule applicability) amounts to finding integer roots of arbitrary polynomials. Thus, to ensure decidability, we next restrict limit programs so that only linear (i.e., essentially multiplication-free) numeric terms are allowed.

Definition 4. *A numeric variable m is* exact-guarded, *or just* guarded,[1] *in a rule if it occurs in the rule body in a function-free exact atom. A positive rule or limit positive program is* limit-linear *(LL-) if, in each multiplication, at most one argument mentions an unguarded variable.*

Intuitively, a guarded variable m in a rule of a positive LL-program $\mathcal{P}$ can be matched only to finitely many integers during the evaluation of $\mathcal{P}$. To see this, note that all exact predicates are EDB in $\mathcal{P}$; thus, if m is guarded because it occurs in a function-free atom over an exact predicate, then m can be matched only to facts explicitly mentioned in $\mathcal{P}$. Note that atoms with other numeric terms involving m, such as $B(\mathbf{t}, m + 1)$, do not make m guarded.

To understand how guarded variables are used to ensure decidability, consider an LL-rule ρ containing a numeric term $m \times n$ with numeric variables m and n. Since ρ is limit-linear, at least one of m and n must be guarded. If m is guarded, then, by the previous paragraph, m can be matched to finitely many integers

---

[1] This notion is unrelated to the guarded fragment of first order logic.

$k_1, \ldots, k_v$ and hence we can replace ρ with its v instances where the term $m \times n$ is replaced by $k_i \times n$. We have thus reduced multiplication of variables $m \times n$ to *linear* multiplication $k_i \times n$, which allows us to obtain decidability in Sect. 4 using methods from Presburger arithmetic.

To simplify the discussion in the rest of this paper, we assume that each LL-program is normalised so that each exact atom is function-free. This can be achieved by replacing each positive exact body atom $B(\mathbf{a}, s)$ with s containing functions by the conjunction $B(\mathbf{a}, m) \wedge (m \doteq s)$ with m a fresh numeric variable. Note that such normalisation can be done in linear time and independently for each rule. Moreover, we note that all exact atoms in rule heads are function-free: the predicates in all these atoms are EDB, and so all such rules are facts.

3.3   Application Examples

Despite the restrictions of Definitions 1 and 4, positive LL-programs can still naturally capture many interesting data analysis tasks. In this section, we show a wide range of practical analytics tasks that can be naturally formulated using limit-linear $Datalog_{\mathbb{Z}}$ programs.

Example 4 (All-pairs shortest paths).   Assume that a directed graph with weighted edges is represented as a dataset $\mathcal{D}_{\mathsf{apsp}}$ over a ternary exact predicate *edge* and a unary object predicate *node* in the obvious way. The following LL-program $\mathcal{P}_{\mathsf{apsp}}$ encodes the all-pairs shortest paths problem, where the ternary min predicate *dist* encodes the distance from any node to any node as the length of a shortest path between them:

$$node(x) \rightarrow dist(x, x, 0), \tag{4}$$

$$dist(x, y, m) \wedge edge(y, z, n) \rightarrow dist(x, z, m + n). \tag{5}$$

Then, $\mathcal{P}_{\mathsf{apsp}} \cup \mathcal{D}_{\mathsf{apsp}} \models dist(a, a', k)$ if and only if the distance from node a to node a' is at most k.   ◁

Example 5 (Diffusion in social networks).   Consider a social network of agents connected by the 'follows' relation. A first agent a_s introduces (*tweets*) a message, and each agent a retweets the message if at least k_a agents that a follows tweet this message, where k_a is a positive threshold associated with a. We can determine which agents tweet the message eventually using limit-linear $Datalog_{\mathbb{Z}}$ as follows. We encode the network structure as a dataset $\mathcal{D}_{\mathsf{tw}}$ consisting of the object fact $tweet(a_s)$ saying that a_s introduces a message, object facts $follows(a, a')$ saying that a follows a', and exact facts $threshold(a, k_a)$ saying that the threshold of a is k_a. We also assume that $\mathcal{D}_{\mathsf{tw}}$ is *ordered*—that is, it contains facts $first(a_1)$, $next(a_1, a_2)$, $\ldots$, $next(a_{c-1}, a_c)$, $last(a_c)$ for some enumeration $a_1, \ldots, a_c$ of all objects (i.e., agents) in $\mathcal{D}_{tw}$. The LL-program $\mathcal{P}_{\mathsf{tw}}$, consisting of Rules (6)–(10), encodes message propagation. Here, *acc* is an 'accumulating' max predicate such that $acc(a, a', m)$ is *true* if there are at least m agents tweeting the message among the agents that a follows and that (inclusively) precede

a' in the dataset order. In particular, Rules (6) and (7) initialise acc for the first agent in the order; note that acc is a max predicate, so if the first agent tweets the message, Rule (7) 'overrides' Rule (6); Rules (8) and (9) recurse over the order to compute acc as stated above:

$$follows(x, y') \land fist(y) \rightarrow acc(x, y, 0), \tag{6}$$

$$tweet(y) \land follows(x, y) \land fist(y) \rightarrow acc(x, y, 1), \tag{7}$$

$$acc(x, y', m) \land next(y', y) \rightarrow acc(x, y, m), \tag{8}$$

$$tweet(y) \land follows(x, y) \land acc(x, y', m) \land next(y', y) \rightarrow acc(x, y, m+1), \tag{9}$$

$$threshold(x, m) \land acc(x, y, m) \rightarrow tweet(x). \tag{10}$$

Then, $\mathcal{P}_{\mathsf{tw}} \cup \mathcal{D}_{\mathsf{tw}} \models tweet(a)$ if and only if an agent a tweets the message according to $\mathcal{D}_{\mathsf{tw}}$.   ◁

Example 6 (Bill of materials). Let $\mathcal{D}_{\mathsf{bm}}$ be a dataset describing parts needed to manufacture an end product. Specifically, for each part a and each subpart a' of a, $\mathcal{D}_{\mathsf{bm}}$ contains object facts $part(a)$ and $part(a')$, and an exact fact $dirpart(a, a', k)$ indicating that a needs k copies of a' as direct subparts; also, let $\mathcal{D}_{\mathsf{bm}}$ be ordered as in Example 5. The graph formed by predicate $dirpart$ is acyclic and has positive edge weights. Rules (11)–(17) form the LL-program $\mathcal{P}_{\mathsf{bm}}$. They compute, using max predicates acc and $subpart$, how many copies of each subpart are used for each part in total. Intuitively, $acc(a, a', b, k)$ is *true* if part a contains at least k copies of subpart a' in all direct subparts of a that precede part b in the order. Rule (14) propagates the value to the next part in case b is not a direct subpart of a; if b is a direct subpart occurring $n_1 \geq 1$ times in a while a' occurs $n_2 \geq 0$ times in b, then Rule (16) increments k by $n_1 \times n_2$ to account for all occurrences of a' in a in copies of b. Finally, Rule (11) asserts that each part is a subpart of itself, while Rule (17) defines k in $subpart(a, a', k)$ for a part a and a subpart a' as the maximum k in $acc(a, a', b, k)$ over all b:

$$part(x) \rightarrow subpart(x, x, 1), \tag{11}$$

$$part(x) \land part(y) \land first(z) \rightarrow acc(x, y, z, 0), \tag{12}$$

$$dirpart(x, z, n_1) \land subpart(z, y, n_2) \land first(z) \rightarrow acc(x, y, z, n_1 \times n_2), \tag{13}$$

$$acc(x, y, z', m) \land next(z', z) \rightarrow acc(x, y, z, m), \tag{14}$$

$$dirpart(x, z, n_1) \land subpart(z, y, n_2) \land \tag{15}$$

$$acc(x, y, z', m) \land next(z', z) \rightarrow acc(x, y, z, m + n_1 \times n_2), \tag{16}$$

$$acc(x, y, z, m) \rightarrow subpart(x, y, m). \tag{17}$$

Then, $\mathcal{P}_{\mathsf{bm}} \cup \mathcal{D}_{\mathsf{bm}} \models subpart(a, a', k)$ if and only if a contains at least k copies of a'. Program $\mathcal{P}_{\mathsf{bm}}$ is limit-linear since n_1 occurs in exact atoms over $dirpart$ and is thus guarded in Rules (13) and (16).   ◁

Observe that in Examples 5 and 6 we use ordered datasets; this is a standard assumption in Datalog and related areas such as *descriptive complexity* [17]. It is important to emphasise that this order can be chosen arbitrarily, and thus it is not a serious restriction.

We conclude this section with the observation that several of these examples demonstrate how limit-linear $Datalog_{\mathbb{Z}}$ express database-style aggregation functions over integers, such as max, min, and sum. This is not a coincidence, and it is possible to prove that the language indeed capture these aggregates.

4 Complexity of Positive LL-Programs

We now discuss the complexity of fact entailment in positive limit-linear $Datalog_{\mathbb{Z}}$. We show that the problem is complete for coNP in data complexity. We also explain how our techniques can be adapted to show coNEXP-completeness in combined complexity, respectively. Thus, positive LL-programs have the same complexity as answer-set programming (ASP) [30], and are one level above the usual positive Datalog, which is P- and EXP-complete [10].

We start, in Sect. 4.1, by establishing a useful characterisation of fact entailment that allows us to manipulate only finite structures when computing materialisations. We next study, in Sect. 4.2, fact entailment, where we show decidability via a reduction to the evaluation problem for Presburger sentences and then provide complexity upper bounds by analysing the shape of the Presburger formulas computed by our reduction. Finally, in Sect. 4.3 we obtain the matching lower bounds.

4.1 Pseudointerpretations

The definition of fact entailment is formulated in terms of the immediate consequence operator $\mathcal{S}$. Unlike usual Datalog, however, this definition cannot be used directly for deciding fact entailment, because all limit-closed interpretations containing at least one limit fact are infinite. In this section, we prove a characterisation of fact entailment in terms of *pseudointerpretations*—that is, certain sets of so-called pseudofacts, which are 'facts' where a special symbol ∞ may occur in place of integers. Pseudointerpretations have a one-to-one correspondence with limit-closed interpretations, and we will see that it is enough to consider only finite pseudointerpretations when deciding fact entailment.

Positive LL-programs admit an important property analogous to the grounding property of function-free positive Datalog: all object and guarded numeric variables may be grounded to constants occurring in the program without affecting the outcomes of fact entailment checks.

Definition 5. *A positive LL-rule is object-and-guarded-ground (OG-ground) if it has neither object nor guarded numeric variables. A positive LL-program is OG-ground if so is each of its rules. The (result of the) canonical OG-grounding of a positive LL-program $\mathcal{P}$, denoted $\mathcal{G}(\mathcal{P})$, is the OG-ground (positive) program that consists of all OG-ground instances $\rho\sigma$ of rules ρ in $\mathcal{P}$ with σ a substitution mapping all object and guarded numeric variables of ρ to constants mentioned in $\mathcal{P}$.*

The first immediate property of OG-ground programs is that all of their numeric terms are linear. Moreover, since we consider only normalised programs, in which all positive exact body atoms use no unguarded variables or function symbols, all numeric terms in exact body atoms in the canonical OG-grounding are integers. As follows directly from the definitions and is formalised in the following proposition, positive LL-programs and their canonical OG-groundings are semantically interchangeable, and the sizes of such OG-groundings can be bounded (for this proposition, recall also that $\|E\|$ is the size of the representation of expression E under binary encoding of integers).

Proposition 1. *The following holds for each positive LL-program $\mathcal{P}$ with the dataset part $\mathcal{D}$:*

1. *$\mathcal{M}(\mathcal{P}) = \mathcal{M}(\mathcal{G}(\mathcal{P}))$; and*
2. *$\mathcal{G}(\mathcal{P})$ can be computed in time polynomial in $\|\mathcal{D}\|$.*

Note that this proposition immediately implies that fact entailment can be checked on the canonical OG-grounding instead of the original program: for every positive LL-program $\mathcal{P}$ and fact γ, $\mathcal{P} \models \gamma$ if and only if $\mathcal{G}(\mathcal{P}) \models \gamma$. Also, it implies that $\|\mathcal{G}(\mathcal{P})\|$ and hence also $|\mathcal{G}(\mathcal{P})|$ (i.e., the number of rules in $\mathcal{G}(\mathcal{P})$) are polynomially bounded in $\|\mathcal{D}\|$. Thus, we can concentrate on OG-ground programs when studying data complexity for positive LL-programs in this and the next section.

We proceed to the definition of pseudointerpretations. Recall that if a limit-closed interpretation $\mathcal{I}$ contains a limit fact $C(\mathbf{a}, k)$, then either a limit integer $\ell \succeq_C k$ exists such that $C(\mathbf{a}, \ell) \in \mathcal{I}$ and $C(\mathbf{a}, k') \notin \mathcal{I}$ for all $k' \succ_C \ell$, or $C(\mathbf{a}, k') \in \mathcal{I}$ holds for all $k' \in \mathbb{Z}$. Thus, to characterise the value of C on a tuple of objects $\mathbf{a}$ in $\mathcal{I}$, we just need the corresponding limit integer or the information that no such integer exists.

Definition 6. *A* pseudofact *is either a fact or an expression of the form $C(\mathbf{a}, \infty)$ for C a limit predicate and $\mathbf{a}$ a tuple of objects. A* pseudointerpretation *is a set $\mathcal{J}$ of pseudofacts such that $\ell_1 = \ell_2$ for all limit pseudofacts $C(\mathbf{a}, \ell_1)$ and $C(\mathbf{a}, \ell_2)$ in $\mathcal{J}$ with $\ell_1, \ell_2 \in \mathbb{Z} \cup \{\infty\}$.*

As expected, limit-closed interpretations and pseudointerpretations naturally *correspond* to each other in a one-to-one manner; this is illustrated in the following example.

Example 7. Let $\mathcal{I}$ be the limit-closed interpretation consisting of facts $B(1)$, $B(2)$, $C(a_1, k)$ for all $k \leq 5$, and $C(a_2, k)$ for all $k \in \mathbb{Z}$, where B is an exact predicate, C is a max predicate, and a_1 and a_2 are objects. Then

$$\{B(1), B(2), C(a_1, 5), C(a_2, \infty)\}$$

is the pseudointerpretation corresponding to $\mathcal{I}$.   ◁

Thus we can transfer all the definitions and notations for (limit-closed) interpretations to pseudointerpretations: for example, a pseudointerpretation $\mathcal{J}$ satisfies a ground atom λ, written $\mathcal{J} \models \lambda$, if the corresponding limit-closed interpretation $\mathcal{I}$ satisfies λ, and $\mathcal{J}$ is a *pseudomodel* of a program $\mathcal{P}$, written $\mathcal{J} \models \mathcal{P}$, if $\mathcal{I} \models \mathcal{P}$. Also, we write $\mathcal{J}_1 \sqsubseteq \mathcal{J}_2$ for pseudointerpretations $\mathcal{J}_1$ and $\mathcal{J}_2$ if $\mathcal{I}_1 \subseteq \mathcal{I}_2$ for corresponding limit-closed interpretations $\mathcal{I}_1$ and $\mathcal{I}_2$.

We next show how the computation of the materialisations of OG-ground programs can be simulated on pseudointerpretations.

Now we show how to apply a positive OG-ground rule ρ to a pseudointerpretation $\mathcal{J}$. A minor problem is that, if we derive a fact $C(\mathbf{a}, \ell)$ with C max and we already have a fact $C(\mathbf{a}, k)$ with $k < \ell$, then we must remove $C(\mathbf{a}, k)$, and similarly if C is min. More importantly, identifying the substitutions that match the body of ρ to $\mathcal{J}$ is considerably more complex than for ordinary interpretations. For example, the body of the rule $C_1(m) \wedge C_2(m) \to C(m)$ where C_1 and C_2 are max predicates does not match to the pseudointerpretation $\{C_1(7), C_2(5)\}$ directly, but the rule is applicable and it derives $C(5)$. We address this difficulty by reducing the problem of a positive OG-ground rule application to *integer linear optimisation*. Specifically, to match ρ to $\mathcal{J}$, we can transform ρ into an *integer program (IP)*—that is, a system of integer linear inequalities—$\psi(\rho, \mathcal{J})$ whose solutions encode exactly the substitutions obtained by matching of the body of ρ to (the limit-closed interpretation corresponding to) $\mathcal{J}$. Thus, to compute the consequences of ρ with a limit atom in the head, we just need the solution that optimises the numeric term in this atom.

Definition 7. *For $\rho = \varphi \to \alpha$ an OG-ground (positive limit-linear) rule and $\mathcal{J}$ a pseudointerpretation, let $\psi(\rho, \mathcal{J})$ be the IP defined as the conjunction of the following comparison atoms:*

1. $(0 < 0)$ if φ contains
   - *an object or exact atom that is not in $\mathcal{J}$, or*
   - *a limit atom $C(\mathbf{a}, s)$ such that $C(\mathbf{a}, \ell) \notin \mathcal{J}$ for each $\ell \in \mathbb{Z} \cup \{\infty\}$;*
2. $(s \preceq_C \ell)$ for each limit atom $C(\mathbf{a}, s)$ in φ with $C(\mathbf{a}, \ell) \in \mathcal{J}$, and $\ell \neq \infty$; and
3. each comparison atom in φ.

Rule ρ is applicable *to pseudointerpretation $\mathcal{J}$ if the IP $\psi(\rho, \mathcal{J})$ is satisfiable. In this case we write $\delta(\rho, \mathcal{J})$ for the pseudofact defined as α if α is an object or exact atom, and as $C(\mathbf{a}, k)$ if $\alpha = C(\mathbf{a}, s)$ is a limit atom, where $k \in \mathbb{N} \cup \{\infty\}$ is the $\max_C$-optimal value of $\psi(\rho, \mathcal{J})$.*

For $\mathcal{P}$ an OG-ground program and $\mathcal{J}$ a pseudointerpretation, let $T_{\mathcal{P}}(\mathcal{J})$ be the smallest (with respect to $\sqsubseteq$) pseudointerpretation satisfying $\delta(\rho, \mathcal{J})$ for each rule ρ in $\mathcal{P}$ applicable to $\mathcal{J}$. A partial pseudomaterialisation $\mathcal{N}^\kappa$ of $\mathcal{P}$, for $\kappa \in \mathbb{N}$, is a pseudointerpretation defined by induction on κ as follows:

$$\mathcal{N}^0 = \emptyset, \qquad\qquad \mathcal{N}^\kappa = T_{\mathcal{P}}(\mathcal{N}^{\kappa-1}), \qquad \text{if } \kappa \geq 1.$$

The pseudomaterialisation *$\mathcal{N}(\mathcal{P})$ of $\mathcal{P}$ is $\sup_{\kappa \in \mathbb{N}} \mathcal{N}^\kappa$, where the supremum is taken with respect to $\sqsubseteq$.*

Example 8. Let ρ be the following OG-ground rule, where C_1 and C_2 are max predicates:

$$C_1(m) \wedge (2 \leq m) \to C_2(m+1). \tag{18}$$

Then, $\psi(\rho, \emptyset) = (0 < 0) \wedge (2 \leq m)$, where the first comparison atom is derived by condition 1 in Definition 7 from the atom $C_1(m)$, and the second comparison atom by condition 3 from $(2 \leq m)$. Clearly, IP $\psi(\rho, \emptyset)$ does not have a solution, and hence rule ρ is not applicable to the empty pseudointerpretation $\emptyset$. However, for the pseudointerpretation $\mathcal{J} = \{C_1(3)\}$, we have that $\psi(\rho, \mathcal{J}) = (m \leq 3) \wedge (2 \leq m)$, where the comparison atoms are derived from the corresponding body atoms by conditions 2 and 3. IP $\psi(\rho, \mathcal{J})$ has two solutions, one assigning 2 to m and the other assigning 3; thus, rule ρ is applicable to $\mathcal{J}$. Finally, C_2 is max, and the optimal value is $\max\{2+1, 3+1\} = 4$; hence $\delta(\rho, \mathcal{J}) = C_2(4)$. Thus, $T_{\{\rho\}}(\mathcal{J}) = \{C_2(4)\}$.   ◁

In fact, there is a direct correspondence between (partial) materialisations and (partial) pseudomaterialisations: for each OG-ground program $\mathcal{P}$ and each $\kappa \in \mathbb{N}$, the partial materialisation $\mathcal{M}^\kappa$ of $\mathcal{P}$ and the partial pseudomaterialisation $\mathcal{N}^\kappa$ of $\mathcal{P}$ correspond to each other (in the sense illustrated in Example 7); therefore, materialisation $\mathcal{M}(\mathcal{P})$ corresponds to pseudomaterialisation $\mathcal{N}(\mathcal{P})$ and thus $\mathcal{P} \models \gamma$ if and only if $\mathcal{N}(\mathcal{P}) \models \gamma$ for every fact γ. This claim may be proved by induction using the following straightforward proposition.

Proposition 2. *For each OG-ground rule ρ with body φ and each pseudointerpretation $\mathcal{J}$, a grounding σ of ρ is a solution to the IP $\psi(\rho, \mathcal{J})$ if and only if $\mathcal{J} \models \varphi\sigma$.*

We next discuss the computational properties of the immediate consequence operator and (partial) pseudomaterialisations, which will be useful in the following sections. We begin by establishing relevant complexity of applying the immediate consequence operator for pseudointerpretations. Note that, in this lemma and the rest of the paper, we assume that all polynomials involved in complexity are effectively computable and hence can be evaluated in polynomial time in the size of input.

Lemma 1. *For every (positive) OG-ground program $\mathcal{P}$ with dataset part $\mathcal{D}$ and every finite pseudointerpretation $\mathcal{J}$, $T_{\mathcal{P}}(\mathcal{J})$ can be computed in time polynomial in $\|\mathcal{D}\| + \|\mathcal{J}\|$.*

Proof. Let $\mathcal{E}$ be the set of all pseudofacts $\delta(\rho, \mathcal{J})$ such that ρ is a rule in $\mathcal{P}$ applicable to $\mathcal{J}$. By Definition 7, $T_{\mathcal{P}}(\mathcal{J})$ is the smallest pseudointerpretation with respect to $\sqsubseteq$ such that $T_{\mathcal{P}}(\mathcal{J}) \models \mathcal{E}$, so it can be easily (in polynomial time) computed from $\mathcal{E}$ by removing subsumed limit pseudofacts. Hence, to complete the proof of the lemma, we next argue that set $\mathcal{E}$ can be computed within the required time bounds.

A rule ρ in $\mathcal{P}$ is applicable to $\mathcal{J}$ if and only if the IP $\psi(\rho, \mathcal{J})$ is satisfiable, and, by construction, $\psi(\rho, \mathcal{J})$ can be computed in time polynomial in $\|\rho\| + \|\mathcal{J}\|$, while $\|\psi(\rho, \mathcal{J})\|$ is linearly bounded in $\|\rho\| \cdot b'$. Moreover, rule ρ, IP $\psi(\rho, \mathcal{J})$

and its normal form as above have the same variables. Thus, by Theorem 5.4 of Kannan [21], there is an (effectively computable) polynomial q such that satisfiability of $\psi(\rho, \mathcal{J})$ can be checked in time polynomial in $2^{q(v)} + \|\rho\| \cdot b'$, where v is the number of variables in ρ; since v does not depend on $\mathcal{D}$ and $\mathcal{J}$, applicability of ρ to $\mathcal{J}$ can then be checked in time polynomial in $\|\mathcal{D}\| + \|\mathcal{J}\|$.

Now assume that a rule $\rho = \varphi \rightarrow \alpha$ is applicable to $\mathcal{J}$. According to Definition 7, $\delta(\rho, \mathcal{J})$ is

- α, if α is object or exact,
- $C(\mathbf{a}, k)$, if $\alpha = C(\mathbf{a}, s)$ is limit and k is the integer $\max_C$-optimal value of s for IP $\psi(\rho, \mathcal{J})$, or
- $C(\mathbf{a}, \infty)$, if $\alpha = C(\mathbf{a}, s)$ is limit and the $\max_C$-optimal value of s for IP $\psi(\rho, \mathcal{J})$ is unbounded (i.e., there is no integer $\max_C$-optimal value).

Hence, computing $\delta(\rho, \mathcal{J})$ in the first case is trivial, while in the last two cases it requires checking the the $\max_C$-optimal value of s for boundedness and, if it is bounded, computing its integer optimal value. By results of Meyer [26, Corollary 5.2] and the duality theorem (see, e.g., [32]), the former can be done in time polynomial in $\|\rho\| + \|\mathcal{J}\|$ (recall that $\psi(\rho, \mathcal{J})$ is satisfiable since ρ is applicable), and, by application of the main result of Papadimitriou [28] using binary search, the latter can be done in time polynomial in in $2^{q'(u)} + \|\rho\| + \|\mathcal{J}\|$ for some polynomial q' and, as above, u the length of ρ assuming all integers taking unit space. Thus, overall, $\delta(\rho, \mathcal{J})$ can be computed with the same bounds.

Finally, to compute $\mathcal{E}$, we need to check applicability of each rule ρ in $\mathcal{P}$ to $\mathcal{J}$ and, if successful, to compute $\delta(\rho, \mathcal{J})$. Since program $\mathcal{P}$ is OG-ground, each rule of $\mathcal{P}$ can contribute at most one fact to $\mathcal{E}$. So $|\mathcal{E}| \leq |\mathcal{P}|$, and the rules can be processed one by one, which gives us, together with the previous results, a procedure for computing $T_{\mathcal{P}}(\mathcal{J})$ within the required bounds.   □

However, the algorithm for rule application following from Lemma 1 and the fact that $|\mathcal{N}^\kappa| \leq |\mathcal{P}|$ for each partial pseudomaterialisation $\mathcal{N}^\kappa$ of an OG-ground program $\mathcal{P}$ by definition do not yet imply decidability of fact entailment as they do not restrict the size of the binary representation of a (partial) pseudomaterialisation—that is, they do not bound the magnitudes of the integers that may be involved.

4.2   Upper Bounds for Positive Programs

In this section, we establish decidability and upper data complexity bound for fact entailment for positive LL-programs. We do this via an encoding of each OG-ground program $\mathcal{P}$ and fact γ as a Presburger sentence that holds if and only if $\mathcal{P} \models \gamma$.

Recall that Presburger arithmetic is the language of first-order logic over a special signature, which consists of constants 0 and 1, the binary addition and subtraction functions $+$ and $-$, and the binary comparison predicates $<$ and $\leq$. Formulas in this language are always evaluated over integers $\mathbb{Z}$ with the usual interpretation of the signature [4,14,15,31]. For convenience, we slightly extend the signature of Presburger formulas by allowing the use of all integers (and not just 0 and 1) as constants (coded in binary) as well as multiplication $\times$ with at least one argument variable-free. These extensions of the syntax have no effect on the expressive power of the language or on any result in this paper, because each integer can be axiomatised using 1, $+$ and $-$, and multiplication by a variable-free numeric term can be rewritten as addition. Finally, we allow for Boolean variables in Presburger formulas, which can be axiomatised using numeric variables in a straightforward way.

Our reduction is based on three main ideas.

1. For each limit atom $C(\mathbf{a}, s)$ in $\mathcal{P}$, we introduce a Boolean variable $def_{C\mathbf{a}}$ to indicate that an atom of the form $C(\mathbf{a}, \ell)$ exists in a pseudomodel of $\mathcal{P}$, a Boolean variable $fin_{C\mathbf{a}}$ to indicate whether ℓ is a (finite) integer or ∞, and a numeric variable $val_{C\mathbf{a}}$ to capture ℓ if it is finite.
2. Each rule of $\mathcal{P}$ is encoded as a universally quantified Presburger formula by replacing each standard atom with its encoding.
3. Entailment of γ by $\mathcal{P}$ is encoded as a Presburger sentence stating that, for every limit-closed interpretation $\mathcal{I}$, either $\mathcal{I}$ does not satisfy some rule in $\mathcal{P}$ or $\mathcal{I}$ satisfies γ.

We begin the description of our encoding by formally introducing the variables $def_{C\mathbf{a}}$, $fin_{C\mathbf{a}}$, and $val_{C\mathbf{a}}$ for limit atoms, as well as analogous variables for other types of atoms, and relating them to the satisfaction of the atoms in a pseudointerpretation.

Definition 8. *For each object predicate A of arity v, each exact predicate B of arity $v + 1$, each limit predicate C or arity $v + 1$, each v-tuple of objects $\mathbf{a}$, and each integer k, let $def_{A\mathbf{a}}$, $def_{B\mathbf{a}k}$, $def_{C\mathbf{a}}$ and $fin_{C\mathbf{a}}$ be Boolean variables, and let $val_{C\mathbf{a}}$ be a numeric variable.*

The encoding ξ_ρ of an OG-ground rule ρ is the Presburger formula (with the same quantifier block as ρ) that is obtained from ρ by replacing each atom α (both in the body and in the head) by formula ξ_α, defined as follows:

- $\xi_\alpha = def_{A\mathbf{a}}$ *if α is an object atom of the form $A(\mathbf{a})$;*
- $\xi_\alpha = def_{B\mathbf{a}k}$ *if α is an exact atom $B(\mathbf{a}, k)$ (recall that this is the only possible form for exact atoms because ρ is normalised and OG-ground);*
- $\xi_\alpha = def_{C\mathbf{a}} \wedge ((s \preceq_C val_{C\mathbf{a}}) \vee \neg fin_{C\mathbf{a}})$ *if α is a limit atom $C(\mathbf{a}, s)$ with $s \neq \infty$; and*
- $\xi_\alpha = \alpha$ *if α is a comparison atom.*

The encoding $\xi_\mathcal{P}$ of an OG-ground program $\mathcal{P}$ is the Presburger formula $\bigwedge_{\rho \in \mathcal{P}} \xi_\rho$.

Let $\mathcal{J}$ be a pseudointerpretation, and let σ be an assignment of all such variables $def_{A\mathbf{a}}$, $def_{B\mathbf{a}k}$, $def_{C\mathbf{a}}$, $fin_{C\mathbf{a}}$, and $val_{C\mathbf{a}}$ for the predicates and constants in $\mathcal{J}$. Then, $\mathcal{J}$ and σ correspond to each other if the following holds for all A, B, C, $\mathbf{a}$, and k as above:

- $\sigma(def_{A\mathbf{a}}) = true$ *if and only if $A(\mathbf{a}) \in \mathcal{J}$;*
- $\sigma(def_{B\mathbf{a}k}) = true$ *if and only if $B(\mathbf{a}, k) \in \mathcal{J}$;*

- $\sigma(\mathit{def}_{C\mathbf{a}}) = \mathit{true}$ if and only if there exists $\ell \in \mathbb{Z} \cup \{\infty\}$ such that $C(\mathbf{a}, \ell) \in \mathcal{J}$;
- $\sigma(\mathit{fin}_{C\mathbf{a}}) = \mathit{true}$ and $\sigma(\mathit{val}_{C\mathbf{a}}) = \ell$ if and only if $C(\mathbf{a}, \ell) \in \mathcal{J}$, for every $\ell \in \mathbb{Z}$.

Note that ℓ in the last case of Definition 8 ranges over all integers but not ∞, and $\mathcal{J}$ is a pseudointerpretation and thus cannot contain both $C(\mathbf{a}, \infty)$ and $C(\mathbf{a}, \ell)$ for an integer $\ell \in \mathbb{Z}$; therefore, $\sigma(\mathit{def}_{C\mathbf{a}}) = \mathit{true}$ and $\sigma(\mathit{fin}_{C\mathbf{a}}) = \mathit{false}$ if and only if $C(\mathbf{a}, \infty) \in \mathcal{J}$.

Also note that each assignment corresponds to exactly one pseudointerpretation. However, each pseudointerpretation may correspond to several assignments since two assignments corresponding to the same pseudointerpretation may differ, for a limit predicate C and objects $\mathbf{a}$, on the value of $\mathit{val}_{C\mathbf{a}}$, if $\mathit{def}_{C\mathbf{a}}$ or $\mathit{fin}_{C\mathbf{a}}$ is set to false in both assignments.

Example 9. Consider the OG-ground program $\mathcal{P}$ consisting of the following rules, for B an exact and C a max predicate:

$$\rightarrow B(1), \qquad B(1) \wedge C(m) \wedge (1 \leq m) \rightarrow C(m+1).$$

Then $\xi_{\mathcal{P}}$ is the following Presburger formula:

$$\mathit{def}_{B1} \wedge \forall m. \, \mathit{def}_{B1} \wedge (\mathit{def}_C \wedge ((m \leq \mathit{val}_C) \vee \neg\mathit{fin}_C)) \wedge (1 \leq m) \rightarrow$$
$$\mathit{def}_C \wedge ((m+1 \leq \mathit{val}_C) \vee \neg\mathit{fin}_C).$$

The following straightforward proposition shows how the correspondence between pseudointerpretations and assignments transfers to the correspondence between programs and their encodings.

Proposition 3. *Let $\mathcal{P}$ be an OG-ground program, and let $\mathcal{J}$ and σ be a pseudointerpretation and a variable assignment, respectively, such that $\mathcal{J}$ and σ correspond to each other. Then, $\mathcal{J} \models \mathcal{P}$ if and only if σ is a solution to $\xi_{\mathcal{P}}$.*

We are now ready to summarise the main properties of our Presburger encoding (we remind the reader that an IP is a conjunction of comparison atoms with linear numeric terms).

Lemma 2. *For $\mathcal{P}$ an OG-ground program and γ a fact, there is a Presburger sentence*

$$\xi = \forall \mathbf{n}. \, \exists \mathbf{m}. \bigvee_{i=1}^{h} \psi_i$$

with each ψ_i an IP such that the following holds, for d and u the maximum sizes of ψ_i and rules in $\mathcal{P}$, respectively, under the assumption that integers take unit space:

- *ξ holds if and only if $\mathcal{P} \models \gamma$;*
- *$|\mathbf{n}|$, h, and d are linearly bounded in $|\mathcal{P}| \cdot u$, $|\mathcal{P}| \cdot 2^u$, and u, respectively; and*
- *each integer in ξ appears in $\mathcal{P}$ or γ.*

Proof. Since fact entailment for positive programs coincides with classical first-order entailment, Lemma 3 implies that $\mathcal{P} \models \gamma$ if and only if the Presburger sentence

$$\xi_0 = \forall \mathbf{n}.\ \neg \xi_{\mathcal{P}} \vee \xi_{\gamma}$$

holds, where $\mathbf{n}$ is the tuple of all variables def_{Aa}, def_{Bak}, def_{Ca}, fin_{Ca}, and val_{Ca} occurring in $\xi_{\mathcal{P}}$ and ξ_{γ}. Next, we transform, in several equivalence-preserving steps, ξ_0 to a Presburger sentence ξ that satisfies the required properties.

Let first ξ_1 be the Presburger sentence obtained from ξ_0 by converting each top-level conjunct ξ_{ρ} of $\xi_{\mathcal{P}}$, for $\rho \in \mathcal{P}$, into the form

$$\forall \mathbf{m}_{\rho}.\ \bigwedge_{i=1}^{h_{\rho}} \zeta_{\rho}^i$$

with each ζ_{ρ}^i a disjunction of literals (i.e., atoms or their negations), where $\mathbf{m}_{\rho}$ are all the (numeric) variables of ρ (i.e., the quantifier-free part of each ξ_{ρ} is converted to conjunctive normal form). By moving all quantifiers in ξ_1 to the front and pushing negations inwards, we obtain the sentence

$$\xi_2 = \forall \mathbf{n}.\ \exists \mathbf{m}.\ \left(\bigvee_{\rho \in \mathcal{P}} \bigvee_{i=1}^{h_{\rho}} \chi_{\rho}^i \right) \vee \xi_{\gamma}',$$

where $\mathbf{m}$ is the (disjoint) union of all $\mathbf{m}_{\rho}$ (assuming without loss of generality that different rules in $\mathcal{P}$ use different variables), each χ_{ρ}^i is the negation normal form of $\neg \zeta_{\rho}^i$, and ξ_{γ}' is the disjunctive normal form of ξ_{γ}. Finally, let ξ be obtained from ξ_2 by rewriting each negated comparison atom to the equivalent (positive) comparison atom (e.g., $\neg(s_1 \leq s_2)$ is rewritten to $(s_2 < s_1)$).

We next claim that ξ satisfies all the required properties. First, ξ is of the required form, because $\mathcal{P}$ is an OG-ground program and hence all the terms are linear. Second, ξ holds if and only if $\mathcal{P} \models \gamma$ because ξ is equivalent to ξ_0 by construction. Third, $|\mathbf{n}|$ is linearly bounded in $|\mathcal{P}| \cdot u$. Fourth, by construction, $\Sigma_{\rho \in \mathcal{P}}\, h_{\rho}$ plus the constant number of conjunctions in ξ_{γ}'—that is, h—is linearly bounded in $|\mathcal{P}| \cdot 2^u$, while each $[\![\chi_{\rho}^i]\!]$ and the size of χ under unit integer assumption for χ a conjunction in ξ_{γ}'—and hence d—is linearly bounded in u. Finally, also by construction, each integer in ξ appears in $\mathcal{P}$ or γ. □

The following lemma, which is due to Christoph Haase and can be proved using ideas of Chistikov and Haase [6], bounds the magnitudes of variable values in the Presburger sentence from Lemma 2 (the proof is out of the scope of these notes).

Lemma 3. *There exist polynomials p_1 and p_2 such that, for every Presburger sentence*

$$\xi = \forall \mathbf{n}.\ \exists \mathbf{m}.\ \bigvee_{i=1}^{h} \psi_i$$

with each ψ_i an IP and the maximal magnitude of an integer in ξ bounded by $b > 1$, ξ holds if and only if it holds over integers with magnitudes bounded by the following, where d is the maximum size of ψ_i under the assumption that integers take unit space:

$$b^{p_1(|\mathbf{n}|+h)\cdot 2^{p_2(d)}}.$$

We now combine the above results to establish upper bounds to the complexity of fact entailment. Lemmas 2 and 3 provide us with bounds on the size of counter-pseudomodels for entailment.

Lemma 4. *For every OG-ground program $\mathcal{P}$ with the dataset part $\mathcal{D}$ and each fact γ, $\mathcal{P} \not\models \gamma$ if and only if there is a pseudomodel $\mathcal{J}$ of $\mathcal{P}$ such that $\mathcal{J} \not\models \gamma$, $|\mathcal{J}| \leq |\mathcal{P}|$, and the magnitude of each integer in $\mathcal{J}$ is bounded exponentially in $\|\mathcal{D}\| + \|\gamma\|$.*

Proof. The backward direction is trivial since $\mathcal{P}$ is positive, so we concentrate on the forward direction. To this end, consider an OG-ground program $\mathcal{P}$ and a fact γ such that $\mathcal{P} \not\models \gamma$. By Lemma 2, there exists a Presburger sentence $\xi = \forall \mathbf{n}. \exists \mathbf{m}. \bigvee_{i=1}^{h} \psi_i$ that does not hold and satisfies the following properties, for d and u the maximum sizes of ψ_i and rules in $\mathcal{P}$, respectively, under the assumption that integers take unit space:

- $|\mathbf{n}|$ and h, and d are linearly bounded by $|\mathcal{P}| \cdot u$, $|\mathcal{P}| \cdot 2^u$, and u, respectively;
- each integer in ξ appears in $\mathcal{P}$ or γ.

Therefore, by Lemma 3, there are polynomials q_1 and q_2, and an assignment σ to variables $\mathbf{n}$ such that σ is not a solution to $\exists \mathbf{m}. \bigvee_{i=1}^{h} \psi_i$ and the magnitudes of all numbers in the range of σ are bounded by the following, where $b > 1$ is a bound on the maximal magnitude of an integer in $\mathcal{P}$ and γ:

$$b^{q_1(|\mathbf{n}|+h)\cdot 2^{q_2(d)}}.$$

This immediately implies the bound on the magnitudes of integers in $\mathcal{J}$.

We are left to show how to construct a pseudomodel $\mathcal{J}$ with $|\mathcal{J}| \leq r = |\mathcal{P}|$ and the same bound on integers. By construction of ξ in Lemma 2, σ is a solution to $\xi_{\mathcal{P}}$ and not a solution to ξ_{γ}. Now, let σ' be the extension of σ to all variables introduced in Definition 8 that assigns *false* to all Boolean and 0 to all integer variables outside of the domain of σ, and let $\mathcal{J}'$ be the pseudomodel corresponding to σ'. By Lemma 3, $\mathcal{J}' \models \mathcal{P}$ and $\mathcal{J}' \not\models \gamma$. Moreover, by definition, the bound on the magnitudes of integers propagates from σ to $\mathcal{J}'$. Let $\mathcal{J}$ be the subset of $\mathcal{J}'$ consisting of all pseudofacts that are either identical to the head of some rule in $\mathcal{P}$ or differ from such a head only in the numeric position of a limit atom. On the one hand, we still have $\mathcal{J} \models \mathcal{P}$ and $\mathcal{J} \not\models \gamma$. On the other hand, $|\mathcal{J}| \leq |\mathcal{P}|$ by construction. So, $\mathcal{J}$ satisfies all the required properties. □

We are ready to present our algorithm for fact entailment: by Claim 1 of Proposition 1 and Lemma 4, nondeterministic Algorithm 1 decides fact entailment for positive LL-programs; in this algorithm, as usual in descriptions of

---

ALGORITHM 1: Fact Entailment for Positive LL-Programs

   Input: positive LL-program $\mathcal{P}$ and fact γ

   Output: *true* if and only if $\mathcal{P} \models \gamma$

  1 compute the canonical OG-grounding $\mathcal{G}(\mathcal{P})$ of $\mathcal{P}$

  2 universally guess a pseudointerpretation $\mathcal{J}$ with bounds on integer
      magnitudes provided by Lemma 4 applied to $\mathcal{G}(\mathcal{P})$ as $\mathcal{P}$

  3 **return** *true* if $\mathcal{J} \not\models \mathcal{G}(\mathcal{P})$ or $\mathcal{J} \models \gamma$ and *false* otherwise

---

nondeterministic computations, by 'universally guess' we mean 'verify all possibilities in parallel', which is precisely the ability of coNP Turing machines. Next, we show that the algorithm works within the announced upper data complexity bound for the problem (we will prove the matching lower bound in Theorem 3 in Sect. 4.3).

Theorem 2. *The fact entailment problem for positive LL-programs is in* coNP *in data complexity.*

Proof. As discussed before the theorem, we are left to show that Algorithm 1 runs within the required complexity bound.

First, by Claim 2 of Proposition 1, Line 1 requires polynomial time (in the size of the dataset part $\mathcal{D}$ of $\mathcal{P}$ and γ) and hence produces an OG-ground program $\mathcal{G}(\mathcal{P})$ of polynomial size. Moreover, since each integer in $\mathcal{G}(\mathcal{P})$ is inherited from $\mathcal{P}$, the magnitude of the integers in pseudointerpretation $\mathcal{J}$ guessed in Line 2 is exponentially bounded by Lemma 4; representing such integers requires polynomially many bits. Furthermore, since $|\mathcal{J}| \leq |\mathcal{G}(\mathcal{P})|$ also by Lemma 4, the size $\|\mathcal{J}\|$ is also bounded polynomially. Finally, as follows from Proposition 2 and the monotonicity property of the immediate consequence operator, Line 3 amounts to checking $\mathcal{T}_{\mathcal{G}(\mathcal{P})}(\mathcal{J}) \not\sqsubseteq \mathcal{J}$ and $\gamma \sqsubseteq \mathcal{J}$, which can both be done in time polynomial in $\|\mathcal{T}_{\mathcal{G}(\mathcal{P})}(\mathcal{J})\| + \|\mathcal{J}\|$ in the straightforward way (when $\mathcal{T}_{\mathcal{G}(\mathcal{P})}(\mathcal{J})$ is computed); moreover, $\mathcal{T}_{\mathcal{G}(\mathcal{P})}(\mathcal{J})$ can be computed in time polynomial in $\|\mathcal{G}(\mathcal{P})\| + \|\mathcal{J}\|$ by Lemma 1, which is polynomial in $\|\mathcal{D}\|$ by Proposition 1 and the above observation on $\|\mathcal{J}\|$. Hence, we conclude that Line 3 requires polynomial time. Therefore, overall, the algorithm works in coNP, as required.   □

Note that Algorithm 1 can be shown to work in coNEXP in combined complexity; however, the analysis of the bounds of integer magnitude is more complex and left out of the scope of these notes.

4.3 Complexity Lower Bounds for LL-Programs

In this section, we establish the lower bound on the complexity of fact entailment matching the upper bound established in the previous section. In particular, we show that the problem is coNP-hard for positive LL-programs, in data complexity (Theorem 3). In fact, only minor modifications of our proofs are required to obtain coNEXP-hardness in combined complexity. Note that the only integer used in our constructions is 1, so the results hold for both unary and binary encodings of numbers.

We start with the positive case, and first give a precise definition of a Turing machine deciding an NP problem, which we rely on in this section. To this end, consider a problem $P \in$ NP over alphabet $\{0, 1\}$. There exists a nondeterministic Turing machine M_P and a number $d \in \mathbb{N}$—called the *degree* of M_P—with the following properties. Machine M_P has a set of states Q that contains the initial state q^{init}, the set Q^{acc} of accepting states, and the set Q^{rej} of rejecting states; it has a work tape, infinite to the right, over alphabet $\Gamma = \{0, 1, \_\}$ with $\_$ the blank symbol, and a transition function

$$\delta : (Q \setminus (Q^{\mathsf{acc}} \cup Q^{\mathsf{rej}})) \times \Gamma \times \{0, 1\} \rightarrow Q \times \Gamma \times \{\mathsf{left}, \mathsf{right}\}.$$

The nondeterminism of M_P is realised by the third argument of the transition function—that is, in each step, computation of M_P splits into two branches, one for 0 as the argument and one for 1; on each branch, M_P enters a new state, writes a new symbol into the tape cell under the head, and moves the head left or right, which is represented by symbols L and R, respectively. Without loss of generality, we require that the two transitions for 0 and 1 always end in different states, and that M_P never moves the head to the left of the first cell of the tape and terminates (i.e., accepts or rejects by entering a state in Q^{acc} or in Q^{rej}, respectively) on an input w in at most $(\max(|w|, 2))^d$ steps, for $|w|$ the length of w. A partial run of M_P on an input w is a sequence of configurations of M_P (i.e., triples of a state, a position of the head, and contents of the tape) starting in the initial configuration for w (i.e., a configuration with state q^{init}, the head over the left-most cell, and w on the tape) that agrees with δ at all steps. We have $w \in P$ if and only if there is an accepting run (i.e., a partial run ending in a configuration with a state in Q^{acc}). In the rest of this section, by a machine deciding a problem $P \in$ NP we mean a Turing machine M_P with a degree d as described above.

Note that, since, by assumption, two transitions differing only in the guessed bit always lead to different states, each partial run $\Pi = C_0, \ldots, C_j$ of machine M_P on an input w has a one-to-one correspondence with the sequence of guesses from $\{0, 1\}$ of length j. Since $j \leq h$ for $h = (\max(|w|, 2))^d$, this sequence is the binary representation of a number in $[0, 2^h - 1]$, and we denote by $\ell(\Pi)$ the number obtained from this representation by prepending 1 to it (i.e., adding 1 as the most significant bit). This operation plays a technical role: it ensures that each number represents a unique partial run; moreover, we can model a 0 guess by doubling the number, and a 1 guess by doubling and adding 1.

The following definition reflects the main idea for the simulation of a non-deterministic Turing machine M_P by a semi-positive LL-program: to decide whether an input w is in P, it is enough to go through the terminating runs Π of M_P on w in increasing order of $\ell(\Pi)$ until finding an accepting run or completing the pass at the rejecting run Π with $\ell(\Pi)$ consisting of $|\Pi| = (\max(|w|, 2))^d + 1$ ones; then, $w \in P$ if and only if the last run explored is accepting. Here and in what follows, $|\Pi|$ is the number of configurations in a partial run Π, which equals the number of guesses plus one.

Definition 9. *For $P \in$ NP, a partial run Π of M_P is searching if one of the following holds:*

- *Π consists of a single initial configuration;*
- *the last digit of $\ell(\Pi)$ is 0 and $\Pi = \Pi', C$ for a searching partial run Π' and configuration C;*
- *the last digit of $\ell(\Pi)$ is 1, the partial run Π'' with $\ell(\Pi'') = \ell(\Pi) - 1$ is searching, and all terminating extensions of Π'' are rejecting.*

The following straightforward proposition establishes that it is enough to go through all searching partial runs when looking for the accepting one.

Proposition 4. *For $P \in$ NP, if a searching partial run Π of M_P on an input w satisfies $\ell(\Pi) \geq \ell(\Pi')$ for each searching partial run Π' of M_P on w with $|\Pi| = |\Pi'|$, then there is an accepting extension of Π if and only if $w \in P$.*

We are ready to present our hardness theorem. It is important to note that the same result may be proven by reduction of other coNP-complete problems (e.g., UNSAT), and those reductions may be slightly easier in some places. However, we will give a more generic reduction based on Turing machines, because it highlights the main ideas of limit $Datalog_{\mathbb{Z}}$ and can also be easily adapted to the combined complexity bound.

Theorem 3. *The fact entailment problem for positive LL-programs not using $\times$ and using only 1 as a numeric constant is coNP-hard in data complexity.*

Proof. Consider an arbitrary problem $P' \in$ coNP over alphabet $\{0, 1\}$ and let M_P be a nondeterministic Turing machine with a degree d deciding the complement P of P' (which is in NP) as described above. Then, each such input $w = u_1, \ldots, u_c$ over $\{0, 1\}$ can be encoded as an (ordered) dataset $\mathcal{D}_w$ over only object EDB predicates *first*, *next*, *last*, $input_0$ and $input_1$ in a way similar to the encoding in Example 5 in Sect. 3.3:

$$first(a_1), \quad next(a_1, a_2), \quad \ldots, \quad next(a_{c-1}, a_c), \quad last(a_c), \tag{19}$$
$$input_{u_1}(a_1), \quad \ldots, \quad input_{u_c}(a_c).$$

Since $c \geq 2$ by our assumption, machine M_P running on w always terminates in exactly $h = c^d$ steps and uses at most h cells on its tape. Therefore, we can refer to each configuration in a partial run of M_P on w by a number requiring d digits in c-ary representation—that is, by a d-tuple of objects in $\mathcal{D}_w$; similarly, we can address each cell used by M_P by a d-tuple of objects. As a result, we can encode the configuration C concluding each partial run Π of M_P on w using the following facts over $(2d + 1)$-ary max predicates $head_q$, for each state q of M_P, and $tape_u$, for each symbol $u \in \Gamma$:

- $head_q(\mathbf{a_t}; \mathbf{a_x}; \ell(\Pi))$, where q is the state in C, while $\mathbf{a_t}$ and $\mathbf{a_x}$ are the d-tuples of objects in $\mathcal{D}$ encoding $|\Pi| - 1$ and the head position in C, respectively; and

- $tape_u(\mathbf{a_t}; \mathbf{a_x}; \ell(\Pi))$, for each $i \in [0, h-1]$, where u is the symbol in the i-th tape cell in C, $\mathbf{a_t}$ is as above, and $\mathbf{a_x}$ is the d-tuple encoding i.

Note that we use ';' instead of ',' to separate tuples of arguments when writing these atoms. We will use this notational convention in this and some later proofs to avoid ambiguity when concatenating several such tuples without explicitly mentioning their sizes.

The idea behind the positive LL-program $\mathcal{P}_P$ constructed below based on M_P (and independent on w) is to populate predicates $head_q$ and $tape_u$ so that they encode all and only searching partial runs on an input word; then, we can apply Proposition 4 and extract the answer of M_P from the encoding of the searching partial run Π with the greatest $\ell(\Pi)$.

Program $\mathcal{P}_P$ consists of Rules (20)–(32) given next. First, it is convenient to have a uniform way of accessing all objects in the dataset. This is achieved by the unary object predicate $object$, defined by Rules (20) from EDB predicates $first$ and $next$, which encode a total order on the objects in $\mathcal{D}_w$:

$$first(z_0) \rightarrow object(z_0), \qquad next(z, z') \rightarrow object(z'). \qquad (20)$$

Rules (21), where $i \in [0, d-1]$, define the $2d$-ary object predicate $succ$ to denote the immediate successor relation on numbers encoded as d-tuples of objects, as explained above, by a lexicographic extension of the order given by $next$ to d-tuples of objects:

$$object(z_1) \wedge \cdots \wedge object(z_i) \wedge next(z, z') \wedge first(z_0) \wedge last(z_{\max}) \rightarrow$$
$$succ(z_1, \ldots, z_i, z, z_{\max}, \ldots, z_{\max}; z_1, \ldots, z_i, z', z_0, \ldots, z_0). \quad (21)$$

It is also convenient to have access to the transitive closure $succ^+$ of $succ$, defined by Rules (22), and the the symmetric closure $differ$ of $succ^+$—that is, the inequality relation,—defined by Rules (23):

$$succ(\mathbf{z}; \mathbf{z}') \rightarrow succ^+(\mathbf{z}; \mathbf{z}'), \quad succ^+(\mathbf{z}; \mathbf{z}') \wedge succ(\mathbf{z}'; \mathbf{z}'') \rightarrow succ^+(\mathbf{z}; \mathbf{z}''), \quad (22)$$
$$succ^+(\mathbf{z}; \mathbf{z}') \rightarrow differ(\mathbf{z}; \mathbf{z}'), \qquad succ^+(\mathbf{z}; \mathbf{z}') \rightarrow differ(\mathbf{z}'; \mathbf{z}). \quad (23)$$

The simulation of M_P starts with Rules (24)–(26), which read the input word and initialise the state, head, and tape of M_P—that is, encode the partial run Π consisting of a single initial configuration. In Rules (24)–(26), $\mathbf{z_0}$ and $\mathbf{z_0'}$ are tuples consisting of variable z_0 repeated d and $d-1$ times, respectively. In particular, the rules initialise the first d arguments of the predicates $head_{q^{init}}$ and $tape_u$, for $u \in \Gamma$, by the first object in $\mathcal{D}$, which encodes $0 = |\Pi| - 1$. Similarly, Rule (24) initialises each component of the second d-tuple in $head_{q^{init}}$ by the first object in $\mathcal{D}$, thus encoding that the head of M_P initially points to the left-most tape cell. Rule (25) load the input into the tape predicates $tape_u$ and $tape_u$, for $u = 0, 1$: the least significant position of the second argument tuple in facts over $tape_1$ encode the 1-bits in the input word, while the same position in facts over $tape_0$ encode the 0-bits; Rule (26) then pads all remaining tape cells with the blank symbol. Finally, the last argument of each predicate initialised by Rules (24)–(26) is set to $\ell(\Pi) = 1$, as explained earlier:

$$first(z_0) \rightarrow head_{q^{\text{init}}}(\mathbf{z}_0; \mathbf{z}_0; 1), \tag{24}$$

$$first(z_0) \wedge input_u(x) \rightarrow tape_u(\mathbf{z}_0; \mathbf{z}_0', x; 1), \tag{25}$$

$$first(z_0) \wedge last(z_{\text{max}}) \wedge succ^+(\mathbf{z}_0', z_{\text{max}}, z_{\text{max}}; \mathbf{x}) \rightarrow tape_{\_}(\mathbf{z}_0; \mathbf{x}; 1). \tag{26}$$

Each transition $\delta(q, u, G) = (q', u', X)$ with $X \in \{\text{left}, \text{right}\}$ and $G \in \{0, 1\}$ is simulated by Rules (27) if $G = 0$ and (28) if $G = 1$; for brevity, we use conjunctions in rule heads, which can be easily rewritten away by several rules. Rules (27) extend the encoding of a searching partial run Π' to the encoding of the searching partial run $\Pi = \Pi', C$ in the case when the last digit of $\ell(\Pi)$ is 0. Rules (27) have an instance for each $q \in Q \setminus Q^{\text{acc}} \cup Q^{\text{rej}}$, each $u \in \Gamma$, and each $v \in \Gamma$; furthermore, $S(\mathbf{x}; \mathbf{x}')$ denotes $succ(\mathbf{x}'; \mathbf{x})$ if X is left and $succ(\mathbf{x}; \mathbf{x}')$ if X is right, and hence $\mathbf{x}'$ encodes the head position after the transition provided $\mathbf{x}$ does so before the transition. To encode the step from Π' to Π, all atoms in the head of Rule (27) have variables $\mathbf{t}'$ as their first d arguments, which are related to variables $\mathbf{t}$ in the respective body atoms by $succ(\mathbf{t}, \mathbf{t}')$. The atoms with variables $\mathbf{y}$, which must be different from the head position $\mathbf{x}$ by $differ(\mathbf{x}; \mathbf{y})$, propagate the unaffected contents of the tape to both sides of the head. Finally, since $G = 0$, we have $\ell(\Pi) = 2 \cdot \ell(\Pi')$, which is reflected by doubling the numeric argument of the head atoms compared to the body:

$$head_q(\mathbf{t}; \mathbf{x}; m) \wedge tape_u(\mathbf{t}; \mathbf{x}; m) \wedge tape_v(\mathbf{t}; \mathbf{y}; m) \wedge$$
$$succ(\mathbf{t}; \mathbf{t}') \wedge S(\mathbf{x}; \mathbf{x}') \wedge differ(\mathbf{x}; \mathbf{y}) \wedge (m + m \doteq m') \rightarrow$$
$$head_{q'}(\mathbf{t}'; \mathbf{x}'; m') \wedge tape_{u'}(\mathbf{t}'; \mathbf{x}; m') \wedge tape_v(\mathbf{t}'; \mathbf{y}; m'). \tag{27}$$

Similarly, Rules (28) extend the encoding of a searching partial run Π' to the encoding of the searching partial run Π when the last digit of $\ell(\Pi)$ is 1. The main difference here is that, by Definition 9, we need to ensure that all terminating extensions of Π' starting with a step corresponding to a 0 guess are rejecting. This is achieved by the atom $allreject_0(\mathbf{t}; m)$, for $allreject_0$ a max predicate defined by Rules (29)–(31) as explained below. Moreover, since $G = 1$, we have $\ell(\Pi) = 2 \cdot \ell(\Pi') + 1$, which is reflected by increasing the numeric argument of the head atoms accordingly:

$$head_q(\mathbf{t}; \mathbf{x}; m) \wedge tape_u(\mathbf{t}; \mathbf{x}; m) \wedge tape_v(\mathbf{t}; \mathbf{y}; m) \wedge allreject_0(\mathbf{t}; m) \wedge$$
$$succ(\mathbf{t}; \mathbf{t}') \wedge S(\mathbf{x}; \mathbf{x}') \wedge differ(\mathbf{x}; \mathbf{y}) \wedge (m + m + 1 \doteq m') \rightarrow$$
$$head_{q'}(\mathbf{t}'; \mathbf{x}'; m') \wedge tape_{u'}(\mathbf{t}'; \mathbf{x}; m') \wedge tape_v(\mathbf{t}'; \mathbf{y}; m'). \tag{28}$$

Predicate $allreject_0$ is defined by Rules (29)–(31) so that a fact of the form $allreject_0(\mathbf{a}_t; \ell(\Pi))$ is derived if and only if all terminating extensions of Π' starting with a step corresponding to a 0—that is, all terminating runs $\Pi', C_1, \ldots, C_j$

with $\ell(\Pi', C_1)$ even—are rejecting; this is done with the help of a max predicate $allreject$ such that $allreject(\mathbf{a_t}; \ell(\Pi))$ is derived if and only if all terminating extensions of Π (including Π itself, if it is terminating) are rejecting. Rule (29), which instantiated for each $q^{rej} \in Q^{rej}$, covers the case when the last configuration is rejecting, while Rules (30) and (31) propagate information one step back in the run when the last guess is 0 and 1, respectively. It is important to note that a propagation along a 1 guess is only possible after the corresponding propagation along a 0 guess—that is, for each $\mathbf{a_t}$ and each k, fact $allreject_0(\mathbf{a_t}; k)$ is always derived before $allreject(\mathbf{a_t}; k)$:

$$head_{q^{rej}}(\mathbf{t}; \mathbf{x}; m) \rightarrow allreject(\mathbf{t}; m), \qquad (29)$$

$$allreject(\mathbf{t}'; m') \wedge succ(\mathbf{t}; \mathbf{t}') \wedge (m + m \doteq m') \rightarrow allreject_0(\mathbf{t}; m), \qquad (30)$$

$$allreject(\mathbf{t}'; m') \wedge succ(\mathbf{t}; \mathbf{t}') \wedge (m + m + 1 \doteq m') \rightarrow allreject(\mathbf{t}; m). \qquad (31)$$

Finally, Rule (32) checks whether all runs are rejecting—that is, whether M_P rejects the input, and hence the input is in P'. The rule triggers if and only if we can derive $allreject$ for the run consisting of only the initial configuration, which, by Proposition 4 and the explanation above, happens precisely when all runs are explored and found rejecting:

$$first(z_0) \wedge allreject(\mathbf{z}_0; 1) \rightarrow goal. \qquad (32)$$

Having completed the construction of $\mathcal{P}_P$, it is a matter of technicality to show its correctness—that is, that, for every input w as above, $\mathcal{P}_P \cup \mathcal{D}_w \models goal$ if and only if $w \in P'$,—and we omit it from these notes. $\square$

Before moving on, we briefly discuss how to adapt the proof of Theorem 3 to show coNEXP-hardness of fact entailment for positive LL-programs in combined complexity. Indeed, we can use the same construction; the only difference is that a machine deciding a problem in NEXP, defined in exactly the same way as a machine deciding a problem in NP, terminates on input w in exactly $(\max(|w|, 2))^{(\max(|w|,2))^d}$ steps, for a fixed degree $d \in \mathbb{N}$, and uses at most this number of tape cells, so the arities of the relevant predicates become polynomially dependent on $|w|$ (e.g., the arity of $head_q$ and $tape_u$ becomes $2c^d + 1 = 2|w|^d + 1$) and Rules (21) have $c^d = |w|^d$ (i.e., polynomially many) instantiations.

5   Fragments with Tractable Reasoning

Tractability (i.e., polynomial time) of reasoning in data complexity is key for problems involving large datasets. Thus, we next give a *stability* condition on LL-programs that brings the complexity of reasoning down to P in data complexity, which matches the complexity for usual Datalog. We then present a syntactic *type-consistency* condition that ensures stability and is simple to verify.

5.1   Stable Positive LL-Programs

The fact entailment algorithm for usual Datalog computes the materialisation iteratively, which can be done in polynomial time in the size of data. We now present a further restriction on positive LL-programs that makes such iterative computation viable for LL-programs. The difficulty in doing so is to detect when a numeric argument *diverge*—that is, when it increases or decreases indefinitely. Hence, to ensure tractability, we should be able to detect divergence after polynomially many rule applications.

Example 10. Consider the LL-program $\mathcal{P}_{st}$ over max predicates C_1, C_2:

$$C_1(0), \qquad C_1(m) \rightarrow C_2(m), \qquad C_2(m) \rightarrow C_1(m+1).$$

Here, both C_1 and C_2 diverge when computing pseudomaterialisation $\mathcal{N}(\mathcal{P}_{st})$ due to a cyclic dependency between C_1 and C_2. The existence of such a dependency, however, does not necessarily lead to divergence. Let an LL-program $\mathcal{P}'_{st}$ be obtained from $\mathcal{P}_{st}$ by adding a fact $C(5)$, for C max, and replacing the second rule by the following rule:

$$C_1(m) \wedge C(m) \rightarrow C_2(m).$$

While C_1 and C_2 still depend on each other, the increase in C_1 and C_2 is bounded by an independent value of C, so neither C_1 nor C_2 diverges.   ◁

To capture these ideas formally, we first extend $\mathbb{Z} \cup \{\infty\}$ with a new symbol $\bot$, which indicates that a fact does not hold for any integer. We also define $\bot < k < \infty$ for each $k \in \mathbb{Z}$; $\bot + \ell = \bot$ and $\infty + \ell = \infty$ for each $\ell \in \mathbb{Z} \cup \{\infty\}$; and $\bot + \infty = \bot$.

Next we formalise the notion of dependency, concentrating first on (positive) OG-ground LL-programs; we will discuss arbitrary positive LL-programs at the end of the section.

Definition 10. *A numeric variable m depends on a numeric variable n in an OG-ground rule ρ if $m = n$ or m occurs in an atom in ρ with a variable that depends on n. A numeric term s_2 depends on a numeric term s_1 if s_2 mentions a variable depending on a variable in s_1.*

We next introduce a key notion of a value propagation graph. Our definition is based on IP $\psi(\rho, \mathcal{J})$ from Definition 7 whose solutions encode matches of the body of an OG-ground rule ρ to a pseudointerpretation $\mathcal{J}$. So, if the head of ρ is a limit atom $C(\mathbf{a}, s)$, then $\psi(\rho, \mathcal{J})$ corresponds to an integer linear optimisation problem $\psi^*(\rho, \mathcal{J})$ that optimises (i.e., maximises or minimises, depending on the type of C) the value of s under $\psi(\rho, \mathcal{J})$. If $\psi(\rho, \mathcal{J})$ is satisfiable (i.e., ρ is applicable to $\mathcal{J}$), then $\psi^*(\rho, \mathcal{J})$ can either be bounded and have an optimal integer value, or unbounded.

Definition 11. *Given an OG-ground program $\mathcal{P}$ and a pseudointerpretation $\mathcal{J}$, the value propagation graph of $\mathcal{P}$ over $\mathcal{J}$ is the weighted directed graph (V, E, Ω) with the following components:*

- *the set of nodes V contains a node $\langle C\mathbf{a}\rangle$ for each limit atom $C(\mathbf{a}, s)$ in a rule head in $\mathcal{P}$;*
- *the set of edges E contains $(\langle C_1\mathbf{a}_1\rangle, \langle C_2\mathbf{a}_2\rangle)$ for each rule ρ in $\mathcal{P}$ applicable to $\mathcal{J}$ that produces the edge—that is, has $C_1(\mathbf{a}_1, s_1)$ in the body and $C_2(\mathbf{a}_2, s_2)$ in the head where s_2 depends on s_1;*
- *the weight $\Omega(e)$ of each edge $e = (\langle C_1\mathbf{a}_1\rangle, \langle C_2\mathbf{a}_2\rangle)$ in E is an element of $\mathbb{Z} \cup \{\bot, \infty\}$ defined as*

$$\Omega(e) = \max\{\Omega_\rho(e) \mid \rho \in \mathcal{P} \text{ produces } e\},$$

where $\Omega_\rho(e)$ is defined as follows, for $\ell \in \mathbb{Z} \cup \{\infty\}$ with $C_1(\mathbf{a}_1, \ell) \in \mathcal{J}$ (which exists by applicability):

- *$\Omega_\rho(e) = \infty$ if the $\max_{C_2}$-optimal value of s over $\psi(\rho, \mathcal{J})$ is unbounded,*
- *$\Omega_\rho(e) = \bot$ if the $\max_{C_2}$-optimal value of s over $\psi(\rho, \mathcal{J})$ is bounded and $\ell = \infty$,*
- *$\Omega_\rho(e) = d_2 \cdot k - d_1 \cdot \ell$ if the $\max_{C_2}$-optimal value k of s over $\psi(\rho, \mathcal{J})$ is $\psi(\rho, \mathcal{J})$ is bounded and $\ell \in \mathbb{Z}$ where, for $i \in \{1, 2\}$, d_i is 1 if C_i is max and -1 if C_i is min.*

The weight $\Omega(\Pi)$ of a path Π in a value propagation graph is the sum of the edge weights along Π; path Π has positive weight if $\Omega(\Pi)$ is a positive integer or ∞.

Intuitively, graph (V, E, Ω) of a OG-ground program $\mathcal{P}$ over a pseudointerpretation $\mathcal{J}$ describes how, for each pseudofact $C_1(\mathbf{a}_1, \ell)$ in $\mathcal{J}$, applying $\mathcal{P}$ propagates ℓ to other pseudofacts. For example, every edge $e = (\langle C_1\mathbf{a}_1\rangle, \langle C_2\mathbf{a}_2\rangle)$ with max C_1 and C_2 indicates that a rule is applicable to a fact $C_1(\mathbf{a}_1, \ell) \in \mathcal{J}$ and that it produces $C_2(\mathbf{a}_2, \ell + \Omega(e))$.

It is easy to check that the value propagation graph increases monotonically during rule application as described in the following proposition.

Proposition 5. *For every OG-ground program $\mathcal{P}$ and pseudointerpretations $\mathcal{J}$ and $\mathcal{J}'$, let (V, E, Ω) and (V', E', Ω') be the value propagation graphs of $\mathcal{P}$ over $\mathcal{J}$ and over $\mathcal{J}'$, respectively. Then $V = V'$, and $\mathcal{J} \sqsubseteq \mathcal{J}'$ implies $E \subseteq E'$.*

We have the following key definition (note that the proposition above guarantees that edge e always exists in E').

Definition 12. *An OG-ground program $\mathcal{P}$ is stable if $\Omega(e) \leq \Omega'(e)$ for all pseudointerpretations $\mathcal{J}$ and $\mathcal{J}'$ such that $\mathcal{J} \sqsubseteq \mathcal{J}'$ and all edges $e \in E$, where (V, E, Ω) and (V, E', Ω') are the value propagation graphs of $\mathcal{P}$ over $\mathcal{J}$ and over $\mathcal{J}'$, respectively.*

Intuitively, iterative rule applications never decrease the edge weights if a program is stable. Program $\mathcal{P}_{st}$ in Example 10 is stable, while $\mathcal{P}'_{st}$ is not stable since $\Omega(e) = 0$ and $\Omega'(e) = -1$ for the edge $e = (\langle C_1\rangle, \langle C_2\rangle)$ in the propagation graphs (V, E, Ω) and (V, E', Ω') of $\mathcal{P}'_{st}$ over the pseudointerpretations $\{C_1(0), C(0)\}$ and $\{C_1(1), C(0)\}$, respectively.

The following straightforward lemma formulates a key property of stable OG-ground programs: a positive-weight cycle for a program $\mathcal{P}$ and pseudointerpretation $\mathcal{J}$ guarantees divergence of numeric arguments along the cycle by repeated application of $\mathcal{T}_{\mathcal{P}}$ to $\mathcal{J}$.

ALGORITHM 2: Pseudomaterialisation of Stable OG-Ground Programs

---

Input: stable OG-ground program $\mathcal{P}$
Output: pseudomaterialisation $\mathcal{N}(\mathcal{P})$
1 set $\mathcal{J} := \emptyset$
2 **repeat**
3   set $\mathcal{J}_{\mathsf{old}} := \mathcal{J}$
4   set $\mathcal{J} := \mathcal{T}_{\mathcal{P}}(\mathcal{J})$
5   compute value propagation graph (V, E, Ω) of $\mathcal{P}$ over $\mathcal{J}$
6   **foreach** node $\langle C\mathbf{a} \rangle$ in V on a positive-weight cycle in (V, E, Ω) **do**
7   replace $C(\mathbf{a}, \ell)$ in $\mathcal{J}$ with $C(\mathbf{a}, \infty)$
8 **until** $\mathcal{J} = \mathcal{J}_{\mathsf{old}}$
9 **return** $\mathcal{J}$

Lemma 5. *For each node $\langle C\mathbf{a} \rangle$ on a positive-weight cycle in the value propagation graph of a stable OG-ground program $\mathcal{P}$ over a pseudointerpretation $\mathcal{J}$ and for every pseudomodel $\mathcal{J}'$ of $\mathcal{P}$ such that $\mathcal{J} \sqsubseteq \mathcal{J}'$, we have $C(\mathbf{a}, \infty) \in \mathcal{J}'$.*

While Lemma 5 ensures that a positive-weight cycle leads to divergence along this cycle, it does not bound the number of applications of the immediate consequence operator needed to obtain such a cycle. The following lemma, which can be proved by induction on j, closes this gap.

Lemma 6. *For each stable OG-ground program $\mathcal{P}$ and each pseudointerpretation $\mathcal{J}$ there is $i \in [1, |\mathcal{P}|]$ such that one of the following holds, where $\mathcal{J}_0 = \mathcal{J}$ and $\mathcal{J}_j = \mathcal{T}_{\mathcal{P}}(\mathcal{J}_{j-1})$ for $j \geq 1$:*

1. *$\mathcal{J}_i = \mathcal{J}_{i-1}$,*
2. *there is a rule in $\mathcal{P}$ that is applicable to $\mathcal{J}_i$ but not to $\mathcal{J}_{i-1}$,*
3. *there is a node $\langle C\mathbf{a} \rangle$ on a positive-weight cycle in the value propagation graph of $\mathcal{P}$ over $\mathcal{J}_i$ such that $C(\mathbf{a}, \infty) \notin \mathcal{J}_i$.*

We are now ready to present Algorithm 2, which computes the pseudomaterialisation of a stable OG-ground program $\mathcal{P}$ in polynomial time in data complexity. The algorithm iteratively applies $\mathcal{T}_{\mathcal{P}}$. After each application, however, it computes the corresponding value propagation graph (Line 5) and replaces all integers by ∞ along all positive-weight cycles in the graph (Lines 6–7); by Lemma 5, such replacements are always sound. Moreover, Lemma 6 guarantees termination of the algorithm—indeed, the lemma says that, until we reach the fixpoint, every $|\mathcal{P}|$ iterations either a new rule becomes applicable or a new pseudofact involving ∞ is introduced to the partial pseudomaterialisation; since $\mathcal{P}$ is OG-ground, each of the two cases can happen at most $|\mathcal{P}|$ times. We next make this argument formal in the proof of the following theorem.

Theorem 4. *For every stable OG-ground program $\mathcal{P}$ with the dataset part $\mathcal{D}$, the pseudomaterialisation $\mathcal{N}(\mathcal{P})$ can be computed in time polynomial in $\|\mathcal{D}\|$.*

Proof. We claim that Algorithm 2 computes $\mathcal{N}(\mathcal{P})$ for a stable OG-ground program $\mathcal{P}$ within the required complexity bounds. To this end, first note that Lemma 5 guarantees that $\mathcal{J} \sqsubseteq \mathcal{N}(\mathcal{P})$ holds throughout the computation; moreover, the algorithm terminates only if $\mathcal{J} = T_{\mathcal{P}}(\mathcal{J})$—that is, only if $\mathcal{J}$ is a pseudomodel of $\mathcal{P}$. Since the pseudomaterialisation $\mathcal{N}(\mathcal{P})$ is the minimal pseudomodel of $\mathcal{P}$ with respect to $\sqsubseteq$, these two observations imply that whenever the algorithm terminates, it outputs $\mathcal{N}(\mathcal{P})$. Thus, it remains to argue that the algorithm terminates within the stated time.

First, note that the pseudointerpretation $\mathcal{J}$ monotonically increases with respect to $\sqsubseteq$ during the execution of the main loop in Lines 2–8 of the algorithm; hence, once a rule becomes applicable to $\mathcal{J}$, it remains applicable in all consequent iterations, and once a pseudofact $C(\mathbf{a}, \infty)$ is in $\mathcal{J}$, it remains in $\mathcal{J}$ in all consequent iterations. Then, Lemma 6 guarantees that after at most $|\mathcal{P}|$ iterations of the main loop, either the algorithm terminates by reaching a fixpoint, or a new rule becomes applicable, or a new pseudofact $C(\mathbf{a}, \infty)$ appears in $\mathcal{J}$. Since both the number of rules and the number of pseudofacts are bounded by $|\mathcal{P}|$, the algorithm terminates after at most $2 \cdot |\mathcal{P}|^2$ iterations of the loop.

Then, the polynomial complexity bound follows since each step can be done in polynomial time by Lemma 1 and the fact that computing the value propagation graph in Line 5 boils down to checking applicability of $|\mathcal{P}|$ OG-ground rules, which is polynomial since the IPs involved have fixed number of variables, while detecting whether a node is on a positive-weight cycle in Line 6 can be done in polynomial time using, for example, a variant of the Floyd-Warshall algorithm [16]. □

Algorithm 2 allows us to decide fact entailment for stable OG-ground programs in P in data complexity and can be shown to work in EXP in combined complexity; both bounds are the same as for usual Datalog. This result naturally extends to positive LL-programs that are not OG-ground. First of all, we generalise the notion of stability.

Definition 13. *An LL-program $\mathcal{P}$ is stable if its OG-grounding $\mathcal{G}(\mathcal{P})$ is stable.*

We are now ready to establish the general result.

Theorem 5. *The fact entailment problem for stable LL-programs is P-complete in data complexity.*

The EXP combined complexity of this problem can be proven as usual.

5.2   Type-Consistent Programs

Stability identifies a large class of positive LL-programs for which reasoning is tractable. Unfortunately, the condition is semantic, rather than syntactic. Moreover, it is not a local condition in the sense that it cannot be verified by looking at each rule in isolation but depends on how different rules interact. Finally, checking stability of an LL-program involves computing the reduct of each stratum, which depends on the materialisation of the preceding strata (in fact, even checking stability of an OG-ground program is coNP-hard). This motivates the following sufficient condition for stability.

Definition 14. *A min-max typing of variables in an LL-rule is a partitioning of all unguarded numeric variables that occur in limit atoms in the rule into* max *and* min *types. Given a min-max typing, a numeric term is of type* max *if it has the form*

$$s + \left(\sum_{i=1}^{v} k_i \times m_i \right) - \left(\sum_{j=1}^{w} \ell_j \times n_j \right),$$

where s is a numeric term not mentioning any max *or* min *variables, $v \in \mathbb{N}$, $w \in \mathbb{N}$, each m_i is a* max *variable with coefficient $k_i \geq 1$, and each n_j is a* min *variable with coefficient $\ell_j \geq 1$; a numeric term is of type* min *if the same holds except that each m_i is* min *and each n_j is* max.

(Positive) rule $\rho = \varphi \rightarrow \alpha$ is type-consistent *if it has a min-max typing with the following properties:*

- *the numeric term of each* max *and each* min *atom in ρ is of type* max *and* min, *respectively;*
- *each comparison atom in φ has the form $(s_1 < s_2)$ or $(s_1 \leq s_2)$, for term s_1 of type* min *and term s_2 of type* max; *and*
- *if $\alpha = C_2(\mathbf{a}_2, s_2)$ is a limit atom, then, for each limit atom $C_1(\mathbf{a}_1, s_1)$ in φ with s_2 depending on s_1, terms s_1 and s_2 have a common unguarded variable that has coefficient 1 in s_1 and does not appear in any other limit atoms in φ, where* dependency *is defined as in Definition 10 except that only unguarded numeric variables are taken into account.*

A positive LL-program is type-consistent *if so are all of its rules.*

Note that in our previous definition a numeric term that mentions only integers and guarded variables is both of type max and of type min.

Type consistency is a syntactic property that, by definition, can be checked rule by rule in polynomial time (in fact, in logarithmic space).

It is easily seen that all the example LL-programs in Sect. 3.3 are type-consistent. In the rest of the section, we show that all type-consistent LL-programs are stable, which, by Theorem 5, implies that such programs have the same complexity of fact entailment as usual Datalog programs.

Lemma 7. *Each type-consistent program is stable.*

Proof. To avoid notational clutter, in this proof we focus on homogeneous limit programs all of whose limit predicates are max. By definition, t is also enough to consider only OG-ground programs.

Consider an arbitrary type-consistent OG-ground program $\mathcal{P}$. It suffices to show that, for each rule $\rho = \varphi \rightarrow C_2(\mathbf{a}_2, s_2)$ in $\mathcal{P}$ with an atom $C_1(\mathbf{a}_1, s_1)$

in φ such that C_1 and C_2 are limit predicates and s_2 depends on s_1, and for all pseudointerpretations $\mathcal{J}$ and $\mathcal{J}'$ such that $\mathcal{J} \sqsubseteq \mathcal{J}'$ and ρ is applicable to $\mathcal{J}$, we have $\Omega_\rho(e) \leq \Omega'_\rho(e)$, where $e = (\langle C_1 \mathbf{a}_1 \rangle, \langle C_2 \mathbf{a}_2 \rangle)$ is an edge in the value propagation graphs $G = (V, E, \Omega)$ and $G' = (V, E', \Omega')$ of $\mathcal{P}$ over $\mathcal{J}$ and over $\mathcal{J}'$, respectively (note that G and G' have the same set of nodes and $e \in E \subseteq E'$ by Proposition 5). To this end, consider arbitrary such ρ, $C_1(\mathbf{a}_1, s_1)$, $C_2(\mathbf{a}_2, s_2)$, $\mathcal{J}$, $\mathcal{J}'$, G, and G'. Note that, since ρ is OG-ground and type-consistent, and s_2 depends on s_1, terms s_1 and s_2 are such that either $s_1 = s'_1 + 1 \times m$ and $s_2 = s'_2 + k_m \times m$ for $k_m \geq 1$ and m a max variable that occurs neither in s'_1 nor in other limit atoms in ρ, or $s_1 = s'_1 - 1 \times n$ and $s_2 = s'_2 - \ell_n \times n$ for $\ell_n \geq 1$ and n a min variable that appears neither in s'_1 nor in other limit atoms in ρ. We next focus on the first case; the second case is symmetric.

First, note that if $C_1(\mathbf{a}_1, \infty) \in \mathcal{J}$, then the max-optimal value of s_2 for IP $\psi(\rho, \mathcal{J})$ is unbounded. Indeed, in this case, for each solution σ to $\psi(\rho, \mathcal{J})$ mapping m to some $k \in \mathbb{Z}$ and each integer $k' > k$, the function σ' mapping m to k' and all other variables to the same values as σ is also a solution, because

- m occurs only negatively on the left-hand side of each comparison atom in φ,
- m occurs only positively on the right-hand side of each comparison atom, and
- m does not occur in any standard atom in φ except $C_1(\mathbf{a}_1, s_1)$;

so, increasing the value of m to k' does not invalidate an atom in φ. Furthermore, since m does not occur in s'_2, $s_2\sigma' = s_2\sigma + k_m \cdot (k' - k) \geq s_2\sigma + (k' - k)$; clearly, this allows us, for each $\ell \in \mathbb{Z}$, to pick σ' such that $s_2\sigma' \geq \ell$. For the same reasons, the max-optimal value of s_2 for $\psi(\rho, \mathcal{J}')$ is unbounded whenever $C_1(\mathbf{a}_1, \infty) \in \mathcal{J}'$. Therefore, $\Omega_\rho(e) \neq \bot$ and $\Omega'_\rho(e) \neq \bot$ for $e = (\langle C_1 \mathbf{a}_1 \rangle, \langle C_2 \mathbf{a}_2 \rangle)$, and we have two cases: either $\Omega_\rho(e) = \infty$ or $\Omega_\rho(e) \in \mathbb{Z}$.

If $\Omega_\rho(e) = \infty$ then the max-optimal value of s_2 for $\psi(\rho, \mathcal{J})$ is unbounded. Since $\mathcal{J} \sqsubseteq \mathcal{J}'$, each solution to $\psi(\rho, \mathcal{J})$ is also a solution to $\psi(\rho, \mathcal{J}')$. Thus, the max-optimal value of s_2 for $\psi(\rho, \mathcal{J}')$ is also unbounded and $\Omega'_\rho(e) = \infty$.

Consider now the case $\Omega_\rho(e) \in \mathbb{Z}$—that is, $\Omega_\rho(e) = k - \ell$ for $\ell \in \mathbb{Z}$ with $C_1(\mathbf{a}_1, \ell) \in \mathcal{J}$ and k the max-optimal value of s_2 for IP $\psi(\rho, \mathcal{J})$. If $C_1(\mathbf{a}_1, \infty) \in \mathcal{J}'$ then, as already argued, the max-optimal value of s_2 for $\psi(\rho, \mathcal{J}')$ is unbounded; hence $\Omega'_\rho(e) = \infty$, and so $\Omega_\rho(e) \leq \Omega'_\rho(e)$. Otherwise, let $C_1(\mathbf{a}_1, \ell') \in \mathcal{J}'$ for $\ell' \in \mathbb{Z}$ and consider the solution σ to $\psi(\rho, \mathcal{J})$ such that $s_2\sigma$ is the optimal value—that is, such that $s_2\sigma = s'_2\sigma + k_m \cdot m\sigma = k$. In particular, we have $s_1\sigma \leq \ell$. Let σ' be a function mapping m to $m\sigma + \ell' - \ell$ and all other variables to the same values as σ. Function σ' is a solution to $\psi(\rho, \mathcal{J}')$, because

- $s_1\sigma' = s'_1\sigma' + m\sigma' = s'_1\sigma + m\sigma + \ell' - \ell = (s_1\sigma - \ell) + \ell' \leq \ell'$ and hence $\mathcal{J}' \models C_1(\mathbf{a}_1, s_1\sigma')$,
- $\mathcal{J}'$ satisfies all other standard atom in $\varphi\sigma'$ since they do not mention m and $\mathcal{J} \sqsubseteq \mathcal{J}'$, and
- $\mathcal{J}'$ satisfies all comparison atoms in $\varphi\sigma'$ since m occurs only negatively in terms on the left and only positively in those on the right of each comparison.

Since $\mathcal{J} \sqsubseteq \mathcal{J}'$ and hence $\ell \leq \ell'$, the following holds, for k' the max-optimal value of s_2 for $\psi(\rho, \mathcal{J}')$:

$$\Omega_\rho(e) = k - \ell = s_2'\sigma + k_m \cdot m\sigma - \ell = s_2'\sigma + k_m \cdot m\sigma - k_m \cdot \ell + (k_m - 1) \cdot \ell \leq$$
$$s_2'\sigma + k_m \cdot m\sigma - k_m \cdot \ell + (k_m - 1) \cdot \ell' = s_2'\sigma + k_m \cdot (m\sigma + \ell' - \ell) - \ell'$$
$$= s_2'\sigma + k_m \cdot m\sigma' - \ell' \leq s_2'\sigma' + k_m \cdot m\sigma' - \ell' = s_2\sigma' - \ell' \leq k' - \ell' = \Omega_\rho'(e);$$

note that $s_2'\sigma \leq s_2'\sigma'$ because m is max and may appear in s_2' only positively. $\square$

6   Related Work

The closest formalism to limit $Datalog_{\mathbb{Z}}$ is the so-called *monotonic programs* of Ross and Sagiv [29]. Their core fragment extends usual Datalog by *cost* predicates whose last position ranges over partially ordered *cost domains*, which have associated built-in and aggregate functions. An example of a cost domain relevant to $Datalog_{\mathbb{Z}}$ is the integers $(\mathbb{Z} \cup \{-\infty, +\infty\}, \leq)$ with built-in functions $+$, $-$ and $\times$, and aggregate functions count and max. Then, the bodies of rules in programs of Ross and Sagiv are conjunctions of *standard* atoms over usual non-cost or cost predicates, *built-in* atoms over built-in predicates associated with the partial order of the cost domain (e.g., $\leq$ and $\equiv$), and *aggregate* atoms using aggregate functions, while the heads are atoms over standard predicates (i.e., neither build-in nor aggregate); additionally, all variables are appropriately typed and safe (in particular, as opposed to $Datalog_{\mathbb{Z}}$, all cost variables should appear in standard cost predicates). In what follows, we omit aggregate atoms since they are inessential for the comparison.

Ross and Sagiv's *interpretation* is a set of facts over standard predicates that does not contain two facts that differ only in their cost positions—that is, their notion of interpretations resembles our pseudo-interpretations. However, the immediate consequence operator of a program applies to an interpretation as in usual Datalog, essentially ignoring the special semantics of cost domains (i.e., there is no analogue of limit closure). Thus, the result of such application may not be an interpretation; to overcome this, the authors consider *cost-consistent* programs—that is, the programs for which the immediate consequence of an interpretation is always an interpretation. Moreover, the partial order of the cost domains induces an order on the interpretations, and *monotonic* programs are those whose immediate consequence operator preserves this partial order (i.e., if one interpretation subsumes another under the order, then their consequences are in the same order relation).

Example 11. Not every Ross and Sagiv's program is cost-consistent. For instance, consider the following program $\mathcal{Q}$, where C is a cost predicate with associated cost domain $(\mathbb{Z} \cup \{-\infty, +\infty\}, \leq)$:

$$\rightarrow C(0), \qquad\qquad C(m) \wedge (n \equiv m + 1) \rightarrow C(n).$$

Then, the immediate consequence $\{C(0), C(1)\}$ of the interpretation $\{C(0)\}$, $\mathcal{R}_Q(\mathcal{J}) =$ is not an interpretation. Similarly, not every cost-consistent program is monotonic, which is illustrated by the following cost-consistent program:

$$C(m) \wedge (n \equiv -m) \rightarrow C(n). \quad \lhd$$

The main property of monotonic programs is that each such program has a unique minimal model, which is the least fixpoint of the immediate consequence operator [29, Corollary 3.5]. However, checking cost consistency and monotonicity of a program can both be shown undecidable in general. Hence, [29] define sufficient conditions for both cost consistency and monotonicity, which are, however, outside the scope of this summary. Nonetheless, knowing that a program is monotonic and thus has a least model does not guarantee decidability of reasoning; in fact, it is possible to show undecidability of fact entailment for monotonic programs with the cost domain $(\mathbb{Z} \cup \{-\infty, +\infty\}, \leq)$ and without multiplication.

Another related formalism is Datalog^{FS} proposed by Mazuran et al. [25], which extends usual Datalog with so-called *frequency support goals* and provides the formal underpinning for the DeALS system [39]. Similar to the language of Ross and Sagiv, fact entailment in Datalog^{FS} is undecidable, and no decidable fragment has been identified.

Datalog$_\mathbb{Z}$ is also closely related to constraint logic programming (CLP). Although a number of decidable CLP languages have been identified [8], none of them allow for recursive *numeric value invention*, which is an integral feature of *Datalog*$_\mathbb{Z}$ necessary to capture several examples in Sect. 3.3.

Recall that some examples from Sect. 3.3 implement aggregation over recursive rules. Several attempts were made to provide a generic semantics for such aggregation (including monotonic programs and Datalog^{FS} considered above in their full power). However, all these attempts yield solutions either for restricted classes of programs that are subject to strong monotonicity assumptions, use only *min* and *max* aggregate functions, or have undecidable fact entailment [7,12,13,22,27,35].

Finally, we remind the reader that in these notes we concentrated on positive limit programs; several extensions of limit and limit-linear *Datalog*$_\mathbb{Z}$ with negation (both stratified and non-monotonic) and disjunction has been also considered [18,20], thus bridging aggregation and answer-set programming (ASP).

7 Conclusion

In these notes we have presented the formalism of limit *Datalog*$_\mathbb{Z}$ programs, which builds upon usual Datalog with integer arithmetic. While having a clear natural syntax and semantics, this formalism is flexible and powerful enough to capture in a natural way a wide range of data analysis tasks. We have also identified several sublanguages with decidable and even tractable reasoning and established the associated computational complexity. Additionally, the proofs of these results demonstrated an application of several common techniques, including reduction to Presburger arithmetic and Turing machine simulation.

References

1. Alvaro, P., Condie, T., Conway, N., Elmeleegy, K., Hellerstein, J.M., Sears, R.: BOOM analytics: exploring data-centric, declarative programming for the cloud. In: Morin, C., Muller, G. (eds.) EuroSys. pp. 223–236. ACM (2010). https://doi.org/10.1145/1755913.1755937
2. Aref, M., et al.: Design and implementation of the LogicBlox system. In: SIGMOD, pp. 1371–1382 (2015)
3. Beeri, C., Naqvi, S.A., Shmueli, O., Tsur, S.: Set constructors in a logic database language. J. Log. Program. **10**(3&4), 181–232 (1991). https://doi.org/10.1016/0743-1066(91)90036-O
4. Berman, L.: The complexitiy of logical theories. Theor. Comput. Sci. **11**, 71–77 (1980). https://doi.org/10.1016/0304-3975(80)90037-7
5. Chin, B., et al.: Yedalog: exploring knowledge at scale. In: Ball, T., Bodík, R., Krishnamurthi, S., Lerner, B.S., Morrisett, G. (eds.) SNAPL. LIPIcs, vol. 32, pp. 63–78. Schloss Dagstuhl - Leibniz-Zentrum für Informatik (2015). https://doi.org/10.4230/LIPIcs.SNAPL.2015.63
6. Chistikov, D., Haase, C.: The taming of the semi-linear set. In: Chatzigiannakis, I., Mitzenmacher, M., Rabani, Y., Sangiorgi, D. (eds.) ICALP. LIPIcs, vol. 55, pp. 128:1–128:13. Schloss Dagstuhl - Leibniz-Zentrum für Informatik (2016). https://doi.org/10.4230/LIPIcs.ICALP.2016.128
7. Consens, M.P., Mendelzon, A.O.: Low-complexity aggregation in GraphLog and Datalog. Theor. Comput. Sci. **116**(1), 95–116 (1993). https://doi.org/10.1016/0304-3975(93)90221-E
8. Cox, J., McAloon, K., Tretkoff, C.: Computational complexity and constraint logic programming languages. Ann. Math. Artif. Intell. **5**(2–4), 163–189 (1992). https://doi.org/10.1007/BF01543475
9. Cuenca Grau, B., Horrocks, I., Kaminski, M., Kostylev, E.V., Motik, B.: Limit Datalog: a declarative query language for data analysis. ACM SIGMOD Rec. (SIGMOD Rec.) **48**(4), 6–17 (2019)
10. Dantsin, E., Eiter, T., Gottlob, G., Voronkov, A.: Complexity and expressive power of logic programming. ACM Comput. Surv. **33**(3), 374–425 (2001). https://doi.org/10.1145/502807.502810
11. Eisner, J., Filardo, N.W.: Dyna: extending Datalog for modern AI. In: de Moor, O., Gottlob, G., Furche, T., Sellers, A. (eds.) Datalog 2.0 2010. LNCS, vol. 6702, pp. 181–220. Springer, Heidelberg (2011). https://doi.org/10.1007/978-3-642-24206-9_11
12. Faber, W., Pfeifer, G., Leone, N.: Semantics and complexity of recursive aggregates in answer set programming. Artif. Intell. **175**(1), 278–298 (2011). https://doi.org/10.1016/j.artint.2010.04.002
13. Ganguly, S., Greco, S., Zaniolo, C.: Extrema predicates in deductive databases. J. Comput. Syst. Sci. **51**(2), 244–259 (1995). https://doi.org/10.1006/jcss.1995.1064
14. Grädel, E.: Subclasses of Presburger arithmetic and the polynomial-time hierarchy. Theor. Comput. Sci. **56**, 289–301 (1988). https://doi.org/10.1016/0304-3975(88)90136-3
15. Haase, C.: Subclasses of Presburger arithmetic and the weak EXP hierarchy. In: Henzinger, T.A., Miller, D. (eds.) CSL-LICS, pp. 47:1–47:10. ACM (2014). https://doi.org/10.1145/2603088.2603092
16. Hougardy, S.: The Floyd-Warshall algorithm on graphs with negative cycles. Inf. Process. Lett. **110**(8–9), 279–281 (2010). https://doi.org/10.1016/j.ipl.2010.02.001

17. Immerman, N.: Descriptive Complexity. Springer, New York (1999). https://doi.org/10.1007/978-1-4612-0539-5
18. Kaminski, M., Cuenca Grau, B., Kostylev, E.V., Horrocks, I.: Complexity and expressive power of disjunction and negation in limit Datalog. In: AAAI. AAAI Press (2020)
19. Kaminski, M., Cuenca Grau, B., Kostylev, E.V., Motik, B., Horrocks, I.: Foundations of declarative data analysis using limit Datalog programs. In: Sierra, C. (ed.) IJCAI, pp. 1123–1130. ijcai.org (2017). https://doi.org/10.24963/ijcai.2017/156
20. Kaminski, M., Cuenca Grau, B., Kostylev, E.V., Motik, B., Horrocks, I.: Stratified negation in limit Datalog programs. In: Lang, J. (ed.) IJCAI, pp. 1875–1881. ijcai.org (2018). https://doi.org/10.24963/ijcai.2018/259
21. Kannan, R.: Minkowski's convex body theorem and integer programming. Math. Oper. Res. **12**(3), 415–440 (1987). https://doi.org/10.1287/moor.12.3.415
22. Kemp, D.B., Stuckey, P.J.: Semantics of logic programs with aggregates. In: Saraswat, V.A., Ueda, K. (eds.) ISLP, pp. 387–401. MIT Press (1991)
23. Loo, B.T., et al.: Declarative networking. Commun. ACM **52**(11), 87–95 (2009). https://doi.org/10.1145/1592761.1592785
24. Markl, V.: Breaking the chains: on declarative data analysis and data independence in the big data era. PVLDB **7**(13), 1730–1733 (2014). https://doi.org/10.14778/2733004.2733075
25. Mazuran, M., Serra, E., Zaniolo, C.: Extending the power of Datalog recursion. VLDB J. **22**(4), 471–493 (2013). https://doi.org/10.1007/s00778-012-0299-1
26. Meyer, R.R.: On the existence of optimal solutions to integer and mixed-integer programming problems. Math. Program. **7**(1), 223–235 (1974). https://doi.org/10.1007/BF01585518
27. Mumick, I.S., Pirahesh, H., Ramakrishnan, R.: The magic of duplicates and aggregates. In: McLeod, D., Sacks-Davis, R., Schek, H. (eds.) VLDB, pp. 264–277. Morgan Kaufmann (1990)
28. Papadimitriou, C.H.: On the complexity of integer programming. J. ACM **28**(4), 765–768 (1981). https://doi.org/10.1145/322276.322287
29. Ross, K.A., Sagiv, Y.: Monotonic aggregation in deductive databases. J. Comput. Syst. Sci. **54**(1), 79–97 (1997). https://doi.org/10.1006/jcss.1997.1453
30. Schlipf, J.S.: The expressive powers of the logic programming semantics. J. Comput. Syst. Sci. **51**(1), 64–86 (1995). https://doi.org/10.1006/jcss.1995.1053
31. Schöning, U.: Complexity of Presburger arithmetic with fixed quantifier dimension. Theor. Comput. Sci. **30**(4), 423–428 (1997). https://doi.org/10.1007/BF02679468
32. Schrijver, A.: Theory of Linear and Integer Programming. Wiley, Hoboken (1999)
33. Seo, J., Guo, S., Lam, M.S.: SociaLite: an efficient graph query language based on Datalog. IEEE Trans. Knowl. Data Eng. **27**(7), 1824–1837 (2015). https://doi.org/10.1109/TKDE.2015.2405562
34. Shkapsky, A., Yang, M., Interlandi, M., Chiu, H., Condie, T., Zaniolo, C.: Big data analytics with Datalog queries on Spark. In: Özcan, F., Koutrika, G., Madden, S. (eds.) SIGMOD, pp. 1135–1149. ACM (2016). https://doi.org/10.1145/2882903.2915229
35. Sudarshan, S., Ramakrishnan, R.: Aggregation and relevance in deductive databases. In: Lohman, G.M., Sernadas, A., Camps, R. (eds.) VLDB, pp. 501–511. Morgan Kaufmann (1991)
36. Van Gelder, A.: The well-founded semantics of aggregation. In: Vardi, M.Y., Kanellakis, P.C. (eds.) PODS, pp. 127–138. ACM Press (1992). https://doi.org/10.1145/137097.137854

37. Wang, J., Balazinska, M., Halperin, D.: Asynchronous and fault-tolerant recursive Datalog evaluation in shared-nothing engines. PVLDB **8**(12), 1542–1553 (2015). https://doi.org/10.14778/2824032.2824052
38. Yang, M., Shkapsky, A., Zaniolo, C.: Scaling up the performance of more powerful Datalog systems on multicore machines. VLDB J. **26**(2), 229–248 (2016). https://doi.org/10.1007/s00778-016-0448-z
39. Zaniolo, C., Yang, M., Das, A., Shkapsky, A., Condie, T., Interlandi, M.: Fixpoint semantics and optimization of recursive Datalog programs with aggregates. Theory Pract. Log. Program. **17**(5–6), 1048–1065 (2017). https://doi.org/10.1017/S1471068417000436

Knowledge Graphs: Research Directions

Aidan Hogan$^{(\boxtimes)}$

DCC, Universidad de Chile, and IMFD, Santiago, Chile
ahogan@dcc.uchile.cl

Abstract. In these lecture notes, we provide an overview of some of the high-level research directions and open questions relating to knowledge graphs. We discuss six high-level concepts relating to knowledge graphs: data models, queries, ontologies, rules, embeddings and graph neural networks. While traditionally these concepts have been explored by different communities in the context of graphs, more recent works have begun to look at how they relate to one another, and how they can be unified. In fact, at a more foundational level, we can find some surprising relations between the different concepts. The research questions we explore mostly involve combinations of these concepts.

1 Introduction

Knowledge graphs have been gaining more and more attention in recent years, particularly in settings that involve integrating and making sense of diverse data at large scale. Much of this attention stems from the 2012 announcement of the Google Knowledge Graph [63], which was later followed by further announcements of knowledge graphs by eBay, Facebook, IBM, Microsoft [53], and many more besides [35]. These *enterprise knowledge graphs* are typically internal to a company, where they aim to serve – per the words of Noy et al. [53] – as a common substrate of knowledge within the organisation, expanding and evolving over time. Other *open knowledge graphs* – such as BabelNet [49], DBpedia [44], Freebase [14], Wikidata [66], YAGO [33] – are made available to the public.

On a more technical level, there are varying perspectives about how knowledge graphs should be formally defined (if at all) [35]. This stems from the diversity of communities and organisations that have adopted the phrase. However, underlying all such perspectives is the foundational idea of representing knowledge using a graph abstraction, with nodes representing entities of interest in a given domain, and edges representing relations between those entities. Typically a knowledge graph will model different types of relations, which can be captured by labelled edges, with a different label used for each type of relation. Knowledge can consist of *simple assertions*, such as Charon orbits Pluto, which can be represented as directed labelled edges in a graph. Knowledge may also consist of *quantified assertions*, such as all stellar planets orbit stars, which require a more expressive formalism to capture, such as an ontology or rule language.

A reader familiar with related concepts may then question: what is the difference between a graph database and a knowledge graph, or an ontology and a

© Springer Nature Switzerland AG 2020
M. Manna and A. Pieris (Eds.): Reasoning Web 2020, LNCS 12258, pp. 223–253, 2020.
https://doi.org/10.1007/978-3-030-60067-9_8

knowledge graph? Per the previous definition, both graph databases[1] and ontologies can be considered knowledge graphs. It is then natural to ask: what, then, is new about knowledge graphs? What distinguishes research on knowledge graphs from research on graph databases, or ontologies, etc.?

If we so wish, we can choose to see the "vagueness" surrounding knowledge graphs as a feature not a bug: this vagueness offers flexibility for different communities to adapt the concept to their interests. No single research community can "lay claim" to the topic. Knowledge graphs can then become a commons for researchers from different areas to share and exchange techniques relating to the use of graphs to represent data and knowledge. In any case, most of the different choices – what graph model to use, what graph query language to use, whether to use rules or ontologies – end up being quite superficial choices.

Anecdotally, many of the most influential papers on knowledge graphs have emerged from the machine learning community, particularly relating to two main techniques: *knowledge graph embeddings* [67] and *graph neural networks* [70] (which we will discuss later). These works are not particularly related to graph databases (they do not consider regular expressions on paths, graph pattern matching, etc.) nor are they particularly related to ontologies (they do not consider interpretations, entailments, etc.), but by exploiting knowledge in the context of large-scale graph-structured data, they are related to knowledge graphs. Subsequently, one can find relations between these ostensibly orthogonal techniques; for example, while graph neural networks are used to inductively classify nodes in the graph based on numerical methods, ontologies can be used to deductively classify nodes in the graph based on symbolic methods, which raises natural questions about how they might compare.

Knowledge graphs, if we so choose, can be seen as an opportunity for researchers to bring together traditionally disparate techniques – relating to the use of graphs to represent and exploit knowledge – from different communities of Computer Science: to share and discuss them, to compare and contrast them, to unify and hybridise them. The goal of these notes will be to introduce examples of some of the principal directions along which such research may follow.

Recently we have published a tutorial paper online that offers a much more extensive (and generally less technical, more example-based) introduction to knowledge graphs than would be possible here, to which we refer readers new to the topic [35].[2] In the interest of keeping the current notes self-contained, and in order to establish notation, we will re-introduce some of the key concepts underlying knowledge graphs. However, our focus herein is to introduce specific open questions that we think may become of interest for knowledge graphs in the coming years. Specifically, we introduce six main concepts underlying knowledge graphs: data models, queries, ontologies, rules, embeddings and graph neural networks. Most of the questions we introduce intersect these topics.

---

[1] We intend to refer to the data model known as graph databases [9], not graph database systems [2].

[2] An abridged version of [35] is currently under review for ACM CSUR.

2   Data Model

Knowledge graphs assume a graph-structured data model. The high-level benefits of modelling data as graphs are as follows:

- Graphs offer a more intuitive abstraction of certain domains than alternative data models; for example, metro maps, flight routes, social networks, protein pathways, etc., are often visualised as graphs.
- When compared with (normalised) relational schemas, graphs offer a simpler and more flexible way to represent diverse, incomplete, evolving data, which can be defined independently of a particular schema.
- Graphs from different sources can be initially combined by taking the union of the constituent elements (nodes, edges, etc.).
- Unlike other semi-structured data models based on trees, graphs allow for representing and working with cyclic relations and do not assume a hierarchy.
- Graphs offer a more intuitive representation for querying and working with paths that represent indirect relations between entities.

A number of graph data models have become popular in practice, principally *directed edge-labelled graphs*, and *property graphs* [4]. The simpler of the two models is that of directed edge-labelled graphs, or simply *del graphs* henceforth. To build a del graph we will assume a set of constants $\mathbf{C}$.

Definition 1 (Directed edge-labelled graph). *A* directed edge-labelled graph *(or* del graph*) is a set of triples* $G \subseteq \mathbf{C} \times \mathbf{C} \times \mathbf{C}$.

We provide an example of a del graph in Fig. 1, describing various astronomic bodies. The data are incomplete, but more data can be added incrementally by adding new nodes and edges. Each triple $(s, p, o) \in G$ denotes a directed labelled edge of the form $s \xrightarrow{p} o$. Nodes in the graph denote entities of interest, and edges between them denote (binary) relations. We see both directed and undirected cycles formed from the relationships present between the entities.

The property graph model is more ornate, and allows for adding labels and property–value pairs on both nodes and edges [4].

Definition 2 (Property graph). *A* property graph G *is a tuple*

$$G := (V, E, L, P, U, e, l, p)$$

where $V \subseteq \mathbf{C}$ *is a set of node ids,* $E \subseteq \mathbf{C}$ *is a set of edge ids,* $L \subseteq \mathbf{C}$ *is a set of labels,* $P \subseteq \mathbf{C}$ *is a set of properties,* $U \subseteq \mathbf{C}$ *is a set of values,* $e : E \to V \times V$ *maps an edge id to a pair of node ids,* $l : V \cup E \to 2^L$ *maps a node or edge id to a set of labels, and* $p : V \cup E \to 2^{P \times U}$ *maps a node or edge id to a set of property–value pairs.*

In Fig. 2 we provide an example of a property graph alongside a del graph representing analogous information. The graph is defined as follows:

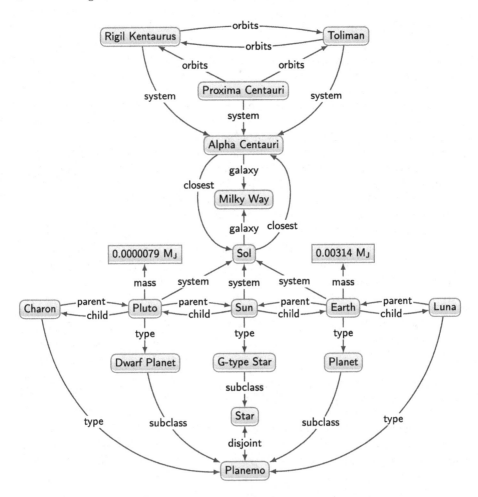

Fig. 1. Del graph describing astronomic bodies

- $V := \{\text{Alpha Centauri}, \text{Proxima b}, \text{Proxima Centauri}\}$
- $E := \{\text{Pb orbit}, \text{Pb system}, \text{PC system}\}$
- $L := \{\text{Exoplanet}, \text{Red Dwarf}, \text{Star System}, \text{child}, \text{system}\}$
- $P := \{\text{distance}, \text{mass}, \text{spectral}\}$
- $U := \{\text{0.05 AU}, \text{0.1221 M}_\odot, \text{1.172 M}_\oplus, \text{M5.5Ve}, \}$
- $e(\text{Pb orbit}) := (\text{Proxima Centauri}, \text{Proxima b})$,
  $e(\text{Pb system}) := (\text{Proxima b}, \text{Alpha Centauri})$,
  $e(\text{PC system}) := (\text{Proxima Centauri}, \text{Alpha Centauri})$
- $l(\text{Alpha Centauri}) := \{\text{Star System}\}$, $l(\text{Proxima b}) := \{\text{Exoplanet}\}$,
  $l(\text{Proxima Centauri}) := \{\text{Red Dwarf}\}$, $l(\text{Pb orbit}) := \{\text{child}\}$,
  $l(\text{Pb system}) := \{\text{system}\}$, $l(\text{PC system}) := \{\text{system}\}$
- $p(\text{Alpha Centauri}) := \{\}$, $p(\text{Proxima b}) := \{(\text{mass}, \text{1.172 M}_\oplus)\}$,
  $p(\text{Proxima Centauri}) := \{(\text{mass}, \text{0.1221 M}_\odot), (\text{spectral}, \text{M5.5Ve})\}$,
  $p(\text{Pb orbit}) := \{(\text{distance}, \text{0.05 AU})\}$, $p(\text{Pb system}) := \{\}$, $p(\text{PC system}) := \{\}$

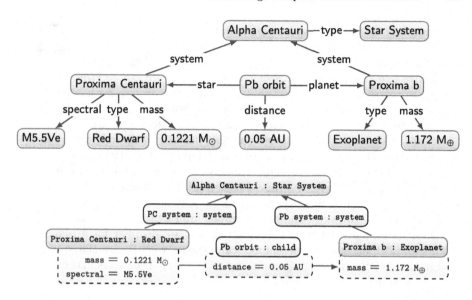

Fig. 2. Del graph (above) and property graph (below) with analogous information describing a planet orbiting Proxima Centauri

While del graphs form the basis of the RDF data model [18], property graphs are used in a variety of popular graphs databases systems, such as Neo4j [48]. Comparing del graphs and property graphs, we can say that del graphs are simpler, but property graphs are more flexible, particularly in terms of the ability to add property–value pairs to edges. However, property graphs can be represented as del graphs (and vice versa) as illustrated in Fig. 2, where edges with property–value pairs in the property graph can be converted to nodes in the del graph, as seen for Pb orbit; edges without property–value pairs in the property graph can be represented directly as edges in the del graph.

We identify two particular topics relating to modelling data as graphs.

Topic 2.1: Representing complex data

While graphs allow for representing many domains of data in an intuitive and concise manner, other forms of data are not so straightforward to represent. Being based on sets of elements, graphs are inherently unordered, which raises the question of how ordered data (lists, tuples, arrays, etc.) should be represented. Likewise statistical data are often associated with particular datatypes (integer, decimal, temporal, etc.), particular units (kilograms, pounds, seconds, hours, etc.), particular levels of precision (error bounds, rounding, etc.). An important topic then relates to modelling more complex forms of real-world data as graphs.

Thus far we have assumed graphs to be populated with a generic set of constants $\mathbf{C}$. However, knowledge graphs in practice may be populated with diverse terms; for example, `Proxima b` is an identifier for a planet, while 0.1221 `M`$_\odot$ is a complex numerical quantity with an associated unit of measure (Solar masses). Recognising this, the RDF data model, based on del graphs, supports the following terms:

- *Internationalized Resource Identifiers* (IRIs) serve as identifiers for nodes and edge labels, which can be linked to from across the Web.
- *Literals* represent datatype values, such as strings (optionally with language tags), numeric values, booleans, dates, times, durations, etc.
- *Blank nodes* are not strictly speaking constants, but rather represent existential terms, used to represent entities known to exist but whose values are unknown, or for enabling syntactic shortcuts [34].

Still there are open questions regarding how units – such as $M_\oplus$ (Earth masses), M_J (Jupiter masses), $M_\odot$ (Solar masses) – can be represented, or how levels of precision should be handled. Although proposals have been made to represent units and precision in graphs [16, 43], often knowledge graphs will adopt an ad hoc representation. There are also open questions regarding how to perform querying and reasoning over statistical data, with automatic translation of units and handling of precision.

Likewise for ordered data, although a number of proposals have been made for representing lists as a graph, these proposals are quite verbose [46].

A more general question arises: how should graph models be extended (if at all) in order to be able to concisely, intuitively and comprehensively model diverse, real-world data? Should we allow only simple terms and use complex graph structures to model such data, or should we support complex terms – e.g., allowing tuples, arrays, tables, trees, edges, graphs, etc., as nodes – to simplify the graph structure? How can we explore such trade-offs and evaluate different proposals? How can we apply querying, reasoning, machine learning, etc., on these different representations?

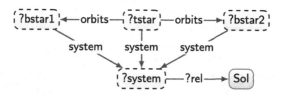

Fig. 3. Del graph pattern looking for trinary star systems related to Sol

---

Topic 2.2: Semantics of property graphs

While the semantics of del graphs have long been explored, the semantics of property graphs are less well understood. In reference to Figure 2, for example, we might ask if the child relation between Proxima Centauri and Proxima b holds. Intuitively we might assume that it does, but we should keep in mind that we may have property–value pairs on the edge that state deprecated = true, or probability = 0.1, for example. An open research question then relates to defining the semantics of property graphs, taking into consideration the semantics of labels and property–value pairs on nodes and edges. (We refer the interested reader to Attributed Description Logics [39], which make progress in this direction.)

Henceforth we will focus on del graphs, as the simpler of the two models.

3   Queries

We may wish to pose questions over the data represented by the graph. While a range of query languages have been proposed for querying graphs – including SPARQL for RDF graphs [29]; Cypher [23], Gremlin [56], and G-CORE [3] for property graphs – the same foundational elements underlie all such languages: *graph patterns*, *relational algebra*, and *path expressions* [4]. Herein we will assume data represented as a del graph, though the concepts we present generalise quite straightforwardly to other graph models, as appropriate [35].

At the core of graph queries is the notion of graph patterns. The most basic form of graph pattern is a graph that additionally allows *variables* to replace constants in any position. We refer to the set of variables as $\mathbf{V}$. We refer to the union of constants $\mathbf{C}$ and variables $\mathbf{V}$ as *terms*, denoted $\mathbf{T}$ (i.e., $\mathbf{T} = \mathbf{C} \cup \mathbf{V}$).

Definition 3 (Directed edge-labelled graph pattern). *A* directed edge-labelled graph pattern *(or* del graph pattern*) is a set of triples* $Q \subseteq \mathbf{T} \times \mathbf{T} \times \mathbf{T}$.

We provide an example in Fig. 3 of a del graph pattern looking for trinary star systems related (in some way) to Sol. Variables are prefixed with "?". A graph pattern is then evaluated over a data graph by mapping the variables of the graph pattern to constants such that the image of the graph pattern under

Table 1. Evaluation of the del graph pattern of Fig. 3 over the del graph of Fig. 1 under homomorphism-based semantics

?bstar1	?bstar2	?tstar	?system	?rel
Rigil Kentaurus	Toliman	Proxima Centauri	Alpha Centauri	closest
Rigil Kentaurus	Rigil Kentaurus	Proxima Centauri	Alpha Centauri	closest
Toliman	Toliman	Proxima Centauri	Alpha Centauri	closest
Rigil Kentaurus	Rigil Kentaurus	Toliman	Alpha Centauri	closest
Toliman	Toliman	Rigil Kentaurus	Alpha Centauri	closest

the mapping is a sub-graph of the data graph. More formally, let $\mu : \mathbf{V} \to \mathbf{C}$ denote a partial mapping from variables to constants, and let $\mathrm{dom}(\mu)$ denote the set of variables for which μ is defined. Further let $\mathbf{V}(Q)$ denote the set of variables used in Q. We can then define the evaluation of Q over G as:

Definition 4 (Evaluation of a del graph pattern). *Let Q be a del graph pattern and let G be a del graph. We then define the* evaluation of graph pattern Q over G, *as $Q(G) := \{\mu \mid \mu(Q) \subseteq G \text{ and } \mathrm{dom}(\mu) = \mathbf{V}(Q)\}$.*

Graph patterns of this form can be seen as transforming graphs into tables. In Table 1 we present the results of evaluating the del graph pattern of Fig. 3 over the del graph of Fig. 1, where each row indicates a *solution* given by a mapping μ per the previous definition. Graph patterns can be evaluated under different semantics by placing further restrictions on μ. Without further restrictions, a *homomorphism-based semantics* is considered where two or more variables in an individual solution can be mapped to a single constant in the data. On the other hand, if we restrict μ to be one-to-one, a (sub-graph) *isomorphism-based semantics* is considered, where each variable in an individual solution must map to a different constant. All of the solutions shown in Table 1 are returned under the unrestricted homomorphism-based semantics, while only the first solution is returned under the restricted isomorphism-based semantics.

Given that graph patterns return tables, a natural idea is to introduce the relational algebra to allow the solutions of a graph pattern to be transformed, and the solutions of several graph patterns to be combined: using π to project variables or σ to select rows returned from a single graph pattern, or using $\cup$, $-$, or $\bowtie$ to apply a union, difference, or join (respectively) across the results of two graph patterns. We can also introduce further syntactic operators, such as left-joins ($\bowtie$, aka optionals), anti-joins ($\triangleright$; aka not exists), etc. As a simple example, given the graph pattern Q of Fig. 3, we may define $\pi_{?\text{tstar}}(\sigma_{?\text{bstar1}\neq?\text{bstar2}}(Q))$ to select only solutions where ?bstar1 and ?bstar2 map to different constants, and subsequently project only the results for the ?tstar variable. Graph patterns extended with the relational algebra are called *complex graph patterns* [3]. Graph patterns extended with projection alone are called *conjunctive queries.*

The features we have seen thus far can only match bounded sub-graphs of the data graph (more formally, we can say that they are Gaifman-local [45]). However, we may be interested to find pairs of nodes that are connected by paths of arbitrary lengths. In order to express such queries, we can introduce *path expressions* and *regular path queries*.[3]

Definition 5 (Path expression). *A constant $c \in \mathbf{C}$ is a path expression. Furthermore:*

- *If r is a path expression, then r^- (inverse) and r^* (Kleene star) are path expressions.*
- *If r_1 and r_2 are path expressions, then $r_1 \cdot r_2$ (concatenation) and $r_1 \mid r_2$ (disjunction) are path expressions.*

In the following we assume that the evaluation of a path expression returns pairs of nodes connected by some path that satisfies the path expression [29]. Other query languages may support returning paths [3,23]. We will further introduce the notation N_G to denote the nodes of G; more formally, we define the nodes of G as $N_G := \{x \mid \exists p, y : (x, p, y) \in G \text{ or } (y, p, x) \in G\}$.

Definition 6 (Path expression evaluation). *Given a del graph G and a path expression r, we define the* evaluation *of r over G, denoted $r[G]$, as follows:*

$$r[G] := \{(u, v) \mid (u, r, v) \in E\} \, (where \ r \in \mathbf{C})$$
$$r^-[G] := \{(u, v) \mid (v, u) \in r[G]\}$$
$$r_1 \mid r_2[G] := r_1[G] \cup r_2[G]$$
$$r_1 \cdot r_2[G] := \{(u, v) \mid \exists w \in N_G : (u, w) \in r_1[G] \text{ and } (w, v) \in r_2[G]\}$$
$$r^*[G] := N_G \cup \bigcup_{n \in \mathbb{N}+} r^n[G]$$

where by r^n we denote the nth-concatenation of r (e.g., $r^3 = r \cdot r \cdot r$).

Let $\mathbf{R}$ denote the set of all path expressions. We next define a *regular path query* and a *navigational graph pattern* [4].

Definition 7 (Regular path query). *A regular path query is a triple $(x, r, y) \in \mathbf{T} \times (\mathbf{R} \cup \mathbf{V}) \times \mathbf{T}$.*

Definition 8 (Navigational graph pattern). *A navigational graph pattern Q is a set of regular path queries.*

---

[3] We implicitly refer to *two-way* regular path queries as inverse expressions are quite widely used in practice [15].

We provide an example of a navigational graph pattern in Fig. 4, searching for planemos in the Milky Way, along with the star(s) they orbit. The evaluation of a navigational graph pattern is then defined analogously to the evaluation of graph patterns, but where pairs of nodes connected by arbitrary-length paths – rather than simply edges – can now be matched. The navigational graph pattern of Fig. 4 will return four results, with ?star mapped to Sun in each, and ?planemo mapped to Earth, Pluto, Charon and Luna.

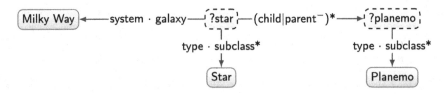

Fig. 4. Navigational graph pattern looking for planemos in the Milky Way and the stars that they orbit

Finally, noting that navigational graph patterns again transform graphs into tables, it is natural to define *complex navigational graph patterns*, which support applying relational algebra over the results of one or more navigational graph patterns. Navigational graph patterns extended with (only) projection are known as *conjunctive two-way regular path queries* (C2RPQs) [9].

The task of finding solutions for a query over a graph is known as *query answering*. While query answering have been well-studied in the literature [4,9], there are a number of interesting problems that arise when considering the evaluation of (complex) navigational graph patterns. We now discuss two topics.

Topic 3.1: *-case optimality

In the context of relational databases, the Atserias–Grohe–Marx (AGM) bound establishes a tight upper bound for the number of tuples that can be returned for conjunctive queries (without projection) over relations with a given number of tuples [7]. This bound can be naturally extended to give a tight bound in the case of graph patterns. For example, consider the following triangular graph pattern looking for planets of binary stars:

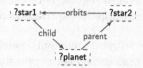

The AGM bound is based on a *fractional edge cover*, where each edge (relation) is assigned a weight in $[0, 1]$ such that, for each variable, when we sum the weights of the edges it appears in, the value is at least 1. In this case, for example, we can assign $\frac{1}{2}$ to orbits, $\frac{1}{2}$ to child and $\frac{1}{2}$ to parent, which is sufficient to (fractionally) cover all variables. The number of results returned by the query is then bounded by $n_o^{w_o} \cdot n_c^{w_c} \cdot n_p^{w_p}$, where n_o, n_c, n_p denote the size of the relations for orbits, child and parent, respectively, while w_o, w_c, w_p denote their fractional edge cover weights. If we find the fractional edge cover that minimises the aforementioned product over all relations, then the bound is tight. In this case, the tight bound is given by $n_o^{\frac{1}{2}} \cdot n_c^{\frac{1}{2}} \cdot n_p^{\frac{1}{2}}$; assuming $n = n_o = n_c = n_p$ for simplicity, we get $n^{\frac{3}{2}}$.

The AGM bound then gives us a general mechanism by which we can estimate the maximum number of results that a graph pattern can return. When we think of methods for enumerating all of the solutions for a graph pattern Q over a given graph, the best we can then hope for is an algorithm that runs in $O(\beta(Q))$, where $\beta(Q)$ is the AGM bound for Q. This is not trivial as the classical strategies for evaluating the aforementioned graph pattern (nested loops, hash joins, etc.) would be to proceed pattern-by-pattern, which would first execute a join such as:

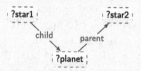

But in this case we must assign 1 to child and 1 to parent to have a fractional edge cover, meaning that the bound for this join would be n^2, which could not be processed within the $O(n^{\frac{3}{2}})$ runtime.

However, there do exist *worst-case optimal join algorithms* [50] that allow for the solutions of such queries to always be evaluated within linear time of the worst-case output size (the AGM bound). The core idea of such algorithms is to apply multiple joins at once, essentially evaluating variable-by-variable, rather than pattern-by-pattern. Such algorithms have been implemented in the context of querying graphs, and have shown that these theoretic guarantees translate into promising results in practice, particularly for more complex graph patterns with cycles (e.g., [51, 1, 38, 36]).

More work is left to do in terms of extending worst-case optimal algorithms to offer similar guarantees when other features of graph queries are present, including path expressions. Furthermore, works that go beyond worst-case optimality, perhaps considering average-case output size, or even instance-optimal join algorithms, are left to explore [50].

Topic 3.2: Native graph querying

Graph patterns return tables of solutions rather than graphs. An interesting research topic to explore is then to consider query languages based on composable operators that transform and return native graph objects – i.e., nodes, edges, paths, graphs, etc. – rather than tables.

We defined the evaluation of regular path queries such that the nodes connecting paths satisfying the path expression are returned. In practice,

it may often be necessary to return not only pairs of nodes, but also the paths themselves that are matched by the expression. Unlike pairs of nodes, paths in the presence of cycles may be infinite! For this reason, often a particular restriction is applied to the paths considered, such as to include only *simple paths*: paths that only visit each node at most once. As an additional complication, differing semantics may affect the complexity of evaluation in non-trivial ways; for example, finding a simple path of even length between two nodes (e.g., matching (orbits·orbits)* in a directed graph is NP-complete [42]). Similarly, the number of even simple paths can be astronomically large, even for small graphs, making them difficult to implement [5]. Finally, it is unclear how paths of arbitrary length should be represented in the results, or what kinds of operators over paths can be defined in the query language; for example, how should we join different tables on a variable mapped to paths?

Practical query languages like Cypher [23] support returning paths, and offer some operators, such as length(·) over paths. G-CORE [3] takes this one step further, and treats paths as "first-class citizens", allowing for returning paths in results, finding weighted shortest paths, and more besides. Still, however, more work is needed to understand how paths in results can be represented, what key operators should be defined for them, what are the appropriate semantics to apply, etc.

On the other hand, we may wish to return graphs from queries. Along these lines, SPARQL and G-CORE support CONSTRUCT queries, which allow for transforming a table of intermediate solutions into an output graph [29, 3]. Recursive extensions of CONSTRUCT queries have further been proposed and studied in the literature [55]. Still, however, CONSTRUCT queries are based on graph patterns that generate tables of intermediate results.

We then pose the idea of a *native graph query language* that is composed of unary and binary operators over graphs that return graphs. In the case of del graphs, which are defined as sets of triples, *selection* can be trivially defined in terms of filtering such triples, while set-based operators – *union, intersection, difference* – can be defined naturally with respect to the sets of triples. An interesting question relates to how joins on two graphs could or should be defined. Are joins even needed? What about aggregation? Would a graph-based definition of operators affect the computational complexity of query answering? Would it have practical benefits?

4   Ontologies

Looking more closely at the graph of Fig. 1, we may be able to deduce additional knowledge beyond what is explicitly stated in the graph. For example, we might conclude that Charon and Luna are instances of Moon; that Toliman and Rigil Kentaurus are instances of Binary Stars; that Luna, Earth, Sun, etc., are all part of the Milky Way, etc. In order to be able to draw such conclusions automatically from a graph, we require a formal representation of the semantics of the terms used in the graph. While there are a number of alternatives that we might consider for this task, we initially focus on *ontologies*, which have long been studied in the context of defining semantics over graphs.

Ontologies centre around three main types of elements: individuals, concepts (aka classes) and roles (aka properties). They allow for making formal, well-defined claims about such elements, which in turn opens up the possibility to perform automated reasoning. In terms of the semantics of ontologies, there are many well-defined syntaxes we can potentially use, but perhaps the most established formalism is taken from *Description Logics (DL)* [8,41,57], which studies logics centring around (unary and) binary relations, and logical primitives for which reasoning tasks remain decidable.

Table 2 defines the typical DL constructs one can find in the literature. The syntax column denotes how the construct is expressed in DL. A DL ontology then consists of an assertional box (A-Box), a T-Box (terminological box), and an R-Box (role box), each of which consists of a set of axioms that describe formal claims about individuals, concepts and properties, respectively.

Definition 9 (DL ontology). *A DL ontology O is defined as a tuple* $(\mathsf{A}, \mathsf{T}, \mathsf{R})$, *where* A *is the* A-Box: *a set of assertional axioms;* T *is the* T-Box: *a set of concept (aka class/terminological) axioms; and* R *is the* R-Box: *a set of role (aka property/relation) axioms.*

Syntactically, DL ontologies can be serialised as (del) graphs. Such a serialisation is defined by the Web Ontology Language (OWL) [31], which draws inspiration from the DL area towards standardising languages for which common reasoning tasks are decidable (or even tractable), and which defines serialisations of OWL ontologies as RDF graphs. In this context, looking at Fig. 1, for example, a triple such as (Planet, subclass, Planemo) can be read as a concept axiom Planet $\sqsubseteq$ Planemo, a triple such as (Pluto, child, Charon) can be read as a role axiom child(Pluto, Charon), while a triple such as (Charon, type, Planemo) can be read as a concept assertion Planemo(Charon).

Regarding the formal meaning of these axioms, the semantics column of Table 2 defines axioms using *interpretations*.

Definition 10 (DL interpretation). *A DL interpretation* I *is defined as a pair* $(\Delta^I, \cdot^I)$, *where* Δ^I *is the interpretation domain, and* $\cdot^I$ *is the interpretation function. The interpretation domain is a set of individuals. The interpretation function accepts a definition of either an individual a, a concept C, or a role R,*

Table 2. Description Logic syntax and semantics

Name	Syntax	Semantics ($\cdot^I$)
CONCEPT DEFINITIONS		
Atomic Concept	A	A^I (a subset of Δ^I)
Top Concept	$\top$	Δ^I
Bottom Concept	$\bot$	$\emptyset$
Concept Negation	$\neg C$	$\Delta^I \setminus C^I$
Concept Intersection	$C \sqcap D$	$C^I \cap D^I$
Concept Union	$C \sqcup D$	$C^I \cup D^I$
Nominals	$\{a\}$	$\{a^I\}$
Existential Restriction	$\exists R.C$	$\{x \mid \exists y : (x, y) \in R^I \text{ and } y \in C^I\}$
Universal Restriction	$\forall R.C$	$\{x \mid \forall y : (x, y) \in R^I \text{ implies } y \in C^I\}$
Self Restriction	$\exists R.\mathsf{Self}$	$\{x \mid (x, x) \in R^I\}$
Number Restriction	$\star n\, R$ (where $\star \in \{\geq, \leq, =\}$)	$\{x \mid \#\{y : (x, y) \in R^I\} \star n\}$
Qualified Number Restriction	$\star n\, R.C$ (where $\star \in \{\geq, \leq, =\}$)	$\{x \mid \#\{y : (x, y) \in R^I \text{ and } y \in C^I\} \star n\}$
CONCEPT AXIOMS (T-Box)		
Concept Inclusion	$C \sqsubseteq D$	$C^I \subseteq D^I$
ROLE DEFINITIONS		
Role	R	R^I (a subset of $\Delta^I \times \Delta^I$)
Inverse Role	R^-	$\{(y, x) \mid (x, y) \in R^I\}$
Universal Role	U	$\Delta^I \times \Delta^I$
ROLE AXIOMS (R-Box)		
Role Inclusion	$R \sqsubseteq S$	$R^I \subseteq S^I$
Complex Role Inclusion	$R_1 \circ \ldots \circ R_n \sqsubseteq S$	$R_1^I \circ \ldots \circ R_n^I \subseteq S^I$
Transitive Roles	$\mathsf{Trans}(R)$	$R^I \circ R^I \subseteq R^I$
Functional Roles	$\mathsf{Func}(R)$	$\{(x, y), (x, z)\} \subseteq R^I \text{ implies } y = z$
Reflexive Roles	$\mathsf{Ref}(R)$	for all $x \in \Delta^I : (x, x) \in R^I$
Irreflexive Roles	$\mathsf{Irref}(R)$	for all $x \in \Delta^I : (x, x) \notin R^I$
Symmetric Roles	$\mathsf{Sym}(R)$	$R^I = (R^-)^I$
Asymmetric Roles	$\mathsf{Asym}(R)$	$R^I \cap (R^-)^I = \emptyset$
Disjoint Roles	$\mathsf{Disj}(R, S)$	$R^I \cap S^I = \emptyset$
ASSERTIONAL DEFINITIONS		
Individual	a	a^I (an element of Δ^I)
ASSERTIONAL AXIOMS (A-Box)		
Role Assertion	$R(a, b)$	$(a^I, b^I) \in R^I$
Negative Role Assertion	$\neg R(a, b)$	$(a^I, b^I) \notin R^I$
Concept Assertion	$C(a)$	$a^I \in C^I$
Equality	$a = b$	$a^I = b^I$
Inequality	$a \neq b$	$a^I \neq b^I$

mapping them, respectively, to an element of the domain ($a^I \in \Delta^I$), a subset of the domain ($C^I \subseteq \Delta^I$), or a set of pairs from the domain ($R^I \subseteq \Delta^I \times \Delta^I$).

An interpretation I *satisfies* an ontology O if and only if, for all axioms in O, the corresponding semantic conditions in Table 2 hold for I. In this case, we call I a *model* of O. This notion of a model gives rise to the key notion of entailment.

Definition 11. *Given two DL ontologies* O_1 *and* O_2, *we define that* O_1 *entails* O_2, *denoted* $O_1 \models O_2$, *if and only if every model of* O_1 *is a model of* O_2.

As an example of a DL ontology, for $O := (A, T, R)$, let:

- $A := \{\texttt{Planet(Earth)}, \texttt{parent(Luna,Earth)}, \texttt{parent(Pluto,Sun)}\}$;
- $T := \{\texttt{Planet} \sqsubseteq \forall\texttt{child.Moon}, \texttt{Planemo} \equiv \texttt{Moon} \sqcup \texttt{Planet} \sqcup \texttt{DwarfPlanet}\}$;
- $R := \{\texttt{parent} \sqsubseteq \texttt{orbits}, \texttt{parent} \equiv \texttt{child}^-\}$.

For $I = (\Delta^I, \cdot^I)$, let:

- $\Delta^I := \{\oplus, \mathbb{C}, \mathbb{P}, \maltese\}$;
- $\texttt{Earth}^I := \oplus$, $\texttt{Luna}^I := \mathbb{C}$, $\texttt{Pluto}^I := \mathbb{P}$, $\texttt{Sun}^I := \maltese$;
- $\texttt{Planet}^I := \{\oplus, \mathbb{P}\}$, $\texttt{Planemo}^I := \{\oplus, \mathbb{P}, \mathbb{C}\}$;
- $\texttt{parent}^I := \{(\mathbb{C}, \oplus), (\mathbb{P}, \maltese)\}$, $\texttt{child}^I := \{(\oplus, \mathbb{C}), (\maltese, \mathbb{P})\}$.

The interpretation I is not a model of O since it does not have that $\mathbb{C}$ is an instance of $\texttt{Moon}$, nor that $\mathbb{C}$ orbits $\oplus$, nor that $\mathbb{P}$ orbits $\maltese$. However, if we extend the interpretation I with the following:

- $\texttt{Moon}^I := \{\mathbb{C}\}$;
- $\texttt{orbits}^I := \{(\mathbb{C}, \oplus), (\mathbb{P}, \maltese)\}$.

then the interpretation of I will satisfy – i.e., will be a model of – the ontology O. Notably even though the ontology O does not entail that $\texttt{Planemo(Pluto)}$, it is still the case that I satisfies O; this is often referred to as the *Open World Assumption*, where ontologies are not assumed to completely describe the world, but rather to be incomplete. Now given the ontology:

$$O' := (\{\texttt{Moon(Luna)}\}, \{\texttt{Moon} \sqsubseteq \texttt{Planemo}\}, \{\}) ,$$

we may – with a bit of thought – convince ourselves of the fact that any model I of O must also be a model of O', and hence that $O \models O'$.

Unfortunately, deciding entailment for DL ontologies using all of the axioms of Table 2 in an unrestricted manner is undecidable. Hence, different DLs then apply different restrictions to the use of these axioms in order to achieve particular guarantees with respect to the complexity of deciding entailment. Most DLs are founded on one of the following base DLs (we use indentation to denote that the child DL extends the parent DL):

$\mathcal{ALC}$ (*Attributive Language with Complement* [60]), supports atomic concepts, the top and bottom concepts, concept intersection, concept union, concept negation, universal restrictions and existential restrictions. Role and concept assertions are also supported.

$\mathcal{S}$ extends $\mathcal{ALC}$ with transitive closure.

These base languages can be extended as follows:

$\mathcal{H}$ adds role inclusion.

$\mathcal{R}$ adds (limited) complex role inclusion, as well as role reflexivity, role irreflexivity, role disjointness and the universal role.

$\mathcal{O}$ adds nomimals.

$\mathcal{I}$ adds inverse roles.

$\mathcal{F}$ adds (limited) functional properties.

$\mathcal{N}$ adds (limited) number restrictions.

$\mathcal{Q}$ adds (limited) qualified number restrictions (subsuming $\mathcal{N}$ given $\top$).

We use "(limited)" to indicate that such features are often only allowed under certain restrictions to ensure decidability; for example, complex roles (chains) typically cannot be combined with cardinality restrictions. DLs are then typically named per the following scheme, where $[a|b]$ denotes an alternative between a and b and $[c][d]$ denotes a concatenation cd:

$$[\mathcal{ALC}|\mathcal{S}][\mathcal{H}|\mathcal{R}][\mathcal{O}][\mathcal{I}][\mathcal{F}|\mathcal{N}|\mathcal{Q}]$$

Examples include $\mathcal{ALCO}$, $\mathcal{ALCHI}$, $\mathcal{SHIF}$, $\mathcal{SROIQ}$, etc. These languages often apply additional restrictions on concept and role axioms to ensure decidability, which we do not discuss here. For further details on Description Logics, we refer to the recent book by Baader et al. [8].

We now discuss a research topic relating to the combination of ontology entailment and graph querying.

Topic 4.1: OBDA on graphs

The area of Ontology-Based Data Access (OBDA) [71] focuses on finding and implementing DL fragments for which query answering can be conducted over an ontology by means of a *query rewriting strategy*. Given an ontology and a graph query, this strategy involves extending the query such that, when it is evaluated over the base data, the solutions include those also given by entailments with respect to the ontology. For example, with respect to the aforementioned example ontology O, a simple graph pattern $\{(?\mathsf{moon}, \mathsf{type}, \mathsf{Moon})\}$ may be rewritten to query for:

$$\{(?\mathsf{moon}, \mathsf{type}, \mathsf{Moon})\} \cup$$
$$\{(?\mathsf{planet}, \mathsf{type}, \mathsf{Planet})(?\mathsf{planet}, \mathsf{child}, ?\mathsf{moon})\} \cup$$
$$\{(?\mathsf{planet}, \mathsf{type}, \mathsf{Planet})(?\mathsf{moon}, \mathsf{parent}, ?\mathsf{planet})\}$$

capturing the various ways in which instances of Moon could be entailed from the base data. The ability of an ontology language (e.g., DL fragment) to have all of its entailments supported in this way for queries using the basic relational algebra (i.e., complex graph patterns) is called *first-order rewritability* (referring to "first-order queries" which are equivalent to relational algebra queries per Codd's theorem). In general, only heavily restricted ontology languages have this property [6], often only conjunctive queries are accepted, and often the rewritten queries are unions of graph patterns (rather than using the full algebra) as illustrated above.

So what happens if the input query is not simply a graph pattern or a conjunctive query, but is rather a (complex) navigational graph pattern? A number of works have studied the complexity of query answering for navigational graph patterns in the presence of ontologies of varying expressivity [54, 64, 12]. However, such queries are not first-order queries, and are not first-order rewritable, where it is thus unclear how regular path queries can be supported in the context of OBDA, for example.

Many database systems, however, support features that go beyond first-order queries; for example, relational database engines support recursion, while graph database engines support path expressions. Such features of query engines have rarely exploited as targets for query rewriting strategies; exceptions include works on supporting transitive closure [62] and recursive rules [72] using SQL recursion, and studies of other forms of rewritability, such as rewriting to Datalog and Monadic Disjunctive Datalog [22].

This leaves the question: given a graph database system capable of answering (complex) navigational graph patterns – as popular in practice – what are the limits to the types of OBDA that the system can support through query rewriting? What kinds of input queries can be supported with respect to which ontology languages? A number of works have explored query rewriting strategies considering navigational queries as targets, but have focussed on particular ontology languages [13, 21]. An interesting topic would be to explore, more generally, what kinds of ODBA typical graph database engines can support, and under what assumptions. Furthermore, experimental works to understand the limitations of such techniques in terms of scalability and performance would be of importance to understand how such systems can be adopted in practice.

5   Rules

Another way to define the semantics of knowledge graphs is to use *rules*. Rules can be formalised in many ways – as Horn clauses, as Datalog, etc. – but in essence they consist of IF-THEN statements, where IF some condition holds, THEN some entailment holds. Here we define rules based on graph patterns.

Definition 12 (Rule). *A rule is a pair* $R := (B, H)$ *such that B and H are graph patterns. The graph pattern B is called the body of the rule while H is called the head of the rule.*

Given a graph G and a rule $R = (B, H)$, we can then apply R over G by taking the union of $\mu(H)$ for all $\mu \in B(G)$. Typically we will assume that the set of variables used in H will be a subset of those used in B ($\mathbf{V}(H) \subseteq \mathbf{V}(B)$), which assures us that $\mu(H)$ will always result in a graph without variables. Given a set of rules, we can then apply each rule recursively, accumulating the results in the graph until a fixpoint is reached, thus enriching our graph with entailments.

There is a large intersection between the types of semantics we can define with rules and with DL-based ontologies [40]. For example, we can capture the role-inclusion axiom parent $\sqsubseteq$ orbits as a rule (written $B \to H$):

$$\{(?\mathtt{x}, \mathtt{parent}, ?\mathtt{y})\} \to \{(?\mathtt{x}, \mathtt{orbits}, ?\mathtt{y})\}$$

or we can capture the concept inclusion Planet $\sqsubseteq \forall$child.Moon as:

$$\{(?\mathtt{x}, \mathtt{type}, \mathtt{Planet}), (?\mathtt{x}, \mathtt{child}, ?\mathtt{y})\} \to \{(?\mathtt{y}, \mathtt{type}, \mathtt{Moon})\} \ .$$

However, we cannot capture axioms such as BinaryStar $\sqsubseteq \exists$orbits.BinaryStar with the types of rules we have seen. Such an axiom would need a rule like:

$$\{(?\mathtt{x}, \mathtt{type}, \mathtt{BinaryStar})\} \to \exists y : \{(?\mathtt{x}, \mathtt{orbits}, y), (y, \mathtt{type}, \mathtt{BinaryStar})\}$$

where the head introduces a fresh existential variable y for each binary star, which itself is a binary star. (Note that if left unrestricted, such a rule, applied recursively on a single instance of a binary star, might end up creating an infinite chain of existential binary stars, each orbiting their existential successor!)

Additionally, rules as we have previously defined cannot capture axioms of the form Planemo $\sqsubseteq$ Moon $\sqcup$ Planet $\sqcup$ DwarfPlanet either. For this we would need a rule along the lines of the following:

$$\begin{aligned} \{(?\mathtt{x}, \mathtt{type}, \mathtt{Planemo})\} \to &\{(?\mathtt{x}, \mathtt{type}, \mathtt{Moon})\} \vee \\ &\{(?\mathtt{x}, \mathtt{type}, \mathtt{Planet})\} \vee \\ &\{(?\mathtt{x}, \mathtt{type}, \mathtt{DwarfPlanet})\} \ . \end{aligned}$$

Here we introduce the disjunctive connective "$\vee$" to state that when the body is matched, then at least one of the heads holds true.

Rules extended with existentials and disjunction have, however, been explored as extensions of Datalog. Datalog$^{\pm}$ variants support existential rules (aka *tuple generating dependencies* (*tgds*)) that allow for generating existentials in the head of the rule, per the `BinaryStar` example, but typically in a restricted way to ensure termination. On the other hand, Disjunctive Datalog allows for using disjunction in the head of rules, as seen in the `Planemo` example. These extensions allow rules to capture semantics similar to more expressive DLs [26, 27, 58].

On the other hand, rules can express entailments not typically supported in DLs, where a simple example of such a rule is:

$$\{(?\texttt{x}, \texttt{orbits}, ?\texttt{y}), (?\texttt{y}, \texttt{orbits}, ?\texttt{x})\} \rightarrow \{(?\texttt{x}, \texttt{sibling}, ?\texttt{y})\} \ .$$

This type of entailment would require role intersection, which is not typically supported by DLs. More generally, cyclical graph patterns that entail role assertions are typically not supported in DLs, though easily captured by rules.[4]

Efficient reasoning systems have then been developed to support such rules over knowledge graphs, including most recently, Vadalog [11] and VLog [17].

> **Topic 5.1: Existential/disjunctive rule mining**
>
> Given a diverse knowledge graph, such as Wikidata [66], manually defining all of the rules that may hold is a costly exercise. To help arrive at an initial set of rules in such cases, a number of *rule mining* techniques have been proposed that, given a graph, a certain *support* threshold, and a certain *confidence* threshold, will return rules that meet the defined thresholds; support is defined as the number of entailments given by the rule that are deemed correct, while confidence is the ratio of entailments given by the rule that are deemed correct. Given that knowledge graphs are incomplete, while we may assume that the triples given by the graph are correct, it is not clear how we might know which triples are incorrect. A common heuristic is to apply a *Partial Completeness Assumption* (*PCA*) [24], where a triple (s, p, o) is considered correct if it appears in G, and incorrect if it does not appear in G but there exists a triple (s, p, o') that does appear in G; other triples are ignored. A seminal rule mining system along these lines is AMIE [24], which incrementally builds rules using a sequence of steps called "refinements", filtering rules that do not meet the specified thresholds. A number of later systems support additional features in rules, such as forms of negation [32]. However, to the best of our knowledge, mining existential or disjunctive rules remains open for knowledge graphs.

6 Context

All of the data represented in Fig. 1 holds true with respect to a given *context*: a given scope of truth. As an example of temporal context, the Sun will cease

---

[4] Cyclical graph patterns that entail *concept* assertions can be captured, in a slightly roundabout way, in DLs with Self Restrictions and Complex Role Inclusions.

being a G-type Star and will eventually become a White Dwarf in its later years. We may also have spatial context (e.g., to state that something holds true in a particular region of space, such as a solar eclipse affecting parts of Earth), provenance (e.g., to state that something holds true with respect to a given source, such as the mass of a given planet), and so forth.

There are a variety of syntactic ways to embed contextual meta-data in a knowledge graph. Within del graphs, for example, the options include reification [18], n-ary relations [18], and singleton properties [52]. Context can also be represented syntactically using higher-arity models, such as property graphs [4], RDF* [30], or named graphs [18]. For further details on these options for representing context in graphs, we refer to the extended tutorial [35].

Aside from syntactic conventions for representing context in graphs, an important issue is with respect to how the semantics of context should be defined. A general contextual framework for graphs based on *annotations* has been proposed by Zimmermann et al. [75], based on the notion of an *annotation domain*.

Definition 13 (Annotation domain). *Let A be a set of* annotation values. *An* annotation domain *is defined as an idempotent, commutative semi-ring $D = \langle A, \oplus, \otimes, \mathbf{0}, \mathbf{1} \rangle$.*

For example, we may define A to be powerset of numbers from $\{1, \ldots, 365\}$ indicating different days of the year. We may then annotate triples such as $(\mathsf{Luna}, \mathsf{occults}, \mathsf{Sun})$ with a set of days in a given year – say $\{13, 245, 301\}$ on which the given occultation will occur. Given another similar such triple – say $(\mathsf{Luna}, \mathsf{occults}, \mathsf{Jupiter})$ annotated with $\{46, 245, 323\}$ – we can define $\oplus$ to be $\cup$ and use it to find the annotation for days when Luna occults the Sun or Jupiter $(\{13, 46, 245, 301, 323\})$; we can further define $\otimes$ to be $\cap$ and use it to find the annotation for days when Luna occults the Sun and Jupiter $(\{245\})$. In this scenario, $\mathbf{0}$ would then refer to the empty set, while $\mathbf{1}$ would refer to the set of all days of the year. Custom annotation domains can be defined for custom forms of context, and can be used in the context of querying and rules for computing the annotations corresponding to particular results and entailments.

In the context of ontologies, a more declarative framework for handling context – called *contextual knowledge repositories* – was proposed by Homola and Serafini [37] based on Description Logics, with a related framework more recently proposed by Schuetz et al. [61] based on an OLAP-style abstraction. These frameworks can assign graphs into different hierarchical contexts, which can then be aggregated into higher-level contexts.

Still, there are a number of questions that remain open regarding context.

Topic 6.1: Complex contexts

Context – in the sense of the scope of truth – is an almost arbitrarily complex subject. To take some examples, context can be recurrent, relative, and conceptual. Such forms of context are not – to the best of our knowledge – well-supported by current contextual frameworks.

In terms of recurrent context, most examples stem from temporal context, where we may state something that recurrently holds true of a given date of a year, or a given day of the week, which we may then wish, for example, to map to intervals on a non-recurrent temporal context.

In terms of relative context, the Wikidata [66] knowledge graph defines a "truthy" context, which includes information that is not deprecated or superseded by other information; for example, a population reading for a city would be considered truthy if there is no other more recent population reading available. However, the contextual notion of "most recent" requires a relative assessment of context dependent on the other data available.

Regarding conceptual context, the triple (Pluto, type, Dwarf Planet) only holds true since 2006. But unlike temporal context, it is the conceptualisation of a Planet, rather than Pluto itself, that has changed. This is an example of *concept drift* [69], where the meaning of domain terms can change over time, which in turn relates to the area of *ontology evolution* [74]. How we conceptualise a domain can thus also be contextual.

The notion of *context* in knowledge graphs can then be arbitrarily complex, where more complex notions of context remain poorly understood.

7   Embeddings

Machine learning has been gaining more and more attention in recent years, particularly due to impressive advances in sub-areas such as Deep Learning, where multi-layer architectures such as Convolutional Neural Networks (CNNs) have led to major strides in tasks involving multi-dimensional inputs (such as image classification), while architectures such as Recurrent Neural Networks (RNNs) have likewise lead to major strides in tasks involving sequential data (such as natural language translation). An obvious question then is: what kinds of learning architectures could be applied to graphs? The answer, unfortunately, is not so obvious. While machine learning architectures typically assume numeric inputs in the form of *tensors* (multi-dimensional arrays), graphs – unlike, say, images – are not naturally conceptualised in such terms.

A first attempt to encode a graph numerically would be a "one-hot encoding". Recalling the notation of N_G for the nodes of a del graph, we introduce a similar notation E_G to denote the edge-labels (i.e., predicates or properties) of a del graph; formally, $E_G := \{p \mid \exists x, y : (x, p, y) \in G\}$. We could consider creating a 3-mode tensor of size $|N_G| \cdot |E_G| \cdot |N_G|$, where the element at (i, j, k) is 1 if $(n_i, e_j, n_k) \in G$, or 0 otherwise; here n_i and n_k denote the ith and k^{th} nodes in an indexing of N_G, while e_j indicates the jth edge label in an indexing of

E_G. Though we now have a tensor representing the graph, for most graphs in practice, the tensor would be very sparse, with few 1's relative to 0's. As a result, using the tensor for the purposes of machine learning would be impractical.

In order to create more practical numeric representations of graphs for machine learning applications, knowledge graph embeddings aim to embed graphs within a low-dimensional, dense, numerical representation. There are many ways in which embeddings may be defined, but typically an embedding will map each node and each edge-label of a graph to an independent vector or matrix. For simplicity, we will assume embeddings that associate nodes and edge-labels to real-valued vectors of fixed dimension d, which we denote by the set $\mathbb{R}^d$.[5]

Definition 14 (Knowledge graph embedding). *Given a del graph G, a knowledge graph embedding of G is a pair of mappings (ε, ρ) such that $\varepsilon : N_G \to \mathbb{R}^d$ and $\rho : E_G \to \mathbb{R}^d$.*

Typically ε is known as an entity embedding, while ρ is known as a relation embedding. The knowledge graph embedding then consists of (typically low-dimensional) numeric representations of the node and edge-labels of the graph G, typically extracted such that the graph G can be (approximately) reconstructed from the embedding. Towards this goal, the graph can be conceptualised as a function $\gamma : \mathbf{C} \times \mathbf{C} \times \mathbf{C} \to \mathbb{R}_{[0,1]}$, where $\gamma(s, p, o) = 1$ if $(s, p, o) \in G$ or $\gamma(s, p, o) = 0$ if $(s, p, o) \notin G$. Instead of accepting the constants s, p, o, however, we could rather consider accepting the embeddings of those concepts: $\varepsilon(s)$, $\rho(p)$, $\varepsilon(o)$. This gives rise to the notion of a *plausibility scoring function*.

Definition 15 (Plausibility). *A plausibility scoring function is a partial function $\phi : \mathbb{R}^d \times \mathbb{R}^d \times \mathbb{R}^d \to \mathbb{R}_{[0,1]}$. Given a del graph $G = (V, E, L)$, a triple $(s, p, o) \in N_G \times E_G \times N_G$, and a knowledge graph embedding (ε, ρ) of G, the plausibility of (s, p, o) is given as $\phi(\varepsilon(s), \rho(p), \varepsilon(o))$.*

Triples with scores closer to 1 are considered more plausible, while triples with scores closer to 0 are considered less plausible. We can now learn embeddings that yield a score close to 1 for triples in (s, p, o), and a score close to 0 for a sample of negative triples not in G. Given that G is assumed to be incomplete, we cannot be certain that triples not in G are false. A common heuristic to generate negative examples is to apply the Partial Completeness Assumption (PCA), taking a triple (s, p, o) from G and replacing a term (often o) with another term appearing in G such that the resulting triple does not appear in G. In practice, the dimensions of the embeddings are fixed to a low number such that rather than "remembering" G, the knowledge graph embedding is forced to generalise patterns in how G is connected. Different knowledge graph embeddings instantiate the types of embedding considered and the plausibility scoring function in different ways [67]. We refer to the extended tutorial for details [35].

---

[5] In practice, knowledge graph embeddings can take complex-valued vectors, or real-valued matrices, or have entity and relation embeddings of different dimensions [67], and so forth, but such details are not exigent for our purposes.

Topic 7.1: Semantic knowledge graph embeddings

The plausibility scoring function assigns 1 to triples deemed likely to be true, and 0 to triples deemed likely to be false. This function is learnt based on the triples found in G. But in the case that G contains ontological definitions, it may entail triples that are not explicitly stated. In such cases, many knowledge graph embeddings only consider the structure, rather than the semantics, of G, and may thus assign entailed-but-not-stated triples a score closer to 0. Ideally, a semantic knowledge graph embedding would assign a plausibility of (close to) 1 for triples that are entailed by G.

A natural strategy is to materialise as many entailments for G as possible and then apply a structural knowledge graph embedding over the extended version of G as usual. However, in the case of ontological defini-

tions that generate new existentials, for example, it is possible that not all entailments can be materialised; in other cases, the number of entailments may simply be too large for materialisation to be practical.

A number of approaches have been proposed for considering entailments in knowledge graph embeddings [68, 28, 20]. Wang et al. [68] use functional and inverse-functional axioms as constraints (under a Unique Name Assumption (UNA)) such that if adding a triple to the graph would violate such a constraint, then its plausibility is lowered; for example, if we define system to be functional, and if we already have that the edge (Sun, system, Sol) holds, then we would reduce the plausibility of triples such as (Sun, system, Alpha Centauri). On the other hand, the KALE [28] system uses a combination of t-norm fuzzy logics and rules to assign plausibility to entailments. However, the approach relies on generating "ground rules" that indicate specific ways in which a triple can be entailed, which can lead to many ground rules for more complex definitions.

A perhaps simpler approach is to again conceptualise entailment numerically. If we state, for example, that parent ⊑ orbits, then we would expect that for any triples (x, parent, y) and (x, orbits, y), the former triple (being more specific) should be less plausible than the latter triple (being more general). Likewise, for example, a triple $(z, \text{type}, \text{Dwarf Planet})$ should always be less plausible than a triple $(z, \text{type}, \text{Planemo})$. This observation is exploited by FSL [20], which then defines soft constraints that associate a cost with contradicting such plausibility orderings. However, only simple forms of entailment are supported.

Hence a relevant topic is to explore how knowledge graph embeddings can be formulated and trained in order to find a numerical representation not only of the structure of a graph, but also its semantics, including potentially complex forms of entailment.

Once trained over G, knowledge graph embeddings directly allow for estimating the plausibility for triples of the form $(s, p, o) \in N_G \times E_G \times N_G$ (i.e., triples using some combination of terms found in G). This can be used for the purposes of link prediction, whereby considering the graph G of Fig. 1 and given a partial triple such as (Toliman, orbits, ?), the embedding of G can be used to predict likely completions of the triples, such as Rigil Kentaurus (already in the graph), or perhaps Proxima Centauri, or even Toliman itself. The embeddings themselves can also be useful independently of the plausibility scoring function as numerical representations of the elements of the graph, where, for example, similar numerical values will typically be assigned to similar nodes and edge-labels based on how they are connected in the graph.

In terms of open questions, a natural topic to explore is the combination of knowledge graph embeddings with ontologies and notions of entailment.

8 Graph Neural Networks

Rather than encoding the structure of graphs numerically, an alternative to enable learning over graphs is to design machine learning architectures that operate directly over the structure of a graph. A natural starting point is to consider neural networks, which already form graphs where nodes are (artificial) neurons, and edges are (artificial) axons that pass signals between neurons. Unlike graphs used to represent data, however, traditional neural networks tend to have a much more regular structure, being organised into layers, where all the nodes of one layer are connected pairwise to all the nodes of the next layer.

To enable learning over graphs of data, an alternative approach is to define the structure of the neural network in terms of the structure of the graph. In this case, the nodes of the graph are interpreted as neurons, while edges are interpreted as axons. Thus nodes can pass signals to each other through edges towards solving a given task. In a supervised setting, we may label a subset of nodes in the graph and then learn functions that aggregate information from the neighbourhood of each node, computing a new state for the node; this may continue recursively until a fixpoint, or for a fixed number of steps. Typically nodes and edges in the input graph will be associated with numerical feature vectors that encode pertinent information for the supervised task. Such a learning architecture is known as a graph neural network (GNN) [59].

As an example, assuming a large del graph similar to that shown in Fig. 2, we may label a subset of planets that are known to be in a habitable zone that could support life. We could then associate nodes with vectors that numerically encode their type, their mass, their density, their composition etc.; we may then further associate edges with vectors indicating the type of relation, the astronomic distance between bodies, etc. Based on labelled examples, a graph neural network can then learn aggregation functions that take the information surrounding the neighbourhood of each node – for example, numerical data about the moon(s) of a particular planet, the star(s) of planet, the distances involved, etc. – and generate the expected output; the same functions can then be applied to unlabelled nodes to generate predicted classifications.

We first define a vector-labelled del graph, which serves as input to a GNN:

Definition 16 (Vector-labelled graph). *A vector-labelled del graph G_λ is a pair $G_\lambda := (G, \lambda)$ where G is a del graph, and $\lambda : N_G \cup G \to \mathbb{R}^a$ is a vector labelling function.*

For simplicity, we will assume that nodes and triples are labelled with vectors of the same dimension (a). Thereafter, there are two principle architectures for GNNs: recursive and non-recursive graph neural networks. Here we focus on non-recursive graph neural networks, where details of the recursive architecture can rather be found in the extended tutorial [35]. Note that in the following definition, we use $S \to \mathbb{N}$ to denote *bags* (aka *multisets*) formed from the set S.

Definition 17 (Non-recursive graph neural network). *A non-recursive graph neural network (NRecGNN) $\mathfrak{N}$ with l layers is an l-tuple of functions $\mathfrak{N} := (\text{AGG}^{(1)}, \ldots, \text{AGG}^{(l)})$, where $\text{AGG}^{(k)} : \mathbb{R}^a \times 2^{(\mathbb{R}^a \times \mathbb{R}^a) \to \mathbb{N}} \to \mathbb{R}^a$ for $1 \leq k \leq l$.*

Each aggregation function $\text{AGG}^{(k)}$ computes a new feature vector for a node, given its previous feature vector and the feature vectors of the nodes and edges forming its neighbourhood. We assume for simplicity that the dimensions of the vectors remain the same throughout, though this is not necessary in practice.[6] Given an NRecGNN $\mathfrak{N} = (\text{AGG}^{(1)}, \ldots, \text{AGG}^{(l)})$, a vector-labelled graph G_λ, and a node $u \in N_G$, we define the output vector assigned to node u in G_λ by $\mathfrak{N}$ (written $\mathfrak{N}(G_\lambda, u)$) as follows. First let $\mathbf{n}_u^{(0)} := \lambda(u)$. For all $i \geq 1$, let:

$$\mathbf{n}_u^{(i)} := \text{AGG}^{(i)} \left(\mathbf{n}_u^{(i-1)}, \{\!\{ (\mathbf{n}_v^{(i-1)}, \lambda(v, p, u)) \mid (v, p, u) \in E \}\!\} \right)$$

Then $\mathfrak{N}(G_\lambda, u) := \mathbf{n}_u^{(l)}$.

In an l-layer NRecGNN, a different aggregation function is applied at each step (i.e., in each layer), up to a fixed number of steps l. These aggregation functions are typically parametrised and learnt based on labelled training data. When the aggregation functions are based on a convolutional operator, the result is a *convolutional graph neural network (ConvGNN)*.

Though initially it may seem as if GNNs and ontologies are orthogonal concepts for graphs, there are some correspondences between both.

---

[6] We can still define a to be the largest dimension needed, padding other vectors.

Topic 8.1

Both GNNs and ontologies can be used to classify nodes. While GNNs can be used to perform classification based on numerical methods and inductive learning, ontologies can be used to perform classification based on symbolic methods and deductive reasoning. An interesting research question is then to understand how these two paradigms might relate in terms of expressiveness. For example, can GNNs potentially learn to make similar classifications based on similar input data as ontologies? In fact, some progress has been made recently on this question.

GNNs are typically based on aggregations of data from a local neighbourhood. This means that there are limitations to what GNNs can distinguish. In particular, GNNs based on local information cannot distinguish certain non-isomorphic graphs [73], but rather can only distinguish graphs that are also distinguishable by a weaker *Weisfeiler–Lehman* (*WL*) test for isomorphism, which involves recursively hashing neighbouring information of nodes up to a fixpoint. More specifically, if the WL test assigns the same hash to two nodes in the graph, then those nodes cannot be distinguished by a GNN of the form previously described. Barceló et al. [10] then recently showed that for any binary classification expressible as an $\mathcal{ALCQ}$ ontology, there exists a GNN of the form previously described that will compute the same classification; they further define a discrete form of GNN that can only capture binary classifications expressible as an $\mathcal{ALCQ}$ ontology.

This rather surprising correspondence between GNNs and $\mathcal{ALCQ}$ constitutes a bridge between deductive and inductive semantics for knowledge graphs. An interesting line of research is then to investigate GNN-style architectures that permit classification with respect to other DLs [10].

9   Conclusions

The growing popularity of knowledge graphs presents an opportunity for research that combines various technical perspectives on how graphs can be used to represent and exploit knowledge at large scale. Within the intersection of these varying perspectives lies interesting research questions in terms of how concepts from graph databases and knowledge representation can be fruitfully combined, how techniques from machine learning relate to logical languages, and so forth.

Here we have mentioned a number of key concepts relating to knowledge graphs – specifically data models, querying, ontologies, rules, embeddings and graph neural networks – as well as a number of research topics that arise from their combination. We have only scratched the surface. Knowledge graphs encompass an even wider range of topics, where we have not touched upon concepts such as shapes and validation, graph algorithm and analytics, privacy and anonymisation, data quality, knowledge graph creation and completion, knowledge graph refinement, etc. Likewise there are many interesting research questions that arise when considering combinations of these concepts. For discussion on these and other topics we refer to the extended tutorial [35].

Acknowledgements. This work was supported by Fondecyt Grant No. 1181896 and by the Millennium Institute for Foundational Research on Data (IMFD). I would like to thank my co-authors on the extended tutorial for the various discussions and contributions that helped to inform these lecture notes. I also wish to thank the anonymous reviewers' for their helpful comments.

References

1. Aberger, C.R., Lamb, A., Tu, S., Nötzli, A., Olukotun, K., Ré, C.: Emptyheaded: a relational engine for graph processing. ACM Trans. Database Syst. (TODS) **42**(4), 20 (2017)
2. Angles, R.: The property graph database model. In: Olteanu, D., Poblete, B. (eds.) Proceedings of the 12th Alberto Mendelzon International Workshop on Foundations of Data Management, Cali, Colombia, 21–25 May 2018, CEUR Workshop Proceedings, vol. 2100. Sun SITE Central Europe (CEUR) (2018), http://ceur-ws.org/Vol-2100/paper26.pdf
3. Angles, R., et al.: G-CORE: a core for future graph query languages. In: [19], pp. 1421–1432
4. Angles, R., Arenas, M., Barceló, P., Hogan, A., Reutter, J.L., Vrgoc, D.: Foundations of modern query languages for graph databases. ACM Comput. Surv. **50**(5), 68:1–68:40 (2017)
5. Arenas, M., Conca, S., Pérez, J.: Counting beyond a Yottabyte, or how SPARQL 1.1 property paths will prevent adoption of the standard. In: Mille, A., Gandon, F.L., Misselis, J., Rabinovich, M., Staab, S. (eds.) Proceedings of the 21st World Wide Web Conference 2012, WWW 2012, Lyon, France, 16–20 April 2012, pp. 629–638. ACM Press, April 2012
6. Artale, A., Calvanese, D., Kontchakov, R., Zakharyaschev, M.: The DL-lite family and relations. J. Artif. Intell. Res. **36**, 1–69 (2009)
7. Atserias, A., Grohe, M., Marx, D.: Size bounds and query plans for relational joins. SIAM J. Comput. **42**(4), 1737–1767 (2013). https://doi.org/10.1137/110859440
8. Baader, F., Horrocks, I., Lutz, C., Sattler, U.: An Introduction to Description Logic. Cambridge University Press, Cambridge (2017)
9. Barceló, P.: Querying graph databases. In: Hull, R., Fan, W. (eds.) Proceedings of the 32nd ACM SIGMOD-SIGACT-SIGART Symposium on Principles of Database Systems, PODS 2013, New York, NY, USA, 22–27 June 2013, pp. 175–188. ACM Press, June 2013. https://doi.org/10.1145/2463664.2465216
10. Barceló, P., Kostylev, E.V., Monet, M., Peréz, J., Reutter, J., Silva, J.P.: The Logical Expressiveness of Graph Neural Networks. In: 8th International Conference on Learning Representations, ICLR 2020, Addis Ababa, Ethiopia, 26–30 April 2020. OpenReview.net, April 2020. https://openreview.net/forum?id=r1lZ7AEKvB
11. Bellomarini, L., Sallinger, E., Gottlob, G.: The vadalog system: datalog-based reasoning for knowledge graphs. Proc. VLDB Endowment **11**(9), 975–987 (2018)
12. Bienvenu, M., Ortiz, M., Simkus, M.: Regular path queries in lightweight description logics: complexity and algorithms. J. Artif. Intell. Res. **53**, 315–374 (2015)
13. Bischof, S., Krötzsch, M., Polleres, A., Rudolph, S.: Schema-agnostic query rewriting in SPARQL 1.1. In: Mika, P., et al. (eds.) ISWC 2014. LNCS, vol. 8796, pp. 584–600. Springer, Cham (2014). https://doi.org/10.1007/978-3-319-11964-9_37

14. Bollacker, K., Tufts, P., Pierce, T., Cook, R.: A platform for scalable, collaborative, structured information integration. In: Nambiar, U., Nie, Z. (eds.) International Workshop on Information Integration on the Web (IIWeb 2007) (2007)

15. Bonifati, A., Martens, W., Timm, T.: An analytical study of large SPARQL query logs. Proc. VLDB Endowment **11**(2), 149–161 (2017)

16. Capadisli, S., Auer, S., Ngomo, A.N.: Linked SDMX data: path to high fidelity statistical linked data. Semantic Web **6**(2), 105–112 (2015)

17. Carral, D., Dragoste, I., González, L., Jacobs, C.J.H., Krötzsch, M., Urbani, J.: VLog: a rule engine for knowledge graphs. In: [25], pp. 19–35

18. Cyganiak, R., Wood, D., Lanthaler, M.: RDF 1.1 concepts and abstract syntax, W3C Recommendation 25 February 2014. W3c recommendation, World Wide Web Consortium, 25 February 2014. https://www.w3.org/TR/2014/REC-rdf11-concepts-20140225/

19. Das, G., Jermaine, C.M., Bernstein, P.A. (eds.): Proceedings of the 2018 International Conference on Management of Data, SIGMOD Conference 2018, Houston, TX, USA, 10–15 June 2018. ACM Press, June 2018

20. Demeester, T., Rocktäschel, T., Riedel, S.: Lifted rule injection for relation embeddings. In: [65], pp. 1389–1399

21. Dimartino, M.M., Calì, A., Poulovassilis, A., Wood, P.T.: Efficient ontological query answering by rewriting into graph queries. In: Cuzzocrea, A., Greco, S., Larsen, H.L., Saccà, D., Andreasen, T., Christiansen, H. (eds.) FQAS 2019. LNCS (LNAI), vol. 11529, pp. 75–84. Springer, Cham (2019). https://doi.org/10.1007/978-3-030-27629-4_10

22. Feier, C., Kuusisto, A., Lutz, C.: Rewritability in Monadic Disjunctive Datalog, MMSNP, and Expressive Description Logics. Log. Methods Comput. Sci. **15**(2), 15:1–15:46 (2019)

23. Francis, N., et al.: Cypher: an evolving query language for property graphs. In: [19], pp. 1433–1445

24. Galárraga, L., Teflioudi, C., Hose, K., Suchanek, F.M.: Fast rule mining in ontological knowledge bases with AMIE+. Very Large Data Base J. **24**(6), 707–730 (2015). https://doi.org/10.1007/s00778-015-0394-1

25. Ghidini, C., et al. (eds.): ISWC 2019. LNCS, vol. 11779. Springer, Cham (2019). https://doi.org/10.1007/978-3-030-30796-7

26. Gottlob, G., Orsi, G., Pieris, A., Šimkus, M.: Datalog and its extensions for semantic web databases. In: Eiter, T., Krennwallner, T. (eds.) Reasoning Web 2012. LNCS, vol. 7487, pp. 54–77. Springer, Heidelberg (2012). https://doi.org/10.1007/978-3-642-33158-9_2

27. Grau, B.C., Motik, B., Stoilos, G., Horrocks, I.: Computing datalog rewritings beyond horn ontologies. In: Rossi, F. (ed.) IJCAI 2013, Proceedings of the 23rd International Joint Conference on Artificial Intelligence, Beijing, China, 3–9 August 2013, pp. 832–838. IJCAI/AAAI, August 2013

28. Guo, S., Wang, Q., Wang, L., Wang, B., Guo, L.: Jointly embedding knowledge graphs and logical rules. In: [65], pp. 192–202

29. Harris, S., Seaborne, A., Prud'hommeaux, E.: SPARQL 1.1 Query Language, W3C Recommendation 21 March 2013. W3C recommendation, World Wide Web Consortium, 21 March 2013. https://www.w3.org/TR/2013/REC-sparql11-query-20130321/

30. Hartig, O.: Foundations of RDF* and SPARQL* - an alternative approach to statement-level metadata in RDF. In: Reutter, J.L., Srivastava, D. (eds.) Proceedings of the 11th Alberto Mendelzon International Workshop on Foundations of Data Management and the Web, Montevideo, Uruguay, 7–9 June 2017. CEUR Workshop Proceedings, vol. 1912. Sun SITE Central Europe (CEUR) (2017). http://ceur-ws.org/Vol-1912/paper12.pdf

31. Hitzler, P., Krötzsch, M., Parsia, B., Patel-Schneider, P.F., Rudolph, S.: OWL 2 web ontology language primer (Second edn), W3C Recommendation 11 December 2012. W3C recommendation, World Wide Web Consortium, 11 December 2012. https://www.w3.org/TR/2012/REC-owl2-primer-20121211/

32. Ho, V.T., Stepanova, D., Gad-Elrab, M.H., Kharlamov, E., Weikum, G.: Rule learning from knowledge graphs guided by embedding models. In: Vrandečić, D., et al. (eds.) ISWC 2018. LNCS, vol. 11136, pp. 72–90. Springer, Cham (2018). https://doi.org/10.1007/978-3-030-00671-6_5

33. Hoffart, J., Suchanek, F.M., Berberich, K., Lewis-Kelham, E., de Melo, G., Weikum, G.: YAGO2: exploring and querying world knowledge in time, space, context, and many languages. In: Srinivasan, S., Ramamritham, K., Kumar, A., Ravindra, M.P., Bertino, E., Kumar, R. (eds.) Proceedings of the 20th International Conference on World Wide Web, WWW 2011, Hyderabad, India, 28 March – 1 April 2011 (Companion Volume), pp. 229–232. ACM Press, March 2011

34. Hogan, A., Arenas, M., Mallea, A., Polleres, A.: Everything you always wanted to know about blank nodes. J. Web Semantics **27–28**, 42–69 (2014)

35. Hogan, A., et al.: Knowledge graphs. CoRR abs/2003.02320 (2020). https://arxiv.org/abs/2003.02320

36. Hogan, A., Riveros, C., Rojas, C., Soto, A.: A worst-case optimal join algorithm for SPARQL. In: Ghidini, C., et al. (eds.) ISWC 2019. LNCS, vol. 11778, pp. 258–275. Springer, Cham (2019). https://doi.org/10.1007/978-3-030-30793-6_15

37. Homola, M., Serafini, L.: Contextualized knowledge repositories for the semantic web. J. Web Semantics **12**, 64–87 (2012)

38. Kalinsky, O., Etsion, Y., Kimelfeld, B.: Flexible caching in Trie joins. In: International Conference on Extending Database Technology (EDBT), pp. 282–293. OpenProceedings.org (2017)

39. Krötzsch, M., Marx, M., Ozaki, A., Thost, V.: Attributed description logics: reasoning on knowledge graphs. In: IJCAI, pp. 5309–5313 (2018). https://doi.org/10.24963/ijcai.2018/743

40. Krötzsch, M., Rudolph, S., Schmitt, P.H.: A closer look at the semantic relationship between datalog and description logics. Semantic Web **6**(1), 63–79 (2015)

41. Krötzsch, M., Simancik, F., Horrocks, I.: Description logics. IEEE Intell. Syst. **29**(1), 12–19 (2014)

42. LaPaugh, A.S., Papadimitriou, C.H.: The even-path problem for graphs and digraphs. Networks **14**(4), 507–513 (1984). https://doi.org/10.1002/net.3230140403

43. Lefrançois, M., Zimmermann, A.: The unified code for units of measure in RDF: cdt:ucum and other UCUM datatypes. In: Gangemi, A., et al. (eds.) ESWC 2018. LNCS, vol. 11155, pp. 196–201. Springer, Cham (2018). https://doi.org/10.1007/978-3-319-98192-5_37

44. Lehmann, J., et al.: DBpedia - a large-scale, multilingual knowledge base extracted from Wikipedia. Semantic Web J. **6**(2), 167–195 (2015)

45. Libkin, L.: Locality of queries and transformations. Electron. Notes Theor. Comput. Sci. **143**, 115–127 (2006). https://doi.org/10.1016/j.entcs.2005.04.041

46. Meroño-Peñuela, A., Daga, E.: List.MID: a MIDI-based benchmark for evaluating RDF lists. In: Ghidini, C., Hartig, O., Maleshkova, M., Svátek, V., Cruz, I., Hogan, A., Song, J., Lefrançois, M., Gandon, F. (eds.) ISWC 2019. LNCS, vol. 11779, pp. 246–260. Springer, Cham (2019). https://doi.org/10.1007/978-3-030-30796-7_16
47. Mika, P., et al. (eds.): ISWC 2014. LNCS, vol. 8797. Springer, Cham (2014). https://doi.org/10.1007/978-3-319-11915-1
48. Miller, J.J.: Graph Database Applications and Concepts with Neo4j. In: Proceedings of the Southern Association for Information Systems Conference, Atlanta, GA, USA, 23rd-24th March 2013, pp. 141–147. AIS eLibrary (2013). https://aisel.aisnet.org/sais2013/24
49. Navigli, R., Ponzetto, S.P.: BabelNet: the automatic construction, evaluation and application of a wide-coverage multilingual semantic network. Artif. Intell. **193**, 217–250 (2012)
50. Ngo, H.Q., Porat, E., Ré, C., Rudra, A.: Worst-case optimal join algorithms. J. ACM **65**(3), 16:1–16:40 (2018). https://doi.org/10.1145/3180143
51. Nguyen, D., et al.: Join processing for graph patterns: an old dog with new tricks. In: GRADES, p. 2. ACM (2015)
52. Nguyen, V., Bodenreider, O., Sheth, A.: Don't like RDF reification?: Making statements about statements using singleton property. In: Chung, C.W., Broder, A.Z., Shim, K., Suel, T. (eds.) 23rd International World Wide Web Conference, WWW 2014, Seoul, Republic of Korea, 7–11 April 2014, pp. 759–770. ACM Press, April 2014
53. Noy, N.F., Gao, Y., Jain, A., Narayanan, A., Patterson, A., Taylor, J.: Industry-scale knowledge graphs: lessons and challenges. ACM Queue **17**(2), 20 (2019)
54. Ortiz, M., Rudolph, S., Simkus, M.: Query answering in the horn fragments of the description logics SHOIQ and SROIQ. In: Walsh, T. (ed.) IJCAI 2011, Proceedings of the 22nd International Joint Conference on Artificial Intelligence, Barcelona, Catalonia, Spain, 16–22 July 2011, pp. 1039–1044. IJCAI/AAAI, August 2011
55. Reutter, J.L., Soto, A., Vrgoč, D.: Recursion in SPARQL. In: Arenas, M., et al. (eds.) ISWC 2015. LNCS, vol. 9366, pp. 19–35. Springer, Cham (2015). https://doi.org/10.1007/978-3-319-25007-6_2
56. Rodriguez, M.A.: The Gremlin graph traversal machine and language. In: Cheney, J., Neumann, T. (eds.) Proceedings of the 15th Symposium on Database Programming Languages, Pittsburgh, PA, USA, 25–30 October 2015, pp. 1–10. ACM Press, October 2015
57. Rudolph, S.: Foundations of description logics. In: Polleres, A., et al. (eds.) Reasoning Web 2011. LNCS, vol. 6848, pp. 76–136. Springer, Heidelberg (2011). https://doi.org/10.1007/978-3-642-23032-5_2
58. Rudolph, S., Krötzsch, M., Hitzler, P.: Description logic reasoning with decision diagrams. In: Sheth, A., et al. (eds.) ISWC 2008. LNCS, vol. 5318, pp. 435–450. Springer, Heidelberg (2008). https://doi.org/10.1007/978-3-540-88564-1_28
59. Scarselli, F., Gori, M., Tsoi, A.C., Hagenbuchner, M., Monfardini, G.: The graph neural network model. IEEE Trans. Neural Netw. **20**(1), 61–80 (2009)
60. Schmidt-Schauß, M., Smolka, G.: Attributive concept descriptions with complements. Artif. Intell. **48**(1), 1–26 (1991)
61. Schuetz, C., Bozzato, L., Neumayr, B., Schrefl, M., Serafini, L.: Knowledge graph OLAP: a multidimensional model and query operations for contextualized knowledge graphs. Semantic Web J. (2020). (Under open review)
62. Sequeda, J.F., Arenas, M., Miranker, D.P.: OBDA: query rewriting or materialization? In practice, both!. In: Mika, P., et al. (eds.) ISWC 2014. LNCS, vol. 8796, pp. 535–551. Springer, Cham (2014). https://doi.org/10.1007/978-3-319-11964-9_34

63. Singhal, A.: Introducing the Knowledge Graph: things, not strings. Google Blog, May 2012. https://www.blog.google/products/search/introducing-knowledge-graph-things-not/
64. Stefanoni, G., Motik, B., Krötzsch, M., Rudolph, S.: The complexity of answering conjunctive and navigational queries over OWL 2 EL knowledge bases. J. Artif. Intell. Res. **51**, 645–705 (2014)
65. Su, J., Carreras, X., Duh, K. (eds.): Proceedings of the 2016 Conference on Empirical Methods in Natural Language Processing, EMNLP 2016, Austin, Texas, USA, 1–4 November 2016. The Association for Computational Linguistics, November 2016
66. Vrandečić, D., Krötzsch, M.: Wikidata: a free collaborative knowledgebase. Commun. ACM **57**(10), 78–85 (2014)
67. Wang, Q., Mao, Z., Wang, B., Guo, L.: Knowledge graph embedding: a survey of approaches and applications. IEEE Trans. Knowledge Data Eng. **29**(12), 2724–2743 (2017)
68. Wang, Q., Wang, B., Guo, L.: Knowledge base completion using embeddings and rules. In: Yang, Q., Wooldridge, M.J. (eds.) Proceedings of the Twenty-Fourth International Joint Conference on Artificial Intelligence, IJCAI 2015, Buenos Aires, Argentina, 25–31 July 2015, pp. 1859–1866. IJCAI/AAAI, July 2015
69. Wang, S., Schlobach, S., Klein, M.C.A.: Concept drift and how to identify it. J. Web Semantics **9**(3), 247–265 (2011)
70. Wu, Z., Pan, S., Chen, F., Long, G., Zhang, C., Yu, P.S.: A comprehensive survey on graph neural networks. CoRR abs/1901.00596 (2019). http://arxiv.org/abs/1901.00596
71. Xiao, G., et al.: Ontology-based data access: a survey. In: Lang, J. (ed.) Proceedings of the Twenty-Seventh International Joint Conference on Artificial Intelligence, IJCAI 2018, 13–19 July 2018, Stockholm, Sweden, pp. 5511–5519. IJCAI/AAAI, July 2018
72. Xiao, G., Rezk, M., Rodríguez-Muro, M., Calvanese, D.: Rules and ontology based data access. In: Kontchakov, R., Mugnier, M.-L. (eds.) RR 2014. LNCS, vol. 8741, pp. 157–172. Springer, Cham (2014). https://doi.org/10.1007/978-3-319-11113-1_11
73. Xu, K., Hu, W., Leskovec, J., Jegelka, S.: How powerful are graph neural networks? In: 7th International Conference on Learning Representations, ICLR 2019, New Orleans, LA, USA, 6–9 May 2019. OpenReview.net, May 2019. https://openreview.net/forum?id=ryGs6iA5Km
74. Zablith, F., et al.: Ontology evolution: a process-centric survey. Knowledge Eng. Rev. **30**(1), 45–75 (2015)
75. Zimmermann, A., Lopes, N., Polleres, A., Straccia, U.: A general framework for representing, reasoning and querying with annotated semantic web data. J. Web Semantics **12**, 72–95 (2012)

Author Index

Printed in the United States
By Bookmasters